Creating the Judicial Branch:
The Unfinished Reform

Robert W. Tobin

Authors Choice Press
New York Lincoln Shanghai

Creating the Judicial Branch
The Unfinished Reform

Authors Choice Press
an imprint of iUniverse, Inc.

For information address:
iUniverse, Inc.
2021 Pine Lake Road, Suite 100
Lincoln, NE 68512
www.iuniverse.com

Originally published by National Center for State Courts

First edition

ISBN: 0-595-32277-8

Printed in the United States of America

Table of Contents

v Preface and Acknowledgments

vii Introduction

1 **Part I The Administrative Requirements of Judicial Independence**

3 Chapter 1 The Judicial Branch: Legal Fiction or Reality?

25 **Part II The Obstacles to Judicial Branch Control of Internal Operations**

27 Chapter 2 Politics and the State Courts: Balancing the Popular Will and Adjudicative Independence

51 Chapter 3 Extracting the State Judiciary from Local Government

81 Chapter 4 Judges and Lawyers: Who's in Charge?

103 Chapter 5 Developing a Management Perspective in the Judiciary

117 **Part III Creating an Independent Judicial Branch: The Court Reform Movement**

119 Chapter 6 Origins of Court Reform and the Movement to Upgrade the State Judiciary

133 Chapter 7 The Unification Movement and the Advent of Judicial Administration

155 Chapter 8 Creation of an Administrative Infrastructure: The State Component

173 Chapter 9 Creation of an Administrative Infrastructure: The Trial Court Component

193 **Part IV The Next Reform Phase**

195 Chapter 10 The Old and New Agendas

207 Chapter 11 A New Look at the Adversarial Process

223 Chapter 12 Broadening the Role of Judges and the Concept of Justice

233 Chapter 13 The Open Service-oriented Court

247   Chapter 14 The Assault on Unification: Specialty Courts and Special Interest
        Groups

257   Chapter 15 Leadership Challenges

263   Index

Preface and Acknowledgments

There comes a time when one has to step back and behold with detachment the events of the recent past, because it is possible to live through great changes and not grasp their scope or significance. This book is an attempt to sort out and understand the changes, sometimes quite dramatic, that have occurred in the state courts since midcentury. What we have witnessed and are still witnessing is a struggle to create a third branch of state government. Thus, the title of the book.

There are a number of personal anecdotes in the book, because I have been actively engaged in state courts for many years, first as a trial lawyer, later as an independent court consultant, and then as an employee of the National Center for State Courts. I have met many of the leading figures in court administration, both judges and court managers, and have been involved in reform efforts in many states. My sympathies lie with the judicial branch, because I am, by career choice, a member of the family. There are, however, some obvious problems in the judiciary that cannot be overlooked and are frankly stated.

The National Center for State Courts has supported this effort with corporate resources and made it possible for this book to be completed. For this, I thank President Roger Warren and Jim Maher, his immediate predecessor as acting president. My special thanks go to my colleague Tom Henderson whose steady encouragement and insightful comments were invaluable and to my diligent editor, Chuck Campbell. Finally, I thank all the people who took the time to comment on early drafts and the many judges, attorneys, and administrators who took the time to talk to me and submit materials.

Robert W. Tobin
Arlington, Virginia
1998

Introduction

This book describes and assesses a recent historical phenomenon, the creation of administratively and organizationally coherent judicial systems within state government. Before 1950, the state judicial branch of government existed mostly in concept, not in operational reality. After 1950, state judges, the organized bar, and many students of the judiciary took a hard look at the way state courts were organized and managed. They concluded that state courts, particularly the trial courts, were externally dominated, highly disorganized, often unprofessional, and poorly managed, to the point where the integrity of the state courts was being seriously undermined. State after state initiated court reform movements and brought about many remarkable improvements. Courts were caught up in a reform wave that swept all three branches of state government but took a unique form in the courts. Unlike the executive and legislative branches, the state courts were not simply seizing management control of their own domain but literally creating a third branch of government. They sought this objective by integrating the various components of the state judiciary into a more coherent whole and generally upgrading the level of professionalism and the quality of justice.

These reforms have been chronicled in numerous publications but usually not in their full historical context. This book views the reforms in a broad perspective and tracks the struggle of the state courts to rise from chaos and achieve credibility as a coequal branch. The book concludes with a look at where court reform is headed.

Part I deals with the early history of courts in the United States and the prevalent legalistic approach to judicial independence that ignored the implications of administrative dependence on the other branches of state and local government. The belief that a tiny appellate court could use its decisions to establish itself as a coequal branch of state government proved to be unrealistic. State supreme courts were like heads without bodies. Judicial independence and separation of powers remained legal concepts devoid of administrative reality, because state trial courts were only nominally part of the state judicial branch. They were so intertwined with local government that they took on the characteristics of their environment and were not part of a coherent whole.

Part II addresses the sorry conditions that existed in state courts in the early part of the twentieth century and sparked the cries for reform. The state trial courts lacked the elementary rudiments of a credible judicial system: independence, accountability, integrity, management, and quality. The reasons for this woeful situation were numerous but, in general, could be attributed to politics, localism run amok, lawyer domination of court processes, and a lack of management orientation among judges.

Politics was most pronounced in judicial selection. Many judges were elected and were beholden to those who supported them, very commonly lawyers who appeared before them. Appointed judges were seldom screened for qualifications, other than their political acceptability to the appointing authority. Politics rather than merit pervaded the whole system and extended into court support divisions, some of which were appendages of urban political machines. Other courts were mired in the local government politics of rural America and were frequently called upon to adjudicate tax, election, and land use cases involving local officials who provided funding for courts and electoral support for judges. Significant numbers of appointed and elected judges in courts of limited jurisdiction were not trained in the law. The overall level of professionalism and accountability was shockingly low.

Trial courts, even those of general jurisdiction, were deeply intertwined with complex local government structures and manifested all the intricate organizational subdivisions of this structure. Court organizational structure defied analysis, even rationality. Geographical and subject matter divisions were blurred and overlapping, confronting court users with a confusing array of forums, few of them paragons of justice. Local fiscal politics and frequent intrusion and manipulation by elected local officials left courts weakened, particularly in budget matters. Courts were, in theory, independent of their environment, but, in practice, they were immersed in it. The value of having courts with sensitivity to local issues was lost in an erratic localism that made individual trial courts into self-contained fiefdoms. Procedures varied from county to county, even from judge to judge. Justices of the peace and municipal judges operated outside any normal procedures and ran pay-as-you-go courts that were both alegal and corrupt.

Because many judges had no real support staff, traveled on a circuit, were part-time, were not attorneys, or lacked any significant administrative authority, they were not in a position to run their own courts. Lawyers willingly filled this void. Prosecutors controlled criminal calendars, and civil attorneys controlled the civil calendar. All the judge had to do was show up. Lawyers could figure out the arcane court structure, negotiate it, and often control it to their own advantage. Their control extended to judicial elections, where lawyers could make or break a candidate for judge. Judges had to rely on lawyers to make their courts work and were tied to lawyers by a common legal culture that made it difficult for judges to exert much discipline.

Judges as a group were not inclined toward management, but were equally disinclined toward delegation of management authority. That is why many basic administrative services in courts were supplied by executive branch agencies of local government or, more commonly, by elected clerks who had their own political constituency and were not subject to any real judicial control. Judges operated by mandate and worried little about procedures or administrative detail.

They sometimes ordered administrative actions or procedures but were singularly ineffective in implementing their orders, because they assumed their orders to be self-executing, as they might be in a court case. By training and temperament, they were not well suited to a management role.

The net effects of these problems were anarchy and mediocrity. By 1950, a movement was under way to address these problems on a grand scale. The first step was widely perceived as creation of a rational statewide organizational structure. The theory was simple—you cannot improve that which does not exist. The first step had to be creation of a system out of the prevailing disorder. Thus was the judicial branch of state government born.

Part III is the story of the reform movement of the late twentieth century. This movement was based on two goals: upgrading the professionalism of the state judiciary and unifying state trial court systems.

The drive to upgrade the caliber of judges was centered on merit selection, judicial education, and judicial discipline. Measured against the conditions in 1950, great strides were made. Measured against the ambitious aspirations of reformers, the results were less heartening. Merit selection is still far from a reality. Though somewhat improved, judicial discipline and judicial performance measurement still leave much to be desired. Judicial education, on the other hand, has been enormously improved. Probably the greatest triumph of the reformers was to introduce some degree of professionalism into lower-tier courts. Overall, the reforms were a great boon to state courts, if not necessarily a smashing success.

The unification movement was more complicated. One objective was court reorganization and simplification of court structure. The second major thrust was to effect administrative unification. The means to this end were establishing administrative rulemaking, creating uniform court procedures throughout the system, centralizing administrative policy in the highest court, making the chief justice the executive head of the system, strengthening the role of chief trial judges, and establishing some vertical lines of authority from the highest courts into the trial courts. The final part of the unification troika was budgetary unification, which involved shifting the primary burden of trial court financing from local governments to the state and making trial court employees state employees. This served the three purposes of increasing the pool of resources, ending funding disparities among courts, and removing trial courts from submersion in the local political scene. It also increased the power of state supreme courts and state court administrators. A majority of states implemented some aspects of unification. On balance, unification was beneficial to courts but did not really resonate with the public or avoid heavy criticism. It appears to have been a foundational step rather than an end in itself.

A less publicized but vitally important part of the unification movement was the creation of administrative infrastructures within the state court systems. Without these management systems, administrative unification would be an illusion. There are now state administrative offices of courts in every state and literally thousands of trial court administrators working with chief trial court judges. In 1950 these managers did not exist; now they are part of a burgeoning profession. Perhaps no other phenomenon of the reform movement so graphically and tangibly illustrates the relationship of administrative self-reliance and judicial independence.

Part IV assesses the early reform agenda and describes the emerging reform agenda. The unification movement failed to generate public respect for courts, because it was an in-house, defensive, and somewhat elitist type of reform. Its concerns were court structure, court administration, rulemaking, court financing, and the selection, education, and discipline of judges. This agenda was tied together by a common theme–"Stay out of our house and we'll put it in order." The newer agenda is more external and person oriented, actively involving the courts in social problems, in collaboration with the citizenry, and in opening up the courts. Courts are being forced to consider lay concerns about the legal process and take on issues that go to the heart of the legal culture. This is a very different agenda than unification but probably could not successfully occur unless unification had prepared the way. These two reform movements will run in parallel, because the struggle to create a coherent, independent, highly professional judicial branch is far from won and because they complement one another. Unification is essentially a platform on which to build. The new reform agenda rests on this platform.

The new reform issues will change the way courts deal with the public and affect the culture of the judiciary and the legal system. Symbolic of these issues is the responsibility of the judiciary to arrest and reverse the declining professionalism of the legal profession, even if this means sharp tensions within the legal-judicial fraternity. Public attitudes toward lawyers are very negative and have led to frequent pro se representation, heavy pressure to provide alternatives to formal adversarial proceedings, and demands to do something about the incivility and shoddy ethics of many lawyers. The public is asking that the legal culture be changed, which is very different from seeking some structural change in the court's superintendence of attorneys.

Another example of the difference between the old and new agendas is provided by jury reform. No one seriously objected to democratizing the jury system by improving lists, to increasing the efficiency of the jury system, and to treating jurors better. Better jury management was part of the general management improvement that characterized the early reform agenda. The legal fraternity was not, however, enthusiastic about more recent reform proposals to change the role of jurors during trial, accurately perceiving this as a challenge to the legal culture. This type of reform often originates at the trial court level, usually with support from the state supreme court. Moreover, this type of reform is sometimes based on social science research rather than legal mythology. It characterizes the second wave of reform that is less respectful of the legal culture, more likely to involve local leadership, and more attuned to greater public participation in court matters.

The adversarial process is in trouble, because it is perceived as lacking both integrity and respect for persons. The system stands accused of producing a shoddy form of justice that is divorced from the truth, demeaning those who participate in the process, and denying access to many who might invoke the aid of the system. There is disagreement about the extent of this trouble but not about the causes of criticism. The formal adversarial process is being weakened and denuded of integrity by tactics and procedures that permit, if not reward, untruth. It is traumatic for participants, costly in money, lengthy, and not particularly reliable as a means of justice. The whole process seems clouded in legal mythology and remarkably hostile to the laity. Inexpensive and less harrowing alternatives abound but are still not fully institutionalized. The underlying premises of the adversarial system are due for reexamination.

Judicial roles are changing in response to the disintegrating social fabric of the country. Family problems, substance abuse, disabilities of age and infancy, and the mental illnesses caused by the social pathologies of contemporary America have placed judges on the front line of a struggle to address social problems. The primary role of the judge remains that of adjudication, but adjudication no longer defines the judge's role. Judges are, for better or worse, engaged in solving problems and are often the gatekeepers who direct troubled persons to resources that can help them or their families recover their dignity and ability to function in society. This is not a traditional arbiter role, nor is it restricted to family, juvenile, and mental health matters. The criminal courts are being called on to help addicted defendants break a cycle of recidivism. This departure from tradition is part of a larger concept of justice. The obligations of justice go beyond dispute resolution and are multidimensional.

The open court is the hallmark of the new agenda. The days of the feudal court are over. This means, in practice, that court proceedings will be more open in terms of public attendance, ability of handicapped persons to participate, and explanation of court actions to the public. Court information will no longer be doled out or sold but made freely available by electronic media and other means. Court facilities will be designed, located, and open for business in a way that facilitates public convenience. Courts will welcome more advisory citizen involvement in their management and will collaborate with local communities in the interest of justice and public service, including support for community courts. Collaboration also means closer involvement with other agencies and less insistence on the separation of the courts.

Unification was by definition hostile to specialized courts, although some specialty courts predated unification and survived it. The impetus for creation of such courts has recently increased. Advocates of specialty courts base their position on the necessity to focus resources on a specific problem and to obtain judges who have the expertise and desire to handle the problem. The underlying assumption of the specialty court advocates is that their agenda will receive low priority from the regular court systems (particularly the unified systems). The traditional specialty courts for juvenile and family matters have received new life because of advocacy groups and federal funding. A variety of boutique courts have arisen; most, like drug courts, are driven by federal funding program objectives and a vocal advocacy group. Business groups have launched drives to make courts more responsive to their desires and have frequently resorted to federal legislation to override state court decisions. The state courts are being pressured by a motley variety of user groups that want court resources, or even court decisions, dedicated to their purposes. Unification is being subjected to centrifugal forces.

The problems facing the courts are big, but the ability to address them is immeasurably greater at year 2000 than it was in 1950. The great judicial leaders of the twentieth century asserted judicial administrative independence and fought the good fight. They gave a legacy to their heirs that enhanced the potential for leadership. Courts have made great progress is getting control of their own branch, imposing some order, introducing management, and improving the professionalism of the courts, but the current leadership needs are different. The newer issues are more "grassroots" in nature and may involve some painful and controversial changes in the legal-judicial culture. Although chief justices will continue to lead in asserting judicial branch prerogatives, the emerging agenda will require a less overtly political and more sophisticated type of leadership. It will also require more direct public dialogue, which may switch many leadership responsibilities to the trial court judiciary or court administrators. The agenda is coming into focus. The sources of leadership are less clear.

PART I

The
Administrative Requirements
of Judicial Independence

Chapter 1

The Judicial Branch: Legal Fiction or Reality?

In politico-legal terms the judicial branch of government interprets, construes, and applies the law and is, therefore, distinguished from the branches that have governing authority. This is a neat functional division—one branch adjudicates, two branches govern. The underlying weakness of this political science approach, as applied to state government, is that it ignores an important historical reality: the lack of administrative cohesion and self-governance of the so-called judicial branch. What passed for a state judicial branch, until very recently, was a group of appellate judges who performed the adjudicative functions of their office but had a very tenuous control over trial courts, which remained local institutions immersed in local political culture, local government operations, and the local legal culture. The judicial branch of state government was, in large part, a legal fiction, rather than an operational reality.

Origin and Development of Legal Concepts Pertaining to Judicial Independence

The early legal literature on separation of powers rarely contains the term *branch*. The closest equivalent is an occasional reference to "department" in *The Federalist*. Courts have generally been uncomfortable with the word *department* because it suggests that the other branches regard the courts as a component of the executive branch. Courts have fought a long battle to combat this view and have chosen *branch* as a more accurate depiction of the coequal status of the courts, the executive, and the legislature. State constitutions generally have a judicial section and sometimes acknowledge the special status of the judiciary by permitting direct submission of the court budget to the legislature.

In actual practice, interbranch relations on budgeting often belie the constitutional language. Even though the West Virginia Constitution prohibits the legislature from cutting the court budget, a budget dispute between the court and the legislature once ended up in front of an ad hoc supreme court composed of trial judges. Governors with no power over the court budget have actually had court budget examiners and placed pressure on the judicial branch to alter its budget. Even if courts are given special constitutional status, they are usually careful not to flaunt their advantage, because a legislature has many weapons, not the least of which is control over judicial pay raises and retirement.

Constitutional provisions notwithstanding, the judiciary has, until late in this century, been a dependent rather than an independent arm of government. Courts have awakened to the idea that the term branch cannot be just a legal concoction based on a constitutional premise but must be given reality by a strong managerial and administrative coherence within the judiciary. A judicial branch exists because it is constructed, not just because the state constitution has a section on courts.

In 1975 Professor Carl Baar's landmark book *Separate but Subservient* was published.[1] The book centered on the vagaries of court financing and the peculiar vulnerability of courts in budgetary matters. The premise, as indicated in the title, was that the inability of state courts to obtain adequate funding undermined separation of powers and judicial independence. In an earlier era when judges and a few assistants constituted the judiciary, the judicial appropriation was so small as to be a nonissue. In the modern era, with a vastly more complex judicial system requiring greater financial resources, the independence of the judiciary is at stake if the courts are totally subservient to the other branches for their funding. The same reasoning could apply to executive branch control over personnel management and other aspects of court management.

It would be misleading, however, to picture the executive branch and the legislative branch as bullies picking on a weaker branch. There were periods in history when the other branches were helpful in bringing about court reforms and acted in the best interest of the courts. It is also misleading to think that the executive and legislative branches of state government were models of administrative coherence and professionalism that put the courts to shame. Until fairly recently, legislatures met infrequently, usually for short periods, and had little in the way of staff or office space. They operated in a state of disorganization that bordered on chaos. The executive branch in many states was rendered weak by short terms for governors, prohibition of gubernatorial reelection, and a plural executive branch that diluted the power of the chief executive by the election of cabinet officers who were quite independent. The historical fact is that the executive and legislative branches of state government were somewhat disorganized and amateurish in the nineteenth century and started to deal with the management and administrative demands of modern society only a few decades before the courts. When the evolution of state government is viewed in perspective, it will be seen that the three branches experienced some of the same growing pains and were proceeding along parallel lines in improving their operations. Therefore, the history of separation of powers should not be viewed solely as one of sporadic warfare but as a history of joint development often marked by comity and self-restraint in interbranch relations.

The eighteenth century gave us separation of powers among agencies of state government; the nineteenth century witnessed the gradual transfer of almost all judicial functions from the state executive and legislative branches to the state courts; and the twentieth century gave us the quest for an administra-

---

[1]   The full title of this book is *Separate but Subservient: Court Budgeting in the American States* (Lexington, MA: Lexington Books, D.C. Heath and Company, 1975).

tively self-sufficient and more highly professional judicial branch, paralleling improvements in state government generally. The attempt to create a coordinated and integrated state judiciary, i.e., a real state judicial branch, is a story that has to be told.

There are two aspects to this story, the legal and the operational. Courts have been rather aggressive in defining their own legal power in relation to the governing branches, but they have only belatedly recognized that independence is more than a constitutional concept. If the courts do not govern themselves, they are not, strictly speaking, a branch of government, much less independent. The legal and the operational supplement one another.

The Legal Arsenal of the Judicial Branch

There are five legal concepts that undergird the state judicial branch: separation of powers; checks and balances, including judicial review; judicial independence; inherent powers; and judicial federalism. These concepts overlap, but are sufficiently distinctive to warrant separate discussion.

Separation of Powers as a General Concept. The term *separation of powers* is invoked frequently and sometimes reverently in the annals of American constitutionalism, both state and federal. The rationale for separation of powers among three branches of government is the protection of liberty by diffusion and counterbalancing of government authority.

The concept has its origins in English legal and political history.[2] The Anglo-Saxon legal system that predated the Norman invasion was intensely local and based on mores and traditions in a particular locale. The Norman kings did not at first try to override this, so kings confined themselves to settling the few disputes that were of such magnitude that they were beyond the power of any local system, such as a dispute between major vassals of the king. This changed with Henry II, who started to pull many formerly local legal matters into a royal tribunal, basically the King in Council. This kingly takeover was based on an ever-expanding system of writs whereby the crown took jurisdiction of different categories of cases by removing them from other courts. As the jurisdiction of the royal courts expanded, specialized tribunals were set up to hear the cases. The king delegated his authority as chief judge to a system of royal courts that featured three types of tribunals, the main one being the King's Bench.

The king, however, did not delegate all his authority and reserved the right to intervene in common-law courts as an ultimate arbiter and to serve as the conscience of the legal system when its formalities interfered with true justice. In short, he reserved the right to provide equitable relief and serve as chancellor.[3]

[2]   See generally, Lawrence M. Friedman, *History of American Law*, 2nd ed. (New York: Simon and Schuster, 1985).

[3]   Henry L. McClintock, *Handbook on the Principles of Equity*, 2nd ed. (St. Paul, MN: West Publishing Company, 1948), 9-13.

The role of chancellor was soon delegated, at first to clerics, later to attorneys who were not clergymen, the first layman being Thomas More. A system of equity courts grew up alongside the courts hearing cases at law. These upper-level English courts built the common law, those principles that transcended the local systems of jurisprudence and started to form a national body of law emanating largely from judicial decisions. The sometimes heated dispute between common-law and equity courts became entangled with the struggle between Parliament and the king, with the parliamentarians favoring the courts of law over the chancery courts, which they perceived as heavily royal in orientation. This conflict carried over into the colonies. The royalist colonies tended to give more leeway to equity courts and set them up as separate courts. In Pennsylvania and Massachusetts, where royalist sentiment was not high, there never were separate equity courts, whereas in the royalist Virginia colony the governor actually doubled as chancellor, reviving the ancient royal prerogative.

When the power of the English monarchy ebbed in the seventeenth century and Parliament asserted its prerogatives, monarchs lost their hold on the courts.[4] The rights secured by Parliament had to be protected by some judicial organ of government. The Act of Settlement in 1701 established the independence of the English judiciary from the monarch. This separation of powers was closely linked to the Rule of Law, the concept that the governing arms are subject to law and that this law must be applied by an organ of government detached from the political process and free to protect the rights of citizens.

The doctrine of separation of powers has two facets: a functional differentiation among the executive, legislative, and judicial branches and a system of checks and balances among the three branches. The nature of the parliamentary system somewhat blurred these distinctions in England; moreover, the lack of a written constitution made the power of judicial review less significant in that country. Blackstone's vision of separation of powers was more fully effectuated in America. The doctrine is, however, not very precise in meaning and has been invoked selectively and molded as much by political decisions as by court opinions. Americans have been quite pragmatic about interbranch relationships:

> Separation of powers—that bedrock principle of constitutional government, that admired doctrine, that distinctive offspring of American political genius—has been conspicuously dishonored throughout its history. It has been violated with style and flourish, as when the first chief justice, John Jay, negotiated a treaty with Britain while holding judicial title, or when John Marshall, in the course of delivering the charter of judicial supremacy in *Marbury v. Madison*, judged the legality of commissions he had signed as a cabinet official.[5]

---

[4]   Charles Keigwin, *Cases on Common Law Pleading with Summaries of Doctrine upon Several Heads of that Subject*, 2nd ed. (Rochester, NY: Lawyers Cooperative Publishing Company, 1934), 1-11.

[5]   John P. MacKenzie, *The Appearance of Justice* (New York: Scribners, 1974), 1.

This pragmatism does not detract from the importance of the concept of separation of powers. The dynamics of government and interbranch relationships are too complex to be placed in a rigid legal mold, but there has to be some overriding principle governing these power relationships and the distribution of functions among the executive, legislative, and judicial branches. Separation of powers provides a flexible conceptual framework for the interaction of the three branches and has been effectively used by the judiciary in building a judicial branch and asserting judicial independence.

Separation of Powers and Differentiation of Functions. In the early colonial period, English colonial administration was relatively passive and detached, but when the English stepped up the intensity of colonial administration, they did so through a single body, the King in Council; i.e., the Privy Council.[6] The centralization of administrative authority under the king, and to some extent his royal governors, made a profoundly negative impression on Americans as evidenced by the list of grievances in the Declaration of Independence; for example, the complaint about the nullification of colonial laws by the Privy Council. Colonial experience with undifferentiated authority led colonial leaders who had read Montesquieu and Blackstone to strongly embrace the separation of powers between the legislative, executive, and judicial branches. Agreeing on the principle was fairly easy, but determining what functions belonged to what branch was difficult and has been worked out over time by a series of interbranch accommodations.

The fact that courts now have control over the performance of judicial functions seems normal and unsurprising, but it took centuries for this to occur. In the colonial period separation of powers was at best embryonic and at worst nonexistent.[7] Massachusetts typified the absence of differentiated government authority. In the seventeenth century, the Massachusetts Bay Colony had a governing body called the General Court.[8] This body was essentially a legislature but had appellate jurisdiction.[9] The Court of Assistants, composed of the governor, the deputy governor, and some magistrates, had original jurisdiction of cases and also some appellate jurisdiction but was really an extension of the executive branch. The local governing bodies were called county courts.[10] In addition to

---

[6]   Roscoe Pound, "Judicial Justice," in Robert Scigliano, ed., *The Courts: A Reader in Judicial Process* (Boston: Little, Brown and Company, 1962), 4-15.

[7]   Friedman, *American Law*, 17-56, tracing English influence on colonial legal systems.

[8]   Massachusetts did not become a united royal colony until 1691. Initially, there were two proprietary colonies that were later melded into the Massachusetts colony. The larger of these two proprietary colonies was the Massachusetts Bay Colony.

[9]   The highest court of Massachusetts is called the Supreme Judicial Court. This sounds redundant but makes sense if it is remembered that there was once a general court that exercised both judicial and nonjudicial functions.

[10]   To this day county governing bodies in some southern and border states are referred to as "courts." Sometimes the members of the county board or commission are called judges. President Harry Truman, who was not a lawyer, served as a county judge in Jackson County, Missouri.

governing authority, these courts had original jurisdiction in some cases and could hear appeals from cases handled by some local judges who were in function, if not title, justices of the peace. Each colony had its own approach, but the Massachusetts system was typical in its intense localism, its failure to clearly distinguish between judicial and nonjudicial functions, its overlapping original jurisdiction, and its confusing appellate structure.[11]

The historical fact is that colonists carried over their local law, the system that affected most English citizens more that the vaunted common law. Despite charters that required observance of English law, the colonists initially developed systems for their colonies that reflected local custom in the areas of England from which they came, served local needs in a thinly settled frontier society, and reflected the religious views of the colonies' founders. A more formal court structure was imposed as colonies matured, but the pattern in America was not unlike that of the mother country, a system of very informal "people's courts" that were responsive to local needs and a more formal upper tier of trial courts. This bifurcation still exists in the United States to some degree and was the norm until the court reform movements focused on the lack of professionalism in limited jurisdiction trial courts.

As upper-tier courts (typically called superior courts or circuit courts) became more formalized and lawyer-judges started to take hold, English legal precedents had more influence, and procedural rules became more complex, causing some reaction against lawyers and judges who were too formal and legalistic for the tastes of many colonists.[12] The English also set up admiralty courts to enforce cases affecting English trade policy and established separate equity courts that generally sat in the capitol and might include the governor as a chancellor. Neither of these courts used juries, and they were not popular with colonists. The colonists felt that the judges were controlled by the king, a grievance expressed in the Declaration of Independence.

In general, however, the courts that affected the lives of most colonists were local courts with lay judges. The fact that the lower courts employed the services of lay judges did not necessarily mean that the judges were your average citizen. Often, they were large landowners or important personages—George Washington, for example. The more populist elements in the colonial era were even skeptical about these judges, not because they lacked legal training, but because they were thought to identify with the upper class. More important, these judges often had functions that might be termed governing functions, pretty well blurring the separation of powers.

In the period after the Revolution, Americans had the opportunity to determine for themselves the proper distribution of governmental authority and to differentiate more clearly among the branches.[13] The Articles of Confederation

---

[11]   One of the most interesting variations were the manorial courts of Maryland, which were based on the rural pattern in aristocratic England where the lord of the manor served as judge on issues within his domain.

[12]   Friedman, *American Law*, 124-138.

[13]   Ibid., 139-143.

gave short shrift to both the executive and the judicial branch, reflecting the colonial experience. The Constitutional Convention adopted the concept of separation of powers at the federal level and carved out a separate judicial department. Some state constitutions had already followed this path before the Constitutional Convention; others followed later. Two things distinguished the state and federal experience. Congress, as one of its earliest acts, created lower federal courts in addition to the Supreme Court (the only court created by Article III of the Constitution) and provided the elements of a relatively coherent judicial branch. Moreover, the separation of powers was much more explicit at the federal level. The states lagged behind many years in actually separating judicial functions.

Although it is now taken for granted that only courts exercise judicial functions, this was not at all clear in the early days of the republic. It was well into the nineteenth century before the state judiciary was able to end the legislative assumption of judicial functions.[14] In colonial times, bills of attainder and bills of pain and penalty were not uncommon and amounted to legislative punishment without the hindrance of a trial. Fortunately, bills of attainder were prohibited in Article I of the United States Constitution, but other forms of legislative justice remained. Legislative divorce existed in many states, ending as late as 1851 in Rhode Island and 1874 in Pennsylvania. The Rhode Island legislature had jurisdiction of insolvency until 1832; in Pennsylvania, the legislature gave equitable relief until 1837 and actually could have granted it up until 1874. The Connecticut legislature administered *cy-pres* relief in cases of charitable trusts and even in ordinary trusts until 1877 and exercised supplementary probate jurisdiction for most of the nineteenth century. Until the late nineteenth century, the Maryland legislature could set aside dismissals for procedural reasons and require causes to be continued or heard at certain terms of court.

Legislatures sometimes served as appellate courts, a function for which they were spectacularly unsuited. The senate exercised appellate jurisdiction in New York until 1846 and the legislature in Rhode Island until 1857. New Jersey did not give its highest court final judicial authority until 1844; New York took this step in 1846. It was one thing to gain control of appellate jurisdiction from the other branches, quite another to sort out appellate jurisdiction within the judicial branch. Appellate jurisdiction and original jurisdiction were not neatly separated in most states during the nineteenth century. Even members of the United States Supreme Court had to ride circuit for much of the nineteenth century. Fortunately, legislative justice had been pretty well phased out by 1900, except for impeachment.

Executive justice disappeared in the seventeenth century but reemerged in a different form in the late nineteenth century when the regulatory functions of government increased, leading to the demand for administrative tribunals. At first, courts stoutly resisted the "usurpation" of their newly won control over judicial functions, but eventually acceded to reality and permitted administrative tribunals to function. Interestingly, in the late nineteenth century many judges and

---

14   Pound, "Judicial Justice," 5-8.

scholars felt that just about any government function could be categorized as executive, legislative, or judicial. The rise of the administrative courts illustrated the folly of this rigidity.

Separation of powers is necessarily a fluid concept. Some government functions do not lend themselves to dogmatic categorization. Thus, courts and the executive branch came to exercise some legislative authority within their own domains: rulemaking in the case of the courts, executive orders and administrative regulations in the case of the executive. The three branches came to various other pragmatic accommodations on the distribution of functions, generally recognizing that one branch might have primary responsibility for a certain function without necessarily excluding the other branches from this whole area of government. Separation of powers has worked, because the three branches have operated with some restraint and shied away from interbranch confrontation wherever possible.

Separation of Powers and Checks and Balances. The judiciary particularly benefits from this concept of countervailing power, because the judiciary, in comparison to the executive and legislative branches, is the weakest component of government and needs a constitutional shield to preserve judicial independence. There was a brief period after the Revolution when state constitutions lionized the legislative branch at the expense of the executive branch, but executive power was gradually restored at the state level. The Articles of Confederation reflected this prolegislative tendency by obliterating the executive branch of the national government, but the Constitution restored executive power at the national level. The judiciary had a harder road to travel in gaining parity with the other branches, its principal and almost sole check on the other branches being the power to invalidate their actions. The other branches of state government usually have a variety of checks on judicial power, although this varies by state. There are also some popular checks on judicial power.

Many of these issues were addressed in the Constitutional Convention and in the early days of the republic when the federal government was being formed.[15] The federal court system was the work of the Federalists and accomplished over the strenuous, sometimes bitter, objection of Thomas Jefferson and his followers. The Jeffersonians did not want lower federal courts and were opposed to the power of federal courts to void state enactments repugnant to the Constitution. Although the Jeffersonians lost these battles, they did win an important concession. Instead of giving exclusive jurisdiction to federal courts in federal questions and diversity-of-citizenship cases, Congress gave state courts concurrent jurisdiction of these matters.

---

[15] Louis Boudin, "Government by Judiciary," and Charles Beard, "Supreme Court Usurper or Grantee?" in Scigliano, The Courts, 23-31 and 32-43, respectively. Beard's article is a rebuttal of Boudin's position on judicial review. See also Elliot Slotnick, "The Place of Judicial Review in the American Tradition: The Emergence of an Eclectic Power," in Slotnick, ed., Judicial Politics: Readings from Judicature (Chicago: American Judicature Society, 1992).

Ultimately, the power of the courts under separation of powers lies in the authority of the courts to judge whether the actions of the other two branches conform to the law, particularly the organic law of the jurisdiction. At the Constitutional Convention and in the early years of the republic, the judicial review issue focused largely on the power of a federal court to void state law and override state courts when their actions or decisions collided with the supremacy of federal law, federal treaties, and the United States Constitution. There is little doubt that the framers of the Constitution and Congress intended that the United States Supreme Court should have this power. The first judiciary act expressly gave this authority.

It was not, however, quite so clear whether the United States Supreme Court was meant to have authority to void an act of Congress. The Jeffersonian position was that each branch should be the ultimate interpreter of the Constitution as regards its own province. Leading Federalists and some members of the Constitutional Convention made it quite clear that the judiciary alone should have ultimate power in interpreting the United States Constitution. The Federalist position, later articulated by John Marshall, was set forth by Alexander Hamilton:

> There is no position which depends on clearer principles, than that every act of a delegated authority, contrary to the tenor of the commission under which it is exercised, is void. No legislative act, therefore, contrary to the Constitution, can be valid. To deny this, would be to affirm, that the deputy is greater than his principal; that the servant is above his master; that the representatives of the people are superior to the people themselves; that men acting by virtue of powers, may do not only what their powers do not authorize, but what they forbid.
>
> If it be said that the legislative body are themselves the constitutional judges of their own powers, and that the construction they put upon them is conclusive upon the other departments, it may be answered, that this cannot be the natural presumption, where it is not to be collected from any particular provisions in the Constitution. It is not otherwise to be supposed that the Constitution could intend to enable the representatives of the people to substitute their will to that of their constituents. It is far more rational to suppose, that the courts were designed to be an intermediate body between the people and the legislature, in order, among other things, to keep the latter within the limits assigned to their authority. The interpretation of the laws is the proper and peculiar province of the courts. A constitution is, in fact, and must be regarded by the judges, as a fundamental law. It therefore belongs to them to ascertain its meaning, as well as the meaning of any particular act proceeding from the legislative body. If there should happen to be an irreconcilable variance between the two, that which has the superior obligation and validity ought, of course, to be preferred; or, in other words, the Constitution ought to be preferred to the statute, the intention of the people to the intention of their agents.[16]

---

[16]   *The Federalist* Number 78 (New York: Tudor Publishing Co., 1937).

Marbury v. Madison settled the issue of judicial review in favor of the Federalist position, much to the chagrin of Thomas Jefferson, whose antipathy to the Federalist-controlled judiciary was legendary.[17] John Marshall, in a cleverly concocted opinion, refused to mandamus Secretary of State James Madison to deliver a commission as justice of the peace in the District of Columbia to William Marbury, a last-minute appointee of John Adams.[18] Marshall thus appeared to buckle under to the Jeffersonians, who were itching for a confrontation with the Federalist judiciary, but he based his judicial restraint on the fact that the congressional act giving the Supreme Court original jurisdiction in mandamus cases was an unconstitutional enlargement of the court's original jurisdiction. The legal merits of Marshall's reasoning are debatable, but the political genius is indisputable. He established the right of the judiciary to void the acts of an elected Congress and did it in a way that made it impossible for the Jeffersonians to challenge him. The Jeffersonians won the case and lost on the bigger issue, but judges did not push their luck. The United States Supreme Court waited some fifty-four years before once again voiding an act of Congress (the Missouri Compromise), this time in the horrendous *Dred Scott* case.

Marshall buttressed the power of the judiciary without ever again, during his long tenure, voiding an act of Congress.[19] He established the power and prestige of his court, and coincidentally all appellate courts, by ending the practice of *seriatim* opinions by individual justices. Ending this practice led to a single majority opinion that spoke the mind of the court in a way that clarified the law and made the position of the court more forceful and authoritative. He established the leadership role of a chief and was able to persuade many of his colleagues to accept his views, much to the dismay of Jeffersonians and later Jacksonians. He lent a certain dignity to the Court's opinions by a method of reasoning and explanation that made it difficult for opponents outside the Court to attack the Court's decisions on purely political grounds. This change was important to the judiciary, because some judges of the period were very openly political and not very judicious in their demeanor. In fact, the impeachment of Justice Samuel Chase in 1803 was based largely on such grounds.

State supreme courts did not rush to exercise judicial review, although state constitutions embraced separation of powers. The same constitutional logic applied at the state level as it did at the federal level. Some arm of government has to interpret the organic law of the jurisdiction and protect liberties of the people. The governing branches are the ones being judged in most instances, and it therefore falls to the judicial branch to determine if the actions of government are repugnant to the state constitution. State legislatures were, of course, already subject to judicial review by state and federal courts for compliance with the federal Constitution. Thus, it was not a big step to reason that the state supreme courts could determine if actions of the governing branches of

---

[17]   1 Cranch 137, 2 L Ed. 60 (1803).

[18]   In this period, one function of the secretary of state was handling the paperwork of the federal government, including the delivery of letters of appointment.

[19]   Friedman, *American Law*, 133-134.

state governments were repugnant to the state constitutions. Nonetheless, state supreme courts used the power of judicial review sparingly. In one instance where judicial review was used in Kentucky to void an act protecting persons subject to foreclosure after the land panic of 1819, popular reaction was so hostile that a second supreme court was created and functioned for almost a decade.

When the judicial system started to emerge as a separate part of government and became more assertive, concern mounted over checks upon judges. Jacksonians were, for example, very much opposed to the fairly free use of the contempt power by some judges.[20] Primary among these checks were those provided by the other branches of government. If elected officials chose the judges and could discipline them, then the public interest was protected. However, the United States Constitution and most state constitutions frowned on using judicial salary appropriations as a means of control, because this had been a point of contention with the English crown. But in later years, when judicial support staffs became large, states found that they could punish judges by limiting appropriations for judicial support staff and nonpersonnel expenses.

The Jeffersonians favored legislative removal of judges, but this was perceived as a rather gross assault on judicial independence. About the only remaining means of removing an appointed judge was by impeachment, an instrument that quickly proved unwieldy and highly political. The historically famous impeachment proceeding against Justice Samuel Chase of the United States Supreme Court in 1803 was nothing more than a Jeffersonian attempt to destroy the judicial branch, because the Court was composed largely of Federalist judges and headed by the greatest Federalist of them all, John Marshall. Enough Jeffersonian senators defected to save Chase from conviction, avoiding what might have been total legislative dominance over the judicial branch. In 1805, an attempt to impeach all but one of the judges of the Pennsylvania Supreme Court narrowly failed.

The judiciary survived some serious misuses of the impeachment process, but the public demand to make judges accountable remained high. One price for acquittal of Samuel Chase was an increased insistence on judicial election of state judges. If judges were to be independent of the governing branches and possess power to void government actions, then they had better be subject to popular control. This control took two forms: election of judges and the use of juries. Both provided popular input into the judiciary, and both were aided by the Jacksonian movement to democratize the institutions of government. The widespread use of juries was a check upon the judiciary in various ways. The underlying idea of the jury was that citizens would be judged by their peers rather than by someone who might harbor elitist inclinations. This popular concern, heightened by colonial experience with judges appointed by the crown in trade and admiralty cases, led to restrictions on the right of judges to comment on the evidence in their jury instructions and even, in some states, led to jury involvement in criminal sentencing.

---

[20]   See generally Arthur Schlesinger, *The Age of Jackson*, chapter 25, "Jacksonian Democracy and the Law" (Boston: Little, Brown and Company, 1945).

The practice of having judges decide the law and the jury decide the facts greatly modified the populist concept of the jury and made it an adjunct of the court. When the jury's role became that of dispassionate trier of facts, then rules of evidence were developed to protect the jury from placing weight on matters that should not be given great probative value or heard at all. Instructions to the jury became very important and at one time were the basis of many appeals before standard jury instructions were devised that saved judges from error, often at the expense of jurors' understanding of the instructions. Notwithstanding these constraints, the jury system constituted a check upon the power of the judiciary.

Judicial Independence. If any single concept links the reforms that have changed state courts in recent decades, it is *judicial independence*. The term has a noble sound and has frequently served as a judicial rallying cry. Although the term sounds precise and clear, its meaning is ambiguous and sometimes controversial. Paraphrasing Dickens: It was the best of terms; it was the worst of terms.

To government officials outside the judiciary, particularly those in appropriating bodies, *judicial independence* may mean lack of accountability by judges and a general license for judicial activists to ignore the separation of powers when the defense of judicial prerogatives is not the issue. There are some interesting historical examples of judges who could not content themselves with a purely judicial role. John Jay negotiated a treaty while holding the position of chief justice of the United States Supreme Court. Justice Abe Fortas, who served as an adviser to President Lyndon Johnson before his appointment to the bench and continued in that role after becoming a justice, was eventually forced to resign from the United States Supreme Court, stating that he did not want to be a party to undermining separation of powers. Chief Justice Earl Warren served as head of the commission to investigate the assassination of President John F. Kennedy. The notorious interference of President Buchanan in the deliberations on the *Dred Scott* decision was actually done at the invitation of a member of the Supreme Court.[21]

To the average person, the term *judicial independence* smacks of elitism and arrogance. Just about any court user hopes that a judge will be objective and enforce procedural due process, but the idea of independent judges also has a pejorative connotation in a democratic society fearful of untrammeled official power.

To judges, the term *judicial independence* encompasses separation of powers, inherent powers of the judiciary, and freedom to adjudicate without external pressure. For purposes of this book, *judicial independence* means what judges say it means. One of the best definitions is provided by Judge John J. Parker, an early advocate of improved court management who was involved in the first set of standards of judicial administration produced by the American Bar Association:

> The judge must not only be independent—absolutely free of all influence and control so that he can put into his judgments the honest, unfettered and unbiased judgment of his mind but he must also be so freed of business,

---

[21]   Carl Brent Swisher, *American Constitutional Development* (Cambridge, MA: Houghton Mifflin Company, 1943), 244-246.

political and financial connections and obligations that the public will recognize that he is independent. It is of supreme importance, not only that justice be done, but that litigants before the court and the public generally understand that it is being done and that the judge is beholden to no one but God and his conscience.[22]

As Judge Parker states, judicial independence is intimately tied up with adjudication of cases, as it has been from the early colonial period when colonists objected to judges answerable to the crown. The term does not mean refusal to account for expenditure of public funds or for operational failures of courts. It does mean protection of the judiciary from external domination or pressure in performing the essential mission of the court.

In the name of judicial independence, judges and their allies have sought to eliminate or at least limit political considerations in the selection, tenure, and salary of judges. They have also sought to make judges more professional and more aware of their responsibilities. They have striven for more control over management of the judicial branch and struggled against budgetary retaliation against judges whose decisions have offended the other branches. They have sought more coherent trial court structures and less tampering with court organization and jurisdiction to suit local political needs. They have tried to bring attorneys under the control of the court rather than vice versa and to generally ward off the intrusion of officials of the other branches. Implicit in all these objectives is the desire to uplift the judiciary as a coequal branch of government. The creation of a "real" third branch is the declaration of judicial independence.

The resource needs of courts have increased in relation to expanding responsibilities, causing appropriating bodies, both state and local, to demand more "accountability" from the judiciary. This is a sensitive word in court circles, not because judges object to being held accountable for the resources they receive, but because they often see the word accountability as a thinly veiled challenge to judicial independence in the exercise of the adjudicative function. The judicial perspective on accountability is dealt with in the *Trial Court Performance Standards*, specifically Standard 4.2, which states, "The trial court responsibly seeks, uses, and accounts for its public resources." Standard 4.2 must be considered in conjunction with the commentary on Standard 4.1, which stresses independence:

> In order for a trial court to persist in its role as preserver of legal norms and as part of a separate branch of government, it must develop and maintain its distinctive and independent status. It must be conscious of its legal and administrative boundaries and vigilant in protecting them.

> Effective trial courts resist being absorbed or managed by the other branches of government.

---

[22]   John J. Parker, "The Judicial Office in the United States," *Tennessee Law Review* 20 (1949): 703, 705-06.

Standard 5.3 combines accountability and independence as elements in winning public trust and confidence, reading as follows: "The trial court is perceived to be independent, not unduly influenced by other components of government, and accountable."

The independence asserted by courts under the concept of separation of powers normally places them in a different budget status than executive branch agencies. The special budgetary status of courts, which is often challenged by officials of the other branches, may be made explicit in case law, the state constitution, or statute.

Judges recognize that they are accountable to the other branches for the public funds that they receive but want it made clear that they are not accountable to the other branches in the exercise of their adjudicative function. Unfortunately, legislative anger over some high-profile exercises of the adjudication function has occasionally resulted in a vengeful attitude and has sometimes been a serious detriment to court success in obtaining resources.

Some legislators complain that the judiciary is too remote and self-absorbed and not really accountable to anyone. The legislative concern generally takes the form of criticizing the manner in which courts request resources. A frequent observation is that the judiciary demands resources without really clarifying their operational needs or adequately explaining what appear to many as arcane procedures. Legislators take the power of the purse as seriously as judges take the concept of independence, so interbranch conflicts often revolve around the two buzzwords *accountability* and *independence*.

A 1995 survey of twenty states by the National Center for State Courts revealed more problems between the judiciary and the executive branch than between the judiciary and the legislative branch. Court officials asserted that the executive branch interfered in financial administration, particularly by impeding the transfer of appropriations between budget categories and by conducting audits. Court officials felt that each new gubernatorial administration changed the ground rules and budget strategy, sometimes intruding into budget matters from which the governor is constitutionally excluded. Relations with the legislature, though not necessarily amicable, were considered more predictable.

Inherent Powers.[23] Another controversial aspect of judicial power is the exercise of inherent powers. This can take the form of punishment for contempt of court, judicial rulemaking, or the mandating of actions of the other branches if the court is sure that such actions are reasonably necessary to fulfill the court's constitutional obligations. Inherent powers have never received the same degree of attention as judicial review, yet inherent powers have been used much more extensively and aggressively than judicial review. The latter is rarely invoked and then only in the context of a case or controversy proper to the judicial function. Admittedly, voiding an action or legal enactment of another branch raises interbranch tensions, but this is a lot less confrontational than ordering an

---

[23]   See generally Felix F. Stumpf, *Inherent Powers of the Courts: Sword and Shield of the Judiciary* (Reno, NV: National Judicial College, 1994).

official or agency of another branch to take an action considered to be discretionary and proper to that branch, such as appropriating money for the judiciary.

Courts have long held that rules of procedure should be a function of judicial rulemaking, not statute. This view is reflected in Section 1.31 of the American Bar Association's 1990 *Standards of Judicial Administration*, volume 1, *Standards Relating to Court Organization*:

> A court system should have authority to prescribe rules of practice and procedure, civil and criminal. The authority should extend to all proceedings in all courts in the system and should include all aspects of procedure. The authority should be exercised through a procedure that involves use of advisory committees and notice to and opportunity on the part of members of appropriate legislative committees and the bar to suggest, review and make recommendations concerning proposed rules.

The problem with rulemaking is deciding when it intrudes into the substantive realm proper to the legislative branch. Rulemaking is a frequent source of interbranch tension.

When the budget process fails to provide the funding necessary to operate the court, the judiciary can also resort to inherent powers. This amounts to an assertion that the judicial branch, as a function of its independence and the separation of powers, has the inherent authority to order the other branches to supply the resources the court deems necessary for performance of its functions. Typically, inherent powers have been invoked at the trial court level in a budget dispute between a court and a local government, normally for some small amount of money. More often than not the requested expenditures were for functions that might be considered peripheral to the court's constitutional mandate; probation expenditures, for example. In the rare instances when the test of power is between a state supreme court and the other branches of state government, the stakes are raised, and the issue is very serious. In 1991 the chief justice of the state of New York filed a case against the governor and the legislature in a budget dispute.[24] In 1996 the Pennsylvania Supreme Court ordered the state legislature to fund trial courts.[25] These state-level fights are hard to win, but at the local level the courts have an advantage. Inherent powers suits against local governments are not struggles among equals. The trial court judge has an arsenal of weapons, not the least of which is that he or she may actually decide the case to which the court is a party or may simply have the power to issue a

---

[24] The chief justice brought suit against the other branches to force a higher appropriation, *Wachtler v. Cuomo*, No 6034, 91/N.Y. Sup. Ct., filed Sept. 25, 1991. The governor sought a stay in the federal courts. *Cuomo v. Wachtler*, No 91-CV-3874 (E.D.N.Y. Oct. 17, 1991). The issue was settled before trial.

[25] In *County of Allegheny v. Commonwealth of Pennsylvania*, 534 A. 2d 760 (1987), the supreme court found that the constitutional provision on court unification required state funding of trial courts but stayed judgment. In 1996 the supreme court effectuated its decision by issuing an order that the state fund trial courts.

mandate without a show cause order.[26] Moreover, the local officials see the supreme court lurking in back of the trial court. Judges see the situation in the same way, so it is not unusual for judges and some chief justices to fear state financing of trial courts, because it is easier to push around local governments than the state legislature.

Supreme courts do not like inherent powers suits by local judges, which are sometimes based on arbitrary reasons and place the court in a difficult position—either showing disloyalty to a judge or rendering a decision that has the appearance of a conflict of interest. Numerous steps have been taken to limit the incidence of inherent powers suits: reducing use of ex parte orders by trial judges (Pennsylvania, Colorado), requiring advance approval of the supreme court (New Jersey), establishing a very high standard of proof in inherent powers suits (Washington), creating separate tribunals that include local government officials (Missouri), and creating a mediation process (New Jersey).

There is a very definite link between inherent powers suits and administrative and budgetary unification. Inherent powers suits may start off as disputes between a trial court and a local government, but they often end up as a dispute between the trial court and the supreme court. The Michigan Supreme Court, at one time, had the state court administrator intervene in inherent powers cases to head off suits, but trial judges forced the termination of this procedure because they felt that the state court administrator was not sufficiently supportive of the court position. The current procedure still calls for intervention by the state court administrator but does not preclude a trial court from proceeding with an action (Michigan Administrative Order No. 1985-6). In Illinois, the chief justice, in annual reports to the legislature in 1986 and 1987, pointed out that the existing structural unification of the state court system would be undercut by local financing until the state assumed ultimate financial responsibility. He pointedly observed that the Illinois Supreme Court had not always sided with trial court judges in inherent powers disputes but that the inadequacies of county financing could not be long ignored. Translation: Do not count on the court to keep its finger in the dike.

Inherent powers suits drive state financing and increased supreme court control. The irony of the inherent powers suits is that trial court judges may win a few local battles but find themselves under more direct supreme court control.

Judicial Federalism. The relationship between state and federal courts is not a peer relationship. Federal judges feel themselves quite superior to state judges, and state judges tend to have a resentful inferiority complex with respect to the federal judiciary. Numerous attempts have been made to have councils of federal and state judges and to encourage dialogue, but despite some improvement in relationships, the two court systems have points of tension that are almost inevitable in a fluid federal system. A period of rapid federal expansion

---

[26]   Under Trial Court Rule 60.5, Indiana judges have very broad power to compel funding of their court.

has coincided with the state court reform movement of the late twentieth century, so that as state supreme courts have succeeded in extending their sway over their court systems, they have felt themselves losing more of their independence to the federal government.

The deep concern over this phenomenon is reflected in the official resolutions of the Conference of Chief Justices (CCJ).[27] This organization of state supreme court chief justices was founded in 1949 at the beginning of the state court reform movement, so its official statements reflect the tensions and issues of the court reform period. Interestingly, federalism is the issue that has generated the most resolutions. These resolutions fall into four broad issue areas:

- the allocation of cases between state and federal courts
- the finality of state supreme court judgments and the primacy of state supreme courts in matters of state law
- the primacy of state supreme courts in administration of the state court system and the bar, in particular admission to the practice of law, attorney ethics, and rules of practice and procedure
- federal preemption of state law

Congress determines the jurisdiction of federal courts and, in so doing, affects the jurisdiction of state courts. Statutes pertaining to diversity jurisdiction are the primary example of this phenomenon, but changes in federal question jurisdiction are also significant; for example, the elimination of a monetary requirement for federal question jurisdiction.[28] State courts live with the overlapping jurisdiction characteristic of our dual court system but do not like it. CCJ has favored eliminating diversity-of-citizenship jurisdiction but has bowed to the reality that the organized bar will never permit loss of the federal option. Therefore, CCJ has focused on reducing the scope of diversity jurisdiction by such means as redefining citizenship or increasing the monetary requirement for federal jurisdiction. Federal judges, by and large, agree with state court judges in this matter.[29] Congress, however, accedes to the trial court attorneys, who like to have a choice of forum.

CCJ has had a more ambivalent attitude on federal question jurisdiction. At one point, CCJ offered to take more federal question cases, but on other occasions expressed its concern over the effects of concurrent jurisdiction on state court caseloads. CCJ objected to the confusion sown by having both state and federal courts dealing with the same issue, especially where the federal preemption of an area was partial.

---

[27]   These resolutions are archived and indexed by the National Center for State Courts, who provides the source of the statements in this section.

[28]   The principal jurisdictional statutes affecting state courts are 28 USC §§ 1331(federal questions), 1332 (diversity).

[29]   This view is reflected in the *Long Range Plan for the Federal Courts* of the Judicial Conference of the United States.

Of highest concern to the state courts has been federal habeas corpus review of state court convictions because it permits federal trial judges to review a conviction affirmed by the highest state appellate court and undermines the finality of state supreme court decisions. For years Congress has debated habeas corpus reform and has, in fact, tightened up federal habeas corpus review. The state courts recognize that reducing the scope of federal habeas corpus places a higher responsibility on state courts, especially in ensuring adequate legal representation, but this is certainly preferable to having state supreme courts second-guessed by federal trial judges.[30]

CCJ has taken a number of other positions related to federal review of state convictions:

- that only a three-judge federal panel should have the authority to set aside the judgment of a state supreme court
- that federal courts should not have jurisdiction of state criminal cases until there has been an exhaustion of remedies
- that state courts should relieve federal courts of habeas corpus volume by adequate review of cases involving federal constitutional rights
- that there be a national court of state review in lieu of review by lower federal courts

These all reflect the concern of state judges over federal domination.

Another "turf" issue of concern to CCJ is preserving the exclusive administrative control of state supreme courts over the state judicial branch and bar. CCJ seeks preservation of state court control of admission to the practice of law, disciplinary procedures for attorneys and judges, promulgating codes of ethics for attorneys and judges, enacting rules for the administration of the court system, and making rules to govern procedures in the courts of the states. CCJ seeks to fend off any attempt of federal regulatory agencies to regulate some aspects of bar admission and ethics, to impose federal standards on child support enforcement proceedings, or to disrupt state court proceedings by stays, as occasionally occurs in bankruptcy proceedings. Similarly, CCJ guards its control over the state judiciary. CCJ opposed legislation that would bring all state court judges within the Age Discrimination in Employment Act of 1967, because the legislation involved a federal preemption of a state prerogative to set the qualifications for state judges.

CCJ has also assumed a protective posture over areas of state law being federalized by legislation. Although this does not come under the heading of judicial federalism, it is one of the areas of state-federal relations about which state judges feel deeply. CCJ believes that product liability law is basically a state court

---

[30] A related issue is certification of state law questions from federal courts to state courts, inasmuch as federal judges must apply state law in diversity cases. The process of certification preserves the state supreme court as the final interpreter of state law.

concern best left to the case-by-case approach of the common law and gradual adaptation on a state-by-state basis. This principle has been applied in objecting to federal legislation limiting product liability in the following areas: manufacturers of small aircraft; producers of child vaccines; producers of toxic substances, particularly in a mass tort situation; and producers of asbestos.

CCJ has expressed opposition to a variety of bills preempting some area of state law, specifically federal attempts to set standards for guardianships and conservatorships; creation of federal cause of action under the Parental Kidnapping Prevention Act; the broad scope of federal civil jurisdiction under RICO; creation of federal civil cause under legislation to prevent telemarketing fraud; creation of a federal civil right for gender-based crimes of violence against women; impingement on state domestic relations law; and the federalization of many street crimes under proposed laws against violent crime. CCJ also expressed concern that health care legislation proposed in 1994 would displant the state courts as the primary forum for health benefit disputes.

The integrity of the state judicial branch is jealously protected against federal attempts to aggrandize the federal role at the expense of the states. The state courts do not wish to be a dumping ground for cases not wanted by federal judges, nor do they like being used as the enforcing agents for federal social policy. There is, however, no defense against federal preemption and the erosion of state law. CCJ is losing this battle.

The Operational Aspects of Judicial Independence and Separation of Powers

A few appellate judges equipped with legal weaponry do not constitute a judicial branch, nor are they truly independent. The judicial branch is not a coequal branch of government unless it has the ability and the authority to manage its internal operations, including its largest single component, the trial courts. When this important component of the judiciary is part of local government and local politics, there is no state judicial branch in any meaningful sense of the word. This was the situation around 1950 when judicial leaders and court reformers started to take cognizance of the relative anarchy that prevailed in trial courts and the detachment of state supreme courts from this problem.

The trial courts were organizationally chaotic, and the judges were often unprofessional and unqualified. To the extent there was any administration of courts, it was under the control of the other branches of government. Lawyers walked into the void and dominated many aspects of court operations, notably scheduling of cases. The immersion of trial courts in local government and politics was compromising the integrity of the judiciary. To speak of these courts as part of a state judicial branch suggested a level of administrative coherence that was belied by the facts. The trial courts were, to an incredible degree, on their own, often for the worse.

The court of last resort and the intermediate appellate courts were treated fairly well by the other two branches under principles of comity, because they made few budgetary demands and were not a real threat to the political status quo. This changed after 1950 when state supreme courts began to protest the way judges were selected and to seek administrative control over trial courts, more state resources for trial courts, and a more rational organization of trial courts. These demands were perceived in two ways by those outside the courts: as a long overdue supreme court interest in improving the trial courts, or as empire-building and centralization at the expense of local autonomy. There was a more fundamental implication. The state supreme courts were attempting to create a state judicial branch that existed in fact, not just in title, and to end the dominance of the other branches, both state and local, over the courts. This shift in the interbranch balance of power was upsetting to many legislators and, for that matter, to many judges, who preferred local autonomy and being part of the local government scene.

A related and very important issue was the ability of judges to manage their own affairs. The judicial branch had no significant track record in public administration and no credibility with the other branches in this field. Moreover, many judges were less than enthusiastic about assuming a management role; some judges felt such a role to be inappropriate. Thus, advocates of a more administratively independent judicial branch found that the judiciary was not unanimous in support of the goal and shared some of the doubts about the ability of judges to manage.

Those urging an administratively strengthened judicial branch addressed what they perceived to be the principal weaknesses within the trial courts:

- haphazard management and the lack of uniform procedures
- inadequacy of local funding for trial courts
- inequitable distribution of local resources for trial courts
- the confusing mishmash of jurisdictional and venue laws
- profusion of separate local courts molded to the whim of local attorneys and politicians
- no coherent means of handling appeals from limited jurisdiction trial courts
- too many judges untrained in the law and operating without any supervision
- highly political means of choosing judges
- no opportunity for judges to receive an initial orientation or to upgrade their skills in training courses
- highly political means of dealing with problems of judicial misbehavior

Basically, state trial courts were too political, too unprofessional, too immersed in localism, too disorganized, too dominated by lawyers, and too bereft of management from judges or anybody else.

The means chosen to improve the trial courts were very simple. The trial courts were to be removed from the local government structure and politics into a uniform statewide judicial branch that operated under the administrative direction of the court of last resort, assisted by a professional manager, and was, if possible, funded by the state. The corollary of these steps was upgrading the judiciary by merit selection, by an intrabranch system for controlling judicial misbehavior, and by creation of judicial education programs. Underlying these reforms was the unspoken premise that unless the top judicial leaders actually have and use the authority to put the judicial house in order, then the judiciary does not deserve to be called a third branch of state government.

PART II

*The Obstacles
to Judicial Branch Control
of Internal Operations*

Chapter 2

Politics and the State Courts: Balancing the Popular Will and Adjudicative Independence

The relationship of state judges to the political process and the popular will has been and still is a dilemma of American democracy. The idea of a judiciary totally insulated from the popular will frightens many people. Even more frightening is the specter of a judiciary that is so politicized that the appearance of justice and the integrity of adjudication are seriously compromised. This conflict of values has had a pendulum effect, so that state courts have been alternately politicized and insulated. By 1950, the pendulum had swung mightily in the direction of political involvement, with serious repercussions for judicial independence and public confidence in the justice system. Since 1950 there has been a swing to the center, but the battle rages.

At the core is the political process of judicial selection. Although critics bewail the deleterious consequences of this process, they do not expect to totally extirpate political practices so firmly rooted in democratic traditions, nor do they urge a passive, apolitical posture for the judicial branch. They favor a more aggressive role for the courts in dealing with the other branches. The reformist position appears to be that adjudication gains credibility if judges are perceived to be independent of the political process but that the judicial branch must assert itself politically as well as legally to establish control over its affairs and to insulate the judiciary from inappropriate political intrusion.

The Origin and Nature of Politicized Selection of Judges

The history of judicial selection reveals the peculiar ambivalence of Americans about the political relationship of the judiciary to the people. In the early days of the Republic, Americans leaned toward a judiciary that was heavily insulated against popular pressure. This view is reflected in Article III of the United States Constitution, which grants federal judges life tenure and protects them from reprisal by salary cuts and from direct control of the electorate. Congress did, however, retain the right to fix the jurisdiction of the courts, an important check that was also preserved at the state level.

The states joined the national government in insulating the judiciary from popular control. The original thirteen state constitutions did not allow for popular election of judges.[1] The two methods of judicial selection were appointment by the legislature or by the governor, the former method being more common in that period. Ten of the states based judicial tenure on good behavior; only Connecticut, New Jersey, and Pennsylvania based judicial tenure on a term of years.

The Jeffersonians and the Jacksonians regarded the judiciary as an undemocratic institution that might thwart the will of the people as expressed through elected governors and legislators. Jefferson's early views on selection of judges were hardly radical, but his confrontation with the federalist judiciary changed his views.[2] He favored selection for a term of years rather than life and was willing to consider the election of state judges. The Jacksonians were less ambivalent and wanted to democratize everything, including the judiciary. The Jacksonians were remarkably successful in their quest for more democracy; courts were simply caught up in the movement, not specially targeted.[3]

Vermont's constitution was the first to call for direct election of judges above the level of justice of the peace. This occurred in 1777, even though Vermont was not officially admitted as a state until 1791. Vermont was not one of the original thirteen states and was considered to be a frontier state with more egalitarian views than the other New England states. Several decades later, in 1812, Georgia permitted some judges to be elected by the voters for four-year terms. In 1816 the new state of Indiana permitted voters to elect judges of the state's principal trial court for seven-year terms. In 1832 Mississippi introduced partisan election of all judges (Mississippi reverted to appointed judgeships after Reconstruction but eventually returned to the democratic model). By 1845 Michigan, Georgia, Indiana, and Vermont had popular election of some judges for a term of years. In 1846 New York followed Mississippi in having all judges elected in partisan elections. This started a general trend to popular election of judges; in 1850 alone, seven states chose this path. By the end of the nineteenth century, popular election of judges for a term of years was the norm. Parallel to this movement was a tendency to end unlimited tenure with removal only for cause and to restrict judges to a term of years, even in those states with legislative and gubernatorial appointment of judges. Americans had clearly chosen to democratize the state judiciary.

There has been some retreat from this robustly democratic posture in the twentieth century. Reformers started to look askance at the methods of judicial selection and complained that the caliber of judges was poor and that their involvement in politics so great as to cast doubt on their objectivity and the appearance of justice. There were some instances of outright corruption to lend weight to these arguments. The reformers took dead aim at partisan elections and legislative selection of judges and were not too enthusiastic about nonpar-

---

[1] For an overview of judicial selection see Larry Berkson, "Judicial Selection in the United States: A Special Report," Slotnick, Judicial Politics, 57-59.

[2] Friedman, American Law, 126-128.

[3] The democratization of the state courts is described in Friedman, American Law, 371-73. See also Evan A. Evans, "Judicial Selection and the Democratic Spirit," Scigliano, The Courts, 57-64.

tisan elections, although they saw them as an improvement. The argument against nonpartisan elections was that under the facade there was often some lively partisanship, with the judges being selected by party organizations to run on a nonpartisan label.

Mainly, reformers sought gubernatorial appointment of judges from a list of qualified nominees chosen by a nominating commission that would, in theory, have a membership that was so broad and diverse that it would escape political domination. To preserve popular participation, voters were permitted to remove judges in a retention election. This general approach (the Missouri Plan) was advocated with some success, particularly as it applied to the appellate courts.

Critics of the plan felt that any judge who had not committed a major felony could obtain approval from a majority of the voters in an uncontested retention election (Illinois requires 60 percent) and would likely serve for life.[4] In actual practice, few judges are rejected, and many voters do not even bother voting in retention elections. The rejection of a judge in a retention election may not be an expression of dissatisfaction with the particular judge but an expression of general dissatisfaction with government or with the judiciary. There are, of course, some notorious retention elections, such as the revolt of the California voters against the Rose Bird court, which led to the lopsided rejection of Chief Justice Bird and two colleagues who were labeled as soft on crime and capital punishment.[5] The Republican governor, formerly state attorney general, intervened on behalf of a fourth justice, sometimes linked with the Rose Bird group, and he survived. Interestingly, Chief Justice Bird based a lot of her campaign on judicial independence despite advice that this was not something that made the hearts of voters beat faster.

The arguments against reforms like the Missouri Plan were that they emanated from elitist groups that wanted judges chosen from a particular stratum of society, rather than by the people they served. Basically, the anti-reform movement rested its case on three democratic principles:

- Why are judges so special that they should be exempted from the democratic process?
- Judges need only common sense and knowledge of the community.
- Politics is a fact of community life in a democracy, not some horrible taboo; no person ascends to a judgeship without political views.

The reformers argued that judges required a degree of detachment and independence that made it inappropriate for them to be selected and removed according to popular whim or to be victimized by reprisals for unpopular deci-

---

[4]   For a description of the politics of retention elections see William K. Hall and Larry T. Aspin, " What Twenty Years of Judicial Retention Elections Have Told Us," Slotnick, *Judicial Politics*, 61-69.

[5]   For a description of this election see John T. Wold and John H. Culver, "The Defeat of the California Justices: The Campaign, the Electorate, and the Issue of Judicial Accountability," Slotnick, *Judicial Politics*, 71-79.

sions. They asserted that adjudication required a special skill and knowledge not conferred simply by receiving more votes than someone else. Underlying this viewpoint was the idea that many fine lawyers are not good politicians, or do not like to undergo the trauma of the election process. This expertise argument was more successful at the appellate level than at the trial court level where judges were more visible and had more direct effect on citizens.

There was some truth in both positions, resulting in a modified retention of the populist model. Despite the concessions to the reformers, the election of judges for a term of years remained common, particularly at the trial court level. Even at the end of the twentieth century, supreme court justices are still chosen by partisan election in Alabama, Arkansas, Illinois, Louisiana, Mississippi, North Carolina, Pennsylvania, Texas, and West Virginia. Supreme court justices are still chosen by nonpartisan election in Georgia, Idaho, Kentucky, Michigan, Minnesota, Montana, Nevada, North Dakota, Ohio, Oregon, Washington, and Wisconsin. In Virginia and South Carolina, the legislature still chooses the members of the supreme court (and other judges, as well).

At the trial court level, election is the most common method of choosing judges. About two-thirds of the states initially choose at least some trial judges in elections. New Mexico even has a contested partisan retention election, as do Utah and Montana (retention elections are usually uncontested). The elective process is tempered somewhat because vacancies are normally filled by executive appointment, so many judges initially come on the bench without having to face the voters. One result of the vacancy appointment system is that judges appointed in a district where their party is in the minority are sometimes voted out of office at the first opportunity.

Some hybrid systems employ several different methods of selection for judges in the same level of the court system. For example, judges of the general jurisdiction court in the two largest Arizona counties are chosen by appointment from nominations by a commission, but other judges of general jurisdiction courts are elected by the voters.

In Ohio, where there is lively partisan politics within the judiciary, there are a number of examples of trial judges of the minority party being voted out of office in the first election after their appointment.[6] Everyone seems to be keenly aware of the political affiliation of judges, in part because judges sometimes make it very clear. I once interviewed a judge in his chambers and was intrigued by the huge picture of Republican governor Jim Rhodes prominently displayed on the wall behind him. Ironically, the general elections are supposed to be nonpartisan, yet party affiliation is usually known because judges are nominated in partisan primaries. Probably no other state has had as many members of the supreme court defeated in theoretically nonpartisan elections.

Neighboring Michigan has a similar system of judicial selection but has not experienced the volatility of Ohio. In 1996 the state witnessed a well-funded, clearly partisan campaign against two incumbent judges in what was ostensibly a

---

[6]   For an analysis of judicial elections in Ohio see Lawrence Baum, "The Electoral Fates of Incumbent Judges in the Ohio Court of Common Pleas," Slotnick, *Judicial Politics*, 81-89.

nonpartisan election. The campaign failed but illustrated that partisan nominations and nonpartisan elections do not mix very well.

Appointing rather electing judges does not mean that the process of selection is apolitical. The appointing authority, normally the governor, can manipulate the process to have his or her favorite candidate included in the list of nominees.[7] Moreover, there is sometimes furious political pressure on the governor to choose particular favorites of legislators. Some governors find this so irritating that they are happy to hide behind the shield of a nominating commission. In Virginia, where legislators choose trial judges (usually deferring to the wishes of legislators from the particular judicial district), the process can be quite unseemly both initially and at the time of retention. Washington-area papers reported that the retention of a judge turned on his refusal in 1994 to approve a permit to carry a concealed weapon for Oliver North (Republican candidate for the United States Senate), despite approving a permit for him in 1992.

In California, where governors control the judicial selection process, there has been no pretense of bipartisanship or balance. The ideological cleavage on some California courts, including the supreme court, has been extreme. Governor Duekmejian, for example, showed a marked preference for former prosecutors, as that had been his career background.   The appointees of Governor Edmund "Jerry" Brown were, on the other hand, somewhat to the left of center. Courts with a mix of Republican and Democratic appointees were sometimes quite divided.

The big difference between elected and appointed methods is that in the former situation the judge is often forced to raise money and to campaign, maybe even take public stands on issues that could become the subject of adjudication. The money often comes from lawyers, sometimes quite grossly. Some Louisiana judges actually have fund raisers at which local attorneys feel obliged to appear. The civil defense bar and civil plaintiffs' bar may openly vie for the inside track. The local folklore is that judges remember those who were on their side, so much so that cases have been settled when the attorneys found out the identity of the judge (or judges on an intermediate appellate panel). One enterprising Texas judge has dinners for small groups of attorneys and their spouses and charges them a significant sum for the honor. There is an element of "mutual blackmail" in attorney funding of judicial campaigns.

Not even the most utopian reformer expects that the judiciary will be totally insulated from politics. The purpose of the twentieth-century reforms was to reduce the more flagrant forms of political influence and to create an atmosphere where judges could make judgments relatively free of political pressures. One measure of the tension between politics and judicial detachment was the difficulty faced by the American Bar Association in defining the ethical aspects of judicial political activity. The original ABA *Canons of Judicial Ethics* in 1924 urged judges to "avoid making political speeches, making or soliciting payment of

---

[7]   Illinois has an unusual process whereby the supreme court can fill any appellate court vacancy. Vacancies on the circuit court are filled by the court. Circuit court judges in Illinois choose associate judges of their court.

assessments or contributions to party funds, the public endorsement of candidates for political office and participation in party conventions." By midcentury the ABA had moderated its stance in the light of political reality, recognizing that judges in some states had to put up money to win political endorsements and had to be politically active. Canon 7 of the 1969 version of the *Canons of Judicial Ethics* frankly permitted political contributions to a party, campaigning, and public identification with a political party.

Realistically, there will always be some crossover between the judiciary and other elected offices. Courts are part of the governmental system, and it is hardly surprising that judges come to the bench after having held some elected public office in state or local government. In fact, such experience is probably helpful to a judge. For example, former Chief Justice Ralph Erickstad in North Dakota had been a leader in the state legislature and used this to great advantage in struggling for court reform. Chief Justice Sandy Keith of Minnesota served in the Minnesota Senate and as lieutenant governor before going on the bench and proved to be particularly sensitive to interbranch relations. Chief Justice Jean A. Turnage of Montana served over twenty years in the legislature before becoming chief, and former Alabama Chief Justice Bo Torbert was instrumental in steering court reform through the state senate before succeeding Howell Heflin as chief.

The judiciary is occasionally a stepping-stone to an elective office. Alabama chief justice Howell Heflin went on to a career in the United States Senate. George Wallace used a circuit judgeship as a springboard to the governorship of Alabama. Frank Licht went from the Superior Court of Rhode Island to the governor's mansion. Conversely, some public figures come to the judiciary from such high public offices as state governor, among them William O'Neill, who became chief justice of Ohio after serving as governor; so did G. Mennen (Soapy) Williams in Michigan and John King in New Hampshire.

There is frequently a political stepping-stone process within the judiciary. A judge may win election to a trial court position and then position himself or herself to run for an appellate judgeship. This internal upward mobility can also occur in a state where judges are appointed. Before unification of superior and municipal courts, California had a tradition of using the municipal courts as an entry-level judicial post pending elevation to the superior court.

Once, the National Center for State Courts was engaged in a study of the financing of the Arkansas courts during a hotly contested election for a position on the state supreme court. A trial judge who was closely identified with the study and was a candidate for election to the supreme court became concerned over the possible effect of the study report on his attempt to move upward. When the project director arrived with the final report, the judge sent an emissary to his hotel room to request that he depart from Little Rock, taking the report with him. The project director declined, and cooler heads prevailed. The next day the report, which was rather detailed and dull, was presented at a press conference and got no negative response from the press, whereupon the judge embraced the report. There was nothing particularly harmful about the incident, but it illustrates the effect of politics on judicial behavior.

Inappropriate Political Intrusions and Public Perceptions

A 1992 public opinion survey in California revealed that 58 percent of the persons surveyed felt that politics influenced court decisions.[8] California has had some sharp ideological divisions among its judges but is not, on a comparative basis, one of the highly political court systems. There is no way to delve into the thinking that led to this survey result, but it was not considered a vote of confidence. The public expects more objectivity from courts than it does from the governor and the legislature and reacts negatively to indications that judges may be carrying a political agenda into the courtroom.

Judges are well aware of the public's skepticism. Nonetheless, the heated discussions on the insulation of the judiciary from politics tend to be a little fuzzy on the subject of what constitutes a political intrusion. From the welter of verbiage on the subject, five main ideas emerge:

- Political campaigning and fund raising demean the judiciary, depriving it of the dignity and detachment that should be associated with the judicial office.

- Judges should be free of the fear of political reprisal if they are to have the requisite independence to do justice.

- Political participation creates the appearance of a quid pro quo for political support and compromises the integrity of the adjudication process.

- An elected judiciary reflects only the dominant political group and is not properly representative of the populace as a whole.

- An elected judiciary becomes part and parcel of the prevailing political system and lacks credibility and detachment in dealing with this system in legal matters.

Political Campaigns. The idea of campaigning or raising money is at odds with the aloof objectivity required of a judge. There is a fundamental discrepancy between being the detached adjudicator and the politico seeking votes wherever they may be found.

One Ohio trial judge reminisced at national meeting about his recent reelection campaign, which he found harrowing for two reasons. He had faced a well-financed opponent who was claiming to be tougher on crime than he (somewhat ironic because this judge, by any standards of toughness, was a rather stern judge). His second problem was that he was a Democrat in a year when it was clear that Republicans were going to sweep the board in Ohio. Although the election was supposedly nonpartisan, it was actually partisan except for the lack of a party label on the ballot. This meant that the usual campaign war chest would be inadequate and that he would have to issue a general financial SOS.

[8]   *Report of the Commission on the Future of the California Courts: Justice in the Balance 2020* (1993), 3.

He had to face voters who were being bombarded by ads saying that he was freeing dangerous felons as fast as they came before him. He had to go to places like the county fair to ask for votes but could not go around assuring everyone that he would incarcerate anyone who came before him. He said it was humiliating to be faced with silly charges and to be unable to respond without compromising his position as a judge with many criminal cases before him. Ultimately, he prevailed (as do all but a few judicial incumbents), but only by appealing to Republican friends, particularly Republican attorneys, to get out the word about him. Fortunately, the Republican attorneys were so disgusted with the campaign against him that he survived. He said that he was not opposed to making judges answerable to the people in some way and felt that he had learned a lot from talking to people in a setting where they could talk to him more freely about their concerns. He could, however, discern no rationale for involving judges in contested elections when they will be exposed to charges to which they cannot reply without compromising their judicial office.

Ohio accords its municipal courts significant jurisdiction in matters arising under state law, so these courts, rather than the forty-nine county courts, are the principal limited jurisdiction courts for the state. From time to time, Ohio considers having a limited jurisdiction trial court system based entirely on county lines; in effect, merging the municipal courts into a countywide court. The problem is that this would upset the political balance in counties where one party controlled a particular municipality but not the county as a whole. Every time the issue of unification comes up in the legislature, the main concern is the ultimate allocation of judgeships between the two parties.

Unification would affect the future of many Ohio municipal judges, who would have a larger election district and more expensive campaigns. A municipal judge explained to a group of out-of-staters that it took about $150,000 to run for municipal judge. If he ran countywide, he'd have to raise double that amount and might lose. These concerns are never far from a judge's mind in a state where judicial politics is highly charged.

Court consultants in a very political state have to worry about the political effects of any report or study as it might provide campaign fodder. Once the National Center for State Courts did a study of a court that did not reflect well on some of the judges. One of the judges stated that he was upset by the report, because he might draw a "real" political opponent and would have to raise more than $300,000.[9] He was not too concerned about being reelected but hated the inconvenience of having to raise more money than he had anticipated.

New York elects most of its judges, but since 1978 the members of the highest court, the court of appeals, have been appointed by the governor from nominees submitted by a judicial nominating commission. Political occurrences in the 1970s speeded this change.[10] For many years, New York allowed the leaders

---

[9] In this jurisdiction it was not uncommon for a nuisance candidate to file in the hope that he would receive a financial incentive for withdrawal.

[10] See Frederick Miller, "Court Reform: The New York Experience," in Lee Powell, ed., *Court Reform in Seven States* (Williamsburg, VA: National Center for State Courts, 1980), 105-129.

of the Democratic and Republican parties to fill vacancies on the court of appeals by agreement. This tradition was particularly strong with the office of chief judge. The long-standing practice was for both parties to nominate the senior associate justice. In 1972 the state changed its election law and permitted candidates for a seat on the highest court to outflank the party conventions and to secure a major party nomination in a party primary. This resulted in a series of political events that dismayed legal and court observers.

In 1973 Chief Judge Stanley Field was slated for retirement. The senior associate judge, also near mandatory retirement age, announced that he would not be a candidate for the top job. Next in seniority was Charles D. Brietel, who, in addition to being a legal scholar, a former prosecutor, and a former counsel to the court, had served on the trial and appellate benches in Manhattan. Brietel was nominated by the Republicans, but the Democratic leadership did not follow the long-standing practice of cross-nomination, leading to a no-holds-barred Democratic primary with six candidates on the ballot. The winner was Jacob D. Fuchberg, a successful and prominent trial lawyer from New York City. In November Breitel defeated Fuchberg and a Conservative party candidate in a very bitter election. The following year, Fuchberg once again went the primary route and won a contested election to fill one of the two vacancies for associate judge; the principal loser was Harold A. Stevens, the court's only black judge. The two elections strained relations within the court, stiffening Brietel's determination to eliminate the partisan ballot in the selection of judges. The only thing that had prevented such electioneering and maneuvering up to 1972 was the iron control of party bosses, hardly a benign alternative.

It is not clear how judicial ethics applies to campaign rhetoric. There seems to be no problem about promising to improve court administration or expressing a general judicial philosophy. Judge James Stovall of Houston once ran for office on the pledge that he would improve the jury system and make it less burdensome for citizens, because he was an advocate of the one-day/one-trial system. Lacking a real issue, some candidates resort to very personal campaigns that demean the judiciary as well as their opponents.

A 1988 race for the Oregon Supreme Court illustrates both the personal and ideological aspects of judicial campaigns.[11] In Oregon's 1988 nonpartisan primary, no candidate for the open supreme court position obtained a majority, so the two highest vote getters had to face each other in the general election. The two men appeared to be remarkably similar; both were Democrats who had held leadership positions in the state legislature and were generally liberal in orientation. The campaign for the general election soon took on a very personal tone, even though the candidates knew each other well and were thought to be friends. One candidate accused the other of being unfit for the high court because of public brawling, misrepresentation of his legal record, and a pending ethics inquiry by

---

[11] For a description of the 1988 race, see Nicholas P. Lovrich and Charles H. Sheldon, "Is Voting for State Judges a Flight of Fancy or a Reflection of Policy and Value Preferences?" 16:3 (1994) *Justice System Journal*, 60-68.

the Oregon bar. In response, the accused candidate questioned the veracity of his opponent, saying that he told half truths 100 percent of the time.

The two men soon divided on some matters of political and legal philosophy, one asserting the it was the role of a judge to interpret the law, not to make it. The same candidate decried the crime rate, curbs on the right to bear arms, and interference with competition to get ahead in life, clearly buzzwords to attract more-conservative voters. The other candidate took a more liberal position and attracted funding from unions and various liberal organizations. Analysis of the election returns in one county revealed that hard-core conservative and liberal voters were influenced by these ideological stands and identified the judge closest to their political philosophy. One judge drew heavily from supporters of George Bush, and the other drew heavily from supporters of Michael Dukakis. The ideological postures of the two candidates for the supreme court had the air of tactical positioning rather than a fundamental philosophical difference, but there is a thin line separating an indication of judicial philosophy from a promise to vote a certain way if a specific issue arises. The campaign did little for the cause of judicial democracy.

Fear of Reprisal. Judges should be free from reprisal at the polls or, for that matter, from fear of not being reappointed because of their decisions. Otherwise, they cannot be truly independent in their essential task of adjudication. This argument is directed at the length and conditions of judicial tenure and the conditions of retention. A judge can be subjected to great pressure if people offended by his or her rulings are in a position to unseat the judge. This prospect does not, of course, upset populists, who feel that judges should be sensitive to community views.

Judges recognize that controversial decisions will engender an adverse reaction and generally accept this as a fact of life. There are numerous examples of legislative retaliation against a high court for political decisions, but this usually takes the form of budgetary revenge, as in California and Maine when the high court had to deal with term limits. The Maine court also had to handle legislative reapportionment in a closely divided two-party state. The Pennsylvania legislature was infuriated by a decision of the Commonwealth Court that required a very large outlay of state funds and promptly struck at the court budget. This sort of thing simply happens. What is more threatening than attacks upon a court budget is an attempt to deny a judge reappointment or reelection. Nothing else so directly strikes at the heart of judicial independence.

Most judges are aware that they face little risk of not being returned to office in a retention election, a contested election, or a reappointment process unless they offend some group that will take the time and effort necessary to unseat them. The most likely source of opposition is the bar. If the local bar mounts a challenge to an incumbent judge, this is particularly threatening, because members of the bar have the professional credentials to convince the voters that the judge is unworthy of the office. Many elected trial judges will confide that they are not too fearful of a challenge unless they deeply offend the local bar. They also count on the bar to discourage possible opponents or to provide a buffer if some special-interest group like Mothers Against Drunk Driving (MADD) decides to target them.

Prosecutors are also quite capable of unseating a judge and may mount campaigns against an incumbent judge they regard as too permissive. There is often a strange love-hate relationship between elected prosecutors and judges. Prosecutors can provide a buffer against weak cases and take the heat from law enforcement agencies, or they can open the floodgates to inundate the courts with weak cases, placing the onus on the courts to dismiss cases and to run the risk of being called soft on crime by the police public relations apparatus. One urban court administrator told a story of being asked to give the local police department a disposition tape that they could use to update their computerized criminal history files. A couple of days later an article appeared in the local paper listing the judges who were "soft on crime" and citing the court administrator as the source of the data for the analysis.

Judges and prosecutors can hurt each other immensely. When judges get disgusted with a prosecutor whom they find legally and managerially incompetent, they can start washing out a lot of cases on motions to quash, speedy trial motions, and other dismissals. A court may even insist on scheduling criminal cases. This type of confrontation can be exacerbated if the judges and the prosecutor are of different political parties. In such cases, the struggle is essentially to see who can place the other in the most embarrassing political position. Elected judges and elected prosecutors can, on occasion, become dangerous political enemies. In 1994 in Orleans Parish, Louisiana, always a colorful political milieu, the prosecutor ran his deputy against a criminal court judge he felt was too lenient, and the criminal court judge backed a strong opponent against the prosecutor. Just before an election, a New England trial court engaged in a titanic battle with the prosecutor over calendar control and charged him with failure to schedule tough cases. The prosecutor, who did not belong to the same party as most of the judges, was defeated, whereupon the struggle for judicial control of the calendar abated.

Watchdog groups like MADD have focused attention on judges who appeared to be too lenient with defendants charged with drunken driving, so that candidates for limited jurisdiction court judgeships frequently run for office on a "get tough with drunks" platform. The truth is that many judges hate to suspend licenses, feeling that they are denying someone a chance to get to work and perhaps undermining the ability of that person to support a family. The local ethos in matters pertaining to the right to operate a vehicle can be a powerful inducement to ignore some of the tough statutes and ordinances passed by state legislators or local officials. MADD or comparable groups challenge this, and judges and prosecutors feel this counterpressure. One lawyer recounted to a court consultant that he had had the dubious honor of being the first attorney to represent a client on a DUI charge before a judge just elected on a platform of sending drunks to jail. The frightened attorney made a deal with the prosecutor that circumvented the awaiting judicial vengeance. The salient fact is that elected judges may be heavily swayed by prevailing community sentiment rather than by the law.

Retention elections are usually pro forma endorsements of the incumbent unless some organized group energizes the voters in opposition. This occurred in Nebraska where a member of the supreme court was targeted by organized groups for his decisions and was defeated despite a late attempt to rally support. In the same period, the mid-1990s, a member of the Tennessee Supreme Court was swept out of office due to a public backlash against the handling of a serious crime. This surprising election result sent shock waves through the Tennessee judiciary because there was no apparent reason for singling out this particular justice as the object of public dissatisfaction. The defeated justice just happened to be on the ballot at an inopportune time.

Where legislators are involved in reappointment, anything can happen. Generally, they reappoint judges unless some organized opposition lobbies against reappointment, at which point volatility sets in. A frequent complaint in reappointment hearings is that the judge is insensitive or lacks appropriate judicial demeanor, charges that are very subjective and tend to rise or fall on the intensity of the opposition and the whims of local legislators in the same district as the judge. In Virginia, where the legislators have power of original appointment and reappointment of judges, the legislators occasionally deny reappointment. Judges tend to regard such denials as a warning shot across the bow, rather than as a serious exercise of legislative authority.

Now that Virginia is a two-party state, a new element has been added to the legislative role. In the 1996-97 session, the Virginia legislature engaged in a bitter struggle to fill a vacancy on the supreme court, because for the first time in the modern era Republicans had achieved parity in the senate and felt that it was time to break the long Democratic monopoly on judgeships. The Democrats were outraged by the idea that Republicans might want to participate in the selection process, and a bitter deadlock ensued, permitting the Republican governor to make an interim appointment.

Rhode Island used to have its legislature choose the supreme court judges. This arrangement favored the lower house and its speaker, because the lower house had more members. For about ten years in the late 1960s and early 1970s, some of the major criminal defense attorneys were members of the legislature, giving that group a political power that they rarely possess in the United States. The speaker of the house was the attorney for some major organized crime figures, but because of his political position was able to become the chief justice. His elevation to the highest court raised grave concerns, which escalated when it became known that he had not severed his ties with his former clients. He was forced to resign, but this did not end the drama. His successor, who was rated as unqualified by the Rhode Island Bar Association, was forced off the court for questionable handling of funds. This called into question the method for selecting members of the highest court, and Rhode Island altered its manner of selection, going to a system of gubernatorial appointment from candidates nominated by a judicial nominating commission. The legislature, however, has retained a major role in selecting members of the nominating commission and in the approval process.

In New Jersey, where appellate judges are subject to gubernatorial reappointment with consent of the senate, the upper house occasionally vents its displeasure about court decisions. Chief Justice Wilentz was almost denied reappointment because of a decision that affected zoning in affluent areas of New

Jersey. The opposition was led by a Republican legislator from the area affected by the decision, and he enlisted strong support from his party (the chief was a Democrat). Intervention by the Republican governor assisted the chief, but the incident illustrated that one unpopular decision can prematurely end a career on the bench.

Even in states with nonpartisan election of judges, incumbents are sometimes defeated by opponents who would, on the basis of their credentials, appear unlikely winners. In 1991 Washington voters replaced a highly regarded chief justice with a relatively unknown candidate in an upset that came as a total surprise. Interestingly, the Washington Supreme Court rotates the job of chief justice to the person closest to election.

In states with partisan judicial elections, incumbent judges can be punished for their party affiliation. In the South, where Democratic domination of state and local government was the norm until recently, partisan balloting ensured a monolithically Democratic judiciary. As the Republican Party started to gain strength and to actively challenge for judgeships, the partisan label started to lose its appeal in areas going Republican. Some politically knowledgeable chief justices in the South have privately observed that Democratic judges become well disposed to nonpartisan elections after a few Democratic incumbents are defeated by Republican rivals.

An illustration of the southern dilemma with respect to partisan elections is provided by North Carolina.[12] Up until the late 1980s, Republicans did not provide any significant opposition in judicial contests at the appellate or superior court level. Generally what happened was that incumbents were returned to office if they bore the Democratic label. Republicans rarely challenged an incumbent Democrat and usually just ran for open seats. When Republican governors were elected, they started to fill vacancies on the superior court with members of their own party, shocking the Democratic leaders in the state. Because Republican strength tended to be localized rather than statewide, the Democrats were normally able to defeat the Republican incumbents on appellate courts. Even superior court judges were elected statewide, despite being nominated in primaries within judicial districts. The statewide election of trial court judges effectively curbed Republican intrusions into the trial court judiciary. In 1988 the Republican Party challenged this practice, resulting in a federal district court decision that statewide election of superior court judges was an unconstitutional gerrymander (*North Carolina Republican Party v. Hunt*, Civil Action #88-263-Civ-5, E.D.N.C). The court ordered that ballots be tallied by district (but also statewide, pending resolution of the issue on appeal), prompting the Republican Party in 1994 to actively challenge Democratic incumbents for the first time. As 1994 was a year of Republican ascendancy in North Carolina and elsewhere, all the Republican challengers won statewide, but two lost within their districts. The specter of a real two-party competition for judgeships shook

---

[12] For a description of the judicial election process in North Carolina, see Theodore S. Arrington, "When Money Doesn't Matter: Campaign Spending for Minor Statewide Judicial and Executive Offices in North Carolina," 18 (1996) *Justice System Journal*, 257-266.

the Democratic political and legal establishments, who were unused to seeing judges with a Democratic label swept away.

In Texas, scores of Democratic judges were swept out of office by Republicans in 1994, leaving some urban courts staffed largely by new judges. This type of dramatic transformation can badly shake up the continuity and performance of a court. Moreover, many capable and experienced judges are removed for reasons that have nothing to do with their performance. The incoming judges were, on the whole, much younger that than their predecessors and more technologically oriented, but lacked a feel for the judiciary as an institution. It used to be that being a judge was the final step in a legal career, but younger judges are more likely to see their office as a stepping-stone to another career. If experience on the bench is important to wise decision making, politically partisan elections do little for the cause of justice.

Appearance of a Political Quid Pro Quo. When judges are elected or defeated because of their stand on a particular case, or type of case, judicial independence is greatly weakened. If given the opportunity, the electorate will try and elicit the judge's views on controversial issues that are likely to arise in cases before the court and will make campaign contributions to support those judges who seem to be saying the right thing. Candidates for appellate judgeships are particularly subject to issue-specific pressures on such contemporary concerns as

- big money verdicts in product liability and medical malpractice cases
- equalization of the tax base for public schools
- voucher plans to permit parental choice on schools
- term limits for elected officials
- same-sex marriage or other aspects of the sexual revolution
- severity of sentences for criminals

In 1994 Alabama was the site of a bitterly contested election for chief justice. It was waged on tort reform, an issue that attracts campaign money. The incumbent, heavily supported by trial lawyers desiring to maintain a pro-plaintiff majority on the highest court, was pitted against a challenger supported by interest groups committed to "tort reform." In addition, the battle was waged on politically partisan lines because the challenger was a Republican seeking an office long held by Democrats. The ads and the rhetoric were anything but restrained, and, to make things worse, the election was eventually decided in favor of the challenger by a court decision on challenged ballots.

Wisconsin was the scene of a heated and well-funded 1997 election for a position on the state supreme court. The contest turned on the issue of school choice and vouchers, with the incumbent justice favoring them and his opponent opposing them. Teachers unions heavily supported the challenger, and groups favoring school choice rallied around the incumbent, who was reelected. Another example of such an issue is school funding, which almost invariably involves an attempt to end reliance on the local property tax and is fraught with all types of ideological and political ramifications. In 1997 a sharply divided Ohio Supreme Court addressed this issue, which will doubtless surface in judicial politics soon.

It can be argued that judges can take stands on issues without necessarily committing themselves to a judgment in a particular case. This is not a very convincing argument. The signals being sent out in judicial elections are very clear indicators of a likely pattern of judgment.

An Elected Judiciary Unrepresentative of the Populace as a Whole. There seems to be a modern consensus that the judiciary should be broadly representative of the populace it serves. There is total disagreement over whether this is best achieved by the elective or appointive process. There is also wide disagreement about what constitutes the appropriate "diversity." Proper representation of minority groups and women is stressed, but it can also be argued that a court should not be totally dominated by liberals or conservatives, by residents of one region or city, or by members of one political party. Ideologies and regions can be as important as race and gender.

In 1980 a major study reported that state trial court judges were 96 percent white and 98 percent male.[13] Since that time there have been significant steps toward diversity, although state courts are far from having a judiciary that is representative of the population. For example, in California, a large, socially liberal state where minority groups comprise more than 50 percent of the population, 14 percent of the state judges were drawn from minorities in 1994; in the same year, 16 percent of the California judges were women.[14] These percentages have to be placed in perspective. They do not represent the ideal, but they show progress.[15] In the last decade there have been national conferences on bias in the courts, and a number of court task forces on minority and gender bias have been formed. Court planning groups have set diversity goals; for example, Recommendation 4.3 of the 1993 *Report of the Commission on the Future of the California Courts*: "An important goal of the judicial selection process should be the selection of judicial officers who are representative of the state's population generally."

Another indicator of progress is that there were nine women chief justices in 1997, ten including the chief justice in the District of Columbia. There were six black chief justices in 1997, five of them in formerly slave-holding areas: the District of Columbia, Maryland, South Carolina, Tennessee, and Georgia.

Despite the progress, there has been much recent criticism of the judiciary for lack of racial, ethnic, and gender diversity, because awareness of the issue has

---

[13]   John Paul Ryan, Allan Ashman, Bruce D. Sales, and Sandra Shane-DuBow, *American Trial Judges* (New York: Free Press, 1980), 128.

[14]   Robert Tobin et al., "California Unification Study" (Williamsburg, VA: National Center for State Courts), project report, 46.

[15]   For an overview of the diversity issues see Dixie K. Knoebel and Marilyn McCoy Roberts, eds. *Proceedings of the National Conference on Gender Bias in the Courts* (Williamsburg, VA: National Center for States Courts, 1990); see also "Achieving Justice in a Diverse America: Report of the American Bar Association Task Force on Minorities and the Justice System," (1992), photocopied.

been heightened. The methods of choosing judges were reexamined in the light of diversity. In general, the elective process for choosing judges favors minorities where the minority population is concentrated. In areas where the minority population does not have adequate voting power, the appointive system seems to work best. In areas where party leaders broker judgeships, minorities will prosper in relation to their political clout and acumen. Advocates of judicial diversity have generally supported the appointment of judges in preference to the election of judges on the theory that this method was more likely to produce a mix of judges that mirrored the populace being served.[16] This pursuit of diversity by appointment inevitably raises charges of cultural elitism, because it collides sharply with the Jacksonian tradition.

The elective process has, in some areas, altered the racial and ethnic make-up of the judiciary. In cities that have become largely black and Hispanic in population, the composition of the judiciary is usually altered by the ballot box, as well as by the appointive methods of selection. There is usually a time lag before this phenomenon occurs, but sooner or later there is a shift. Cities like New Orleans, Detroit, Washington, D.C., and Atlanta have witnessed an increase in judges drawn from minority groups. Although minority candidates for judgeships may be the beneficiaries of a bloc vote on their behalf, women candidates who are not members of a minority group do not normally receive a solid female vote. Women appear to benefit from an appointive system.

When election districts are changed, minority groups sometimes protest the change if it dilutes their voting strength, so judicial election districts are sometimes drawn to satisfy minority groups. In Louisiana, great efforts were made to create an appellate court election district that would ensure that heavily black New Orleans could elect a member of the supreme court. Judges of the Detroit Recorders Court expressed concern over being consolidated with the Wayne County Circuit Court, because the county population is less black in composition than the city of Detroit.

Another issue of diversity involves the politics of the judges. It can be argued that the judiciary ought to reflect the political makeup of the community it serves. The unending criticism of the ideology of federal judges stems in large part from the winner-take-all attitude of presidents toward the judiciary. If one party controls the White House for a number of consecutive terms, the judiciary gets flooded by judges of the president's party.[17] Below the level of the United States Supreme Court, senators of the same party as the president exercise considerable control over appointments to the federal judiciary and are not given to sharing judgeships with the other party. The federal judiciary has paid a price in credibility, because it has never been properly representative of the political complexion of the country.

---

[16]   This view was articulated in the report of Governor Robert Casey's 1988 Judicial Reform Commission in Pennsylvania and has been generally embraced by reformers.

[17]   See Sheldon Golden, "The Bush Imprint on the Judiciary: Carrying on a Tradition," Slotnick, *Judicial Politics*, 97; see also Evan A. Evans, "Political Influence in the Selection of Federal Judges," Scigliano, *The Courts*, 64-69.

There has been more sensitivity to political diversity in state courts, particularly in states where judges are appointed. Nominating commissions are sometimes balanced politically, either officially or unofficially, a clear recognition that political affiliation should be a factor in allocating judgeships fairly.[18] Article IV, Section 3, of the Delaware Constitution requires that there be a balance between the major political parties in each court and in the system as a whole. The constitutional reference to a "major political party" appears to eliminate independents as candidates for judgeships. Another interesting side effect of Delaware's bipartisan judiciary is that it is hard to add a single judge to a court because it might upset the political balance. This creates a dilemma when a court needs an additional judge but cannot justify adding two judges.

Some states, New Jersey, for example, have traditionally divided judgeships equally between the major parties. Rhode Island had a tradition of political division of judgeships at the appellate and superior court levels, but when a district court was created, the dominant Democratic Party took all the judgeships, much to the chagrin of some Democratic judges who felt that some of the persons appointed were not qualified and certainly not worth sacrificing the principle of bipartisanship.

Closely linked to political balance is geographic balance. Circuits dominated by one large county can end up with all the judges, offending the sensibilities of the smaller counties. The same imbalance can occur at the state level if justices of the supreme court are elected. Illinois has achieved a political balance on its highest court by having justices elected from five regions that reflect the balance of party strength in the state. At least one justice of the supreme court must be drawn from each of the three major regions of Tennessee. In Ohio, where the supreme court is selected statewide, control of the court may swing quite sharply between the two parties even though the election is theoretically nonpartisan. Because each major party has cities that are bastions of support, it is not unusual for these cities to be overrepresented on the court.

The Pennsylvania Supreme Court, where all seven justices are elected at large, has generally been Democratic in composition because of the voting power in Pittsburgh and Philadelphia. This one-party domination became a heavy political burden when the court ordered a Republican governor and Republican legislature to assume responsibility for funding the state trial courts. The court appointed a former member of the court with Republican credentials as a master to sort out the issues and facts and report back, but the distrust of the court in Republican circles was tough to overcome. Ironically, the highest court was allied with county officials, largely Republican, who were deeply concerned about being aligned with a Democratic court against a legislature and governor of their own political persuasion.

Integration of the Judiciary into the Prevailing Political Milieu. Judges are sometimes products of an unattractive political milieu. It is fairly common knowl-

---

[18]   For comparative information on judicial nominating commissions see David Rottman et al., *State Court Organization 1993* (Washington DC: U.S. Department of Justice, Bureau of Justice Statistics, 1995), 78.

edge, for example, that the key to a Philadelphia judgeship is party support obtained by a generous contribution. Party endorsement is tantamount to election, even if the candidate is not particularly well qualified. The Democrats control most of the judgeships and court jobs, but the Republicans receive their allotment and have in recent years controlled the family court. By some political calculus, the parties arrive at a modus vivendi on how to divide the number of positions in each court. Candidates for judge receive the blessing of party leaders and are cross-endorsed, giving a bipartisan coloration to the process. In theory, a maverick can buck the slate, but this is somewhat quixotic. Some of the judges who emerge from the selection process are not local legal luminaries. Veteran observers of the Philadelphia court scene recall instances when some new judges were totally unknown to experienced judges and senior court personnel.

New York clings vigorously to the idea of electing trial judges, but there are not many real elections. Party leaders make up slates, so judgeships are more of a gift from the party than a triumph for elective democracy. Republicans control judgeships in some parts of the state, Democrats control judgeships in other parts, and everyone is happy. If necessary, the majority party in some area of the state can accommodate the needs of the minority party.

Circuit judges in Maryland have to stand for election but actually apply to a nominating commission that sends recommended names to the governor. The commission is not totally apolitical, so the names of politically well-connected candidates usually find their way to the governor, at which point a furious lobbying battle breaks out on behalf of candidates. Persons chosen by the governor appear on the ballot at the next general election. Outsiders can run, and occasionally they win. For example, a black activist in Baltimore upset the anointed candidate. Generally, outsiders do not have much of a chance.

Judges should not be in a position where they may be under pressure to pay back their political benefactors, notably contributors to their campaigns and party officials who endorse them. This pressure rarely comes as a request that a judge rule in a certain way. Very often, the pressure relates to the role of a judge, particularly a presiding judge, as a dispenser of court money and as an employer. Thus, a judge may be asked to favor some particular vendor or to hire someone as the price for party support in a judicial election. More commonly, judges bestow financially rewarding assignments on attorneys and law firms that have supported them politically.

Some courts have lively elections for chief judge, occasionally involving some promises to fellow judges. In the machine jurisdictions you do not become chief judge unless you are committed to the local patronage system. Some chief judges have been saddled with mediocre employees, because this is the price of the job. One urban court administrator recounted a story about his request to the local party apparatus to send over a switchboard operator, because the party always had first shot at court jobs. The party-endorsed applicant appeared to be well qualified except for one defect—being hard-of-hearing. Even the party faithful agreed that this was a bit much.

In states where the legislature has traditionally micromanaged the courts, legislators may become quite involved in the internal affairs and allocations for "their judges." When Massachusetts went to state financing, legislators passed a budget that had a separate line item for every minor subdivision of the trial court system. The obvious purpose was to deny the judiciary the freedom to reallocate freely and to give legislators a say in the resources for each component of the court system. This control was largely motivated by patronage considerations but had the unfortunate effect of making the courts look like an extension of the legislative political machinery.

Most state-funded courts have avoided this type of intrusion by presenting a broadly generic judicial budget that is not subject to political raids by legislators attempting to win resources for "their courts" at the expense of some other courts. In New Jersey, where the early court reforms were frankly aimed at insulating the courts from the prevailing political ethos, the judiciary quickly developed a knack for making the court budget arcane enough to ward off political forays on behalf of regions with powerful political support in the legislature.

In a highly unified, state-funded court system like Connecticut, you do not expect a lot of legislative pressure on local matters, but legislators will occasionally intervene on matters like location and quality of court facilities and allocation of court personnel. Legislators have blocked the closure of underused courthouses, forced their priorities into the court capital improvement plan, and brought about the building of courthouses in locations not favored by the judiciary. The governor, who controls the bonding process, can have his or her own set of courthouse priorities. The courts have not been able to escape this political intrusion into the priorities of the judicial branch.

Generic budgets also protected urban courts from the endemic animosity of rural legislators against a state's large population centers. A court-consulting group studying the criminal justice system in Charlotte, North Carolina, sought information on the state budget allocation for Mecklenberg County (North Carolina courts are state funded). They discovered that this budget was so carefully hidden from legislative prying that even the state court administrative office had some problem in supplying the information.

Some courts are still part of the local patronage system. Most party leaders are well aware that they cannot ask a judge to render a decision based upon political considerations, but they are not loath to remind judges of patronage obligations. Judges, for their part, are not unaware of party obligations and will sometimes become very active in the reelection campaigns of fellow judges if there is a threat that the court might be taken over by judges of a different political party. Some trial courts are so divided along political lines that judges tend to associate only with members of their own party. This split may not be along Republican-Democratic lines. In some courts dominated by one party, there may be factional divisions.

In a northeastern trial court where politics was obtrusive, a prosecutor appeared in court wearing a campaign button. The judge ordered him to remove it. He refused, asserting his rights as a citizen. The judge pointed out that she was a Democrat, that he was a Democrat, and that his button reflected support for a Democrat. She asked him how this might appear to Republican attorneys looking for a fair shake, and he ultimately backed down. The incident illustrates how open partisanship destroys the appearance of justice.

In some American jurisdictions, judges come up through the local political organization. A very common route in some urban courts is to start as an assistant prosecutor, then to ascend to the position of prosecutor or deputy prosecutor, or at least the head of a trial section, and then to be elevated to the bench. Another hallmark of such court systems is the selection of many judges from a local law school that caters to the offspring of ethnic, blue-collar families. For example, DePaul Law School has traditionally supplied many of the judges in the Cook County (Chicago) courts. You do not see many graduates of Ivy League law schools on the state trial bench in Cook County and elsewhere.

An indication of the prestige attached to a particular trial court is the number of judges who come from law firms to the bench. Lawyers frequently come from law firms to appellate courts but are less likely to go on the trial bench, even if they are appointed. This is not just a question of money. It is often a question of prestige, because a politicized court does not attract successful lawyers. It may also be that government legal service is now the principal path to a trial court judgeship.

Even at the appellate court level there is some evidence of this pattern of elevating government attorneys to the bench. A position as state attorney general is often a step to the highest court. At any point in time, 10 to 15 percent of the state chief justices have served as attorney general. In states where the governor has strong control over judicial appointments, state political credentials are more important than local credentials or private-practice credentials. Sometimes, attorneys in state agencies or legal advisers to governors are appointed to the appellate bench.

The Politically Assertive Judicial Branch

When the United States Judicial Conference was created, opponents predicted that it would become an organized lobby for judicial interests, which it is.[19] The problem is defining what is an appropriate judicial interest. In the first flushes of judicial activism in the 1960s, the conference started taking stands on issues that were arguably outside their sphere: the legality of pending wiretap legislation, the scope of legal services for the poor, and the activities of federal grand juries. In some cases the views of the conference were solicited by legislators; sometimes, the views were volunteered, much to the chagrin of some senators, notably John McClellan of Arkansas and Sam Ervin of North Carolina.[20] The latter headed the Judiciary Subcommittee on Separation of Powers and launched an investigation of the Judicial Conference. Senator Ervin made the cogent observation that if the judicial conference wanted to be politically active they should not meet in secret.

[19]   MacKenzie, *Appearance of Justice,* 135.

[20]   Ibid., 149.

They certainly do not act as judges when they vote to approve or disapprove of pending legislation, or adopt rules of financial disclosure for their colleagues. Why then should the conference meet in secret? I believe that when judges act as policymakers and lobbyists, it follows that their discussions should be public.[21]

This same problem occurs at the state level when judges attempt to influence the political process. Legislators expect judges to take stands on the court budget, changes in procedures and structures of courts, jurisdictional issues, court reforms, or higher judicial salaries and benefits. In fact, many legislators complain that the only time they hear from judges is when they want an increase in their salaries or retirement benefits. Most legislators recognize that judges have a legitimate interest in penal sanctions and sentencing laws, but the further courts get from areas that directly concern the internal workings of the judiciary, the more they encounter legislative resentment.

Legislators have their own view of how judges should participate in the legislative process. Some legislatures hear an annual state-of-the-judiciary speech by the chief justice and consider this to be an appropriately formal and ceremonial means of interbranch communication. They can accept and even invite judges and judicial organizations to provide testimony and materials on pending legislative matters, but if judges appear to be aloof, they incur the wrath of legislators and executive branch officials who regard this as a sign of arrogance. When judges attempt to exert public pressure on a legislature or to engage in intense personal lobbying, then some legislators become incensed at this activism. It's almost as if legislators reserve the right to intervene in the internal affairs of the judiciary but do not like the idea of the judicial branch taking an active role in the legislative arena. They are used to executive branch agencies drafting bills and expect the governor to have a legislative agenda, but they are still uncomfortable with the judiciary having a legislative agenda and initiating legislation.

There is obviously some point beyond which judges cannot go without seeming to be unduly political and injuring the judiciary in the process. Some judges are inordinately skillful in the way they conduct themselves politically and are able to exercise a lot of influence without incurring charges of impropriety. Judges walk a narrow line.

That the judiciary has become more active in the political process is undeniable, but it is not at all clear what guidelines ought to govern this involvement. Judges themselves have some serious reservations about how much they should participate in the legislative process or attempt to influence the executive branch. Judges like to think of themselves as the nonpolitical branch of government but know that this is a purist fantasy. Ironically, court reform was the principal impetus for more active judicial involvement in politics. In some instances, the reform effort rose or fell with the political acumen of the top judges.

---

[21]   Ibid., 150.

The political involvement of the judicial branch is a given. Whether this ought to involve judges is debatable. Judges can operate through agents who represent them in political give-and-take, although everyone knows that lurking in the background is a chief justice or powerful chief judge. When court reforms were being debated in the Alabama legislature, there was some wild dealing, much of it in bars around the capitol. The legislators knew that somewhere in the background was Chief Justice Howell Heflin and sometimes ended discussions with his agents by saying, "Tell Howell, I'm with him." If necessary, the chief justice would contact people directly, but there is some limit on how far judges can involve themselves in deal making. If some key player will deal only with the top judge, then it may be necessary.

Astute and experienced chief justices quietly influence legislation by a few phone calls without anyone being the wiser, thus preserving the nonpolitical image of the courts. Sometimes, this influence is exerted on behalf of court-related functions, such as indigent defense (which is always under budget attack). However, not too many chiefs achieve this political position. Legislators will always listen to a chief justice just as county commissioners will listen to a chief judge, but this does not necessarily mean much unless the judge is a political force. The mere title of judge does not buy you much in the way of influence.

One court administrator recalled an incident when the chief justice of his state made a call upon the governor during a period of budgetary austerity. The chief was a highly respected man held in great awe by lawyers. The young governor was obviously pleased and flattered that the chief would come to see him. It was clear to the state court administrator that the governor would have agreed to just about anything, but the chief opened the discussion by inquiring, "Governor, what can we do to help during the budget crisis?" The courts did not do well in that year's budget process, because the chief was a gentleman of the old school and loath to enter into political discussions with the governor.

The more active and sophisticated political involvement of the judicial branch is exemplified by the growth of government relations offices in the judicial branch. Such offices would have been considered heretical not too long ago but are now fixtures in state administrative offices of courts. The range of interest for government relations offices goes way beyond strictly judicial matters into any area of legislation that affects the courts in some important matter; for example, no-fault insurance or revisions in family law. Fiscal notes and impact statements estimating the effects of bills on the courts are now quite common. The Washington State courts even developed a mathematical model to analyze the budgetary impact of proposed statutes on courts.

The National Center for State Courts has a government relations office, which is the link of state court judges and court administrators to the federal government. State chief justices regularly contact or visit federal legislators and executive branch officials about issues of importance to the state courts, such as the continuation of the State Justice Institute, which was established to fund improvements in the state courts.

When federal grant programs for courts first became important in the mid-1970s, judges complained that they should not be subjected to the ignominy of competing for block grant funds with the police, corrections, and prosecutors, arguing that the judiciary would be demeaned by this tawdry political struggle. Most courts overcame their aversion and got into the fray. The Alabama courts chose as their bargaining agent a trial judge known as something of a wheeler-dealer. He went into the smoke-filled room with a goal of getting a certain percentage of the block grant money for courts and emerged victorious. The reality is that the courts have to fight for their share with the executive branch as well as the administrative branch, but, for some reason, state judges find this more demeaning to the judiciary than cajoling a state legislature.

Divisions within the judiciary have undermined the political influence of state courts. It is not uncommon for judges to be found on different sides of the same issue but professing to speak for the judiciary. In some states, trial judges would not dream of challenging the chief justice politically. In other states, they not only might oppose the chief on legislative matters but are often capable of marshaling more support than the chief, even on a matter as fundamentally judicial as the power of trial courts to make rules. Virginia is a state where the courts have, in general, taken a fairly low profile in dealing with the legislature, which seems to have the view of "don't you call us, we'll call you." In New Jersey, a trial judge that independently lobbied in Trenton for anything, particularly for a purpose opposed to that of the supreme court, would be subject to sanctions. In other states, trial court judges may actively lobby against the supreme court, as they have frequently done on issues of unification.

California trial judges can effectively block any state-level initiative of the supreme court or judicial council. For years, superior court judges in Los Angeles County and other large southern California counties effectively opposed constitutional amendments to consolidate the superior and municipal courts, because their counties had large legislative delegations. A proposed constitutional amendment on consolidation cleared the legislature and was eventually approved by the voters only by having an opt-in provision. This is a tribute to the political power of the judges in some large metropolitan counties.

When New Mexico went to state financing of trial courts, it permitted its general jurisdiction courts to bypass the supreme court and to lobby the legislature directly for their respective courts. Needless to say, this did little for judicial budget strategy and resulted in judges lobbying against each other for a finite supply of funds. Trial court judges often prefer this arrangement, as it makes them independent of the supreme court and the state court administrative office. Some legislators found this arrangement more trouble than it was worth politically, because courts are not particularly popular with voters. Moreover, judges lose a bit of their aura when they line up with the other lobbyists.

To further destroy the unity of the judicial message, trial courts may disagree among themselves. A leading trial judge in Fargo, North Dakota, became the focal point for opposition to a plan to consolidate the district and county courts, even though this was not the position of the supreme court. To complicate matters, many county court judges lined up against the district court judges. This is what drives legislators crazy. The North Dakota legislature, tired of the divisions in the judiciary, imposed its own views, which included downsizing the judiciary.

An interesting aspect of the political struggle in North Dakota was that the legislature was willing to give broad latitude to the courts in determining administrative districts, court venue, and allocation of judges. This was a bottom-line approach—we won't micromanage if you'll be more efficient. This is the type of administrative independence that courts require to protect themselves against political manipulation of intrabranch operations. Perhaps more important is preventing the political process from foisting unqualified judges on the court system and undermining the integrity of adjudication.

Courts have been not been entirely successful in promoting merit selection and ending political intrusion of the other branches of state and local government. The good news is that the courts have come a long way since 1950. State courts are certainly much freer of local government politics and less vulnerable to political intrusion by the other branches of state government. Political considerations still play a large, although reduced, role in judicial selection, and it is much harder now for a highly unqualified candidate to become a judge. The political pressures on the adjudication process are coming more from public interest groups than from political parties. Politics in courts is a perennial issue, but the struggle has been joined in recent decades with some positive results for the state courts. This improvement is attributable to many factors, but none greater that the rise of state courts from inertia and the creation of a self-assertive, independent judiciary.

Chapter 3

Extracting the State Judiciary from Local Government

J udges in trial courts set up primarily to hear state cases are officials of the state judicial branch. Unlike legislators, who represent a region of the state, judges have to be detached from the local environment to provide a common brand of justice under state law. However, state trial courts have traditionally been viewed as an emanation of the local legal and political culture and as being so immersed in localism that they could not realistically be considered part of a state court system.

Judicial localism served important purposes in a rural, frontier society marked by sharp regional differences and by an isolated parochialism reinforced by primitive transportation. Up to the 1960s, the courts fitted easily into the framework of local government and often acquired distinct local characteristics. Sometimes these characteristics were structural; more often they were procedural and operational, reflecting the views of the local legal and political communities. In every state, there were significant differences in the level of local expenditures for courts due to local economics and labor markets, crime levels, and views about staffing and judicial programming. Such variations were not unique to courts. Variations in per capita expenditures could be found from community to community in other service areas, such as sanitation, policing, and schools.

Inevitably, reformers started to focus on the major flaws of judicial localism:

- The trial courts lacked organizational and administrative coherence, reflecting the crazy-quilt nature of local government.
- There were broad variations within the trial court system in standards, procedures, and levels of professionalism.
- There was an inequitable distribution of resources among trial courts and inappropriate judicial involvement in local government fiscal politics.
- The trial court judiciary was dependent on court-related agencies directed by elected officers who were not subject to court control and intent on their respective political agendas.

To correct these flaws, reformers launched a campaign to extract state trial courts from local government control and from the local culture. This change was perceived as necessary to preserve judicial objectivity and the appearance of justice, to promote the common statewide treatment of cases arising under state law, to improve the level of professionalism, to bring about more procedural uniformity, to simplify court structure along common statewide lines, to reduce funding inequities, to strengthen court control over court operations, and to better deploy judges.

Influence of Localism on Court Organizational Structure

Unlike the federal courts, which achieved a highly compact organizational structure before 1900, state courts, well into this century, had a very chaotic organization with a number of local variations in both structure and mode of operation. There were often three or more tiers of trial courts, with some trial courts hearing appeals from other trial courts either in a formal appellate process or by conduct of a new trial. Some trial courts of general jurisdiction had an appellate division, which served as an intermediate appellate court and heard appeals on the record, mostly from their own trial divisions. Appeals from limited jurisdiction courts were rarely on the record (now some have audio equipment to record testimony), so the typical appeal from these courts was a retrial (trial *de novo*) in a higher trial court, usually with a right to trial by jury. Serious motor vehicle violations constituted the bulk of these appeals, which were largely frivolous delaying actions. Trials *de novo* often languished in the higher trial court because they had low priority.

Trial courts of general jurisdiction had more organizational coherence than courts of limited jurisdiction but tended to operate in their own unique fashion. Under these general jurisdiction courts (typically called circuit courts or superior courts, occasionally district courts), there was an overlapping profusion of county courts, municipal courts, town and village courts, and justice-of-the-peace courts. The tendency of legislatures to pass special laws to create courts in individual counties further complicated the mix.

Before court unification in Alabama, there were a number of courts created by special legislation applying to only one county. The residence requirements for divorce differed by county, as did the age at which a person ceased legally to be a juvenile. One special law to create a court abolished all courts of comparable jurisdiction in the county. What had occurred was that the attorneys in this county did not like the local judge and had the legislature create another court with a judge of their choosing. No one seemed to realize that the existing court had been abolished, and it continued to function.

The complexity of state court organizational structure can be appreciated by viewing the multistep process by which Connecticut introduced order into its court structure through consolidation (see Table 1).

The type of organizational disorder that formerly existed in Connecticut was often exacerbated by jurisdictional statutes or constitutional provisions specifying the types of matters that a court could handle and the territorial scope of the court's authority. All too often, the jurisdictional statutes were influenced by

Table 1
Steps in Simplifying Connecticut Court Structure (1959-1978)

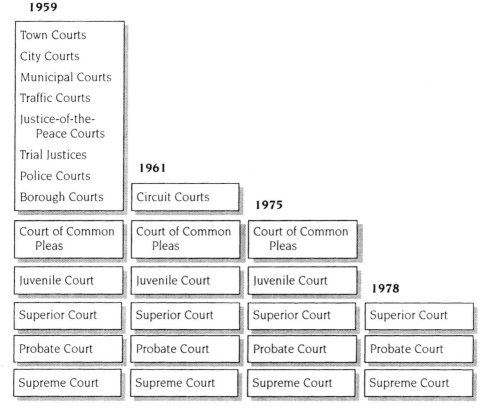

Source: Based on Anthony B. Fisser, "Structural Change in and its Implementation in the Connecticut Court System," appearing in Lee Powell, ed., *Court Reform in Seven States*, (Williamsburg, VA: National Center for State Courts and the American Bar Association, 1980), 85.

localism at the expense of coherence, and by the legislative penchant for micro-managing the judiciary. Sometimes, there were very rigid jurisdictional lines restricting each trial court to certain types of cases; for example, civil cases with an amount in issue of less than $5,000. Rigid jurisdiction created inflexible barriers to transfer of cases and resources, thus reducing speed and efficiency.

Sometimes, the jurisdictional statutes erred on the side of looseness, creating a very confusing overlap of concurrent jurisdiction. This jurisdictional overlap invited disputes among courts, frequent transfer of cases, and the practice of "forum shopping" in which attorneys sought out the courts most favorable to their cause. It was not at all unusual for attorneys in one state judicial district to obtain special legislation on the allocation of cases among courts in their district.

The geographic jurisdiction of trial courts was, quite naturally, influenced by government boundaries and reflected the complex organizational structure of American local government. Some courts had territorial jurisdiction within a city, others within a county, others within a region, and others statewide. Legislatures occasionally contrived districts that did not conform to any other governmental boundary. Some municipal courts were actually given extraterritorial jurisdiction. Courts of uniform statewide jurisdiction were broken into geographic regions composed of one or more counties. These regions were commonly called "circuits" or "districts" and might be served by judges traveling from county to county. Because local politics often determined the geographic structure of upper-level trial courts, some districts were strangely configured.

General jurisdiction trial courts could, in theory, act upon any proceeding arising under state law, but usually there were limitations imposed by venue requirements determining where a particular type of case could be heard. and establishing some rational pattern to the geographic allocation of cases among courts of similar jurisdiction. Venue is usually tied to individual counties, even though county lines date back many years and are, in large part, based on transportation conditions and demographic patterns that no longer exist. Many rural counties are so sparsely populated that they cannot really provide a full range of government services, but they are almost invariably entitled by law to be treated as a court site, a lingering manifestation of judicial localism. Another quirk of court venue was to accommodate competitive communities and local attorneys by having separate venue districts in the same county. Thus, for example, Guilford County, North Carolina, even after unification, contained two separate venue districts, one for High Point and one for Greensboro.

Americans have rarely been content with courts of general jurisdiction. Sooner or later, some movement starts for a court of specialized jurisdiction on the theory that certain types of cases require a special expertise or ability. This argument is most frequently made on behalf of juvenile and family courts. There are other special courts. For example, the water courts of Colorado are a regional phenomenon of the arid West. Separate probate courts are found in a number of states, either as full-blown trial courts (e.g., Michigan and Massachusetts) or as quasi-administrative courts under a nonlawyer judge (e.g., Connecticut and Rhode Island). For unique local reasons, New York City and New Orleans have separate trial courts for civil and criminal matters. Environmental courts, like the one in Vermont, drug courts, and domestic violence courts are products of the modern era and the tendency of special interest groups to seek special courts.

American courts inherited the English legal tradition that made a distinction between cases at law and equity. This distinction was so sharp that England established separate courts and separate procedures for law and equity. Cases at law included criminal cases and common types of civil disputes, such as trespasses upon land, negligence cases, or contract violations that lent themselves to adjudication according to relatively well established methods and ordinary remedies (e.g., money damages usually sufficed in civil cases at law). Equity jurisdiction covered matters that were not considered cases at law and that required some extraordinary remedy, such as an injunction. Trusts, estates, partnership matters, and various aspects of title to land were handled in equity courts. American equity courts also inherited matters pertaining to marriage, which had been handled by ecclesiastical courts in England. The great bulk of cases were considered cases at law, but the equity cases were usually more complex. Moreover, there was no right to trial by jury in an equity case.

In America, these distinctions were preserved to varying degrees, depending on the local legal culture. Some states created separate law and equity courts (usually called chancery courts); in other states, the same court handled law and equity matters (as was the case in federal courts from 1791 onward) but operated under different procedures for both. In 1900 the distinctions between law and equity were still striking and were widely targeted as anachronistic by legal reformers. It was well into this century before there was a strong movement toward procedural merger of law and equity in state courts, a trend sparked by the action of the federal courts in effecting a procedural merger of law and equity in 1938.

Mississippi, Tennessee, and Arkansas still maintain separate courts for law and equity throughout the state. You can get in big trouble in these three states for suggesting that a separate chancery court does not make much sense. The separate chancery court is strongly rooted in tradition and is deeply intertwined with the whole pattern of local government in those states.

Much of the criticism of state courts was directed at limited jurisdiction courts that were not only organizationally incoherent but almost autonomous. These courts handled the bulk of cases coming into the state court system and were the courts with which citizens most frequently came into contact. These courts were often highly unprofessional and poorly run, creating an image of the courts that did little to inculcate respect for the law. State law and the court organizational chart might make it appear that these courts were subject to supervision of the supreme court and the chief judge of a general jurisdiction trial court. In actuality, the supervision tended to be minimal, until recent years, even though the great majority of limited jurisdiction court judges were not law trained. Judges of the upper court and attorneys held these lower trial courts in low regard. Much of the early court reform movement was directed at imposing some control over these courts and making them more professional.

The prototypical limited jurisdiction court was the justice-of-the-peace court run by a lay judge. Justices of the peace (JPs) were a basic part of the English system and later the colonial court systems. In 1915, forty-seven of forty-eight state constitutions provided for JPs. As late as 1945, every state had JPs. The intense localism of these courts was such that it was rare if anyone at the state level had a comprehensive list of JPs, knew exactly where they were located, or if they actually functioned. Most JPs were part-time and had very little judicial work to do.

In an earlier America that was more rural, less connected by transportation systems, and often lacking in the local presence of a law-trained judge or even a law enforcement official, states relied heavily on JPs even though their principal qualification was that they had obtained the requisite number of votes. They were generally elected to serve a district within a county, were compensated by fees, and, more frequently than not, operated out of their home or place of business. Hearings might be held in barns, the back of a store, or a living room.

JPs generally had authority to issue arrest warrants, a great convenience to local law enforcement officers who might otherwise have to go miles to find a judge and would then probably be reluctant to interrupt a judge who had gone home. JPs rarely had the authority to issue search warrants, but they frequently had the authority to conduct preliminary hearings in felonies. JPs generally had authority to hear minor criminal and traffic cases, as well as small-claims cases. As the title implies, justices of the peace also issued peace bonds and often intervened in heated domestic or neighborhood disputes. When a drunken male parent showed up at the door in a rage, family members would often seek out the justice of the peace. Later on, when most states eliminated justices of the peace, reformers found that JPs had actually performed some important services that had to be continued in a different way.

Municipal courts were another common form of limited jurisdiction court, with some of the smaller ones having the same characteristics as JP courts. Some municipal courts in major cities were very large, high-volume courts with full-time judges. Some municipal courts were not restricted to adjudicating municipal ordinance violations and had concurrent criminal jurisdiction, and occasionally concurrent civil jurisdiction, with state courts of limited jurisdiction. In California and Ohio, municipal courts were important elements of the state trial court system and held significant jurisdiction. But the typical municipal court was an ordinance court that occasionally convened under the aegis of a lay judge or some local attorney serving as a part-time judge. Sometimes, mayors served as the judges of municipal courts, thus earning some of these courts the title of "mayors' courts." The number of municipal courts was and is amazingly high, although the number is declining as more and more cases once heard in municipal courts now are heard before the law-trained judges in state courts.

New Jersey alone has over five hundred municipal courts, but the number varies from year to year because smaller municipalities open and close their courts for a variety of reasons—usually an estimate of whether the court will show a profit. Most municipal courts are moneymakers, so there is always some opposition to folding those courts into a statewide court of limited jurisdiction. This consolidation can be achieved but only by assuring the municipalities that the fines collected on their ordinance cases will be transmitted from the state courts to those municipalities. In Alabama, the opposition of municipal courts to court unification was so fierce that municipalities were given the right to opt in or out of the unified court system.

Many limited jurisdiction courts were county courts. These courts were not particularly different from other courts of limited jurisdiction unless they were staffed by law-trained judges. Lawyers in urban counties sometimes insisted that their county court have a law-trained judge, so it was not unusual to have two classes of county courts: one with law-trained judges and one with lay judges. The employment of law-trained judges usually increased the subject matter jurisdiction of the court, because legislators and the supreme court were more likely to entrust significant jurisdiction in civil and criminal cases to such courts.

Some county courts were constitutional in origin and might even have governing powers; others were created by statutes of general application and others by legislation specific to one county. In Ohio, some counties still have county courts while others do not.

A classic example of the anomalous status of many county courts is provided by Texas, which has a group of constitutional county courts and a group of county courts at law. The constitutional courts are really governing bodies that also have some judicial powers, so they can be staffed by nonlawyer judges. The county courts at law must employ lawyer-judges unless otherwise provided by law (meaning the legislature may decide to scrap the requirement in some counties or all counties). The latter courts have an open-ended monetary jurisdiction in civil cases, leaving it up to the legislature to determine this limit, whereas the constitutional county courts have a fixed upper monetary limit in civil cases. This bifurcated county court system is one of the best surviving examples of what was once a common situation.

Texas also provides a good example of autonomous general jurisdiction courts. To this day, judges of the general jurisdiction court of Texas (the district court) are constituted as individual judges of a particular district. There are 394 separate districts listed in the *1997 BNA Directory*, excluding the judges in special criminal courts. Each court has a separate number and is regarded as a separate court. If you walk down the hall of a courthouse with several district judges, there will be a sign posted indicating the number of the court. The numbers indicate the order in which the district courts were created, so in one courthouse you may see widely separated court numbers. There is now some administrative cohesion of the district court judges located in large urban courts, but Texas still exemplifies what was once a common organizational pattern.

Until well into this century, each judge ran his or her courtroom as a separate administrative entity, operating in splendid isolation from other judges who might belong to the same court. This tradition defeated any attempt to look at court operations systematically. This individualism first eroded in large multi-judge trial courts where some power had to be ceded to a central authority, but the cession of power occurred slowly and unevenly.

Because courts were slow to develop a systemic approach, they were also slow in building administrative systems and administrative skills within the courts. The prevailing view was that the courts were so simple that they would function well if judges worked diligently. If management support was considered necessary, it would be supplied by local government. Courts were therefore intertwined with the often mediocre administrative processes of local government. Supreme courts were slow to intervene in this localism, because they only gradually accepted their responsibility for the effective management of the trial courts, confining themselves to appellate review and limited use of administrative rulemaking. Legislatures filled this void in part by enacting laws governing court operations, very often with a series of local exceptions.

When trial courts came under criticism for poor management, it soon became apparent that no one could really speak for the courts. The state supreme court often stayed aloof, and there were many voices at the trial court level, none of them speaking with authority on behalf of the courts. Individual judges could speak for themselves; clerks could speak for their offices. There were no clear lines of authority and no accountability to court users and taxpayers. Localism and individualism combined to deny the courts a coherent voice.

Variations in Standards, Procedures, and Professionalism

Judicial localism has to be put in perspective. Court reformers stress localism's idiosyncratic nature, but it has its appealing points. When each state, at an early point in its history, created a statewide court of general jurisdiction divided into suitable geographic components, judges of these courts commanded a certain prestige and were important figures in most communities. There was a certain local possessiveness and pride about judges and about local courthouses. Everyone was aware of the style and eccentricities of the their judge or judges and accommodated themselves accordingly.

In most parts of the United States, the courthouse remains an important center of community life. In rural America, the arrival of a judge for court days was and is a gala event that draws spectators. People like it if their county receives many judge-days and are especially proud if one or more judges are resident in their locality, because it is a sign that the town or county is recognized as important. Conversely, losing a resident general jurisdiction judge can be traumatic. Court reformers singing the praises of efficiency and rational allocation of judges have often underestimated the fierce opposition of citizens fearful of losing "our judges."

In the 1970s during the Alabama court reform movement, I was asked to visit Circuit Judge Jack Wallace, who was located in Barbour County in southeastern Alabama. Bullock County was also in the circuit, but being smaller than Barbour, did not warrant a great deal of judicial time. Jack Wallace was the brother of Governor George Wallace, who had preceded him as circuit judge. As the brother of the governor, Jack was an important figure in the eyes of the judiciary, because he could serve as an intercessor with his brother, who was not enthusiastic about the court reform movement. The governor eventually took a neutral position, apparently influenced to some extent by the emerging political importance of Chief Justice Howell Heflin.

Judge Wallace was a genial man and an astute observer of the Alabama scene. His relationship to the governor gave him a certain cachet of which he was aware, but he observed that many people in the circuit would have come to him about personal problems even if he were not related to the governor. When I arrived for our interview, the benches outside his office were filled with people who were clearly not among the affluent members of the community. Poor people depended on the judge to protect them or help them, not just because they elected him, but because they viewed the judicial role in broader terms than mere adjudication of disputes. People came to the judge with tales of family woes and needs, requests for intercession with various agencies, and a variety of other personal problems. One could easily discern the deep sense of loss that would occur if the county lost its resident judge, who was something of a patriarchal figure.

The courthouse where Judge Wallace presided was in Clayton, a sleepy little town that was the county seat and was being surpassed in importance by Eufala, a neighboring community famous for its antebellum mansions and high social tone. In Barbour County, as in many other American counties, the original county seat often proved to be secondary in importance to other towns and sometimes was replaced as the principal court site. Residents of dying counties and dying county seats know that the end is near when judges stop coming around. Judicial presence is an important symbol of civic viability, so a judge can become a very major figure in a small or medium-sized community and, to some extent, in an urban setting.

The nostalgic aspects of judicial localism cannot, however, obscure its sometimes quirky individualism, the cult of personality surrounding many judges, and the resulting variations in justice. Because there are not many constraints on a judge, particularly in a rural area, it is easy for a judge to slip into idiosyncratic patterns of action. Such individualism is natural and salutary within bounds and will exist to some extent even in a unified court system with tighter controls. In a totally localized system, however, there are few constraints on such behavior. Some examples from personal experience and anecdotes recounted by judges and court administrators capture the idiosyncrasies that characterize judicial localism.

- A North Carolina judge issued an order from the bench to a city official to close off traffic on a street adjacent to the courthouse, because the auto noise was distracting the jurors. This might not have made a difference in some rural county seat, but the city sealed off a block of a street in the downtown area of a major city.

- A judge in an Alabama court placed his seat near a window so that he could spit his tobacco outside. The sheriff obligingly set up barricades on the sidewalk to protect pedestrians.

- A judge in Ohio once called Eastern Airlines on behalf of a court consultant to order that the consultant's plane be held until he arrived and then advised the consultant to stop worrying because everything was taken care of. The judge was something of a czar in his county and apparently felt that his writ extended to interstate commerce, but, unfortunately, the plane contumaciously left on schedule.

- A rural judge in Louisiana jailed a ferry boat operator for adhering to the ferry schedule even though he had been summoned by bullhorn to return to the dock to pick up the judge.

- A New York city judge interrupted a trial to lecture an attorney on the civic disloyalty involved in challenging the city's flagrantly erratic tax assessment system. This judge, who was hearing tax certiorari cases because she had been recommended for this role to the chief judge by city officials, was totally committed to municipal patriotism as interpreted by the mayor.

- A young woman working on a court study in West Virginia recounted that she had spent the afternoon seated next to the judge of a domestic relations court who had opened court by introducing her as a "friend of the court." He carried on a running conversation with her as he dispensed justice, or, as she put it, "Chuck and I tried eleven cases."

- One Mississippi judge made almost 40 percent of the commitments to a state juvenile institution, even though he was in a medium-sized county. His view of how to treat juveniles was very popular locally, as was his decision to ignore the *In Re Gault* decision and continue his paterfamilias approach.[1]

There is some humor in these events, but the truth is that judges can very easily lose their perspective in a highly localized environment, whether rural or urban. The more extreme examples of judicial deviation from legal and judicial standards can be appealed, if the abuse occurred in a court proceeding, or taken before a judicial discipline commission, but these means are inadequate to deal with deeply entrenched habits of judicial localism.

A strange aspect of localism is that a community can become inured to judicial incompetence or unfairness. A state court administrator told a story about what he termed an "alegal judge," defined as a judge totally unaware of or indifferent to the law. This judge functioned in a limited jurisdiction court where his erratic brand of justice was well known but somehow accepted because the court staff and the attorneys were somehow able to keep him in bounds and to prevent him from self-destructing. This went on for years until the judge was transferred temporarily to a neighboring jurisdiction to fill in for another judge. Deprived of his support system, he plunged the whole court into legal chaos in less than a week, causing a barrage of complaints. When investigators looked into the complaints, they discovered that this judge had been rendering the same type of decisions for years but had been protected by a community that tolerated him because they could cushion the system against him. He was a peculiarly local phenomenon.

Judicial localism is also reflected in treatment of visitors. Visiting judges are welcomed but usually do not enjoy the same personal relationship with the community as a resident judge. Over the years, many judges tell stories about going into a county as the "outsider judge" and trying to figure out the local mores. Rural judges transferred into urban courts and urban judges going to rural courts report culture shock on a grand scale. In Illinois and New York, judges outside the major metropolitan areas are routinely assigned to assist the chronically backlogged courts of Chicago and New York. Some downstate Illinois circuits actually rent apartments in Chicago to house their judges assigned to Cook County.

---

[1]   387 U.S. 1 (1967). In this case the United State Supreme Court held that the constitutional guarantees of due process applied to juvenile delinquency proceedings.

Court employees often remark on the changes that occur every time a new judge comes to the court, even in fairly fundamental matters of procedure set by court rule. Not surprisingly, state legislatures often try to divide circuits, so that some counties can have their own judges rather than having to adapt to the ways of a visiting judge. It is particularly galling to have a larger neighboring county supply all the judges. Many a county seeks its own judge even if the county's size does not warrant it.

Visiting attorneys may encounter an even more chilly reception than a visiting judge. The term *home cooking* captures the favoritism for local attorneys matched against "outsiders." Many attorneys going to a foreign county feel it necessary to have some local attorney at their side even if that person is not active in the trial. Criminal defendants from other counties also have some disadvantages. Prosecutors are not above urging a jury to send a message to the county from which the defendant came—the message obviously being that troublemakers invading the county will be dealt with severely.

Judicial localism lends itself to fiefdoms. General jurisdiction trial courts can easily become subdivided into spheres of influence built around chief judges in various parts of the state. Large urban courts tend to view all other courts with disdain. In Minnesota the term for anything beyond the center of civilization in the Twin Cities is *outstate*. In Illinois, the operative Cook County term is *downstate*, a term so sweeping that it includes counties that are geographically north of Chicago. The cleavage between New York City and the rest of the state is pretty extreme, to the point where the term *upstate* can include Long Island suburban counties.

Metropolitan court systems almost invariably "do their own thing." The Los Angeles court system is so large that it operates almost like a state system and regards the rest of the state system as sort of a subculture. The trial court systems in Philadelphia and Pittsburgh operate as independent entities, as does the circuit court for Cook County, Illinois. Sometimes, the insistence of urban courts on their uniqueness is a thin cover for protection of a political patronage system that would be threatened by having court employees transferred to a state payroll and hired on a merit basis. Judges in these urban courts perceive quite correctly that unification will explode the local culture with which they are comfortable.

On occasion, a state supreme court has seen fit to invade the domain of a metropolitan court to correct a serious problem that was not being addressed. In 1990 the Pennsylvania Supreme Court literally took over the running of the Philadelphia courts as the result of a budgetary impasse between the courts and the city of Philadelphia and retained direct control until 1993. About twenty years before this, the Michigan Supreme Court took control over the Detroit Recorders Court (now gone), appointing an intermediate appellate court judge to set the court in order and giving him wide latitude. Generally, high courts are pretty wary about intruding into the lower courts.

Rural courts have their own style, often pretty informal and breezy. A circuit judge in the mountain South recounted an incident on the opening day of the court session in a small county with one big courtroom where everyone gathered, including the people called for jury service. The judge called the calendar and sorted out the cases for his brief stay in the county. In the first criminal case, the prosecutor said that he and the defense attorney had made a plea agreement and that the defendant was in the courtroom. The judge told him to bring the defendant forward, whereupon the prosecutor turned and summoned the defendant, "Will the boy who broke into the store on Route 7 please come forward?" The defendant jumped up and ambled by the assembled jurors on his way to the bench. The judge pointed out the impropriety of having a defendant identify himself as a criminal in front of prospective jurors, but this was regarded as a legal technicality. This judge also added that in many rural counties, lawyers representing criminal defendants were under pressure from other lawyers not to go to trial and use up the judge's time that could be better employed in hearing civil cases where someone might actually make some money.

In communities with few attorneys, adherence to rules of procedure can become a bit lax because no one wants to upset the local camaraderie. It is considered gauche to seek dismissals because someone misses a deadline by a month or so. Attorneys with statewide practices started complaining years ago about the onerous burden imposed by having to operate under different rules in every county in the same circuit, not to mention the differences between circuits.

Many people are shocked to wander into a typical urban criminal court at arraignment. It is often as noisy and disorderly as an oriental bazaar, with a cast of characters that makes Damon Runyon characters look staid. Some strange things happen: attempted escapes, unbelievably noisy confrontations, and squalid negotiations. The cynicism and despair in such courts is palpable. Literally anything can happen when so many people with antisocial tendencies are assembled. A court administrator recalled sitting in a big-city arraignment court when the bailiff entered to announce the coming of the judge and sought to be heard over the pandemonium. Order of sorts descended on the court as the judge entered, but from the bowels of the crowded room there came a loud, obscene salute to the judge, " F____ you!"

A court consultant engaged in the a study of the District Court of Providence, Rhode Island, was lounging in the back of an arraignment court watching the show and was shocked to hear the presiding judge introduce him from the bench to the assembled felons, gendarmes, and barristers. He was compelled to rise and receive a standing ovation from the local underworld. In some states, this would have been considered a breach of court decorum, but in the relatively folksy climate of Providence, this introduction was considered an act of courtesy.

Differences among trial courts are often reflected in local rules. Typically, local courts are accorded the privilege of adopting local rules not in conflict with administrative and procedural rules of the supreme court. The problem was and is that no one may be assigned to see if the local rules conflict with supreme court rules. Sometimes, copies of the local rules never find their way to the supreme court. This lack of supervision is a constant irritation to attorneys who have to deal with multiple sets of local rules.

Another feature of judicial localism was the small pool of general jurisdiction judges in each judicial district. Until fairly recently, it was not unusual to see circuits with one or two judges. This raised all types of problems, not the least of which was that the respect for the competence of the single judge might be so low as to seriously impede justice in a region of the state. When judges had to recuse themselves, not an unusual event in a rural area where the judge had once practiced law and had numerous family and business affiliations, some judge would have to be imported. In one Mississippi circuit, a newly elected judge came from the only significant litigating firm in the region and had to recuse himself in roughly half of the cases that came before him. Problems occurred with vacations and illness, not to mention the implementation of an attorney's right of refusal. In North Dakota and various other states, attorneys do not have to accept the judge assigned to the case, and a substitute judge has to be imported from elsewhere in the state if there is no local backup. A limited jurisdiction court judge was rarely used to replace a general jurisdiction court judge, so a judge might have to be imported from a great distance even though there was a resident limited jurisdiction judge.

County chauvinism being what it is, many judges find themselves traveling to a county to hear a single case. In some rural areas, a general jurisdiction court judge might visit a county to hear one case, only to be followed a day or so later by a limited jurisdiction court judge coming to hear one or two cases. Many rural judges spend an inordinate time traveling between counties and handle relatively few cases. Much of this waste stems from the lingering and powerful attachment to county government, even in states where many counties are losing population. Localism is at war with common sense, modern technology, and rapidity of travel. Regional trial centers for sparsely settled areas will doubtless be created, but no one is holding their breath.

In Vermont, imbued with the local town-meeting tradition, two assistant judges chosen from the community flank an incoming superior court judge and can, in fact, outvote the judge, much to the chagrin of the attorneys and judges of the state. The people of Vermont simply wanted local input into the decisions. Some local observers feel that the idea has a lot of merit, particularly in cases where knowledge of local mores and the characters of the parties to litigation are important to a just decision.

In some states, there is a tradition of moving judges about frequently so that they will not become too immersed in the local scene. Connecticut rotates its trial judges annually, although not every judge is reassigned geographically. North Carolina moves superior court judges about with some frequency, so it is possible for a judge to serve for years without ever being assigned to his or her own county. This practice, which is very expensive and inefficient, stems from bad experiences in the Reconstruction period and is simply rotation for the sake of rotation.

The complaints directed at the dubious professionalism of general jurisdiction state courts mired in local legal culture paled into insignificance when compared to the torrent of complaints about judges of limited jurisdiction courts, particularly justices of the peace (JPs). In 1956 the Institute for Judicial Administration pithily summed up the problems of JP courts: lack of legal training, part-time service, compensation by fee, inadequate supervision, archaic procedures, and makeshift facilities.[2]

---

[2]   Martin Mayer, *The Lawyers* (New York: Harper and Row, 1967), 466.

Particularly questionable was the form of compensation for JPs. They collected fines, fees, and costs and were permitted to retain the fees attributable to their function under state law, although this conflict of interest was not legally or ethically defensible. Moreover, some justices of the peace were pretty casual about bookkeeping. During a study of the West Virginia justice-of-the-peace system, a consultant was given access to auditor reports. Not infrequently, an auditor would note that some justice of the peace was not issuing receipts and appeared to be taking all the money he collected. These reports were turned over to county prosecutors who almost invariably ignored them, because JPs were an integral part of the county political process. One JP had been turned over for prosecution four straight years and was still going strong.

JPs were often in competition with one another for "business" and sought to curry favor with law enforcement officials. This was done by never finding a defendant innocent, by never refusing a police request for a warrant, and by sharing the proceeds of their cases with police officers. Once while skimming through a JP docket book searching for one "not guilty" verdict, a court researcher located an exoneration on about the eighth or ninth page. The worried JP, embarrassed by this lapse, blurted, "I can explain that." In theory, a justice of the peace could collect his fee from the county if a "not guilty" verdict was rendered, but many counties ignored this, and most JPs did not even bother to submit a bill for fees in such cases.

One enterprising Georgia JP passed out presigned arrest warrants to local law enforcement agencies, saving their officers the trouble of having to appear before a judicial officer. He periodically replenished the supply and obtained his money from the police. This type of service captured the local warrant issuance market from the other JPs.

JPs located near busy highways tended to make more money than those at other locations. A study in the 1970s revealed that a few Mississippi JPs made more than $50,000 per year because they were located near major highways but that most JPs made less than $1,000. When blacks were first elected as justices of the peace in some areas of Mississippi, members of the highway patrol would drag arrestees for miles to reach a white JP, leaving black JPs to wonder why they had fewer cases than their white predecessors. When court reform led to the abolition of the justice-of-the-peace system in Alabama, black JPs observed wryly that no one cared about reform until blacks started to be elected. Disgust with court reform as a white elitist movement turned many blacks against court reform, and it was only the high regard of many blacks for Chief Justice Howell Heflin that prevented wholesale defections to the opponents of court reform in Alabama.

JPs were often uneducated and made some strange decisions. Occasionally, some justice of the peace would get carried away during a preliminary hearing in a serious felony case and pronounce a guilty verdict. A young court researcher once visited a JP office and was able to locate exactly one law book, a state code that had been published some thirty years before. The JP indicated that he still relied heavily on this book.

Some states, West Virginia, for example, had JP juries, meaning that a party could request trial by jury in front of the JP. The jury selection process was quite informal. The constable (the court officer who was the equivalent of a sheriff in a court of general jurisdiction) would wander around the area adjacent to the JP's office and round up a jury. Predictably, friends of the parties were standing around waiting to be selected. One member of the West Virginia Supreme Court defended this practice from a populist perspective, calling justice-of-the-peace courts "the people's court." He added that if someone did not like the casual method of jury selection that they could ask for a trial *de novo* in a higher trial court.

Justices of the peace represented the ultimate step in localism and drew the most criticism from reformers. They were in business for themselves and were essentially unskilled judicial entrepreneurs. To the extent they belonged to anything, it was the local political system. They were certainly not part of a state judicial branch, except by the wildest stretch of the imagination.

Like JPs, the judges of municipal courts were often paid from the fees that they collected, until the United States Supreme Court pointed out the inherent conflict of interest in permitting a judge to benefit from the fees that he or she assessed against a defendant.[3] Municipal courts were an extension of the municipal political system with all that entailed, sometimes corruption, sometimes patronage and nepotism. Most commonly, however, local politicos wanted municipal courts to bury traffic tickets or go easy on DUI cases. Courts with traffic jurisdiction are popular targets for favors, so much so that some municipal government leaders have fought hard to keep traffic courts under their control.

Higher authorities often ignored the operations of municipal courts, so these courts often lacked a real judicial environment. When New Jersey started recording trials in municipal courts to facilitate appeals, the language of judges improved considerably. Before this, profanity and insulting statements from the bench had occurred with some frequency, particularly in the northern urban counties where civility was not highly prized.

In the 1950s, some prosperous farmers in the area of Perrine, Florida, engineered the incorporation of the town so that their sons, who had just graduated from law school, could become the municipal judge and municipal prosecutor. The idea was to pick up some nice fee income from the traffic cases generated on U.S. Route 1, which ran though the center of the town on its way from Miami to Key West. Unfortunately, the farmers did not anticipate that the black voters of the town might elect their own slate of local officials. The municipal charter was promptly surrendered after a couple of years of lucrative judging, an occurrence that went largely unnoticed even though the state legislature was involved. Even to this day, municipal courts operate in the penumbra of the state court system and do not receive much attention from state-level court officials.

No one desires or expects to see robotic uniformity in trial courts at any level. There will always be some accommodation to local culture, but there has to be, and there is, some movement away from the intense localism of the past toward a perception that trial courts are part of a statewide system to render justice efficiently and fairly according to common procedural guidelines and professional standards.

---

[3]   *Tumey v. Ohio*, 273 US 510 (1927). See also *Ward v. Monroeville*, 409 US 57 (1972).

Financial Aspects of Localism

Counties that once protested the loss of "their courts" to the state started to change their mind when the cost of trial court operations escalated. Counties have, since the mid-1980s, been in the forefront of those demanding that trial court expenditures be paid by the state. Trial courts sometimes find themselves in the difficult position of being caught between state and local governments, each trying to fix responsibility for court financing on the other. This was disastrously illustrated in California, where a vacillating state takeover of financial responsibility wreaked havoc on court budgets for the better part of a decade.

There is, however, no doubt where trial courts are headed. They are steadily turning to the states for financing and withdrawing from local governments. The principal reason for this shift is the increasing cost of court operations and the desire of counties to rid themselves of this burden. Most state supreme courts aligned themselves with county officials in favor of state financing. The most vocal opposition to state financing often came from trial judges, particularly those in urban and suburban areas where local funding was satisfactory and where judges experienced relatively little administrative control from the state-level judiciary. The collateral effects of state financing are extraction of the trial court judiciary from local government and a consequent increase in the independence of the trial courts from local governments. There are strong reasons why this transition to state financing became necessary: incessant resort to inherent-powers suits by judges, inequitable distribution of resources, and inappropriate involvement of trial judges in local government personnel and financial problems. Fiscal localism has not worked.

To make their point about court financing, some counties began to balk at funding courts at the level the courts thought necessary, and a number of serious budgetary confrontations occurred, some of them resulting in court orders to provide the requested level of appropriations. Supreme courts were very uncomfortable with these suits and occasionally used their opinions in these cases to fulminate against local funding of trial courts.

Inherent powers suits often become excessively emotional. Judges tend to exaggerate the likely effect of not getting their way and may threaten to close down court operations or to jail county officials for contempt. Local officials grandstand for the voters, basking in their brave defense of the local exchequer against the arrogant judges. Both secretly hope that their bluff will not be called, but all too often the rhetoric gets out of hand, and litigation ensues. The county officials may occasionally desire this, so that they can tell voters that they were *ordered* to give money to the courts.

Court consultants hate to be drawn into an inherent powers suit to buttress whatever argument the court is making. If the consultant suggests that the court budget request is ill-founded and that the court ought to seek an accommodation, the judges feel betrayed. The appropriating body regards the consultant as a flunky of the courts and unworthy of respect. Rarely do these suits make much sense when viewed objectively. The issue becomes one of brute force and does not reflect well on the judiciary even if they win. What is happening is that the judges and county officials are giving testimony to the fact that many counties cannot adequately finance the operations of a modern trial court. The irrationality does not lie with the parties to the inherent-powers suit but with a funding system that pits them against one another in a struggle for resources that may not exist.

County funding of trial courts has proven inequitable and has been a major reason why reformers attacked financial localism. Although high levels of urbanization in some counties may justify some differences in levels of financing, studies of county-financed trial courts in state after state have revealed unjustifiable variations in the level of county funding for trial courts of similar jurisdiction. It was not unusual a short while ago to find counties where judges were dipping into their own pockets to pay some basic court expenses, while judges in a nearby county of similar demography were flanked with an entourage of court employees and given ornate offices. In the 1980s when midwestern states underwent a severe agricultural depression, it was a study in stark contrast to travel from the courts in a depressed agribusiness county to the courts in a nearby county where the local economy was based on the presence of a state university or a major insurance company. The ability to do justice was markedly different.

It is interesting to compare the reaction to budget cutbacks by a court in a traditionally poor county and a court in a normally affluent county. Judges in the latter court fall into a state of outrage, envisioning all types of dire consequences and brandishing the judicial sword. Judges in the poor county are more likely to recognize the general fiscal weakness of the county and to figure out some way to survive. In theory, the judges of both rich and poor courts are invested with the same responsibility and dignity, but they operate on very different levels, because they live in two different worlds. This contrast between the haves and the have nots was one of the reasons why California went to state financing of trial courts. The northern counties of the state were funding courts at a survival level, while the courts in the large southern counties lived in relative affluence. At a time when a court in the northern part of the state was holding court in a trailer, Los Angeles County had about $20,000,000 sitting in courthouse construction funds. When the state of California started giving out block grants to counties for courts, judges in San Diego County thought that this would provide an opportunity to enhance judicial benefits. California is one of the few states where judges of a general jurisdiction court have different benefit packages depending on what county they are in. Every time the idea of unification comes up, judges in the affluent counties insist on preserving their advantage.

If state financing of trial courts takes the form of a unitary state budget, as it usually does, trial court judges are lifted out of the local government administrative systems covering purchasing, budgeting, internal control of court-collected funds, and personnel management. If the court personnel are unionized, the collective bargaining units change, and collective bargaining switches to the state level.[4] The very nature of unitary budgeting insulates trial judges from inappropriate involvement with local administrative politics.

---

[4]   Employees of the superior courts of California are employees of the court and not the county; unions are not welcome. Municipal court employees are county employees and are often unionized. This difference in personnel practices has been a major obstacle to unification of the two courts.

There is such a thing as being too insulated. If a locally funded trial court is able to carve out its own domain, there is a risk that the judges will be unaccountable to anyone other than themselves in administrative matters. Judges can disrupt county personnel and budget systems by making arbitrary hiring, firing, and salary decisions that are at odds with the personnel and budget systems covering all other county employees. A county executive in New Jersey did a time-and-motion study of personal courtroom employees of judges in his county. These employees worked if the judge was on the bench, but if the judge was not hearing cases or was on vacation, they sat idle and could not be assigned to any other court. They always took their vacations at a different time than the judge to maximize their downtime. The executive used the study to force the court to be more efficient but was attacked in the press and in person by the chief judge, who saw this request as a threat to judicial independence. The same judge was unenthusiastic over state financing because the supreme court might also complain about such personnel practices. His goal was not protection of judicial independence but protection of judicial prerogatives.

An urban court engaged in a budget fight with the county called in the National Center for State Courts. One of the budget issues was whether criminal court judges needed two reporters each. The judges felt that this kept their courts operating continuously without the danger of reporters falling behind in transcript preparation. The study showed no justification for this practice, confirming the county position, which was also the position of the state court administrator. The judges were shocked that the National Center did not side with them and started talking about issuing a mandamus to the county. Their contempt for the state court administrator was also expressed. Nonetheless, they preferred county funding to state funding for the very simple reason that they had a better chance to outmuscle the county than the state supreme court.

In the early 1990s, Philadelphia reached the point of bankruptcy. Trial courts, which are city funded, were asked to share the fiscal pain. They responded by ordering the city to fund an increase in the court budget. City officials complained to the state supreme court, which took over the trial courts and forged a five-year, no-growth budget arrangement with the city. The president judge of the Philadelphia Court of Common Pleas unsuccessfully tried to block the supreme court takeover in federal court.[5] This confrontation arose in the context of an increasing tension between the supreme court and the other branches of state government due to a decision of the court holding that the unification provision of the state constitution implicitly required state financing of trial courts. The court did not, however, effectuate this decision with a mandate until 1996, at which point an interbranch squabble ensued.[6] The Philadelphia courts were deeply

---

[5]   The United States District Court for the Eastern District of Pennsylvania issued a preliminary injunction against the Pennsylvania Supreme Court in 1991. The United States Court of Appeals for the Third Circuit overturned this decision, holding in favor of the supreme court.

[6]   Pa. State Association of County Commissioners v. Commonwealth of Pennsylvania, 681 A. 2d 699 (Pa. 1996).

affected by this dispute over state financing.[7] They needed assistance but were very wary about a form of state funding that would affect the autonomous nature of the Philadelphia court system and its deep roots in the political ethos of the city.

Locally funded courts are more often compromised by overinvolvement in local administrative practices than by unbridled autonomy. In heavily politicized jurisdictions, judges may tie into local hiring practices that do not place a high premium on merit (e.g., Cook County, Illinois). There are courts where nepotism rules are circumvented by having judges hire each other's relatives. Judges sometimes like to compensate those close to them, like secretaries and court reporters, at a salary rate that does not conform to the normal scales for such positions. Any personnel consultant who is in a trial court for more than a couple of days will encounter some irate employee who blurts out all the discrepancies in the personnel system, which sometimes include featherbedding. A court consultant attended a session in the Boston Municipal Court, where the judge was handling enforcement orders in landlord tenant cases, and observed that there were three bailiffs assigned to the court, who justified their presence by separately announcing the same case. The court was like an echo chamber.

Judges sometimes get directly involved in budget negotiations with county officials whose actions may come before them for adjudication. Judges occasionally protect their budget by agreeing to raise the level of court-collected revenues for the county general fund. Judges may use a local government purchasing system that is politically flawed. One urban court administrator discovered that the court was paying a premium rental price for facilities in the downtown area at a time when there was a 60 percent occupancy rate. The local government purchasing office was doing its bit to keep big campaign contributors happy.

A veteran state court administrator gave the following advice to persons undergoing a transition to state financing of trial courts: "Grab the revenues and pick the banks." Choosing depositories sounds benign, but local banks often play politics to win government accounts. Clerks are heavily involved in choosing banks, but judges also get involved. One of the big weaknesses of localism was that court registry accounts often sat in favored banks with no interest being gained. Some states have created state-level accounts for all trust funds in courts to maximize returns (e.g., New Jersey). In state-funded systems, court revenues are usually deposited in state accounts that are swept almost daily. There are inevitably howls when a state court administrator breaks up cozy local arrangements.

Potentially more damaging to the reputation of the judiciary is the misuse and theft of court-collected funds by court employees, even those under the control of offices closely identified with the judiciary, like a clerk's office. Under state financing, the responsibility for internal controls passes to the state court administrator. Auditing responsibility also changes. Some judges resist audits as an invasion of judicial independence or try to hire friendly auditors, a practice that

---

[7]   An interesting parallel is provided by the city of New York, which was plunged into bankruptcy a few years earlier and finally consented to state financing of the state trial courts.

is facilitated by localism. In a nutshell, state financing ends the administrative and personnel vagaries of locally funded courts.

Relations with Court-related Local Agencies

Trial courts are the hub of a network of agencies that perform functions that are essential to court operations. Some local agencies provide courts important services that are not fundamentally court functions. Other services, those provided by elected clerks, for example, are so integral to court operations that judicial control of these functions is essential. Although trial judges may appear to be mini-monarchs of their domains, they are often only the titular head of an uneasy coalition of court-related agencies pursuing their individual agendas. One of the most prominent aspects of judicial localism is the array of agencies loosely clustered around a court and cooperating as they see fit. Nothing is more vexing for a judge than to have operational improvements thwarted by court-related agencies.

Another problem is the perception of the judge as part of the local governmental system. Many disputes arise pertaining to local governments, such as personnel matters, tax issues, and disputed elections. The culture of judicial localism makes it difficult for a judge to maintain the necessary detachment in hearing such matters.

In brief, judicial localism deprives the judiciary of

- control over functions that are essential to the courts and that arguably belong under the administrative aegis of a court
- the necessary judicial detachment in adjudicating disputes involving the agencies with which it is intertwined

The relationship between trial court judges and elected clerks exemplifies the difficult position of trial court judges in relation to local government. The judges are members of the state judicial branch but are heavily dependent on an elected county official for performance of functions essential to the court, mainly recordkeeping, courtroom clerking, collection of revenues, and even calendaring. Clerks are important members of the county hierarchy and do not approach judges with docile subservience, even though clerks have many legal obligations to courts and normally try to please judges. As befits their status as elected local officials, clerks operate with administrative independence of the judiciary. The practical effect of this independence is to draw judges into the local orbit and to make it necessary for judges to work out a modus vivendi with the court official who provides the bulk of the court staff.

In state after state, elected clerks have been the most effective and vocal opponents of unification, correctly perceiving that it would eventually integrate them into the judicial branch, threaten their political position in county government, and make them subject to greater control by judges. Clerical opposition to absorption can be fierce in states where clerks have a much more powerful political base than judges. Nowhere is this power discrepancy more noticeable than in Virginia, where clerks are essentially the administrative and budgeting arm of the general jurisdiction court.

Because elected clerks are involved in local politics and by the nature of their office try to please attorneys, many judges have deep reservations about clerks scheduling cases. One of the first steps taken by the unified New Jersey court system was to remove the calendaring function from the elected clerks and bring it under direct judicial control. Judges in highly politicized jurisdictions encounter situations where case records are mislaid or mysteriously lost as a "favor." In some machine counties, it was an absolute necessity for an attorney to slip some money to a clerk at the time of filing. Fortunately, the great majority of courts are free of such shenanigans, but the relationships between elected clerks and attorneys can very quickly become a problem.

Aside from their elected status and their constitutional status in some states, there are a number of other factors that facilitate the independence of clerks from judicial control:

- They generally submit their own budget and take credit for the revenue generated by the court.
- They often perform functions outside the court, among them handling voting records, maintaining land records, issuing licenses, and in Florida, serving as the principal county financial official.
- They may be constitutional officers.
- They often have political power in the jurisdiction where they are elected.
- The clerks form a formidable legislative lobby that often carries more weight than any judicial lobby.

Typically, the budget of the elected clerk is the largest of the court-related budgets. A judge may not like the way a clerk budgets for court functions but has little say about it. The clerk may even do better with local funding authorities than the court itself. If the clerk is a constitutional officer, county budgeting practice often accords the clerk the courtesy of a lump-sum budget. Moreover, clerks are often viewed as money producers, because court revenues flow through the clerk's office, substantially reducing the net operating cost of the office. Many clerks fear state financing, because it breaks up their budget relationships with the county and forces them to go through the chief judge.

Well into this century, many clerks were on the fee system. This meant that the office was self-supporting and that operating expenses were paid from a fee fund and not the general fund. The amount left over after expenses belonged to the elected clerk. This raised some interesting problems when clerks in urban areas starting making more than judges. Even in the 1970s, some clerks in urban areas of Alabama and Mississippi were making more than $100,000 per year. Sometimes, when fee income became very high, the legislature would place the particular clerk on a salary payable by the county.

Fortunately for the cause of court reform, most fee clerks were not well compensated. In one Alabama county, a new clerk was shocked to learn how little he was taking in and decided to keep the clerk's office closed for large parts of each day while he made a living. The chief justice had to remind the clerk of his obligation to the court and the community. Despite the relative paucity of fee income in many counties, Alabama clerks were among the early opponents of court unification and state financing, mostly out of fear of the unknown and concern over what type of compensation they would receive. Proponents of reform promised a clerical salary level that marked a sharp improvement for most clerks, politically isolating the clerks in the more populous counties who made out well on the fee system.

The reaction of clerks to state financing is an interesting study in localism. In some states, they simply became appointed officials and went into the state civil service system (Kansas, South Dakota, and Iowa, for example). In some states, they opted out of the system and remained part of local government (West Virginia, for example). In Maryland and North Carolina, the clerks are elected, but their office budget is included in the state judicial budget, greatly restricting their ability to use their employees as campaign workers. When New Jersey went to state financing in 1995, clerks were given the option of coming under state financing or staying entirely in the county orbit. The whole process of absorbing clerks into the judicial branch becomes very complicated if the clerk has many important noncourt functions, such as license issuance and election responsibilities. Often, unification leads to severance of court and noncourt functions of clerks.

Clerks quickly detected that the logic of court unification required that they choose between being an independent local official or being a civil service employee of the state judicial branch. One veteran clerk observed that the attitudes of clerks toward going into the state system varied with how close they were to an election. In the 1964 landslide election of Lyndon Johnson, many veteran Republican clerks in the Midwest lost their positions. Several knowledgeable observers feel that this had a major psychological impact on many clerks, both Democratic and Republican.

Veteran clerks often achieve a position of political power in their county, a fact that is not lost on judges. Clerks in some Illinois counties are so influential in judicial elections that candidates come to them for support; not just vocal support, but the loan of the clerk's office staff, which constitutes a great campaign resource. Politically powerful clerks can save an incumbent judge from defeat in a retention election. A downstate Illinois clerk helped a judge who had initially been appointed to fill a vacancy but was not a member of the dominant political party in the county. He was targeted for defeat and went to the clerk, who was the major figure in the majority party. The clerk liked him and sent out the word to let him keep his seat. In counties like this, and there are a number of them, it is ludicrous to think of the clerk as a vassal of the judiciary. One clerk in northern Illinois made it a point to remind the judges about his wide margin of victory in the most recent election.

In one Louisiana parish, the clerk, a local political czar, was elected as a judge but did not altogether abandon his former duties. He was photographed helping his successor sort through election ballots in what promised to be a contested election. This, of course, is a flagrant breach of judicial decorum, but even under less outrageous circumstances, it is very hard for any judge to rule credibly on the peccadilloes of a local government of which he or she is an integral part.

When judges and clerks square off legislatively, as they occasionally do, the judges often lose. Virginia judges occasionally try to break the stranglehold of elected clerks on the administration of courts but are almost invariably defeated. In Illinois, as in many other states, the clerks' association is adept at getting legislatures to raise fees and charges and to permit various special-purpose fees specifically targeted for clerical offices. The Illinois clerks lobbied through a data-processing fee imposed on parties to litigation but had to obtain approval from the chief judge for expenditures. Unhappy with this, the clerks lobbied through an additional fee for records system improvement that required no judicial approval of expenditures.[8]

Florida clerks have a very powerful position because the local government tradition in that state made them the principal administrative officer of the county, as well as a court official. This power has been eroded by home rule in metropolitan counties, but there are many Florida counties where the clerk of court is the budget officer and auditor. In a county as large as Pinellas County (St. Petersburg, Clearwater), the clerk can audit the courts. To think of the clerk in such counties as part of the judicial branch is fatuous. Elected clerks are still a powerful force, and they generally do their job conscientiously. They are, however, an anachronism. There can be no true judicial branch until clerical offices become part of it.

Clerks are often involved in the jury system, although there are some states that have jury commissions. Jury commissions have been targeted for extinction because they have been notoriously political and no friend of efficient jury management. Some northern states used jury commissions as political dumping grounds and had statutes dividing the commission membership between the two parties, suggesting the partisan nature of jury selection. In some depressed areas a call to jury service was like a relief check, and jurors were called on the basis of need and political clout. When West Virginia started reimbursing counties for jury expenses, the state did not at first have tight controls, so that the first year under the new system was open season on the state treasury for those counties that were using jury service as a supplemental welfare system.

The problem with political control of the jury system, whether by a jury commission or a clerk, is obvious. Jury panels can be stacked, and racial and ethnic bars to jury service can be enforced.[9] At midcentury, Florida clerks controlled

---

[8]   Judges often have mixed emotions about raising fees and costs, because they have to assess them and incur the wrath of court users. A legislative audit of Florida judges revealed that trial judges were balking at assessing the high fines, fees, and costs being imposed by the legislature. The judges clearly felt them to be unfair.

[9]   South Carolina had an ancient statute that required jurors to be selected by a blind person or a male child of ten years or younger, reflecting a somewhat skeptical attitude toward the objectivity of court clerks.

the jury machinery and had their own ideas about who was worthy to serve. In the 1950s, a famous Key West politician was indicted for felonies related to the construction of a highway to Key West. The indictment was driven by state authorities, and the governor appointed a special prosecutor. The case against the official was overwhelming, but the handpicked jury did not feel it necessary to deliberate before acquitting the defendant.

At midcentury, blacks in Florida and elsewhere in the South were only marginal citizens and might be called for jury service in some counties if they were thought to be trustworthy. Attorneys of the Civil Rights Division of the United States Department of Justice discovered one Tennessee county where the same black juror appeared regularly on jury panels because he had a local reputation as a "good nigger." This was supposed to insulate the jury system against charges of racial exclusion. The strangely local and idiosyncratic nature of juror calls was inevitably the subject of many court suits and the target of court reformers.

Sheriffs are major figures on the court scene and are powerful players in local government. Persons raised in urban areas seldom appreciate the authority of a sheriff in many parts of the country. In the South, they were the principal enforcers of segregation laws. Department of Justice attorneys often had to negotiate with them on desegregation of public facilities (in many sections of the United States, sheriffs have responsibility for public buildings, not just their security but their operation and maintenance).

In some counties, sheriffs exercised very broad authority, but there was usually a ruling oligarchy lurking in the background to impose some limits. The response of sheriffs to civil rights activities and their treatment of people apprehended for participation in such activities was a major concern of the Department of Justice. On one occasion, an attorney in the Civil Rights Division of the Department of Justice persuaded such an oligarchy to restrain a sheriff who had formed a plan to disrupt a civil rights march by leading a rival march flanked by the sheriffs of two neighboring counties.

Courts rely on the power and authority of sheriffs in many ways: service of process, prisoner transportation, courtroom security, building security, operation of detention facilities, and acceptance of bail in off hours. Sheriffs have sometimes been very helpful in setting up video arraignments in jails, even funding the operation, because it substantially reduces their prisoner transportation burden. Sheriffs may also be a principal provider of cases through their law enforcement role, although this role has diminished over the years as local police departments and state police organizations have expanded.

As security issues have risen to the fore, courts have often reconsidered their relationship to sheriffs and to local government. Some sheriffs are, to put it generously, not highly professional. One downstate Illinois judge invited a visiting court consultant to look at his system for summoning the sheriff to his court in case of emergency. Basically, it was a bell that reverberated somewhere in the sheriff's office, causing a team of deputies to speed to the court within seconds (the sheriff's office was close by). He ruminated briefly on the likelihood of this almost immediate assistance and tried not to think too much about whether anything would actually happen if he pushed the button.

A common sight in many courts is a security checkpoint staffed by security persons provided by a contractor. Whether this expenditure is paid for by the courts or by the sheriff is sometimes an issue. Some judges prefer to exercise control over personnel guarding access to the court areas of public buildings and want to have this expenditure in the court budget.

Judges have seen many strange things happen: erroneous release of prisoners, courtroom escapes, confused prisoner identity through mix-ups in fingerprints, incredible midnight bail decisions, and failure to serve process. Many judges are appalled by the caliber of the deputies assigned to the court or engaged in prisoner transportation. One disgusted judge recalled an incident in which a young deputy discharged his gun into the video terminal connected to the state police network while demonstrating his "quick draw" capability.

One Tennessee judge recounted his experience in a county where the sheriff assigned his aging uncle as a courtroom deputy. The deputy could never remember the judge's name, so that when he announced the arrival of the judge in court, he either gave the wrong name or went completely blank. The judge always had to whisper the correct information and complained to the sheriff that he would prefer a deputy who was able to perform the duties of his office, to no avail. The ancient deputy was always there when the judge returned.

Deputies are often assigned to courts because they are close to retirement and do not want to be out on the street. Sometimes, the sheriff charges the court for these deputies, who are inevitably among the highest paid because of their seniority.[10] One judge wryly remarked that it gave him a great feeling of assurance to know that he had these agile and alert protectors in case of a direct attack. A frequent court scene was and is a cadre of middle-aged, overweight deputies lounging around the bench somewhere.

One judge described a bomb search by deputies after a threat. The procedure amounted to walking to the center of a room, taking a sweeping look, and then pronouncing the room free of explosives. Other judges reported strange failures of detained prisoners to appear in court because someone forgot to put them on the bus.

Sheriffs often have close ties to the bond business. Bail bondsmen often loiter around jails to pick up clients, sometimes with the aid of the sheriffs, who have their favorite bondsmen. Sheriffs can accept bond if there are no bond commissioners. In jurisdictions where people occasionally put up a residence to guarantee the court appearance of a relative, some deputy might be the one to make this complicated decision.[11] When cash bail was introduced, there were interesting problems of cash bail posted at night not finding its way from the sheriff to the local treasury.

---

[10] Normally, sheriffs budget for court service in their own budgets, but, occasionally, they charge the courts so that the court must budget for bailiffs under some form of intergovernmental transfer.

[11] An interesting sidelight on this type of bail is that no one wants to force the sale of the residence of a person generous enough to risk their home for a troubled relative.

Commercial bail bondsmen have often been a corrupt influence in the courts. Bondsmen were loosely supervised, and sometimes did not have the requisite financial ability to support their bonds. They nonetheless enjoyed support from judges and prosecutors who sincerely felt that courts could not function without bondsmen making recalcitrant defendants appear in court. Many judges were deeply opposed to broad use of pretrial release on personal recognizance.

One of the great mysteries in most courts was what happened when a bond was forfeited. In theory, there was a show cause hearing and then issuance of an order to pay in the amount of the bond. In practice, bondsmen were given grace periods or permitted to make a deal to pay less than the face amount of the bond. The prosecutor was the usual enforcer of the bond, immediately creating a conflict of interest because prosecutors relied on bondsmen to produce defendants in court. Judges, sheriffs, and prosecutors were all involved in the tawdry bail process that was the ultimate illustration of localism gone awry.

Although usually pictured as weird outcasts, some bondsmen were very powerful political brokers. One deputy court administrator in an urban area recalled that he was approached by bondsmen who offered to get him the job of trial court administrator, which had just fallen vacant. The price of the aid was unstated but hinted at by vague allusions to doing favors for friends. He declined the assistance but was quite certain that they could have secured the job for him because of their influence over some top judges. The generally sleazy nature of the bail bond business led to repeated attempts to abolish it. In June 1976, Kentucky, one of the first states to unify its court system, abolished commercial bail bondsmen and created a state-operated pretrial release system, the harbinger of a concerted attack to free courts from this odious aspect of localism.[12]

Sheriffs can be a great bottleneck causing court delay, either because they are slow or sloppy in transporting prisoners or, more commonly, because they fail to serve process. Some courts get around this by having their own process servers, permitting private organizations to make service, or using various mail or electronic means of serving process. Nonetheless, sheriffs often give low priority to serving court process, especially bench warrants (called *capiases* in some states). Deputies often joke about how bench warrants are at the bottom of the stack. Basically, these warrants get served only if the defendant is apprehended on a new charge. Once the word gets out on the street that bench warrants are not being served, no one worries too much about coming to court or paying fines on installments.

In fairness to the sheriff and police agencies that bury bench warrants, it must be said that courts were also heavily at fault, because many judges did not care about enforcing their own orders in routine cases. Occasionally, a state legislature or state supreme court has started programs to make trial courts more enforcement oriented, but trial courts have not generally been proactive in this area.

Professor Mary Ann Glendon of Harvard Law School described an encounter with the Cook County Sheriff's Office when she appeared to ask for

---

[12]   William Davis, "Implementation of Court Reform in Kentucky," in Powell, *Seven States*, 1.

service of a replevin order and observed a number of deputies sitting around socializing. One of them finally ambled over to the desk where she was standing and informed her that the press of business would make service impossible unless she was prepared to make it worth his while. She ultimately succeeded in getting help by stating in conspiratorial tones that her principals would be very grateful.[13] This is not a technique found in the case management texts but pretty well captures the vagaries of patronage offices assisting the courts.

As courts have withdrawn from the local government milieu to gain more control over their own operations, they have had to deal with their relationship to sheriffs, sorting out those functions of the sheriff that could be performed by court personnel and those that must of necessity be performed by the sheriff. A distinction can be made between the police and custodial functions of a sheriff and the bailiff function of a sheriff. Many courts see the latter function as that of a court attendant to the judge and do not feel that one must be a sworn deputy to fulfill the role. Bailiffs are now often on the court payroll.

Similarly, courts are attempting to exercise more control over service of civil process by sheriffs where this function is being done poorly. Courts have started to use methods other than issuance of bench warrants for failure to make timely payments of fines and fees and to seek alternative methods of dealing with nonappearance in court. It is not very cost beneficial to use sheriffs to serve process for nonpayment of fines, and many courts have switched to methods similar to those used by commercial lending institutions. Courts have recognized that many court needs are not well served by an elected sheriff.

Courts deal with many law enforcement agencies other then sheriffs' offices and schedule the cases initiated by these departments. Occasionally, a local police department also provides security services to a court or is engaged in service of criminal process. Scheduling of police witnesses is a complicated matter even when only one agency is involved. If a court serves many local police agencies, the sheriff's office, and state police organizations, scheduling becomes very involved. Policemen, at least uniformed policemen, often have regular court days. This practice was designed to evenly spread out cases so that neither the court nor the police department would be overly burdened. When radar was first used for traffic violations, the old court-day system broke down a bit because a couple of radar teams could fill up the courtroom, but the system of court days endures, particularly for traffic cases. However, many units in a police department do not function on a court-day basis, and even the court-day system breaks down if a case involves officers from different operational units.

Local police departments have close but not necessarily warm relationships with courts, particularly if the court is intimately tied to the same local government as the police department. Large police departments invariably have a scheduling unit that arranges court appearances of police witnesses and interacts with court employees. There is often a lot of "blame game" tactics between such units and court employees, but these opposing personnel may cooperate in identify-

---

[13] Mary Ann Glendon, A *Nation Under Lawyers* (New York: Farrar, Straus, and Giroux, 1994), 72-73.

ing bottlenecks. For example, when drug cases took over the police calendar, backlogs developed because toxicology reports were hard to obtain quickly, leaving many drug cases hung up for months on the issue of substance identification. Courts and police have largely overcome this problem (police now often use field testing) and have cooperated on adoption of uniform traffic tickets and broader use of the summons to expedite the flow of cases through courts.

In the New England states, there was an institution known as the police prosecutor. Prosecuting attorneys rarely ventured into limited jurisdiction courts, so that policemen were both witnesses and prosecutors. Some police departments scheduled the criminal cases for the judges and prepared calendars. It was not until the 1970s that the Providence, Rhode Island, police department turned over the scheduling of criminal cases to the courts. The police involvement made sense in a way, because the department assigned officer court days and knew the scheduling problems in each department. If officers outside the traffic division made traffic arrests, it caused scheduling problems, because these officers might not have the same court-day schedule as the traffic division. Driving-under-the-influence cases also caused scheduling problems, because one officer might make the arrest, another transport the defendant, and a third test for intoxication. Detectives often shared cases, so two or more detectives might have to be scheduled together; sometimes, the detectives worked with uniformed officers, further complicating the scheduling. Drug and vice squad detectives had many cases per officer, because many of their cases might arise from the same "big bust." It was hard to schedule their cases without keeping them in court all the time, but vice and narcotic squad detectives never seemed unduly concerned if their cases washed out. Drug and gambling cases turned on a motion to suppress the evidence as illegally seized, so these motions were scheduled with the trial to save police witnesses a second court appearance if the denial of the motion did not lead to a plea.

The police department knew the ways of Providence politics and did not worry too much about cases resulting from the traditional preelection drug bust. The top officials in the department also knew what attorneys had clout with the city administration, and so these attorneys had access to much information and had an unusual ability to keep cases bottled up in the department. The department liked to control the calendar to ensure that their informants were protected if they were arrested. Detectives checked the arrests to identify "their boys" who might not be known to any other officer. Detectives viewed cases with a police perspective that would not occur to a court employee. The police, wise in the ways of local romance, identified one attempted rape defendant, the son of a local politico, as a basically good, high-spirited kid with "hot pants." There was one serious assault charge against a woman that was described as her periodic attack on her boy friend, more of a mating ritual than a crime. These cases had been discreetly buried.

About 1970, a consulting firm was hired to move the calendar function from the police to the court, a transfer only permitted because the mayor was concerned about police overtime. His own people seemed to be relatively unconcerned about the army of police seated in court each day. He was willing to give up the rewards of doing favors for attorneys and politicians in return for budget relief. The state courts, for the first time, seized control of the criminal calendar of the district court and started to see that some cases had been languishing in the department for some time. It is very important that courts do not let police agencies run the courts, a goal that is much more difficult to achieve if they are products of the same political environment.

Prosecutors and trial courts are linked in many ways because they are the core elements of the local criminal justice system. General jurisdiction judicial districts and prosecutorial districts are usually the same. Both prosecutors and judges are usually funded by the same government and are products of the same political milieu. They have to coordinate closely in case scheduling and interact in court proceedings, plea bargaining, sentencing, and bail hearings. This linkage is so strong that county budgets for courts often link the prosecutor and the court under a common budgetary heading, almost as if the prosecutor was part of the judicial branch. When counties first prevailed upon state legislatures to assume the cost of judicial salaries, prosecutors and their top assistants also were placed on state salaries. When courts went to state financing, prosecutors often attempted a similar transition.

It is very awkward if the courts are state financed and the prosecutor locally financed, because their budget decisions are not driven by similar considerations; for example, an experiment with setting up prosecution teams assigned to a particular judge. If the judiciary and prosecution cannot coordinate their budget decisions and even have different fiscal years, a variety of problems can arise. Problems can occur on space allocation because local governments will favor the locally funded entity. Problems may occur on criminal justice information systems if the county is funding the development and the courts become a state entity.

The logic of unification suggests that courts and prosecutors should act in tandem to free themselves from localism, but unification of prosecution is not really feasible in most states. Except for a few states where the attorney general is directly involved in trial prosecution (e.g., Rhode Island), the attorney general has much less authority over prosecutors than a supreme court does over trial courts. In North Carolina, where courts and prosecution are state funded, prosecutors chose to have their state budget appropriation included in the court budget rather than the budget of the attorney general.

Public defenders, unlike prosecutors, are rarely elected officials and operate to some extent under the aegis of the court, because defenders are very vulnerable politically and essential to the functioning of the criminal justice system. Judges may be members of defender boards and may do battle for defenders if the budget for indigent defense is about to be cut. For budget reasons, public defender offices often handle only a portion of the indigent cases. Moreover, they are prohibited from representation when there might be a conflict of interest, as in multiple-defendant cases. Sometimes, contract attorneys are used for conflict cases, but most commonly, indigent defense is supplied by appointed attorneys. The appointed attorney is still essential to the indigent defense system.

Courts are heavily involved in the selection of indigent defense counsel and perhaps even the administration of the indigent defense program. What this means is that courts are closely tied to defense, even though they must be neutral in court. This anomaly is not lost on prosecutors, but the simple fact is that courts have assumed the burden for ensuring adequate indigent defense. This means at times that the court must oppose a local culture that is not hospitable to indigent defense. The level of funding for indigent defense is heavily influenced by ideology as well as economics. The logic of indigent defense spending suggests some state role to counteract these local inequities.[14]

As the result of the court unification movement in the late twentieth century, the excesses of localism in courts have definitely been reduced, although certainly not eliminated. Justices of the peace are largely gone, and those that remain are under more supervision. There are fewer municipal courts, and a bit more professionalism in the many that remain. Unified state courts of limited jurisdiction are better organized and more professional. State financing has reduced the problems of fiscal localism. Procedures and jurisdictional laws are more standardized, and some clerks have been absorbed into the courts. The struggle of courts to create order out of the fragmented mess at midcentury has been fairly successful. A judicial branch is taking form where none really existed.

---

[14] In state-funded systems, legislatures frequently assault an indigent defense budget, and so courts often try and avoid having this item of expenditure in the court budget. In any event, a state supreme court is in a better position to confront the problem than individual judges scattered throughout the state.

Chapter 4

Judges and Lawyers: Who's in Charge?

J udges and lawyers are part of the same legal culture, share many common attitudes and experiences, and are mutually dependent. Lawyers need the services of judges to fulfill their professional role and are officers of the court upon whom judges lean to make the court function. Moreover, judges are simply at home with attorneys, because they have so much in common and speak the same language. Due to this affinity, judges often have to live with the public perception, not altogether inaccurate, that they run their courts to suit the convenience of lawyers and are not unduly concerned about the individuals who are defendants in criminal cases, parties to civil cases, or witnesses. Many judges feel uncomfortable about exercising strong control over attorneys, because they are both part of the legal fraternity.

Pressures have been building for judges to be more assertive in dealing with attorneys, particularly in the scheduling and management of cases. Just as judges have distanced themselves from politics and local government, so have they assumed a less clubby attitude toward their fellow attorneys. The dilemma for judges is that the ties binding judges and attorneys are very strong, and yet judges cannot truly say that they are in control of the courts if they do not challenge the bar on some basic issues.

The Ties that Bind

Linkage in Public Perception. In a country currently awash in lawyers, it is hard to believe that there were hardly any lawyers in the American colonies in the seventeenth century nor any particular system for training lawyers.[1] Moreover, many colonists thought this paucity of lawyers was great, because contempt for lawyers was quite widespread in the United States and in England. In the eighteenth century, more lawyers started to appear in the colonies, along with some very rudimentary systems of apprentice training and accreditation, usually under the aegis of courts, but the number of lawyers was still quite small. There were only

[1]   For a discussion of the early development of the legal profession in the American colonies, see Friedman, *American Law*, 94-102.

seventy-one lawyers in Massachusetts in 1775, up from fifteen in 1740.[2] A number of these attorneys had been trained in England and felt the scorn directed by colonists at the colonial legal system. Much of this resentment stemmed from the fact that these attorneys generally represented the interests of the more powerful segments of colonial society and government. Lawyers who engaged in foreclosures or any legal action that seemed directed at the poor were objects of hatred and ridicule and, on occasion, mob attack. They were, however, necessary to the functioning of the increasingly sophisticated system of justice growing up in the colonies.

The early perception of lawyers was that they served the privileged classes, spoke jargon, created convoluted procedures, and were not highly trustworthy. Prototypical of the big-shot lawyers of the early Republic was Daniel Webster, who was well compensated to place his grandiloquent oratory at the service of the rich and the powerful, mainly, the Second Bank of the United States. A more common stereotype in this period was that of the itinerant and long-winded lawyer-politician of the frontier. There was some empirical basis for this image because western states often acquired the less successful members of the bar from other states and were notoriously lax in determining who could practice law. This image persisted even though there were some obvious exceptions, such as Abraham Lincoln and Stephen Douglas, both of whom practiced law in heavily rural central Illinois and were men of great talent, certainly not the rustic buffoons of popular myth. Moreover, Lincoln typified the new breed of office lawyers that started to emerge in the period immediately preceding the Civil War when the changing nature of legal practice demanded a fixed office location.

In the late nineteenth century, the legal profession started to gain more self-awareness and to recognize that there were a substantial number of poorly qualified lawyers.[3] Legal education became more sophisticated, bar associations started to emerge, the judiciary became a bit more active in matters of admission and discipline, and steps were taken to curb some of the more flagrant examples of incompetence and malfeasance. By then, however, lawyers were playing "catch-up ball" in the image game, and they have never caught up.

In August 1997 incoming ABA president Jerome J. Shestack cited a 1997 national poll by Lou Harris and Associates indicating public dissatisfaction with the use of media by lawyers. The poll showed that 58 percent of the public believes that it is never appropriate for lawyers to use media to influence public opinion on pending cases, but 91 percent of those surveyed were convinced that lawyers do use the media for this purpose. In addition, 55 percent of poll respondents said that the high degree of publicity accorded some cases lowered their opinion of lawyers. Shestack pointed out that such practices were unethical according to the ABA *Model Rules of Professional Conduct* and urged a higher degree of professionalism, adding that such practices demean the legal system in the eyes of the public.

---

[2]   Ibid., 100.

[3]   For nineteenth-century development of the legal profession, see generally Friedman, *American Law*, "The Bar and Its Works," 303-333, and "The Legal Profession," 606-620.

Table 1
Ratings of the Honesty and Ethical Standards of Lawyers
(1976 and 1996)

Rating	1976	1996
Very high	6%	3%
High	19	14
Average	48	39
Low	18	27
Very low	8	14
No opinion	1	3

In fact, the public view of lawyers and legal ethics is still in decline, as shown by Gallup poll data cited in the *Sourcebook of Criminal Justice Statistics* (see Table 1). In that survey, the public rated only one of twenty-five professions (car sales) as being lower in ethical standards than the legal profession. As far as professional ethics go, lawyers have nowhere to go but up.

Public perceptions are not, of course, always correct, but there has been a remarkable consistency in the public view of lawyers, even among those who might be considered more sophisticated members of the public. A 1992 survey of corporate executives revealed that 47 percent of the respondents felt that a major reason for the high cost of civil litigation was that defense lawyers were dragging out their cases to jack up their fees.

State court systems have their own problems of public confidence but also appear to suffer by their close connection to the legal profession. The *Sourcebook of Criminal Justice Statistics* contains 1996 national survey data about confidence in local courts. The 1996 national survey data in *Sourcebook of Criminal Justice Statistics* indicates that the level of public confidence in local courts is not very high (see Table 2). This negative view is stronger among minority groups, dwellers in urbanized areas, and persons in lower-income brackets.

The national totals on the first line of Table 2 have been confirmed in state-specific surveys. Courts are sinking in public esteem in somewhat the same way that lawyers are. For better or worse, judges and lawyers are linked in the public mind.

Common Orientation Toward Public and Civic Roles. It is noteworthy that twenty-five of the fifty-six signers of the Declaration of Independence were lawyers and that thirty-one of fifty-five delegates to the Constitutional Convention were lawyers.[4] It should also be noted that many persons who

---

[4] Charles Evans Hughes, "The Supreme Court, Constitutional Foundation," in Scigliano, *The Courts*, 17; see also Friedman, *American Law*, 101.

Table 2
Levels of Confidence in Local Courts*

	A great deal	Quite a lot	Some	Very little
National	11.7%	22.3%	43.2%	22.8%
Race/ethnicity				
White	21.1	23.4	43.0	21.5
Black	5.7	11.4	54.3	28.6
Hispanic	18.1	20.8	31.9	29.2
Income				
Over $60,000	12.4	27.1	47.2	13.3
$30,000 to $60,000	12.4	20.6	47.6	19.4
$15,000 to 29,999	9.7	21.1	42.7	26.4
Less than $15,000	11.8	22.8	32.3	33.1
Region				
Midwest	15.1	26.0	41.1	17.7
Northeast	9.1	20.6	47.3	23.0
South	10.5	22.3	43.8	23.4
West	12.1	18.6	41.6	27.7
Community				
Urban	6.3	19.4	47.5	26.9
Small city	7.5	27.2	38.7	26.6
Suburban	14.2	21.5	45.3	19.0
Rural/small town	13.6	22.1	41.9	22.4

* Refusals and "don't know" responses omitted.

described themselves as lawyers in this early period did not actually derive their living from the practice of law; Thomas Jefferson, for example. They simply were trained in the law and the philosophy of law as expounded by the great commentators on the common law and various giants of jurisprudence. These part-time lawyers occasionally provided legal services but often confined their use of the law to their participation in government and public life. The profession of law was very fluid then and, to some extent, still is.

From the founding of the Republic, lawyers have often sought and won elective offices. Twenty-three of the first thirty-six presidents were lawyers.[5] Richard Nixon, Gerald Ford, and William Clinton are among the modern lawyer-presidents. Among the earlier presidents who were lawyers are John Adams, Thomas Jefferson, Andrew Jackson (who also served as a frontier judge), James Buchanan, Abraham Lincoln, Chester Arthur, James Garfield, Grover Cleveland, and William

[5]   Mayer, The Lawyers, 11.

Howard Taft (who also served as chief justice of the United States Supreme Court and dean of the University of Cincinnati Law School).[6] About 50 percent of the governors elected in the century after the Civil War were lawyers.[7]

Alexis De Tocqueville was amazed at the public role of lawyers in the United States and their orientation toward politics. An aristocrat to the core, he noted that the American lawyers had positions of authority and political influence that might have been reserved for the aristocracy in a less democratic land: "In America, there are no nobles or literary men, and the people are apt to mistrust the wealthy; lawyers consequently form the highest political class."[8]

Lawyers everywhere seemed to find their way into public office and assumed important communal roles contributing substantial amounts of their time to charitable and civic undertakings. De Tocqueville observed that, "They fill the legislative assemblies, and are at the head of the administration." [9] State trial judges were important figures in the community, not just because of their role as judges, but because they were considered part of the local government hierarchy and were sometimes very active in civic affairs, if not politics itself. American judges, like attorneys, have moved in and out of political life with a frequency rare in other legal cultures. De Tocqueville observed that the courts were an extension of the legal profession, which he referred to as a party that imperceptibly controlled American democracy.[10] Perhaps more than any other early observer of the American scene, de Tocqueville perceived the legal profession as a "body" with its own purposes and ends.

When lawyers dominated state legislatures, they were not above passing self-serving legislation, much to the chagrin of the public and nonlawyer legislators. The number of lawyers in state legislatures has declined in recent decades, but some of the resentment against lawyers remains. The surest way to kill a bill in most legislatures is to label it a "lawyers' bill." Judges lament that the number of lawyer-legislators has declined because the state judiciary counted on lawyer-legislators to support judicial positions.

The omnipresence of lawyers in politics and government did little to enhance the public's esteem for lawyers.[11] The average American's view of politicians and lawyers was equally jaundiced. When Jacksonian politics drew state judges into the political orbit, they were indistinguishable from lawyer-politicos, and elected judges were subjected to the same taunts reserved for other officials.

Shared Professional Rites. The law has its own peculiar jargon and rituals. The esoteric and arcane rites of the legal community have always irritated the

[6]   Friedman, *American Law*, 616.

[7]   Mayer, *The Lawyers*, 12.

[8]   Alexis de Tocqueville, *Democracy in America*, abridged edition, ed., Richard D. Heffner (New York: New American Library, 1956), 125.

[9]   Ibid., 126.

[10]   Ibid., 126, 127.

[11]   Mayer, *The Lawyers*, 8, 9.

public but have served the practical purpose of establishing a monopoly over the mysteries of the law.[12] This monopoly was, in later periods of American legal history, protected by laws preventing the unauthorized practice of the law. Lawyers felt competitively threatened by organizations that provided title searches, real estate closings, debt collection, or estate planning and with varying degrees of success tried to ward off these intrusions into these staples of general law practice. Bar associations started setting recommended fees for the prime purpose of keeping fees up rather than having them driven down by price competition.

This monopolization did not always sit well with nonlawyers, particularly if they perceived that judges were allied with lawyers. One of the most popular books of the 1950s was Norman Dacey's *How to Avoid Probate*, which summed up what many Americans already suspected. The average probate of a will was not very complex, and yet compensation of lawyers was traditionally based on the percentage of the money in the estate rather than on their actual work, which often consisted of filling in blanks on forms. Probate work is, in fact, very administrative in nature and is often delegated to secretaries or paralegal assistants, and yet judges have gone along with the inflated compensation for attorneys. Legislatures bowed to public protest and developed fast-track procedures for small estates and some reforms of lawyer compensation. The changes did little to allay public dissatisfaction.

The role of lawyers in the average real estate transaction is often marginal. Real estate lawyers are necessary in complex transactions but are not generally perceived as necessary in the sale of residential property. In Arizona, the voters, by a four to one margin, adopted a constitutional amendment to restore the public right to buy real estate without paying a lawyer, overriding a supreme court decision favoring attorneys.[13] There is little doubt where the public stands. They do not want judges creating busywork for attorneys.

Further cementing the lawyer monopoly well into the nineteenth century was the peculiarly limited availability of legal source materials, in particular reports of cases in appellate courts.[14] Access to the materials carried with it a certain power, quite apart from the ability to interpret the materials. Sometimes, judges themselves compiled cases and commentaries that were made available to lawyers as source materials. Interestingly, the lectures of judges to lawyers in some of the embryonic law schools were closely guarded, because they represented a monopoly on knowledge

Another source of frustration to the public, but bread and butter to lawyers and judges, was the complex and very technical system of common-law pleadings and very technical rules of procedure. Legislatures eventually responded to public dissatisfaction, as well as to some dissatisfaction within the legal profession itself, and enacted simpler and more coherent rules of procedure.[15]

---

[12]   Ibid., 64-70.

[13]   Ibid., 64.

[14]   See general discussion by Friedman, *American Law*, 318-333.

[15]   See general discussion of reforms in civil procedure by Friedman, *American Law*, 146-147, 391-398.

Rules of evidence appeared almost unintelligible to the public, and worst of all, to many jurors. These rules evolved over time and combined many aspects of public policy and constitutional law with protections against evidence of dubious probative value reaching lay jurors, who were assumed to be of very limited intelligence. No one has ever been able to adequately explain why a deathbed statement is presumed to be truer than a statement made at any other time, but it is from such propositions that the law of evidence was molded.

Legalese, of course, was the most irritating aspect of the legal cult. It was characterized by verbal overkill and stilted phraseology. Legal documents abounded in "wherefores," "whereases," and "party of the first part." Lawyers frequently trotted out quaint Latin phrases, such as "res ipsa loquitur" and "de minimis non curat lex." A favorite silly opener was "comes now the plaintiff, through his attorney." Many legal contracts seemed to place a premium on obfuscation of whatever underlying agreement might have existed before its burial in legal prose.

The great invention of lawyers and judges was the common law, that reservoir of legal principles embedded in the words of appellate judges. Those interested in ferreting out the inner meanings of court opinions to support some desired legal outcome could spend hours poring through law books containing court opinions. A favorite professorial exercise for first-year law students was (and is) the analysis of cases to find the bedrock core of the opinions (i.e., the holdings) and to distinguish this from the dross or dicta in the court opinions.

Simpleminded Jacksonians wanted to know why the law could not be stated in some simple form that an average person could understand, perhaps contained in a statute or a code.[16] The western states, where there was not a great body of case law, were more likely to adopt codes than states in the East. Even in the West, lawyers and judges had trouble with the idea that a statute meant what it said and engaged in "interpretation" that sometimes had the effect of repeal. Democratic resentment against the common law grew during the nineteenth century, because the lionization of case law was perceived as an artificial device by which lawyers and judges controlled the development of the law at the expense of the popular will as expressed through legislatures.

Harvard Law School, the father of all law schools and the home of the casebook method, treated statutes as unwelcome intrusions into the purity of the common law.[17] The evolution of the law through judicial decisions was thought to be the best way to keep the law alive and to prevent it from becoming ossified in code enactments. The struggle to preserve the common law lives on in the American Law Institute and in ALI's restatements of the law, which are basically attempts to keep the common law alive and to reduce its wisdom to workable categories that can be effectively applied by judges and attorneys.[18] The burgeoning of statutes and regulatory rules, some in the form of federal pre-

---

[16] See general discussion of the codification movement by Friedman, *American Law*, 403-406.

[17] See general discussion of the Langdell reforms in legal education by Friedman, *American Law*, 612-617.

[18] Ibid., 676.

emption or uniform state laws, has made it difficult for the restatements to have continuing force. Judicial concern over this trend has been reflected in resolutions of the Conference of Chief Justices protesting the attempts of the United States Congress to legislate in the area of product liability, rather then permitting the states to follow the traditional case-by-case approach in developing the law.

Attachment to the Myth of the Solo Generalist. In the early days of the American court system, lawyers were classic loners, roving advocates, and general practitioners.[19] Some of the eastern states toyed with the idea of a barrister and solicitor distinction like that in England, but this was never seriously considered in a new nation characterized by egalitarian ideas and a very fluid and individualistic concept of legal practice.

Trial judges were every bit as solitary and itinerant as attorneys and extremely jealous of their judicial authority, which they exercised in a highly individual fashion. Lawyers and judges frequently rode circuit together, forming a tight-knit legal community with a level of camaraderie that even then seemed a bit incestuous and would now seem quite inappropriate. Common legal background, frequent professional interaction, isolation from the laity, and the sheer loneliness of strange towns created close ties.

Most lawyers and judges knew a little bit about a lot of things but were not particularly profound in their knowledge, because it was seldom necessary for them to be great legal scholars in an age when society and the law itself were still fairly simple in structure. The average practice was routine and tedious, occasionally spiced by a lively or interesting dispute. Success as a lawyer or judge depended largely on common sense and general knowledge, despite the facade of legal mystery shown to the laity. Few fortunes were made in the law. Very often, it served as a stepping-stone to other fields or occupations, such as politics and government.

As time has gone on, judges and lawyers have had to surrender some of their lone-wolf characteristics and associate themselves with larger units. This weakened the close personal ties that once existed and encouraged specialization. In the twentieth century, specialization among lawyers became common. Solo generalist practitioners became, with few exceptions, the least affluent members of the legal profession. People sought expertise and specialists. Law schools responded by offering a broader variety of specialty courses and even graduate degrees. Law firms were organized along specialty lines, and many small boutique law firms arose on the basis of expertise in one or two areas. The idea of certifying lawyers in specialty areas, as is done with doctors, started to surface more frequently, particularly in continuing legal education curricula. In 1984 the Conference of Chief Justices expressed interest in legal specialization as a means of obtaining competent counsel. Certification of attorneys in death penalty cases started occurring.

Even though the realities of law practice and legal economics have brought about some degree of specialization by lawyers, the judiciary still remains the

---

[19]   See discussion of early American law practice by Friedman, *American Law*, 94-102, 303-314.

last bastion of the legal generalists. This has proven very troublesome for attorneys in highly specialized areas of the law, particularly those where bench trials are the norm. Trial judges are not fungible, and everyone knows it. The concept of the generalist judge is colliding with the reality of a technological and scientific world and a very complex economy. Although some lawyers chafe under this heritage of the past, the myth of the generalist lives on in the judiciary and still has a lingering nostalgic appeal for attorneys.

The Bonds of Maleness and Ethnicity. The clubby environment of the legal profession was, and to some extent still is, very male. Women were denied admission to the bar until the late 1800s and were not a significant part of the legal profession and of the judiciary until very recently.[20] As late as the 1960s, women trial attorneys were a rarity. Needless to say, there were very few women judges. In 1970 an incident occurred in New England when a woman judge had to be smuggled into a male club where the judges of her court were having a meeting. She was secretly admitted through a side door to avoid the ignominy of rejection or expulsion. She was not surprised at the choice of the meeting site; most trial benches were quite frankly "good ole boy" networks.

Professor Mary Ann Glendon of Harvard Law School recalled early court appearances where she had to convince the presiding judge that she was actually an attorney:

> The first time I appeared before Judge Julius Hoffman . . . in the U.S. District Court, he interrupted my opening remarks to inquire: "Are you a lawyer, little lady?" Shortly after that incident, I was appointed to represent an indigent prisoner charged with murder. . . . When I sat down between the client and my co-counsel . . . the Cook County Criminal Court judge asked me if I was the person accused of killing the taxi driver.[21]

The legal culture was also clannish along racial, ethnic, and religious lines. The American Bar Association was quite frankly racist early in the twentieth century and was a veritable bastion of WASP attorneys from the more important firms that started to emerge in the late nineteenth century.[22] At midcentury, prestigious law firms in the major cities were just starting to take in Catholics and Jews and doing that very gingerly, following the path of tokenism. Blacks were not even on the radar screen, because very few black attorneys were being graduated. In the hinterlands and the urban ethnic enclaves, the dominant culture reflected itself in other ways. The political route to judgeships in many parts of the United States was through the Masonic lodges, just as the route to political success and judgeships in many urban areas was through ethnic and Catholic associations. The state courts and the legal profession reflected male, northern

---

[20]   Friedman, *American Law,* 639.

[21]   Glendon, *Nation Under Lawyers,* 61.

[22]   Friedman, *American Law,* 638.

European domination. The modern obsession with diversity is starting to make itself felt in courts, but ever so slowly.

Common Training and Formation. The English legal profession was developed in that wonderful institution the Inns of Court, where aspiring lawyers went as apprentices to receive a very practical, technical in-house training from experienced lawyers. Divorced from a university setting, the training was not very theoretical or jurisprudential in nature and encompassed those persons who would eventually go on to judicial careers, as well as those who would continue to practice law.

Colonial Americans, generally following the English model, chose an apprentice type of legal training.[23] Unfortunately, the Americans did not have anything as structured as the Inns of Court, so legal education was a pretty haphazard process. Moreover, this method of training gave existing lawyers the power to control the size of their profession and the nature of the local competition. The quality of education varied remarkably and was generally quite mediocre. Occasionally, law students did have the opportunity to learn under the tutelage of a gifted lawyer-teacher; for example, Thomas Jefferson under the legendary George Wythe.

Americans also followed the English model in not creating a separate educational track for judges, so lawyers and judges received the same education and saw themselves as part of the same legal fraternity. The idea was that some attorneys would simply don robes, and not necessarily on a permanent basis. Even today, attorneys sometimes serve temporarily as part-time judges in the very courts where they practice. Some judges are still permitted an outside law practice if they do not practice in the courts where they sit. Judges are often aware that the attorneys standing before them played a role in their selection or election and may have a role in their reappointment or reelection. The fluid nature of the American judicial system creates a number of ethically ambiguous situations.

As the profession grew, judges were increasingly drawn into certifying lawyers and determining what they should learn during their apprenticeship.[24] More often than not, local courts, rather than the supreme court, exercised this responsibility. To say that this responsibility was carried out rather casually in the early days would be an understatement. There are numerous accounts of lawyers winning judicial approval of their right to be lawyers on the condition that they go elsewhere to practice. Many judges were themselves products of the school of "office training" and not inclined to be overzealous in testing attorney qualifications. A brief conversation over a meal or drink could be the basis for licensing an attorney.

The late nineteenth century witnessed a more serious effort to upgrade the quality of legal education and the quality of the profession itself. The erratic nature of legal education did lead some judges to assume the role of teachers,

[23]   Ibid., 97-101.
[24]   Ibid., 652-654.

often as an adjunct of the judicial function. Actually, the earliest versions of legal education were often conducted by judges; for example, the courses provided by Justice Joseph Story while a member of the United States Supreme Court. The idea of full-time law professors did not come upon the scene until the last part of the nineteenth century, when university-based law schools started to take over squeeze out the apprentice method of legal education.

In the late nineteenth and early twentieth centuries, the emergence of law schools, organized bar groups, bar examinations, and boards of bar examiners greatly upgraded the professional preparation and qualifications of lawyers, as has the more vigilant superintendence of state supreme courts over the legal profession. In the late twentieth century, specialized education for judges came into being through such programs as that provided by the National Judicial College in Reno. Despite these changes, the formation of lawyers and judges remains essentially the same. They remain offshoots of the same family.

Lawyers as an Extension of the Judiciary. Judges rely on attorneys to help them carry out their functions. The orders by which a court exercises its authority are often drafted by the litigating lawyers. Motions and petitions are often accompanied by proposed orders. After disposing of an issue where there is no proposed order, a judge may ask the prevailing attorney to draft an order, clear it with opposing counsel, and return it for signature of the judge. Many orders, particularly those in routine motions, are pretty standardized, but some must be quite tailored. Many laymen are surprised that judges delegate a function so integral to the judicial role and are not comforted by the thought that the judge reviews the attorney product before signing it. The lay view is that the judge is above the attorneys, not a comrade in arms.

Judges also rely on attorneys to direct them to relevant points of law. Many experienced judges need little help on basic procedural issues but may need guidance on less-common issues. A judge may ask for a brief on a crucial point. Sometimes, a judge will take an issue under advisement to consider the legal authorities cited by the attorneys and perhaps to do some independent research. Later, the judge will announce his or her decision. Some judges are notorious for taking practically everything under advisement and then delaying their decisions, prompting some courts to have rules requiring judges to account for cases held longer than a certain time period. The key fact is that trial judges rarely have much legal staff support and rely on lawyers to educate them and to draft orders.

This traditional relationship is being overtaken by technology that permits judges to access legal authorities more quickly and efficiently than ever before and to transcend the limits of a small legal library. Judges will no longer have to rely on attorneys as much and can actually look up cases on a terminal at the bench if speed is of the essence. Moreover, judges can formulate their own search commands and be freed of the limitations of what might be inadequate legal research. Nonetheless, judges still rely heavily on attorneys in the performance of their functions.

Financial Relationships. When judges are seeking salary increases, they need allies. If a judicial compensation commission runs interference, then this need is less urgent, but judges often turn to the bar for help and almost invariably receive it, although it may not be worth much in legislatures that are not exactly pro-lawyer. Conversely, judges often determine attorney compensation. Attorneys appointed by the court to represent indigents are usually compelled to receive judicial approval for bills they submit. Bills of services to persons who are wards of the court or for probate work are subject to court approval. Where a party is compelled to pay attorney fees for the other party, as in domestic relations cases, the court often becomes involved in approving the bill. Judges may also be involved in selecting attorneys who contract with the court to provide services to indigents.

Unfortunately, there is some skepticism about the zeal of judges in dealing with their brothers in the law in any matter concerning income. Most judges are conscientious in reviewing attorney fee requests and sometimes have administrative staff support in making such reviews, but some judges are not at all zealous and approve bills that are substantially undocumented. County officials are vehemently critical of judges who allow attorneys to inflate their bills. Although these charges may be based on ignorance and hearsay, the amount of money being paid from the public treasuries is rapidly rising because of the appointments of attorneys in family cases where virtually every member of the family has separate representation at public expense. There are small counties in the Midwest where 3 to 4 percent of the budget is used to pay attorneys.

In many cases, attorneys need judicial approval for their fees that are to be paid from estates or by litigants. Individual citizens who have watched this process are sometimes shocked and angered, because judges tend to buy into inflated views of the worth of an attorney's time. In guardianship and probate work, fees may run $175 to $200 per hour in some jurisdictions, even though the legal work is usually very pedestrian and is often referred to a paralegal or an experienced secretary. A five-minute phone call becomes a fifteen-minute phone call that costs $50 dollars, even though the attorney initiated the phone conversation and prolonged it. One guardian-conservator reported an instance where an incompetent attorney failed to show up for a hearing and included in his bill a charge for a phone call to apologize. The guardian-conservator challenged the whole bill on the grounds that the attorney did nothing helpful and that she operated on her own quite well. The judge granted a reduction in the bill, mainly because the attorney, who was a regular in the court, failed to show up to defend his bill. If this incident is multiplied by one million, it equals the mounting public disgust over the incestuous financial ties between bench and bar.

Mutual Evaluation. Judges form opinions about the abilities of the attorneys who appear before them and may communicate their views by means other than their decisions. Attorneys seek to win the respect of judges, because judicial approval enhances their professional reputations. What is not so commonly recognized is that attorneys can seriously injure a judge's career. In some instances, attorneys participate in a formal evaluation of judges as part of an official judicial branch process. Sometimes, like judges, they use less formal means to make their views known. Negative evaluations of judges may affect their ability to advance within the judicial profession or may even deny them reelection or reappointment. Judges and attorneys do sometimes make negative evaluations of one another, but usually with objectivity rather than malice. They are painfully aware that they are under constant mutual evaluation and are dependent on one another to be fair. As lay people are not really able to evaluate a judge in a legal sense, judges are particularly vulnerable to strong criticism from attorneys.

Tensions Arising from Judicial Control of Attorneys

Stronger court control of branch operations and the legal profession sometimes pits judges against attorneys. There are many points of tension, among them:

- protecting clients who are not well represented by their attorneys
- attempting to satisfy public demand for changes in the adversarial system
- superintendence of the legal profession
- strong control of case scheduling
- attempts to deal with a diversified bar

Client Protection. Judges are sometimes placed in the difficult position of bypassing the attorney-client relationship to help a person who is being poorly served by his or her attorney. The judge has to weigh professional deference to an attorney against the right of justice owed to a party in court. Judicial decisions made on such issues determine who is actually running the court.

Attorneys may wish to withdraw from a case, or the client may ask them to withdraw. Usually, this requires judicial approval. This can be a pro forma approval, or it can involve a serious consideration of the circumstances. Sometimes, the issue is money. There are plenty of courts where continuations or withdrawals are granted because a client has not paid a fee, although this is not normally stated in open court but through some local code words: "Your honor, I'm invoking Rule 13." Judges understandably tend to sympathize with attorneys who have deadbeat or cantankerous clients, but if the attorney-client relationship means anything, it must occasionally be protected against feckless and unreasonable abdication of responsibility.

Plea bargaining always involves a judge asking a defendant if the defense attorney has explained the consequences of the plea. This can become a very pro forma routine, because no one wants to embarrass an attorney in open court. Moreover, judges, prosecutors, and defenders often have an implicit alliance to keep a high plea rate so that the system will not founder.

A judge can take over a court proceeding if he or she decides that an attorney is not performing up to some minimum standard of representation. The old vaudeville gag line was, "I don't mind you trying my case your honor, but try not to lose it." Some judges intervene in every case, some never do it, and some do it selectively. The simple fact is that many attorneys are not competent and that this is a very frequent cause of reversal and the granting of postconviction relief, not to mention pain for the client. At what point does judicial passivity give way to concern for justice? Judge John Sirica in the Watergate trials was openly skeptical over the narrowness of the prosecution and probed for the full truth despite the truncated scenario scripted by the attorneys on both sides.

Modifying the Adversarial System. Judges and lawyers are united in the belief that the adversarial system is a way of sorting out issues, eliciting the truth, preserving rights, and bringing pressure on all involved to resolve the issues before trial. The centerpiece of the system is the trial, the quintessential legal event in which lawyers are the stars. No other event better illustrates the unique ties of judges and lawyers. Judges rely on lawyers to elicit the facts in an orderly way, to sharpen the issues, and to observe the rules of legal combat. Lawyers need a fair arbiter.

Laypersons participate at trial as parties, witnesses, and jurors. Their participation is limited by rules of procedure and evidence, and they are kept under control by lawyers and judges lest they sully the legal purity of the proceeding. The lay participants are very much aware that they are being admitted to the inner sanctum of the law under terms set by the legal profession. In no other area of current legal practice have members of the public split so sharply with the legal profession as they have on the value of having two attorneys oppose one another in a formal setting under very stilted rules.

Judges are uncomfortable with the lay uprising. They prefer to have lawyers define the issues and serve a buffer between parties and the judge. The idea of courts without lawyers is very unsettling. Even the idea of greater freedom for witnesses and jurors is disturbing. Judges need lawyers in control in order to keep the courts running smoothly and to keep legal proceedings within bounds. For their part, lawyers count on judges to protect their monopoly and hope that judges will not desert them under public pressure to create more informal, less adversarial means of handling disputes.

The lay revolt against the legal system is testing the loyalty of judges to the legal fraternity, and the first fissures in the attorney-judge bond are starting to appear. When judges endorse alternatives means of dispute resolution, pro se representation, and increased juror participation in trials, they are diminishing the role of lawyers. Judges are not always comfortable with such innovations but are permitting and, in some cases, actively promoting them. The implications for bench-bar relations are clear.

Superintendence of the Legal Profession. State court judiciaries have long asserted that they have the inherent power to regulate the legal profession and to govern the bar. This authority encompasses admission to practice, discipline (including disbarment and monetary sanctions), regulation of the organized bar, fee arrangements, unauthorized practice of law, and care of client funds held in trust by attorneys.[25] State courts have held their power over the legal profession to be exclusive and have barred the legislative branch from intruding into regulation of the legal profession. State courts have also bridled at the attempts of federal agencies to regulate the legal profession. They resisted the attempts of the Federal Trade Commission to regulate attorney behavior in the area of discipline, ethics, and commercial and business practices. The Conference of Chief Justices has challenged the Department of Justice insistence on permitting its attorneys to directly contact persons who are represented by counsel. This is a serious violation of state codes of ethics for attorneys and a direct challenge to the bar superintendence powers of state supreme courts.

For lawyers, the advantages of judicial control of the profession were obvious: limiting the number of unqualified lawyers entering the profession by instituting bar examinations, restricting unauthorized practice of law, curbing or disbarring attorneys who disgraced the profession, and generally upgrading the profession by higher educational requirements. Perhaps more important, the state judiciary threw the separation-of-powers cloak around the profession, saving lawyers from regulation by unfriendly legislators. State supreme courts were also instrumental in the formation of state bar associations.

State bar associations have, over the years, exhibited a strange mix of altruism and self-serving defensiveness. They have supported a number of court reforms, established procedures for investigating grievances against attorneys, and encouraged attorneys to contribute their time for representation of the needy and for civic betterment programs. Bar associations have established their own internal systems for investigating and punishing errant attorneys. State bar associations and the American Bar Association can be credited with many other contributions to court improvement. On the other hand, the organized bar has occasionally opposed reforms that threatened their professional monopoly, that appeared to undercut the independence of lawyers, or that might be economically disadvantageous to lawyers. State bar associations now include such a mix of lawyers that it is very hard for them to develop consensus on any controversial issue.[26] The civil plaintiff's bar has gone off on its own and formed powerful lobbies. The inability of state bar associations to take an objective view of the profession undermines the cause of reform, leaving courts as the best hope for addressing problems that the profession cannot deal with.

State supreme courts have claimed and exercised authority to create a unitary or integrated bar to which all attorneys must belong. This integration parallels the general trend to unification within courts themselves and was aimed at the excessive localism of the legal profession, particularly as regards admission to practice, which was traditionally localized. The quaintly local nature of bar examinations at midcentury was illustrated by the District of Columbia practice

---

[25]   See discussion of court governance by Stumpf, *Inherent Powers*, 15-34.

[26]   Some bar leaders see local bar associations as more likely sources of change simply because they are more cohesive.

of having one examiner for each area of law. Bar review courses focused on the eccentricities of these examiners; for example, "Every third year Joe asks a question on the Statute of Frauds."

In the same period, local bar examiners in Connecticut still determined the results of bar examinations. In one part of the state, prospective attorneys of Italian extraction were failing the exam at a very high rate for two reasons: the examiners could identify the test taker, and Irish and Yankee attorneys did not want to lose their Italian clients. This incident underlined the fact that attorneys cannot be given the opportunity to close doors to potential competitors through local control of bar admissions.

State bar exams can also be used to exclude competition. For example, Florida lawyers wanted to limit the flow of attorneys from the North who were being drawn to the state by its climate. So, up until 1954, graduates of the three state law schools were admitted to the bar without an exam, whereas everyone else was given a very tough exam. Louisiana attorneys tried to protect their legal monopoly by preserving the civil-law tradition that was unknown outside the state and opposing legislation to link their state with the rest of the world by enactment of uniform laws in the commercial and business areas. Lawyers are inclined to make themselves indispensable and few in number but have, for the most part, failed. Even the advent of a national section of the bar examination has not been a major obstacle to entering the legal profession.

Bar governance can be regulatory in that the supreme court makes general policy and promulgates rules pertaining to the profession. It can also take the form of decisions in cases of individual attorney misbehavior or of imposition of sanctions at the trial court level. Individual judges have inherent powers to impose sanctions on attorneys who disrupt the administration of justice in specific cases, and so it is not surprising that the big bench-bar conflicts often originate in the trenches when a trial judge disciplines an attorney. Often, the misbehavior is so egregious that there is no dispute, but there are instances where the issues are not as clear, and the attorney is prestigious enough to take on the judge. Around 1970, there were two prominent criminal defense attorneys who, between them, represented over half the criminal defendants in Providence, Rhode Island, and actually had a heavy caseload elsewhere in the state. They were scheduled in so many places that criminal calendars frequently broke down, because they were not ubiquitous. This, of course, increased their popularity among criminals. One exasperated judge, after repeated futile attempts to get one of these attorneys into his court, held the attorney in contempt for failure to appear, whereupon the attorney arose in righteous wrath invoking the constitutional right of defendants to the attorney of their choice. In the ensuing showdown, the judge was deserted by his colleagues, not just because they had reservations about the contempt, but because the attorney in question had major political power in the state. Generally, however, state courts back up trial judges in the imposition of sanctions that arise in litigation before the judge.

Most serious problems between courts and attorneys are conflicts between the judiciary and the organized bar, rather than conflicts with individual attorneys. These disputes usually fall in one of four categories: attorney dissatisfaction with the judicial position on the unauthorized practice of law and the protection of the lawyer monopoly; attorney resentment over interference with attorney-client relationships; attorney objections to forms of alternative dispute resolution that reduce the need for attorneys or limit attorney access to judges; and stringent court control over the pace of litigation.

Lawyers watch for trespasses against their turf. At various times, bar associations have done battle with title companies, debt collection agencies, institutional trust departments, in-house corporate legal offices, and insurance company adjusters. All were charged with unauthorized practice of law even when the offending group had attorneys on the payroll. The contemporary enemy is the pro se litigant, and here the bar splits. The patricians do not have much interest in cases so simple that individuals can represent themselves, but the legal proletariat feels threatened because they handle minor matters. At issue is the relevance of the adversarial system in cases that are not very complex. The judiciary is uncomfortable with pro se litigation but is slowly adapting to it, much to the chagrin of many lawyers. The Los Angeles Bar, for example, provides pro bono attorneys to serve as small-claims judges in a pro se court.

Attorney discipline cases may involve disrespect for a judge or court orders, but more often, they involve betrayal of or disservice to a client. Lawyers will not defend a colleague who has taken client trust funds or failed to file a complaint within the required statute-of-limitations period, but they often get very upset about the sanctions, particularly disbarment. Veteran observers of the New Jersey scene feel that a lot of the animosity between the supreme court and the bar over differentiated case management stemmed from two disciplinary cases where the supreme court, through very tough sanctions on dishonest attorneys, sent out a message to the bar.

Particularly galling to attorneys are supreme court regulations that seem to impinge on the attorney-client relationship. Many courts require that contingent fee agreements be filed with the court. The implication is clear—the court is protecting the client against unscrupulous attorneys and preventing postaward disputes about the fee arrangement. Court regulations governing attorney handling of client trust funds have proven very controversial, not because lawyers are champions of chicanery but because they are not always very orderly in discharging their responsibilities and are nonetheless exposed to strict sanctions. Underlying the discomfiture is the hurt feeling, "Don't they trust us?"

Caseflow Management. The degree of attorney control over case scheduling and movement has historically been very strong. Around 1970, a court consultant doing a study of the court system in a large North Carolina county asked for calendars. He was given a civil calendar that was prepared for the court by a scheduling committee of the local bar association and a criminal calendar prepared by the prosecuting attorney. The judges who were interviewed saw their role as being available to handle disputes when their services were needed and felt no particular obligation to manage cases to conclusion. Case statistics ranged from nonexistent to cursory because the judges saw them as something to send to the supreme court for the annual report rather than as a management aid. Everyone thought the scheduling system worked well, and, in fact, this court was considered to be very good in comparison to other courts in the state. This type of bar control was not at all uncommon elsewhere.

In that period, the idea of a court as a passive civil forum available to legal gladiators was very widespread. When a suit was filed and issue joined, it might lay dormant for years unless some motion was made or dismissal was sought as part of a settlement. In some jurisdictions, answers were (and are) filed in less than 50 percent of civil cases. Sometimes, this was because insurance companies intervened early to prevent defense firms from running the meter, but also because of a casual attitude that filing a suit was a preliminary indication of irritation and not to be taken very seriously. Very often, no step was taken to have a default entered, so the court had no idea what was happening to these cases. The cases just languished.

Courts were embarrassed if civil caseload statistics showed a mounting accumulation of moribund cases, and some courts did not even include these cases in statistical reports. Some courts instituted a certificate of readiness that was basically a request by the attorneys to the court to get serious about the case and to set it down for trial at some future point. Usually, but not always, the certificate had to state that discovery was completed. At this point, the case was considered active and appeared in the court statistics, but attorneys usually controlled the pace of the case. The court posture was, "We are there for you." Thus, court civil statistics often only reflected that part of the caseload where the attorneys had indicated a readiness to have the dispute adjudicated. No one really cared about the civil cases gathering dust, except perhaps the parties to those cases.

In the mid-1970s a trial court judge in Vicksburg, Mississippi, was interviewed by a team of consultants interested in differentiated case management and strong court control over calendars. The judge, a very polite southern gentleman, was clearly uncomfortable with playing the aggressive role suggested by the team and was a little bit on the defensive. He observed that he was an elected judge and not looking for any opposition within the bar. He added a comment on the social camaraderie of the judges and attorneys in the area. For the reasons he cited, caseflow management has been a tough sell. It requires judges to be much stricter with attorneys than they like to be and entails the risk of a major confrontation with the organized bar, always a politically risky undertaking for an elected judge. The judge pretty well captured the judicial ethos of the period.

In the late 1970s court reformers focused national attention on delay and advocated strong judicial control over the movement of cases. Lawyers quickly developed a love-hate relationship with court-scheduling programs that were established under the rubric of "caseflow management." Lawyers appreciated the improved speed, more rational scheduling, and the idea of having their important cases given special attention. They, however, resented tighter deadlines and extra work in filing various informational requests of the court. They resisted added preliminary events, such as status hearings and compulsory settlement conferences, and generally disliked tighter sanctions for procedural violations. Some lawyers disliked the fact that cases were routed to arbitrators or mediators or assigned to a simple case track that encouraged pro se representation.

Changes in scheduling require and often receive bar support, but the level of support may be lukewarm, veiling an underlying hostility and skepticism. It is not unusual for a chief judge to view scheduling reforms more optimistically than attorneys. Consecutive interviews with a judge and a trial attorney on a new differentiated case management system often elicit contradictory views, the judge loving the system and how it works and the attorney viewing the scheduling experiment with skepticism and predicting its demise. Attorneys will usually go along with any new system up to a point, but their support has to be won over time.

In New Jersey, a promising bench-bar agreement on differentiated case management (DCM) between the supreme court and the state bar came under fire from some local bar associations. New Jersey does not have an integrated bar, so the state bar does not speak with great authority and is occasionally contradicted by local bar associations. In several counties, attorneys complained that DCM would deprive them of their principal income because they depend on small civil cases that were being placed on a fast track and simplified to the point where attorney representation might not be necessary. This objection proved to be a serious obstacle, because lawyers are wary about an informality that suggests that their services are superfluous. In many states, New Jersey included, lawyers have been opposed to the use of parajudicial officials for the very simple reason that the majesty of legal confrontation is demeaned by having someone other than a judge presiding. It is hard to charge big fees for talking to a mediator.

Much of this tension centers on discovery issues. It is no secret that case delay caused in large part by prolonged discovery. Attempts to limit discovery have not been particularly successful. Professor Mary Ann Glendon quotes a famous corporate trial attorney who boasted of an ability to drag out the simplest antitrust case almost indefinitely, and then she sums up the discovery dilemma: "The discovery system has proved difficult to reform, not for want of constructive ideas, but because plaintiffs' and defendants' lawyers have joined forces to resist measures to limit abuses."[27]

Trial judges and court staff make pretty accurate assessments of the attorneys who regularly appear in their courts. They know the hard-nosed litigators and the timid settlers, the legally astute and the perennial bumblers, the ethical and the unethical, the firebrands and the decorous, the dilatory and the punctual, those who overtry every case and those are rarely prepared. This knowledge is important to caseflow management, which is more an art form than a branch of management science. Judges and court staff often display an uncanny knack for estimating which cases will settle before trial and the length of those cases that go to trial, basing their prediction, in large part, on their knowledge of the attorneys involved. Caseflow management has, of course, an information base that reflects case type and complexity, parties, witnesses, attorneys, litigation events, dispositions, and time sequences, but this database does not include the personal and intuitive knowledge of the attorneys, how they operate, and the local legal culture. This knowledge can be used to manage attorneys, and they know it.

---

[27] Glendon, *Nation Under Lawyers*, 56.

Attorneys make similar assessments of judges and will, if the scheduling system permits, try to steer their case to a particular judge. If judges in the same court are all over the map on a particular issue, there will be strenuous efforts to manipulate the scheduling process. Attorneys would rather manage the court than have the court manage them, but caseflow management tilts the system toward judicial control. The case management scenario illustrates one of the least publicized aspects of the establishment of a state judicial branch—the struggle to make the courts more people oriented and less lawyer oriented. Judges are placing some strain on their traditional alliance with lawyers and assuming a broader view of their duties to court users and the general public.

Elite Bars. The concentration of commercial and financial establishments in major cities in the late nineteenth century and the beginning of the regulatory state changed the nature of law practice. This change led to the formation of partnerships and a species of lawyer that seldom appeared in court, served corporations, had some narrow specialty areas, and earned a lot of money.[28] These lawyers formed the core of a new elite that over time identified with the federal judiciary and had relatively little to do with the state courts. This elite formed ties with the more prestigious law schools and drew apart from the more mundane legal world of crimes and personal injury suits.

There is a very definite socioeconomic cleavage in the legal profession. Some lawyers get on the fast track in the affluent firms; some develop lucrative specialties or go into boutique law firms; a few make a good living as litigators; and some serve as in-house counsel for businesses. Many find their way on to the public payroll in a variety of legal capacities, but many other lawyers exist on the periphery of the profession and often drop out. The lawyers who frequent state courthouses include a large number of marginal lawyers, who are just entering the profession or struggling to survive. This rich-poor cleavage accounts to some degree for the difference in prestige between the state and federal judiciaries. The state courts end up with the attorneys who are not in the upper economic stratum of the profession. Any movement toward pro se litigation or simplification of legal procedures strikes the most insecure portion of the lawyer population. These attorneys are the ones most dependent on judges to protect their tenuous position in the profession.

Yet, it was often the lawyers from elite firms that were active in bar associations and sponsored reform movements in the state courts. Chief justices have often appointed the head of the state bar association to be the chair or a major member of court reform committees, even if this person did not have a practice that took him or her into the state courts. In one southern state, the state bar president was appointed to chair a court reform committee and appeared at the opening meeting with a copy of *The Federalist* under his arm. This prompted one attorney to state what everybody else was thinking, "We're in big trouble!" As it

---

[28]   Friedman, *American Law*, 633-648.

turned out, the state bar president did a great job, even though he was not intimately familiar with the state courts.

In the disorders that followed the assassination of Martin Luther King, thousands of arrests were made. Because government attorneys could not represent the persons charged, urgent appeals went out over radio and TV for private attorneys to converge on the District of Columbia Court of General Sessions to help process the many defendants. Hanging over the whole bail procedure was the fact that no one wanted to release a bunch of defendants who would go back out and join the mob scene. Yet there was no place to put anybody because every detention facility within a twenty-five-mile radius was filled. Under District of Columbia law, release on personal recognizance or minimal cash bail was the norm, but the judges were under heavy pressure not to supply reinforcements to those in a state of disorder.

Included among the lawyers volunteering their services to the court during the emergency were many lawyers from prestigious corporate law firms. Most of them were unversed in criminal law and had never set foot in the somewhat sleazy atmosphere of the District of Columbia General Sessions Court, which was staffed by judges of dubious competence who worked in close rapport with a seedy group of criminal lawyers called the Fifth Street Bar. After a stirring talk by a young public defender, who displayed mysterious documents like warrants and bail bonds, the would-be criminal lawyers marched off to various courts that were working through the night. It proved to be a culture shock that shook the whole District of Columbia court system.

During a bail hearing in one court, the judge lectured the defendant on the evils of stealing TV sets, sending a young corporate lawyer into spasms of outrage. "My client hasn't been convicted of anything. This is a bail hearing not a sentencing. This is totally inappropriate—your honor." The respectful salutation was delivered as an afterthought with a sardonic tone. The judge was shocked because members of the Fifth Street Bar did not talk that way or toss in their sleep over the treatment of their clients. All around the court that night, young uptown lawyers were exposed to the realities of the criminal justice system of the District of Columbia and were appalled. Within months of the disorders, the wheels of reform were rolling, leading to a major court study and legislation that completely reorganized the District of Columbia court system and eliminated the tawdry general sessions court.

The District of Columbia incident indicates an underlying trend in state courts—the fact that many attorneys no longer know about or really care about state courts. They deal with federal courts or federal agencies, they have an office practice centered on giving advice to corporate clients, or they are engaged in some specialized practice that involves specialized tribunals external to the state court system or requires no tribunal at all. State judges are seldom drawn from this section of the bar. Very often, they have been government attorneys, prosecutors or public defenders, or have engaged in general practice. State judges often express concern that they are being transformed into police courts and family courts and that the elite bar is going elsewhere, even when their legal proceedings could be handled in a state court. Some state judges go on the bench with the idea of presiding over important trials that are stimulating and intellectually challenging, but find the routine of judging to be at odds with their vision of being a superjurist.

The fear that state courts may be losing some of the more challenging cases to other forums is not idle conjecture. A National Center for State Courts study of tort verdicts in Iowa in the 1980s revealed that product liability cases were often taken into federal courts rather than state courts, except in a few regions of the state. Interestingly, the same law firms chose different forums in different regions, sometimes choosing state courts, sometimes choosing federal courts. It was clear that this choice was influenced to a large degree by an assessment of the judges.

Some members of the elite bars choose arbitrators or federal courts, if this is possible, and if they do use state courts, they may insist on special deference. Thus, state court systems may take special steps not to lose their aristocratic clientele. They may set up special courts for them, as they do in the Delaware Chancery Court, or set up special calendars for "major cases." There are some jurisdictions where the bar exercises a veto power over the judges assigned to certain calendars and insists on having the services of judges who are respected by lawyers for their legal acumen. In short, judges sometimes make special accommodations for the lawyers and law firms that they are losing to other forms of dispute resolution, even if this is at the expense of the average litigant or attorney who has to be content with the less talented members of the court.

On the other hand, some state judges feel resentment against the rarely seen and richly compensated lawyers from big firms. It is particularly galling for judges to see young associates in major firms being paid only a little less than senior judges and having every expectation that they will quickly exceed the judges in income. The state courts have paid a price for not acting more quickly than they did to put their houses in order. They have lost the active engagement of many eminent lawyers.

With the legal profession as fragmented as it is, and many of its prominent members only tangentially concerned with state courts, the potential for reform of the profession is diluted. This places a very high level of responsibility on the state courts. Otherwise, the unhealthy condition of the legal profession will invite regulation from outside the judicial branch. The court reforms of the late twentieth century did include more court controls over the legal profession and did encourage continuing legal education. There is little doubt, however, that not enough was done to uplift the legal profession. This is a principal item on the new reform agenda.

Chapter 5

Developing a Management Perspective in the Judiciary

When court reformers urged courts to free themselves from other branches in matters of administration, there was no wild rush to rally around the concept. One of the major problems was general skepticism about the willingness and ability of judges to manage. Many judges shared this skepticism and felt that it was inappropriate for judges to manage. In addition, the collegial nature of the judiciary did not create a natural basis for executive authority, and this diffusion of management authority among equals had the potential to degenerate into anarchy. The judiciary had a serious management credibility problem.

The concerns were legitimate and not really disputed by judges. If the state judiciary wanted to fend off micromanagement by other branches, they had to create management mechanisms where few existed and to employ the services of professional managers. This importation of a management culture into the legal world did not come easily to judges. In a sense, judges were competing with their own professional heritage in trying to assert their administrative independence of the other branches. The obstacles they struggled to overcome were formidable.

Management Responsibility Accepted Rather than Sought. The Sedgwick County District Court in Wichita, Kansas, during a period of twenty-two years, had five presiding judges appointed by the Kansas Supreme Court. The first presiding judge was a legend because of his dynamic leadership. The second and third presiding judges were appointed on the basis of seniority and assumed the position because they felt obligated to serve. The fourth and fifth presiding judges were chosen for management ability and desire to lead. Under the fifth judge, a series of reforms in caseflow management took place. This judge stated that he wanted "to lead."[1] This is not a particularly surprising statement for a leader to make, unless that leader is a judge. The truth is that many judges in top management roles do not have the desire to be a strong executive.

Most judges ascend to the position of chief judge through the legal profession and may never have had any significant management experience. They may

---

[1]   William Hewitt, Geoff Gallas, and Barry Mahoney, *Courts That Succeed: Six Profiles of Successful Courts* (Williamsburg, VA: National Center for State Courts, 1990), 153.

be uncomfortable with a management role and may assume the position of chief judge for a variety of reasons other than a desire to manage. Among these are a sense of obligation, a response to urging from fellow judges, or simply an acceptance of the line of succession in the particular court. Perhaps the greatest motivation is that the position of chief is a great honor carrying with it special prestige and authority. In some courts, the position of chief is the last career stage before retirement.

The position of chief justice or chief judge has symbolic importance. On ceremonial occasions or in interbranch relations, the judiciary needs a single person to speak for the branch. The symbolic role, as important as it is, does not constitute leadership in the management of the branch. Over the years, however, many judges elevated to chief have seen their role in terms of symbolism.

As management burdens in courts have increased, there has been more awareness among judges that a chief judge has to have some management ability and a desire to exercise it. This has reflected itself in the criteria that judges themselves are applying in the selection of a chief; mainly, less reliance on seniority and automatic rotation. Moreover, there are a number of judges who have actively sought management responsibility. Nonetheless, many courts are still led by judges who have accepted rather than sought the post of chief and who make no claim to management ability.

Management as an Extra Burden, a Distraction from Adjudication. Another manifestation of the low priority of judicial administration is the difficulty of getting the chief justice and chief judges to allocate time for administration. Many chief justices and chief trial court judges pride themselves on carrying a full caseload. This shows team spirit but often imposes a very heavy burden on the chief judge and detracts from his or her administrative effectiveness. Interviews with chief judges reveal, to a surprising degree, that they are very sensitive to peer criticism for not taking a full load. Some cut back their caseload a little, often upon the urging of their fellow judges. But they need this assurance. There is almost a guilt attached to taking too much time away from the primary function of adjudication.

A related problem is getting all the judges of a court to give serious consideration to management issues. Many courts rely heavily on committees to involve the judges in management matters and to help formulate court policy. Many judges, including associate justices of the highest court, contribute a great deal of time to such committees.

On three or four occasions, I have had the opportunity to make a presentation to a state supreme court on some administrative matter that was under study. The members of the court were invariably polite but clearly regarded the presentation as a digression from more serious matters. Rarely, if ever, were questions asked. One justice of the Mississippi Supreme Court, at the end of my enthralling presentation in rapid Northeastern style, observed that he had not understood one word I said. This is more a reflection on my ability to present than supreme court interest in administration, but many others have experienced the same amiable toleration from justices.

Most courts of any size have time set aside for en banc meetings on administrative matters. The amount of time varies a lot by court but is generally so limited that not much of anything can be done other than to hear an informational report from a chief or some committee head. Many courts meet monthly or bimonthly on administrative matters and then only spend an hour or two on the subject. The basic reality is that judges generally do not devote a great deal of time to the administration of their courts, even judges who have a major administrative responsibility.

Collegial Tradition that Militates Against Strong Executive Leadership. In forty-two states, the chief justice of the court of last resort is designated as the head of the judicial branch;[2] eight states remain officially collegial in leadership. Rulemaking, however, remains an en banc function of the court in all states, unless limited by the legislature, and even in those states where the chief justice is given executive responsibility, the chief justice may in practice operate in a collegial fashion. The tradition of collegiality in appellate adjudication is so strong that it has quite naturally carried over into the administrative style of state supreme courts.

Courts of last resort tend to fall into one of three categories of leadership: 1) a strong executive system, 2) a modified executive system, and 3) a traditional collegial system.

The first two systems are most commonly found in states that have experienced some degree of administrative unification. The legal and political authority of a supreme court over lower courts in administrative matters is a major factor in determining whether a collegial leadership model will be discarded in favor of an executive system. Generally, the individual powers of a chief justice are strengthened by unification, because more central authority is required to run a unified system. Yet collegial leadership is sometimes retained despite a strong unification trend, as in West Virginia.

Only a few judicial systems could be characterized as examples of the strong executive model of judicial administrative authority. The Hawaii and New Jersey court systems have, at times, appeared to come close. In these jurisdictions, the chief justice is appointed by the governor, not chosen by rotation or by the court itself. The chief assumes a role of chief executive officer, who is able to authoritatively speak and act for the judiciary. Supreme court colleagues have little to do with administration, other than rulemaking. Normally, they fill only consultative roles, or the chief justice advises them of major changes before they become effective

Connecticut has a strong executive system, but not one centered in the supreme court. Since unification of the trial courts in 1978, great executive authority has been reposed in a chief court administrator, who has very broad authority over the trial courts and considerable policymaking power. This official is always a judge, because it would otherwise not be feasible to wield so much power over judges.

---

[2]   Rottman et al., *State Court Org.*, 115, Table 13.

A more common pattern is what may be described as a modified executive model. This authority structure may represent an intermediate step between largely unstructured judicial leadership to a highly concentrated, strong executive model. It may also reflect the ultimate accommodation of traditional collegiality to the demands of modern judicial administration. It appears unlikely that most court systems will choose a strong executive-type system or institute the processes to support such a system.

In the modified executive model, the chief justice is still administrative head of the court system but presents major policy issues to the full supreme court for resolution and assumes relatively little personal initiative. The court relies on the chief justice to see that day-to-day operational decisions conform to the established policy and court views, even though, as a practical matter, responsibility for these decisions is delegated to the state court administrator. Many state constitutions appear to envision this type of court administrative model.

The actual authority exercised by a chief justice in a modified executive model system may be determined by such factors as constitutional provisions, the status attached to independent election of a chief justice, the level of administrative support available from a state court administrator, and the personality of a chief justice. This model is not so clearly defined as others, leaving the chief justice free in many instances to act with or without consulting the other justices or, conversely, free to eschew his authority in favor of group decision making.

A third form of administrative authority structure in court systems is the collegial model, which is almost always a significantly weaker administrative design than the moderate executive format. The collegial model is a very ancient one in the judicial realm, tracing its heritage to the traditional appellate panels. The equality of the judges was evidenced by the seriatim manner of adjudicative decision making, in which each panel member gave an individual opinion as to how the case should be resolved. Until the modern era, parties and scholars often were forced to extract on their own rulings from these disparate opinions. Influenced by these time-honored practices, the collegial model features great deference to the group and only the slightest assumption of independent authority by the chief justice. The model, of course, suffers from all weaknesses inherent in the commission form of government or any kind of management by committee. It may, however, be quite adequate in a small state with largely decentralized court management. It also seems to be particularly appropriate in five-member supreme courts.[3]

The reluctance of appellate judges to invest a lot of authority in the chief justice is amply illustrated in Pennsylvania, where the practice is to divide the various administrative responsibilities of the court among the individual judges. Thus, for example, one associate justice might be assigned the budget portfolio.

---

[3]   Eighteen states have courts of last resort with five members, not including Oklahoma, which in addition to a nine-member court of last resort has a five-member court of criminal appeals. Twenty-six states have courts of last resort with seven members. Six states have courts of last resort with nine members (Texas has two nine-member courts because of a split in civil and criminal jurisdiction). Rottman et al., *State Court Org.*, 18, Table 2.

This functional division of responsibility reduces the role of the chief to administering whatever administrative function is assigned to him or her.

Trial courts have different administrative traditions, because trial judges adjudicate as individuals and are not as collegial as appellate judges. When trial judges started to surrender their autonomy, and to empower one of their number to allocate work and deal with issues that affected the court as a whole, the chief judge was usually kept on a tight leash. Chief judges have legal authority to impose administrative authority on their fellow judges but use it sparingly. There is, of course, the occasional martinet, but this is not the basic judicial style for dealing with other members of the court.

A candidate for the most intimidating chief judge was Cook County's (Chicago) John Boyle, whose sheer size and irascibility added to his political clout made him a formidable figure. Court employees still recount with awe his clashes with the appropriating bodies that questioned his needs. Few in the courts would dream of crossing him. Those who did ended up in assignments that were only slightly better than Siberia. In large metropolitan courts, the status of an individual judge is not as high as it is elsewhere, and it is in such courts that judges feel more like judicial proletarians than independent figures on a peer level with the chief judge.

Another factor that undermined collegiality was administrative unification. As state supreme courts became more involved in trial court operations, attempts were made to have chief judges of trial courts appointed by the chief justice or supreme court, thus freeing the chief judge from control by his colleagues and enhancing his or her authority.

Collegiality does not necessarily mean harmony on either a trial court or an appellate court. Some courts are torn by personality differences, ideological cleavages, partisan politics, and internal differences over court operations. As diversity increases on the bench and the old-boy network loses its cohesiveness, there may be even more cliques than there have been in the past. Chief judges spend a great deal of time catering to the concerns of their colleagues and preventing divisions while staying within the acceptable bounds imposed by the local judicial culture. Chiefs must be a unifying influence, a duty that sometimes conflicts with the idea of being a strong executive.

Management Mechanisms Based on Legal Models. Judges are used to having issues presented to them for resolution and to choosing between fairly well-defined positions. They are not, for the most part, proactive. There have been, of course, chiefs who pursued personal agendas. Chief Justice Howell Heflin in Alabama was elected to his position after being active in bar association reform proposals and was committed to unifying and professionalizing the Alabama courts. It is fair to say, however, that judges in positions of management authority tend to react to proposals they receive rather than to initiate policy.

Some of the early state court administrators recognized that it would be necessary to cast administrative issues in terms that were familiar to judges. Ed McConnell in New Jersey introduced the idea of an administrative agenda that paralleled the appellate docket. He presented written and oral arguments on a particular management issue, usually noting the solution that he favored. The court then made a decision or deferred if they were not ready to decide. Occasionally, they voted, but they generally achieved consensus without this formality, if, in fact, they made any decision at all.[4] The judges were familiar with the format and found it suited their style. It depended heavily on reacting to ideas presented by persons outside the court; for example, proposed legislation, ideas from staff, or recommendations from committees appointed by the court. The problem with this format is the difficulty of getting closure on any serious policy issue.

Because the role of the court is reactive, the person who controls the administrative agenda has great influence. The chief justice or chief judge may personally control the agenda, but as a practical matter, many courts rely on a court administrator to propose issues for resolution and to provide background information. The court administrator may play a ministerial role, simply writing down suggested agenda items, but may sometimes shape the agenda. Generally, however, there are various means to bring issues before the court of last resort, and even those may be funneled through a court administrator. Among these are committee reports, proposals from judicial conferences, bar proposals, and ideas of individual justices. Some courts require a formal petition to bring a matter to the court's attention, and it is not all uncommon for administrative decisions to be reflected in orders.

Courts vary on the level of detail they require on administrative issues. Usually, there is not much detail, because judges may not have the time to digest it. Very complex issues are normally referred to a committee that sorts out the facts and makes recommendations. Where the issues are well beyond the expertise of the court, for example, decisions on computer technology, the judges depend on staff and consultants. In any event, the persons who prepare the background information have a considerable degree of influence on the court's administrative decisions, which may sometimes be far more important than decisions on cases.

At the trial court level, there is less formality in administrative decision making, but the trappings of legalism are still apparent. Judges simply feel comfortable with mechanisms that are familiar to them.

Focus on Microcosmic Issues. Legal education trains one to analyze facts and pertinent law in relation to a very specific issue. The whole common-law tradition is based on building up a body of principles from decisions rendered in concrete situations. The casebook method of teaching is ordained to situational analysis rather than systemic thinking. Lawyers by training and inclination tend to be microcosmic in their thinking.

Court management, however, calls for a broad view of the legal system and its complex dynamics. Caseflow management is basically the application of a

---

[4]   In the early stages of developing administrative policy mechanisms, some courts actually had the junior member state his or her position first.

systems approach to the processing of a cases from inception to disposition. The multiple interactions of courts with criminal justice agencies and social service agencies have increased enormously in the last few decades, absolutely requiring a broad view of system operation and dynamics. Yet anyone familiar with administrative agendas for courts can testify that interspersed with serious policy issues may be relatively minor matters. Many courts are still in the process of distinguishing the matters that require their attention from those that should be disposed of at a lower level in the system.

The full court is often compared to a corporate board that makes policy, with the chief as the chairperson of the board and CEO. It is the chief's job to see that policy is executed and to monitor the day-to-day operations of the court. This corporate board model is useful for encouraging courts to avoid issues relatively petty and to concentrate on broader issues. In general, however, the corporate analogy is very weak.

- There is no neat line between policy and implementation, because policy is refined and honed in the light of experience.
- The members of the board are actually government employees, not stockholder representatives.
- Most boards do not expect the CEO to check back with them on every major decision.
- The CEO/chairman may not even be designated by the board (i.e., the court).
- The CEO is not chosen with reference to executive ability.

The reality is that most courts are still grappling with how to manage without being swamped in trivia. Judges alternately feel overwhelmed and left out. No existing paradigm captures the search of the judiciary for a balance between their management responsibilities and their adjudicative role.

Solving Problems by Judicial Fiat in the Form of Rules, Directives, and Orders. Judges tend to address management problems by issuing rules or orders. Judges occasionally resort to issuing orders in budgetary disputes with the other branches, a uniquely judicial response to what actually may be a management problem within the court itself. Very often judges, in discussing changes or reforms, will produce a set of rules or directives, the implication being that the matter has been solved. In fact, rules are often unenforced or cannot be effectively enforced without management support.

In the early stages of court reform, supreme courts relied heavily on rule-making authority to institute change. In New Jersey, which featured rule-driven reform, administrative judges in trial courts were appointed by the chief justice and given the primary responsibility of enforcing rules, so that rule enforcement became the primary means of exercising administrative authority. Administrative judges also used orders to achieve their local objectives; for example, bringing calendar clerks under direct judicial control.

In 1971 the Ohio Supreme Court attacked case backlog in trial courts by issuing Rules of Superintendence that were quite specific on case processing and mandated an individual judge calendar to more clearly fix accountability for delay. Individual courts were left to implement the rules as they saw fit. The driving force behind this reform was Chief Justice C. William O'Neill, formerly governor of Ohio. During his tenure as chief, a position to which he was elected, he actively sought compliance with the rules and created a great public awareness of the delay issue. There is no question that his acute political sense and personal following had a lot to do with the effectiveness of his leadership, which was widely hailed in court circles. Interestingly, there was little administrative support or oversight for implementing rules. In the thinking of the period, passing rules was synonymous with reform.

The rule-driven court tends to underestimate the complexity of implementing policy. Several decades ago, a court consultant briefed a supreme court on a project to implement a constitutional amendment requiring establishment of a magistrate court system. The project involved a facility plan for the magistrate court, new case procedures, new bookkeeping systems, a magistrate-training plan, records management procedures, and various other aspects of administration. After a summary of what was going on, one justice turned to his colleagues and asked: "Why are we going through all this? Isn't the constitutional provision self-executing?" His colleagues assured him that the implementation project was necessary, as the consultant sat in stunned silence. This is an extreme example, but anyone long involved in court administration has encountered similar assumptions about the miraculous power of the law to effect orderly change.

A more modern manifestation of problem solving through rules is incivility between attorneys. Judges have been concerned over increasing acrimony among attorneys and have discussed it at length. Some courts have predictably addressed this problem through rules. These rules or standards are usually aspirational, but they reveal the judicial penchant for mandating actions that cannot be effectively addressed by orders.

Looking to the Past for Precedent and Avoiding Risk. Judging is, and should be, a reasonably conservative and predictable process. Judges do not lightly depart from precedent, an orientation that almost inevitably affects judicial views toward management and planning.

Courts lag behind other parts of government in technology and management advances. In perhaps no other component of government does one so frequently hear the expression "if it ain't broke, don't fix it." This aphorism is defective in two regards: a system, process, or organization does not have to be in a state of disintegration to warrant change for the better, and some aspects of court operation may appear "broke" to court users even if they appear fine to judges.

The area of management that is most affected by the judicial need for precedent is planning. In the glory days of the Law Enforcement Assistance Administration (LEAA), millions of dollars were expended to encourage courts to institute a planning process, and most courts responded affirmatively to this federal initiative. Inevitably, the planning process was governed by the quest for federal grants, producing plans that were largely wish lists for federal funding of various programs. In the mid-1970s, I was involved in doing a plan for the Alabama courts. It was largely a list of programs that were going to receive federal funds. No one seemed to regard it as a blueprint for the future although it was touted as the first court plan. Its main appeal seemed to be that no one really felt bound by it.

Judicial planning bodies started to atrophy and disappear when no longer driven by federal grant requirements. Nonetheless, the courts received some exposure to the planning process and recruited a number of very talented and innovative persons as planners. Many of these persons currently have high positions in court management.

A more recent federal initiative has fueled interest in futures commissions that lay out goals for the judiciary. Rarely, however, are goals and objectives of this type linked to the actual process of budgeting and management for courts. The ideas in futures reports usually become noble and disembodied concepts that are occasionally invoked but are divorced from real operational goals.

Courts engage in planning if they are forced to do so by some external pressure that makes planning inevitable. Among these pressures are the construction of new facilities, major advances in technology, or a transition to court unification and state financing. This is not strategic planning; rather, it is the type of planning required to complete a project that has very definite time goals and concrete end products. Judges prefer to react rather than initiate.

Apex of a Command Structure or Coordinators of a Loose Coalition. Trial judges, particularly those with administrative responsibility, are at the hub of an intergovernmental and interagency network and find that their control is limited by a variety of factors. An elected clerk may not be amenable to direct control and may have more political power than the judge. Bailiffs may be employees of an elected sheriff to whom they answer. Probation officers may be executive branch employees who are at the service of the judge but not directly subject to his or her management supervision. Various criminal justice agencies play important roles in the successful operation of the courts but are not under direct control of judges. A variety of executive branch social and educational agencies interact with the court but are not under control of judges. To further complicate things, the mix of court-related agencies with which a judge deals may include state, local, and private agencies.

Chief judges are generally pragmatic about accepting the limits on their power and assume the role of coordinator in dealing with external agencies. However, judicial temperament and tradition sometimes cause a chief judge to assume a more authoritarian role. It is difficult for the rule-driven court to accept the idea of the chief judge as catalyst and coordinator, but this is a closer approximation of the judge's role than that of authoritarian manager.

The traditional command structure is changing, even in dealing with court employees. There was a time when a judge was enthroned high above a group of underlings who were poorly paid, poorly educated, and very restricted in their role. As court administration matures, judges are starting to be drawn into participatory management with staff members who are highly skilled and more involved in administrative decision making. The staff persons are not drones but important players on a team of which the judge is the captain, not the remote authority figure. This development is embryonic but more or less inevitable in the technological court world of the future.

Reluctance to Delegate or Share Administrative Authority with Court Managers. Although judges are aware of the need for more cohesion in the judicial system and the necessity of dealing with the outside world through one person who speaks for the court system, they have been reluctant to give up authority to one of their own, much less to cede authority to a nonjudge administrator.

Judges often speak of court administrators as persons who free judges to be judges, the underlying idea being that administrators are technicians or administrative aides who relieve judges of detail. One nationally prominent court administrator recalls that he was several times dismissed from meetings of judges with the comment, "The technical part of the meeting is over. You can go now." Court administrators are not accepted as comanagers.

Court managers write numerous articles about "the executive component of courts," a concept of shared executive authority where the chief judge and professional court manager act as a management team.[5] Court historians occasionally invoke the memories of famous teams: Arthur Vanderbilt and Ed McConnell in New Jersey and Ed Pringle and Harry Lawson in Colorado.[6] There are a number of other examples of effective teams combining the talents of a chief and a court manager in major court improvements. Typically, the chief dealt with judges and major figures outside the judiciary and provided his or her support to implementing court policy. The court manager did not issue directions to judges but generally handled all the management tasks associated with implementing major change efforts. These team efforts have not been the norm and appear to have resulted more from a remarkable affinity between the judge and manager, rather than from an institutionalized approach to court management.

One chief justice tells the story of accompanying his state court administrator to a training session on the formation of executive teams. As they left at the end of the conference, the chief suggested somewhat wryly that they initiate their new relationship by sharing a cab to the airport. Once seated in the cab, they discovered that they were going to different airports, whereupon the administrator exited to seek his own transportation. There was no punch line at the end of the story, but the implication was clear enough.

Some states have not warmed to the idea of having court administrators who are not judges. Illinois offers an interesting insight into the use of a judge as court administrator. In 1962 the administrative authority of the state supreme

[5]   Practically all the literature of judge-administrator relations is written by court administrators or scholars. Judges rarely concern themselves with the subject.

[6]   It is interesting that Chief Justice O'Neill of Ohio and Chief Justice Heflin of Alabama are never mentioned in team context (both were elected). Some state supreme courts are so collegial that reform is associated with a state court administrator; Alaska, for example.

court was increased and the administrative director of courts made a constitutional officer. The provision went into effect in 1964 as part of a general unification effort that was very unpopular among Illinois judges. Under the terms of the provision (Illinois Constitution of 1970, Article VI, §16), the court administrator helps the chief justice execute his or her administrative authority, which is undefined. Critics of this phraseology think that it makes the court administrator an administrative assistant rather then a real manager.

In any event, the Illinois Supreme Court hired Circuit Judge Roy Gulley as court administrator, because he was well respected among his peers and could help overcome the resistance of judges to unification. He remained in office eighteen years and very carefully read the minds of the seven-judge court, which is elected by geographic district and for that reason is balanced between the two major political parties. The court did not want any active involvement in trial court administration, any expansion of the administrative office beyond that required by statute or rule, and any great involvement in administrative detail. Judge Gulley handled transfers of judges between districts, presenting transfer orders to the court for approval. He also staffed the various court committees dealing with matters of procedure and superintendence, provided synopses of cases and statutes for judges, handled relations with the legislature, and generally conducted the low-key operation desired by the high court. His office, in fact, had very little to do with management, other than routine budget and personnel matters, but had a lot to do with the legal matters that transcended individual cases.

Judge Gulley was left largely unsupervised until some new members of the court wanted to play a more active role in court administration, at which point Judge Gulley resigned. The court chose as interim court administrator a senior lawyer skilled in rulemaking who later went on to be a judge, as did one of his top legal assistants. Samuel Conti of the National Center for State Courts became court administrator and advocated a very activist role for the court and for the administrative office, using the administrative agenda of the court as a forum to advocate ideas for change. After a short period in which some major changes were made, Sam Conti left his post and was replaced by a judge who reverted to a lower-key style with which the court was comfortable.

Illinois is not cited as typical of how a judge-administrator operates, because Connecticut has had very active court management from judge-administrators. The Illinois Supreme Court simply preferred an administrative office of courts staffed heavily with senior lawyers who assisted the court with rules, judicial education, and sending out analyses of cases to judges. The court was unsympathetic to a court manager seeking to move the court from its strongly legalistic tradition into programmatic undertakings and court management issues.

Another interesting insight into the judicial view of court managers is provided by the California Trial Court Budgeting Commission. The entity was created to establish budget policy for the allocation of state trial court appropriations, which take the form of reimbursements to counties in California. The commission was composed of judges, with staff support from the state administrative office of courts. The original concept was to exclude court managers; this was subsequently amended to include them as nonvoting members. The judges were not really versed in making budget policy, but they engaged in on-the-job learning. The irony of this is that one of the nonvoting members was the Los Angeles Superior Court administrator, who holds perhaps the most important court administration position in the United States. The idea that judges, any set of judges, are managerially superior to professional court managers is much more pervasive than the literature would suggest.

The need for judges to delegate more management authority is obvious, but the desire to retain control is almost as strong. Judges consider court managers to be necessary but are still not ready to accept them as a partner on an executive team.

Privacy in Matters of Adjudication Extended to Areas of Administration. Judicial independence requires privacy in adjudication. The public may see a trial or oral argument in appellate court, but they do not go into jury deliberation rooms, conferences of appellate judges, or the chamber of trial judges who are engaged in reaching a decision. It is only natural for judges to extend this concept of privacy to other areas, such as the governance of the judicial branch. In the era of sunshine laws, this may be an anomaly. Why should courts cloak their governing practices in secrecy any more than the other branches of government?

One area where the courts have usually sought some outside participation is the rulemaking process, although this participation is often limited to lawyers. Courts have often involved a wide range of citizens in studies or court reform efforts, but courts do not generally open up their administrative policymaking for a variety of reasons:

- Administrative policy and matters of judicial branch governance are so intertwined with case-specific matters that courts may often consider both types of issues in the same meeting.
- Courts are reluctant to air differences in public, although many serious differences may exist on some fundamental management issue.[7]
- There is no mechanism for public participation.
- The concept of privacy as an aspect of judicial independence is so strongly rooted that it embraces virtually all aspects of court decision making.

It is not clear exactly how courts might open up their administrative processes, but it is clear that courts have to distinguish between the privacy surrounding adjudication and the necessity for more administrative openness. Some administrative decisions of courts significantly affect citizens, who have

---

[7] Judges sometimes ask a court administrator to leave a court meeting if they know a dispute is brewing, although it is probably important for the administrator to know the thinking of the court.

every right to know what the court is considering. For example, in both South Dakota and North Dakota public hearings have been held on the allocation of judgeships and judges.

A possible model of openness is provided by the North Dakota Rule on Rules. North Dakota has used this open approach in dealing with the downsizing of the trial court judiciary to carry out a legislative mandate. Whenever a judgeship falls vacant, a hearing examiner conducts a public hearing on whether the judgeship should be filled or left vacant. This report is filed with the supreme court, which then conducts an open hearing in which more testimony is taken from a variety of citizens. Interestingly, the decision in several cases was that there was no need to fill the judgeship, but the result is less important than the process. A matter that might have been resolved within the judiciary without much outside participation was handled openly, because it obviously affected the people of North Dakota.

Blurred Lines of Authority. Some courts are set up on paper as models of a vertical chain of command with neat functional boxes and established authority relationships. There is considerable doubt as to whether the textbook public administration ideas of organization are of much value in courts, but in any event, courts rarely operate along traditional public administration lines, because judges are not great respecters of lines of authority. Trial judges sometimes bypass a presiding divisional judge to go to their chief judge or bypass their chief judge by going to a chief justice. Chief justices, chief judges, and all other judges feel few qualms about bypassing their court managers to deal directly with staff.

Any court consultant has witnessed examples of judicial disregard for the lines of authority. One court consultant tells a story about being in the office of a chief justice who received a call from a clerk in some outlying area. The clerk had apparently run out of some supplies stocked at the state level. The chief carefully wrote down the information and gave a note to his secretary, who went to the employee of the administrative office of courts who dispensed supplies. Later, the state court administrator complained to the chief that he ought to route all such calls to the administrative office and not bypass the lines of authority. The chief was genuinely surprised by the reaction.

Another court consultant recalls sitting with a state court administrator and observing an associate justice of the state supreme court entering the office of the court budget officer. The state court administrator commented that this justice routinely bypassed him and the chief justice to get items directly into the budget.

One reason for these problems is that some courts still do not have any formal organizational structure. They did not historically think in these terms and have been slow to adapt to the idea that branch management may require something more than a loose conglomeration of offices and divisions. Many court consultants have asked for a court organizational chart and found that the court had to order someone to create it. The final chart might look neat, but had no operational validity. Reporting relationships in many courts are so fluid that they defy description.

Judicial Independence as an Excuse for Failure to Manage. The defense of judicial administrative independence sometimes leads perversely to the disorder and lack of accountability noted above. The desire to maintain a necessary independence from the other branches can translate itself into a staunch defense of poor management by the judiciary and may encourage individual judges to resist centralized judicial management. In short, judicial independence can color judicial management attitudes to the point where lack of efficiency and accountability are defended in the name of separation of powers. This, of course, does nothing for the management credibility of the judicial branch and is not what judicial independence is all about. Judges have to be more, not less, management oriented.

Fortunately, time and experience are on the side of the judiciary. Judges have been making a great effort to fulfill the managerial role thrust on them by contemporary reality, and there are numerous examples of judges who have proven to be excellent managers. It would, however, be unrealistic to expect that the judicial culture would adopt a management perspective overnight and produce numerous executive geniuses. Judges were not meant to be CEOs, nor were courts set up to be boards of directors. There is a style of management compatible with adjudication. It involves delegation to professionals, delegation to fellow judges, use of policy advisory boards, a sense of the judicial management role, and a more positive view of management. This new style is evolving, and while not yet one of the great triumphs of twentieth-century court reform, it is a very definite step forward.

PART III

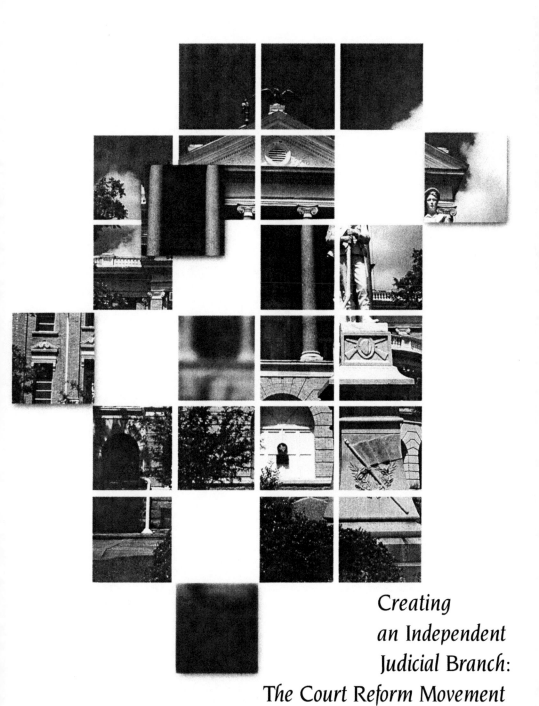

Creating
an Independent
Judicial Branch:
The Court Reform Movement

Chapter 6
Origins of Court Reform and the Movement to Upgrade the State Judiciary

Democratic governmental institutions, courts included, are characterized by gradual ongoing change. In courts, where the resistance to novelty is deeply rooted, the pace of change can be glacial. Measured against this inherent conservatism, the scope and pace of court reform in the last half of the twentieth century has been rapid and quite impressive. The politics of court reform and unification does not lend itself to structured analysis, because each state moves to a different political rhythm. Moreover, there is no accounting for the gifted political leader who occasionally arises in time of need. One thing is clear. Courts came alive in the late twentieth century and made changes that could not have been envisioned as late as World War II.

Origins of the Court Reform Movement

Not all the reform activity occurred after 1950. A strong basis for later innovations was established in the first half of the century when a number of steps were taken to improve the management of courts.[1] The original impetus for this reform movement is generally credited to Roscoe Pound, a great legal educator and student of the law, who outlined the goals of court improvement in a 1906 speech to the American Bar Association.

The American Judicature Society (AJS), the first organization to promote the efficient administration of justice, was created in 1913. This organization focused on judicial selection, tenure, compensation, and retirement, rather than on court operations. AJS can be credited with providing the major impetus for merit selection of judges. The merit selection method proposed by AJS underwent a number of changes over the years, ultimately emerging as the Missouri Plan in 1940 when the state of Missouri adopted merit selection of judges through the use of a nominating commission. AJS was also instrumental in initiating the judicial council movement and in encouraging broader use of rulemaking power to lend coherence to court operations and procedures.

---

[1]   For the history of early court reform initiatives see Fannie J. Klein, ed., *The Improvement of the Administration of Justice*, 6th ed. (Chicago: American Bar Association Press, 1981), 1-16; and Larry C. Berkson, Steven W. Hays, and Susan J. Carbon, eds., *Managing the State Courts: Text and Readings* (St. Paul, MN: West Publishing Company, 1977), 7-17.

In 1913 Wisconsin created a judicial council as a planning and policy body for its courts. Many other states followed suit, so at the height of the council movement in the late 1940s, thirty-seven states had such bodies. Some states also had judicial conferences, which primarily meant periodic meetings of all judges. Some conferences were deeply involved in rulemaking, but they were generally informal gatherings. The exceptions were the Judicial Conference of the United States and the Judicial Conference of New York, which were formal conferences with limited rather than general membership.

Judicial councils, which typically included judges, bar members, representatives of court-related agencies, and sometimes legislators, were designed to ascertain the needs of the court system, to propose policy and planning objectives for court improvement, and, in particular, to make recommendations on legislation. In some states, notably Utah and California, the judicial council had considerable administrative authority, but in most states, these councils failed to achieve their early promise. The reasons for their failure were lack of staff support, lack of connection to an implementing authority within the judiciary, the sheer difficulty of a part-time group overseeing and attempting to improve the operations of a complex system, and the difficulty of effecting any improvement in the older eastern states that were more fixed in their ways and more burdened with anachronistic practices. The council movement did, however, represent an important first step in building judicial branch awareness of the need to address court improvement systematically.

Paralleling the early reform movement in the state courts were some important changes in the federal court system. The federal courts started a process of self-examination under William Howard Taft, the only person in American history to hold the offices of both president and chief justice of the United States Supreme Court. In 1914 he delivered a strong critique of the federal courts, advocating, among other things, ending the separation of law and equity, placing the responsibility for rulemaking under the Supreme Court, and conferring on the federal judicial system the power to reallocate judges to reduce backlogs.

His suggestions were taken seriously, leading to the creation of the Conference of Senior Circuit Judges in 1922. This organization became the Judicial Conference of the United States in 1948. This conference drew its membership from a cross-section of federal court judges with the chief justice as chair. The conference surveyed the business of the federal courts, assigned judges to circuits or districts, monitored the effect of rules of procedure, recommended legislation to Congress for improving the federal courts, and proposed rules of procedure to take effect upon adoption by the United States Supreme Court, which, since a 1934 enabling act, has had rulemaking power for the courts. Congress, however, reserved the right to modify or reject these rules.

Chief Justice Taft was instrumental in the erection of a building for the United States Supreme Court, which formerly occupied space given by Congress. The new court facility, completed in 1935, is a magnificent building adjacent to the Capitol and a tangible reminder of the presence of the judiciary. In 1939, in recognition that the Conference of Senior Circuit Judges needed some staff support and an administrative arm to perform the various services vital to the day-to-day administration of the courts, Congress created the Administrative Office of the United States Courts (USAOC). Up to that point, the Department of Justice had provided administrative services to the judiciary. Construction of the Supreme Court Building and creation of the USAOC reduced court dependence on the other branches of government and were milestone events in court administration and interbranch relations.

In 1939 Congress created the Judicial Councils of the Circuits. Each year the chief judge of each circuit (the federal appellate regions) must call a meeting of the trial and appellate judges in their circuits. These councils can enact orders for the effective administration of the business of their courts. Each council files a quarterly report with the director of the USAOC. These councils are an integral part of the still rather decentralized administrative machinery of the federal court system.

The state counterpart of Chief Justice Taft was Arthur Vanderbilt, a New Jersey attorney who in 1930 started a struggle for court reform in his state as chairman of the New Jersey Judicial Council. When Arthur Vanderbilt became president of the ABA in 1938, he created an ABA section on judicial administration, headed by Judge John Parker, and asked this section to develop standards on court administration. These so-called Vanderbilt-Parker standards became a starting point for postwar improvements in court administration.

After World War II there was a burst of reform in state and local government. State legislatures were targeted for reform because they met at infrequent intervals and lacked trained staff and adequate facilities.[2] In 1966 thirty states held biennial sessions; by 1990 all but seven met in annual session. In 1988 there were 33,000 staffers in state legislatures, a quantum leap from the 1960s. Similarly, state executive branches were going through a series of reforms to increase the authority of governors, to strengthen gubernatorial staff support, and to reduce the number of independently elected executive branch officers.[3] For example, since the 1950s, over twenty states have changed their laws to require that the lieutenant governor and governor run on the same ticket.

It was no fluke, therefore, that the state judicial branch also attempted to strengthen itself and to launch a reform effort. From 1950 onward, the state court reform movement followed two paths, one focused on upgrading the judiciary and the other on a set of reforms lumped under the label "unification."

Upgrading the State Judiciary

In 1964 the president of the Association of the Bar of the City of New York made a rather startling appraisal of the judiciary: "Let us face this sad fact: that in

---

[2]   See generally Karen Hansen, "Our Beleaguered Institution," in Bruce Stinebrickner, ed., *State and Local Government*, 7th ed. (Guilford, CT: Dushkin Publishing Group, Brown and Benchmark, 1995), 91-94.

[3]   See generally David R. Berman, *State and Local Politics*, 7th ed. (Dubuque, IA: Brown and Benchmark, 1994), 145-172.

many—in far too many—instances, the benches of our courts in the United States are occupied by mediocrities—men of small talent, undistinguished in performance, technically deficient and inept."[4] The speaker was Samuel I. Rosenman, a former judge and an adviser to Presidents Roosevelt and Truman. What makes his observations particularly notable is that they were made to attorneys in a setting where public criticism of the judiciary is not common, particularly from a bar association president.

Samuel Rosenman was not alone in his negative views. There was little dispute that the problems in the state judiciary at midcentury were low judicial competence, inadequate compensation, inadequate orientation for new judges, little or no continuing judicial education, no method of judicial performance evaluation, and lack of methods, other than impeachment or recall, to control and discipline judges who engaged in improper behavior. Reformers focused on merit selection of judges, judicial disciplinary commissions, and on judicial colleges or other systematized methods of education for judges. A corollary of these reforms was the attempt to obtain adequate compensation for judges, primarily through judicial compensation commissions.

Merit Selection. The problem of incompetence was attributed to lay judges and the politicized judicial selection process. Merit selection was seen as the best means to eliminate lay judges and to improve the quality of law-trained judges.[5] Unifying limited jurisdiction trial courts was also a means of eliminating lay judges.

Merit selection was being urged long before 1950. Various plans of merit selection were advanced in state legislatures during the 1930s, usually meeting fierce opposition from those with a vested interest in the political process of selection. The principal methods of selection were popular election, usually by partisan means, gubernatorial appointment, and legislative appointment. None of these methods placed a premium on selecting the most qualified candidate.

Fortunately, some qualified candidates made it through the political process; for example, the legendary Benjamin Cardozo.[6] Justice Cardozo, arguably one of the premier jurists of this century, actually started his career by election to the New York Supreme Court (a general jurisdiction trial court). In 1913 he ran as an anti-Tammany Democrat in the First Judicial District that then included Manhattan and the Bronx. A somewhat austere and introverted man with a strong sense of rectitude, he did not directly engage in politics, but his supporters, who included many prominent New York attorneys, organized the effort to elect him. He won a narrow victory, defeating his machine-endorsed opponent by less than 3,000 votes. He personally attributed his victory to Italian voters who mistook him for one of their own, although he was a Sephardic Jew of Portuguese ancestry. There was a certain irony to his election because his father,

---

[4] Mayer, *The Lawyers*, 488.

[5] See Berkson et al., *Managing the State Courts*, 132-141.

[6] Richard Polenberg, *The World of Benjamin Cardozo: Personal Values and the Judicial Process* (Cambridge, MA: Harvard University Press, 1997), 50-51, 121-122.

Judge Albert Cardozo, had been forced to resign from the New York Supreme Court for decisions that were apparently influenced by his close connection with Tammany.

Cardozo was later elevated to the New York Court of Appeals but never totally escaped his political past. In 1926 the chief justice of the court resigned and, according to the political practice of the state, Cardozo should have received bipartisan support to be chief. New York Democrats, still remembering his anti-Tammany origins, tried to block his appointment, favoring a Republican chief in return for Republican support for filling the court vacancy with a Democrat chosen by the party. Only a furious fight on behalf of Cardozo won over Governor Al Smith, who ended the Democratic insurrection. The New York Court of Appeals, during Cardozo's tenure, achieved a reputation as one of the finest appellate courts in American history, notable for some important developments in the law. Cardozo ended his illustrious career on the United States Supreme Court but might never have reached that pinnacle if his merit were not so apparent that his supporters were willing to fight the political status quo on his behalf.

Early merit selection plans differed on the appointing authority (some favored appointment by the chief justice rather than the governor), but they usually featured a nominating commission that recruited candidates, screened qualifications, and recommended three or more qualified candidates to the appointing authority. The appointee had to survive a retention election to stay in office, preserving some means of popular participation in the selection of judges.

The ABA became an early supporter of merit selection. Because much of the reform impetus came from bar associations, it is not surprising that merit selection plans often included bar participation in the nominating group or some process for bar comment on the candidates. Some legislatures minimize or eliminate bar participation on nominating commissions by denying the bar the right to choose the lawyer members of the commission. Rhode Island, for example, recently created a judicial nominating commission with only the governor and the legislature having authority to choose members.

When Missouri adopted merit selection in 1940, it became a model, but, interestingly, the plan permitted trial judges outside the metropolitan areas of Missouri to be chosen by partisan election. Critics thought the retention elections were worthless as a popular check on the judiciary, because from 1940 to 1964 only one Missouri judge was defeated in a retention election. Champions of merit selection argued that this passivity indicated public satisfaction with the judges being chosen. In fact, there was a broad consensus that the caliber of judges improved under merit selection. After World War II, some other states moved toward some form of merit selection, usually gubernatorial appointment from nominees of a commission. In some states, merit selection applies only to the filling of vacancies, but so many judges enter the courts through vacancies that merit selection is used more broadly in these states than one might assume.

Not even the most enthusiastic supporter of merit selection would deny that the process of nomination is subject to political manipulation. Missouri, the home of merit selection, provides some interesting examples of the vagaries of merit selection.

In 1982, three vacancies on the seven-judge court opened up in five months' time, and one sitting judge (Rendlen) purportedly manipulated the merit plan to handpick three new members of the court (Billings, Blackmar, and Gunn). After taking office, the three new judges allied with Rendlen to form a majority bloc of four out of the seven seats and began to run the court without always consulting the three minority judges. These dominant four judges became known as the "Gang of Four," and their actions provoked two members of the minority (Donnelly and Welliver) into public accusations against Rendlen and the majority for their misdeeds. One judge (Donnelly) even called for Rendlen's impeachment. To prevent Welliver from becoming chief justice, the majority of the court abandoned its institutional tradition of choosing as chief justice the seniormost judge who had not yet served in this capacity. Welliver complained publicly about his shabby treatment. Newspapers in the state carried many reports of the dispute. As press coverage swelled to a crescendo in spring 1985, Gunn—one the three judges recruited in 1982—resigned the court for an appointment to the U.S. District Court bench in St. Louis, allegedly relieved to escape the poisoned atmosphere on the state supreme court.

With Gunn's resignation, the merit nominating process began anew. The appellate judicial commission provided Governor Ashcroft a list . . . of three nominees which included two sitting judges with considerable experience. The other nominee was a thirty-three-year-old gubernatorial aide (Robertson) who had no judicial experience, having worked for the governor most of his eight-year legal career. After a short interval, the governor passed over the experienced judges and appointed Robertson.[7]

The reformers had better success at the appellate court level than they did at the trial court level. Although many general jurisdiction court judges are chosen by merit selection, this method is not the norm.[8] Alaska, Colorado, Delaware, Hawaii, Iowa, Massachusetts, Nebraska, Utah, and Vermont have adopted merit selection for full terms and for filling vacancies (i.e., gubernatorial appointment from recommendations made by a nominating commission).[9] In some of these states, senate confirmation is also required. Maryland uses a judicial nominating commission and gubernatorial appointment, but the appointees must be approved by the electorate and are occasionally beaten by an unendorsed candidate. Rhode Island recently went from legislative appointment to what might be termed a pseudo-reform in which merit selection is used but the legislature has heavy input into the nomination process. Twelve states use merit selection for filling vacancies, but use elections (ten nonpartisan and two partisan) for a full term. Three states use unrestricted gubernatorial appointment for full terms and

---

[7]   Greg Casey, "Public Perceptions of Judicial Scandal: The Missouri Supreme Court 1982-88," 13 (1988-89) *Justice System Journal* 289.

[8]   See Rottman et al., *State Court Org.*, Table 6, "Selection and Terms of Trial Judges."

[9]   It should be noted that the listed states have unified court systems and are state funded.

for filling vacancies.[10] Fourteen states use elections (seven partisan and seven nonpartisan) for the full term and unrestricted gubernatorial appointment for filling vacancies. Two states use unrestricted legislative appointment (South Carolina and Virginia). Connecticut has a hybrid system in which the legislature appoints judges but acts upon recommendations from the governor, who chooses from a list of candidates proposed by a nominating commission.

The remaining states cannot be fitted into any mold. In states like Arizona, Indiana, and Kansas, some judicial districts use merit selection, but others use elections. In Wyoming, the governor makes appointment for a full term from nominees submitted by a commission but may fill vacancies without going through the nomination process. In Illinois, Louisiana, and Indiana, the supreme court can make interim appointments to the bench. The only appropriate summation is that the reformers have made themselves felt but are still fighting deep-seated aversions to elitist selection practices that circumvent the citizenry. Moreover, there is considerable skepticism about the nonpolitical nature of merit selection. The one thing that can be said for merit selection is that it probably eliminates the spectacularly unqualified candidates. The political price for pushing the candidacy of a person who has been publicly rated as unfit is usually too high. The big triumph of reformers has been to make judicial qualifications a more visible issue.

Judicial Compensation. There is an obvious tie between the quality of the state judiciary and judicial compensation. Reform groups, notably the ABA, have tried to raise the level of judicial compensation. Everyone accepted the fact that judicial salaries would never match the income of successful legal practitioners, but it is particularly galling to state judges to see young associates in major law firms making salaries higher than those of state judges. A more reasonable target for state judicial salaries was to achieve parity with federal judges. This was the norm advanced by the ABA, but it remains a fantasy. In 1997 the average salary of a state trial judge ($91,108) was about 70 percent of the salary of a federal district court judge ($133,600). State legislatures are erratic in their treatment of judicial salaries and not above holding them hostage to obtain leverage or to vent ire. The reformers advocated judicial compensation commissions—blue-ribbon groups that would periodically review judicial salaries and remove the salary issue from politics. This reform never got off the ground. The salaries of state judges have really not increased much, or at all, in real-dollar terms during the decades of court reform.

Judges have fared better in pensions and benefits. Because many judges come to the bench in middle age, judicial pension plans vest with relatively brief periods of service at very high percentages of salary. Survivor benefits and disability are similarly attractive. Moreover, judges can continue to work after retire-

---

[10]   The term *unrestricted* does not necessarily mean that the governor ignores merit selection. A number of governors have, by executive order, set up merit selection panels to guide them, but this practice does not bind the next governor or, for that matter, the governor who sets up the panel.

ment. Many states have a separate retirement plan for judges, which is rarely, if ever, actuarially sound because of the high average age of the participants. These benefits have been one of the principal monetary inducements for service in the state judiciary.

Judicial Discipline. Reformers fared better in judicial discipline, where the consensus was broad and deep that the existing means of controlling judicial behavior were so inadequate that judges were not really accountable to anyone. The two main methods of punishing judicial misbehavior were impeachment by a state legislature and recall. Some states have procedures for removal of judges by a concurrent vote of both legislative chambers by a super-majority, usually two-thirds. Other states permit the legislature, by a majority vote in both houses, to direct the governor to remove an errant judge. Legislative removal procedures, other than impeachment, simply do not occur any more.

Recall and impeachment are sometimes used but are widely regarded as impractical. Recall procedures require massive gathering of petitions and the funds for a political campaign. Legislatures have neither the time nor the political interest to handle an impeachment and generally get involved when the offending judge is on the supreme court, as in the case of Justice Rolf Larsen of the Pennsylvania Supreme Court, who was convicted on impeachment charges and removed from office in 1994. Moreover, the impeachment sanction, removal from office, may be appropriate for a major act of wrongdoing, such as illegal behavior, but is too severe for relatively minor behavioral problems, such as sheer laziness. Finally, impeachment proceedings are often marred by political considerations where the ideology and politics of the judge and of the court become dominant considerations. Like most impractical methods of judicial discipline, impeachment is rarely employed.

In 1960 California set up what was to be a prototype of a commission to investigate complaints of judicial misbehavior. Every state now has some body to investigate complaints against judges, most of them composed of judges, lawyers, and lay members.[11] Some of these commissions also can adjudicate charges, but it is more common to have a separate body sit in judgment. The adjudicatory body may be a separate commission or the court of last resort itself. The grounds for discipline vary from state to state, as do the sanctions. Common grounds for discipline are physical or mental disability, persistent failure to perform judicial duties, willful misconduct in office, habitual intemperance, bringing the office of judge into disrepute, and conviction of an offense involving moral turpitude. Sanctions range from removal to private reprimands. Forced retirement, public reprimands, and suspension are other common sanctions. The biggest problem is confidentiality and the premature revelation that a judge is under investigation. Some states end confidentiality when charges are filed; others attempt to preserve it until sanctions are ordered, or even beyond that point.

---

[11] Rottman et al., *State Court Org.*, 104, Table 12, "Judicial Discipline: Investigating and Adjudicating Bodies."

There is a tension between public accountability on the one hand and preserving respect for the judiciary and exposing judges to public opprobrium for unproven allegations on the other hand.

Anyone who works in a variety of courts will encounter judicial misbehavior. It is just a fact of life. Occasionally, these behavioral problems involve serious breaches of ethics, court rules, or statutes. Usually, they are less harmful. The most common problems are neglect or incompetent handling of judicial business and lack of proper judicial demeanor. Most judges are very considerate to persons in their courts because they well know that courts appear intimidating, even to attorneys, but some judges are notoriously impolite and abusive, taking advantage of their great authority. Most judges are scrupulous in adhering to the law and moving their cases expeditiously, but some judges, through age, health, incapacitating personal problems, or poor training, are not capable of running a court. There was a time when there was no real means to deal with this problem except by the action of a chief judge, who assumed responsibility for warning a colleague or altering the assignments of a problem judge. Sometimes, a court resorted to forced retirement of a judge under pressure from colleagues. Mandatory retirement laws resulted from experience with older judges whose skills started to slip badly, but the idea of mandatory retirement was widely criticized, because it forced retirement upon judges whose skills were unimpaired and who were an asset to the judiciary. Federal legislation against age discrimination buttressed the argument against forced retirement.

More-serious problems exist in some courts with a weak ethical ethos. A disproportionate number of problems occur in courts where there is a lax atmosphere. In such courts, judges may be involved in systematic defalcation, as they were in the bail scandal that shook the Chicago courts in the 1980s. Even worse is the sale or deliberate distortion of justice. I recall an incident that occurred when I was working after normal work hours on a court project. A prominent criminal defense attorney and his client entered the courthouse in the company of a judge who was not currently assigned in that part of the state. They went into an empty office and remained about ten minutes. Later, I found an order of dismissal signed by the judge even though he had no previous contact with the case, which was a misdemeanor within the jurisdiction of the court. At no time was a prosecutor involved, and the probability was that in the chaotic scheduling system of that era, the dismissal would not even have been noticed. Later, I found a number of case papers in the back of a file with the notation "Hold for Judge ___"—the same judge who had just issued the order of dismissal. The attorney of record in the cases being held was the defense attorney who had just obtained an ex parte dismissal. It was clear that some clerk was involved in concealing cases until this particular judge was rotated back through this court division.

Chief judges may become aware of questionable conduct by colleagues and take steps to control it; for example, assigning a suspect judge to cases that offer little temptation. During a study in a northeastern court, I was struck by the fact that all condemnation cases had been assigned to one judge for years, despite a general pattern of rotation of judicial assignments. A veteran clerk took me aside and explained that the county had been growing rapidly and that both state and local governments had been condemning a lot of land for roads and other governmental purposes. Much money was involved, and several judges assigned to that calendar had succumbed to temptation. The chief kept looking for a judge he could trust. When he found one, he simply left him there.

Incidents such as these are minor and atypical but illustrative of problem behavior. Judicial misbehavior may be individualistic, but very often it involves others and is part of a general pattern in a particular court. An urban trial court administrator commented to NCSC employees that some employees in his court were passing the word in criminal circles that a payment to a certain clerk could steer a case to a certain judge and guarantee a very lenient judgment (unfortunately, this was not an idle boast). Corrupt judges usually have a marketing agent, perhaps a lawyer or clerk. They do not like to take money directly and need some help in collecting and in making sure that the random case assignment system is not random.

An interesting instance of organizational ethos is provided by the Oklahoma Supreme Court scandal of the 1960s, which gave great impetus to the movement for judicial discipline mechanisms. In 1964 it was discovered that a bribery ring involving four justices of the supreme court and a former Oklahoma City mayor and prominent appellate attorney had been in existence for twenty years. The lawyer-mayor had once served as a special member of the supreme court, and each of the four justices had at one time been chief justice. The corrupter was the attorney, who at first worked through one judge to whom he made "campaign contributions." This judge drew some colleagues into the bribery scheme. The number of cases involving the corrupt attorney over the years was significant, and the corruption was instrumental in many key cases, some of them decisions on new points of state law. The shock waves from this scandal went beyond Oklahoma. It showed that corruption did not stop at the justice-of-the-peace level. It could penetrate the highest court of a state and involve judges who were held to very high public standards.

It is no surprise that campaign contributions became the basis for influencing appellate judges in Oklahoma and that lawyers were the contributors. Such contributions do not normally have the corrupting influence that they did in Oklahoma, but they do little to enhance public perceptions of judicial objectivity. A *Wall Street Journal* article of July 21, 1998, on campaign contributions to judges cited a study indicating that 42 percent of the campaign contributions of $100 or more to the seven justices of the Supreme Court of Texas elected since 1994 came from lawyers and law firms with cases before the court. Of the 530 civil cases in which the court rendered opinions from 1994 through October 1997, 60 percent involved attorneys or interested parties who had contributed to at least one of the seven justices.[12] The same article cited another study indicating that some New York City trial judges were awarding guardian ad litem appointments primarily to lawyers who contributed, or were in law firms that contributed, to the judges' political campaigns.

---

[12] The Supreme Court of Texas is a civil appellate court. Another appellate court hears criminal appeals.

Corruption in an appellate court has unique aspects. One judge cannot necessarily guarantee a particular outcome, but one judge can divulge court actions to parties before they are made public.[13] A chief judge of an appellate court is in a better position than his peers to influence the outcome. An example of this dates from Thomas E. Dewey's glory days as a prosecutor. Dewey brought to light what many lawyers already knew: that Martin T. Manton, presiding judge of the federal Circuit Court of Appeals, was selling the judgments of his court to the extent that he could control them.[14] Only one law firm ever complained and that was to another judge, who had no authority to look into the matter.[15]

Judicial Education. Reformers, in addition to seeking a limit on the political involvement of judges, sought to improve judicial behavior and performance by promoting judicial education—both initial orientation for new judges and continuing legal education for sitting judges.[16] The reformers stressed the almost total lack of opportunities for judges to learn necessary skills and substantive knowledge. In a national survey of judges conducted by the Institute of Judicial Administration in 1965, only 12 percent reported receiving any formal training or orientation on taking office.

Unfortunately, lawyers are not trained to be judges in law school and do not suddenly become great judges when they ascend to the bench. Many people, including a number of attorneys, assumed that a lawyer needed only brief on-the-job training, unlike lay judges, who obviously needed a lot of instruction (many early judicial education programs were focused exclusively on lay judges). However, even lawyers with extensive trial experience have a lot to master and need all the help they can get. It is a very daunting experience to preside over a court for the first time. In large courts with many specialized components, judges may start off on the simpler calendars, but judges in less specialized courts do not have this opportunity to learn the job by handling relatively simple nonjury cases. They are simply thrown into the arena.

The movement to provide judicial education started in 1956 with the Appellate Judges Seminar sponsored by the Institute of Judicial Administration and New York University School of Law. The centerpiece of judicial education later became the National Judicial College (formerly the National College of Trial Judges) established in Reno in 1964 as an emanation of ABA seminars for trial judges that started in 1961 under the sponsorship of the Joint Committee for the

---

[13] Sometimes the leaks are political in nature. A decision of the Pennsylvania Supreme Court mandating state financing of trial courts was leaked to the press before its official issuance, prematurely sparking a political controversy.

[14] Mayer, *The Lawyers*, 500.

[15] Estes Kefauver, chairman of a House Judiciary Committee that investigated federal judge Albert W. Johnson for taking bribes, reported that not one bar association had been willing to help the committee. The judge resigned rather than face impeachment.

[16] See generally Berkson, *Managing the State Courts*, 142-49; see also S. W. Hays and C. G. Graham, eds., *Handbook of Court Administration and Management* (New York: Marcel Dekker, 1993), 92-94, 107-08.

Effective Administration of Justice.[17] Thousands of judges have completed courses in the National Judicial College. As many as 2,500 judges per year attend the college, which offers a curriculum of fifty or more courses. Since 1986, the college provides, in conjunction with the University of Nevada-Reno, a master's degree for judges in judicial studies. From the outset, many states used the college to provide orientation to new judges. Although some states have their own judicial colleges (California and Michigan, for example) and practically all states have judicial education programs, the popularity of the National Judicial College continues.

The Institute for Court Management (ICM), which was founded in 1970 and later merged into the National Center for State Courts, offers many courses open to judges but has never attempted to compete with the National Judicial College. The ICM programs tend to stress management issues. If there has been a major omission in judicial education, it has been a systematic way of helping chief justices and administrative judges fulfill their management functions.

Judicial education is so closely related to judicial qualifications and performance that most states make continuing judicial education mandatory. Even in states where it is optional, attendance is high, either out of interest, professional pride, peer pressure, or a general understanding that judges should attend. Compared to the dismal educational opportunities in the 1950s, judicial education has come a long way.

Appropriating bodies have not always appreciated the importance of judicial education, and so judges often struggle to obtain resources for education. Counties have been notoriously reluctant to fund judicial education, so funding has always come primarily from the state general fund, even in states where the trial courts are locally funded.[18] Even at the state level, judicial education is often the first victim of a budget cutback. During a budget crisis in Maine in the early 1990s, the judicial education budget was simply eliminated, but the chief justice made it a personal priority to keep the judicial education program alive by seeking alternative funding sources and putting together inexpensive programs. The problem very often is finding funds to pay travel and lodging costs for judges who have to come from afar, but some judges will attend sessions at their own expense. Sometimes, the obstacle is tuition, but some judges have been willing to pay tuition themselves.

Very helpful to courts in funding judicial education was the tremendous surge of federal grant money into justice agencies during the 1970s through the Law Enforcement Assistance Administration (LEAA). Among the efforts of LEAA to upgrade the justice system was the funding of the National Commission on Criminal Justice Standards and Goals. This commission stressed the need for judicial education, a goal that that was backed by LEAA money. LEAA strongly supported the American Academy of Judicial Education, which opened its program in 1970, and was generally supportive of judicial education programs.

[17]   Section 1.25 of the 1990 version of the ABA *Standards Relating to Court Organization* calls for continuing judicial education.

[18]   Rottman et al., *State Court Org.*, 92, Table 10, "Funding Sources for Mandatory Judicial Education."

Judicial Evaluation. There is a connection between judicial education and evaluation of judicial performance. Education should focus on those areas where there are weaknesses. The problem is developing criteria to measure performance and winning judicial acceptance for their use. Judicial performance measurement is a very sensitive issue.

In the 1990s, the state courts embraced the *Trial Court Performance Standards*, a landmark event in court administration. For the first time, there were national performance standards, but there was one caveat to the embrace. The standards were to be applied to courts, not individual judges, because the evaluation of individual judges has to be based on more appropriate, judge-specific criteria. There are, however, some standards that address the fairness and legality of court decisions and implicitly evaluate judges as a group. When the Los Angeles Municipal Court implemented the *Trial Court Performance Standards*, judges thought it inappropriate for a panel of lawyers or law professors to review a sample of court files to ascertain judicial adherence to the law and the proper application of the law to the facts.[19] They did not object to using appellate court actions as a measure, because judges made these decisions after serious consideration as part of the overall judicial process. Moreover, the Los Angeles judges did not object to relatively objective measures, such as examining sentences by the race, ethnicity, and gender of the defendants. They were understandably reluctant to have their actions second-guessed by some ad hoc group of lawyers.

There has been progress in developing standards for certain types of judicial behavior. In the United States, the federal court system and forty-eight of fifty state court systems have adopted a *Model Code of Judicial Conduct* composed of general standards and specific rules pertaining to judges. In general, the code requires judges to uphold the integrity and independence of the judiciary, to avoid impropriety and the appearance of impropriety, and to perform their duties with diligence and impartiality. Each of the fifty states has a permanent government agency within the judicial branch to investigate complaints and, if necessary, to impose sanctions on judges who have violated the state's code.

The *Model Code of Judicial Conduct* stresses ethical considerations, but there are other forms of judicial performance evaluation that focus on the ability of a judge to execute his or her function with professional skill. In the United States, about twenty-three states have some semblance of judicial performance evaluation, but perhaps ten have a highly developed system. Most states view judicial performance evaluation as an aspect of judicial education and as a means of developing judicial education programs that address weaknesses revealed in assessments. A few states see evaluation as a means of informing the electorate before a retention election.[20] In Colorado, one of the states with pre-electoral

---

[19] Standard 3.1 states that: "Trial court procedures faithfully adhere to relevant laws, procedural rules, and established policies." Sampling cases to determine adherence to the law is a sensitive issue, even if applied to the court as whole rather than individual judges.

[20] Some states have a merit system for initial selection that requires judges to seek approval of the electorate after serving a term.

evaluations, there are several instances of judges deciding not to seek reelection after seeing the results of their evaluations. Evaluations are based on criteria developed in the particular state and then included in surveys and question-naires. States vary in the number and types of persons who are included in such surveys. Some restrict the surveys to lawyers; others include litigants, witness-es, jurors, or court employees.

The reform movement of the late twentieth century concentrated on establishing the professional credibility of the state judiciary and largely suc-ceeded. There is no objective way to compare the state judiciary at midcentury and the state judiciary at century's end, but there is broad consensus that the quality of the state judiciary has improved greatly in the last fifty years. For one thing, the number of lay judges has greatly diminished. Perhaps more important is the great progress in judicial education, in control of judicial behavior, and in highlighting the importance of qualifications in the selection of judges. The state judiciary still has some substantial weaknesses, but these do not minimize the achievements of the last fifty years. The state judiciary is entering the new mil-lennium in far better condition than it was in 1950.

Chapter 7

The Unification Movement and the Advent of Judicial Administration

he identification of court reform with unification started in New Jersey under Chief Justice Arthur Vanderbilt. As early as 1955, the Conference of Chief Justices urged all states to measure court administration against the standards proposed by Chief Justice Vanderbilt. In 1978 the Conference of Chief Justices endorsed the ABA *Standards of Judicial Administration*, which incorporated the concept of unification. Although unification has its drawbacks and has received its share of criticism, it has, for better or worse, been central to state court reform in the United States.

Unification is best understood in the light of the problems it was designed to solve. *Structural unification* was designed to end the organizational chaos and confusion caused by accommodation of court structure to local government structures and to local legal cultures. It was also necessary to eliminate the profusion of unprofessional limited jurisdiction courts. *Budgetary unification* involved state financing of the trial court system and centralized judicial budgeting. This aspect of unification was viewed as a means to bring court employees into a state-funded personnel system, governed by supreme court policy, to effect a more equitable and efficient allocation of resources, to remove judges from local fiscal politics, and to secure a more stable and abundant funding base for court improvement. *Administrative unification* was necessary to lend some operational coherence to the trial court system in each state. This aspect of unification was characterized by central policymaking and planning (not necessarily centralized management) and broader use of rulemaking power.

The path to court reform through unification has been incremental. In most states, initial efforts failed and led to some realistic analyses of the obstacles to success and how to overcome them. Early euphoria gave way to hard-nosed politics. Voter education was stepped up, opinion makers were wooed, and citizen groups were energized. A postelection analysis in Kentucky revealed that voter approval of a constitutional revision of the court system was highest in counties where public forums had been conducted. Court reform experience also indicated that the packaging of proposals was crucial. One way to kill any reform is to consolidate it with an unpopular proposal, and so court reformers had to make hard choices about seeking a comprehensive judicial article or fighting for discrete reforms. Timing of reform proposals was also important. In New York the poor financial condition of New York City made it easier to win support for state financing, an idea that had been anathema to city politicians for years. Leadership within the judicial branch was also very important but not necessarily crucial, because some reforms were achieved through gubernatorial or legislative leadership with relatively minor support from the judiciary. Even where the leadership came from within the judicial branch, the change agent was not necessarily the supreme court. Judicial councils and judges of lower courts have occasionally been the moving force.

Administrative, budgetary, and organizational unification have been implemented unevenly. Some states are highly unified; others have not experienced much change. By 1996, depending on the criteria applied, fifteen to eighteen states had highly unified court systems, and an equal number of states had achieved a considerable degree of court unification.[1] Even in the minority of states where unification was not embraced, the issue of unification was usually considered. Despite its failures and defects, unification has framed the debate for court improvement and raised awareness of the judicial branch as a coherent entity with a mission.

Structural Unification

Structural unification is the visible, symbolic manifestation of building the third branch of state government. Fifty years ago, very few people could even conceive what a state judicial branch would look like, much less appreciate its importance to the credibility of state court systems and judicial independence. The reformers strove to remove trial courts from the crazy-quilt structure of local government organization and to place them within a uniform statewide organizational structure. This reform made the state judicial branch a tangible reality.

The 1974 ABA *Standards Relating to Court Organization* advocated statewide courts of uniform jurisdiction, ideally a single-tier trial court with divisions as necessary.[2] The standards also allowed for unification of trial courts in two tiers with a court of uniform statewide general jurisdiction and a court of uniform statewide limited jurisdiction. By 1974 some states had already moved toward a more unified structure, but most were still pondering the issue. The standards gave official and authoritative voice to the forces of reform. The ABA also provided a model judicial article to facilitate the legal and political deliberations in each state.

For most states, the idea of a single-tier court was utopian and a bit threatening. It raised specters of a monolithic judiciary and seemed to ignore the unique role of lower courts in the mass processing of cases. Even a unified trial court with two tiers appeared a political impossibility in states where judicial

---

[1]   Based on Rottman et al., *State Court Org.*, Part VIII, 1993 Court Structure Charts. See also David Rottman and William Hewitt, *Trial Court Structure and Performance: A Contemporary Reappraisal* (Williamsburg, VA: National Center for State Courts, 1996). All references to trial court structure in this chapter are based on Rottman et al., *State Court Org.*

[2]   In 1990 the ABA released its *Standards Relating to Court Organization*, updating the 1974 standards but retaining the basic principles of court organization.

localism was solidly entrenched. Moreover, many states had judicial articles that had not undergone major amendment or revision in living memory and seemed impervious to change. Despite the apparent obstacles, one state after another embarked upon court reorganization after 1950. Some settled for a bit less than the ABA ideal (e.g., New York), some chose the two-tier trial court model (e.g., Kentucky), and some sought the ultimate in structural unification, a one-tier trial court (e.g., Wisconsin).

By 1950 very few people could seriously question that state trial court organization was a mess. In the 1950s New York City alone had 190 separate trial courts, each with its own staff, own budget, and its own jurisdiction; the upstate courts were not much better.[3] The fragmentation of the New York trial court system and its heavy politicization led to a series of studies and reform proposals in the 1950s and 1960s. After a number of false starts, the voters in 1962 affirmed a gubernatorial and legislative initiative to reorganize the courts, providing a political victory for Governor Nelson Rockefeller. The new court organization profoundly affected New York City, where the numerous limited jurisdiction courts were merged into two citywide courts, one a civil court, the other a criminal court. However, the trial court organization in upstate counties was not greatly altered, so the New York court structure is not fully unified although the New York courts refer to themselves as a unified system. It turned out that upstate Republican leaders were more interested in reforming New York City than in disturbing the status quo in upstate counties.

In 1976 Kentucky created a unified two-tier trial court system.[4] Before 1976, Kentucky had limited jurisdiction courts characterized by lack of professional judges, immersion in local politics, and jurisdictional confusion. In 1968 Kentucky voters, by a four-to-one margin, rejected a constitutional amendment that would have reorganized the court system by merging the various limited jurisdiction into a statewide court of uniform limited jurisdiction. Voters feared loss of local control and were unenthusiastic about state financing and merit selection of judges, which were part of the reform proposal based upon the ABA model article. Moreover, the vote on judicial reform became an issue in a bitterly contested gubernatorial election, with both candidates courting county officials who were opposed to unifying the courts. Following the defeat, more attention was given to citizens' concerns. Surveys were conducted, great voter education efforts were undertaken, influential citizen groups were enlisted in support of the judicial article, and bipartisan support was obtained. In 1976 the amendment was approved comfortably statewide but did not do well in rural areas, where the voters feared they would lose their local judges and would not be well served by full-time lawyer-judges who were not residents of their counties.

Kentucky has 120 counties, many of them with a very small population. It was apparent that many counties had such a small volume of cases that they did

[3]   For description of New York court reform politics, see Miller, "New York Experience," in Powell, *Seven States*, 105-129.

[4]   For description of Kentucky court reform politics see Davis, "Court Reform in Kentucky," in Powell, *Seven States*, 1-39.

not deserve much judicial time, but allocation of judges is a delicate issue, one that inevitably rises in connection with unification of limited jurisdiction courts. To accommodate the concerns of small counties for some judicial presence, the judicial article permitted the use of trial commissioners, whose duties would be prescribed by the supreme court and who were required to be attorneys (unless none were available or qualified). The Kentucky courts, to lend some factual content to a largely emotional debate revolving around local pride, arranged for a weighted caseload study that led to a report recommending that there be 123 district court judges, a number supported by the supreme court. The governor thought 92 judges would be adequate; the legislature, reacting to local pressures, thought that 176 judges would be required. The final number was 113 judges, which by some strange quirk of political calculus was about right. The observation of the state court administrator was that this was the first time in Kentucky's history that there had been some rational connection between the number of judges and the caseload. Thus was the Kentucky District Court born.

When a two-tier trial court is created, dividing the workload between the limited jurisdiction court and the general jurisdiction court becomes an issue. This allocation can be based on political whimsicality or on a workload analysis that leads to jurisdictional lines dividing the caseload in a way that matches the judicial resources in each court, as was done in Kentucky. Even where allocation of caseload is fairly scientific, it must be based on the situation at the time the jurisdiction of each court is fixed. Unfortunately, court workload is dynamic and volatile, so rigid jurisdictional barriers inevitably lead to one court being overburdened while the other is not fully occupied.

Underlying some of the rational quantitative veneer for allocating caseloads between two trial court levels are some personal considerations. Judges of limited jurisdiction are often viewed as being of limited ability and unworthy of significant jurisdiction. The general conception is that limited jurisdiction court judges are good at moving routine cases but not quite up to handling a felony case or a complex civil case, raising the point of why a uniform limited jurisdiction court with lawyer-judges was created in the first place. In states where this condescending outlook is prevalent, the jurisdictional statutes minimize the role of the limited jurisdiction courts.

What sometimes modifies this condescension is the desire of general jurisdiction court judges to relinquish cases they find very onerous, typically family and juvenile cases. This is normally done by having specialized courts or by using quasi-judicial officials. It can also be accomplished by having the lower-tier courts handle family and juvenile cases, as they do in North Carolina. In Nebraska and Kentucky, a lower-tier court has juvenile jurisdiction. There is some practical basis for having judges of lower-tier courts handle juvenile cases: they are more apt to stay in one county, more likely to be knowledgeable about the local scene, and more readily available.

One option of a chief judge of a general jurisdiction court in a two-tier system is to assign judges of the limited jurisdiction courts to the higher court temporarily. This gives the chief judge the opportunity to choose a judge that he feels is particularly well qualified. In Massachusetts, at one point, superior court cases were backed up to an extreme degree while district court judges, who were not at all busy, were seldom used.[5] A study in California revealed that some superior court judges asked for temporary assignment of a superior court judge from outside their counties rather than using their own municipal court judges. A Los Angeles superior court judge who farmed out many cases to municipal court judges in his district was dubbed a "traitor" by members of his own court. The California Constitution now permits counties to have a one-tier system but does not require it. Most counties have taken advantage of this power, but superior court judges in other California counties would not dream of combining the superior and municipal courts. This attitude, which is common among judges in general jurisdiction courts, is one of the negatives of two-tier structural unification.[6]

Eight states have gone to single-tier courts: Idaho, Illinois, Iowa, Kansas, Minnesota, North Dakota, South Dakota, and Wisconsin. Connecticut has a single-tier system, except for some probate courts with routine functions. Some of these states have even absorbed municipal courts so that the state trial court hears ordinance cases, but some of these states have retained a system of municipal courts. It is interesting that the one-tier states are heavily concentrated in the Midwest. This could be attributed to several factors: court structure was not as chaotic in the Midwest as it was in older states, midwestern states are traditionally more receptive to reform messages, and the demography of largely rural states favors a simpler structure.

Wisconsin provides an example of a state that created a single-tier trial court by merging county courts into the circuit courts and leaving the municipal courts with ordinance jurisdiction.[7] The leadership in Wisconsin came from three successive chief justices who were consistently strong supporters of court reform. The governor was cooperative, and a variety of civic groups and professional associations were enlisted in support of court reform, the centerpiece of which was the one-tier trial court. The issue did not become partisan in the legislature, and such problems as did appear involved abortive legislative attempts to shift control over the bar and judicial behavior to the legislative branch. Differences also arose over how the court reform proposals would be submitted to the voters. The legislature wanted each issue to be considered separately, hoping that voters would shoot down the creation of a state-funded intermediate appellate court. Court reformers thought the intermediate appellate court proposal would be helped by linkage to the one-tier court proposal. The chief accepted the legislative proposal to present the issues separately.

---

[5]   In this period Massachusetts had a popular Republican governor and a heavily Democratic legislature. When this happens, the legislature is loath to create new superior court judgeships to be filled by gubernatorial appointment. The same situation paralyzed the process of creating new judges in California, where there had been, before 1999, a continuous string of Republican governors in a state legislatively controlled by Democrats.

[6]   The term *superior court* suggests the presence of an inferior court. There used to be local courts that were actually given the title of inferior court, but for obvious reasons the name did not catch on.

[7]   For description of the early court reform movement in Wisconsin, see Robert J. Martineau, "Judicial Reform in Wisconsin: Some More Lessons for Reformers," in Powell, *Seven States*, 87-103.

There was amazingly little opposition in Wisconsin to a one-tier trial court because of the strongly organized bipartisan support and the difficulty of finding a good argument against something that seemed quite sensible. Everyone could appreciate the inefficiency and sheer wastefulness of having two judges visit the same county several days apart to hear a few cases within the jurisdiction of their own court or of having one judge sit idle while a judge of an adjacent court of higher jurisdiction was overworked. Moreover, county judges loved the idea of becoming circuit judges, and those circuit judges who feared their prestige was being diminished could find no way to voice their grievances persuasively. Another reason for success was that the unification proposal was not linked with a proposal for state financing of courts and could be presented as an inexpensive reform cloaked in vague promises of improved efficiency.

Connecticut is one of the most structurally unified court systems. It has a single-tier trial court served by all trial judges and meets the fundamental test of organizational unification. However, this one-tier trial court is split into a high number of specialty courts and geographic and administrative units. There are housing courts in major population centers. The juvenile courts are geographically separate from other courts and have their own districts. There are a profusion of "geographic area courts" that hear most criminal cases below the serious felony level and some small civil cases, but are often geographically separate from judicial district courts that hear family cases and major civil and criminal cases. There are functional divisions within the superior court (family, criminal, housing, juvenile, and civil). Many administrative appeals handled at the trial court level are centralized in one court in Hartford. The judicial mechanisms for hearing child support enforcement cases are also separate. To this mix are being added some boutique courts. Structural unification permits many organizational variations within the same overall framework.

A curious aspect of single-tier systems is their tendency to create a second level of judges within the same tier. Illinois and Iowa have different types of judgeships within the unified court. Illinois has a large group of judges called associate judges, who are chosen by the circuit judges. Some states used associate judges as a temporary means of grandfathering in judges of limited jurisdiction courts who were not qualified to be judges in the unified court. This became an institution in Illinois, although the associate judges have essentially the same jurisdiction as circuit judges. Iowa, which initially rejected the idea of a second-string judiciary, has a number of associate judges and many magistrates, virtually a three-tier judiciary within a one-tier court. Staunchly populist Minnesota believes that each person is entitled to a real judge regardless of the complexity or gravity of the case. This belief was accompanied by resistance to broad use of quasi-judicial officials, but even in Minnesota, district court judges who opposed the merger of their court with county courts won the concession that they would not have to hear cases formerly triable in county courts. Some judges were scandalized by the possibility of having to hear a traffic case or an eviction case.

Experience indicates that there is a practical need for some kind of minor judiciary and that the inclination of judges to create different levels of responsibility is not just an ego trip but a rational response to variations in the caseload.[8] There appear to be at least two but possibly three levels of case processing, each requiring a different type of judicial role. Single-tier trial courts are not immune to this.

The term *structural unification* implies a rigidity belied by the actual practice in the states. Any organizational structure in a dynamic environment has to be adaptable. Where there are statewide tiers of trial courts, localism is curbed without sacrificing flexibility. Unified courts can adapt themselves to changed circumstances faster and less confusingly than a court system rooted in local government structure. Moreover, they can do this without reverting to disorder. The great achievement of structural unification was to give organizational form to the concept that the state judicial branch is more than a group of semi-independent judges loosely held together by a common appellate process. It is an integrated organism.

Budgetary Unification

Until recent decades, the major state financial responsibility in courts was support of appellate courts, and even this responsibility was sometimes shared with local governments if the appellate court was geographically decentralized. This method of financing reflected the historical reality that trial courts were not treated as an integral administrative component of the state judicial branch.

Until the 1970s, the burden of trial court financing did not weigh heavily on most local governments, because court expenditures were relatively modest. The major expenditures were salaries and fringe benefits for general jurisdiction trial judges, both of which had been at least partially assumed by most states before 1970. As the resource needs of trial courts started to increase rapidly after 1970, so did the demands for state financing.[9] These demands were reflected in the ABA standards and were a major item in the reform agenda.

State financing of trial courts is not necessarily linked to centralized judicial budgeting, because state financial assistance can, and sometimes does, take the form of grants or reimbursements to local governments. Nonetheless, there has been a strong tendency to conceptually link state financing and centralized budgeting. In actual practice, centralized judicial budgeting has been adopted by practically all states that have assumed responsibility for trial court financing, the major exception being California, which introduced a system of county reimbursement.

---

[8]   This has even happened in the federal court system, where magistrates have gradually created a minor judiciary with the earmarks of a federal court of limited jurisdiction.

[9]   The information in this section is drawn largely from Robert W. Tobin, "Status of State Court Financing 1988," project report (National Center for State Courts, Williamsburg, 1989); and Tobin, *Funding the State Courts: Issues and Approaches* (Williamsburg, VA: National Center for State Courts, 1996).

State financing of trial courts is not necessarily linked to structural or administrative unification, although these three types of change are often grouped conceptually. New Jersey achieved a high degree of administrative unification in 1948 by placing great authority in the chief justice and by creating an office of court administration. Decades later, New Jersey effected a structural unification of its superior court and in 1995 went to state financing. Illinois, Idaho, Minnesota, and Wisconsin are examples of states that created structurally unified trial courts without adopting state financing. It is clear that states can, and frequently do, adopt some discrete aspect of unification.

In the first group of states to adopt state financing, fiscal unification was a major factor in the reform proposals. By the mid-1970s, a number of states (none of them highly populous, industrial states) had switched to state financing of trial courts.[10] In some states where unification focused on limited jurisdiction courts, the level of state financing was greater in the courts undergoing reform than it was for the general jurisdiction courts, where significant functions remained locally funded.[11]

The court reform movement received strong support from many sources in the 1970s. The National Center for State Courts, which provided an educational, technical, and intellectual impetus for court reform, was deeply involved in unification, particularly state financing of trial courts. The Law Enforcement Assistance Administration (LEAA) of the Department of Justice was very supportive of state financing of trial courts and made grants to the National Center for State Courts to help states make the transition to state financing. The American Bar Association also called for state financing of trial courts in its 1974 *Standards of Judicial Administration*. The climate for court reform was favorable, and state financing was at first viewed favorably.

By the late 1970s, state financing started to come under critical examination. The proponents of state financing and uniform budgeting were challenged to produce empirical evidence that state financing had beneficial effects on caseflow, efficiency, or even the total resources available to the court system.[12] Fiscal relief of local governments was not emphasized in the debate, although it frequently was an important factor in state assumption of trial court operating costs.

By 1980, fiscal relief for local governments became more than a supporting factor in state assumption of trial court operating costs. It emerged as the dominant factor due to the escalating operating costs of trial courts and the consequent budgetary tension with local funding authorities. In the halcyon days of the 1960s and 1970s, this problem was present, but was usually not the dominant reason for

---

[10]   E.g., Alaska, Alabama, Colorado, Connecticut, Hawaii, Kansas, Kentucky, Maine, Missouri, New Mexico, North Carolina, Rhode Island, and Vermont.

[11]   E.g., Maryland, Nebraska, Virginia, and West Virginia.

[12]   Certain necessary expenditure increases are built into state financing without reference to efficiency: 1) making up for deferred county spending in the period before state assumption; 2) upgrading personnel and services to meet statewide standards; 3) improving salaries and fringe benefits; and 4) equalizing regional disparities.

going to state financing. In the early 1980s, when a general recession reduced governmental revenues, the call for relief drowned out the reform debate. Local government officials started to become the principal advocates of state financing.

Why did this occur? Obviously, local fiscal problems were one cause, but it is also clear that the nature of court operations changed dramatically in the 1970s. The number of judges jumped, as did the level of judicial compensation. Local governments, even if they were not responsible for judicial salaries, were responsible for providing facilities, staff, and equipment for each new judge, not to mention absorbing additional jury costs.

Exacerbating the problem was an increase in the personal staff of judges, causing some states to assume the costs of court reporters or persons serving a judge in a confidential capacity. Constitutional requirements regarding indigent defense, treatment of juveniles, and protection of the mentally incompetent created a set of large and volatile expenditures, which could be imposed by judicial mandate. The demands of modernized court administration introduced a cadre of trained managers into the court system and created demands for various new technologies: records automation, recording devices, computer-aided transcription, and word-processing equipment. Breakdown in family structure caused large expenditures for social support services, counseling, juvenile detention facilities, foster care, and child support enforcement. A collateral effect of social disintegration was the need for more juvenile and adult probation officers. No longer did a court consist of a judge, a reporter, and some clerks. Courts were becoming complex administrative entities.

Even when impecunious rural counties started asking for relief from the expenses of trial courts, urban areas, particularly metropolitan areas, generally opposed state financing of courts. The urban areas saw state financing as a shift of authority to officials outside their orbit and a threat to urban political systems. Then came the local government fiscal crisis of the late 1970s and early 1980s. Financially beleaguered Massachusetts counties almost overnight pushed a state court financing bill through the legislature. Fiscal problems in Detroit contributed to the support for state financing in Michigan, but state funding was originally restricted to trial courts in Wayne County (Detroit), with a commitment to include the rest of the state later (which only started in a limited way in 1997). Even mighty New York City sank into serious financial problems that paved the way for state financing of courts.

The fiscal problems of local government may, of course, exist side by side with reform objectives, as they did in some of the first states to go to state financing, but after 1980, the fiscal objectives generally outweighed the reform objectives. This led to a renewed impetus toward state financing. By 1996, twenty-nine state court systems were primarily state funded, including California, New York, New Jersey, North Carolina, and Massachusetts. Although in a minority, county-funded systems are found in some of the most populous states, among them Ohio, Pennsylvania, Illinois, Texas, and Florida. Oklahoma is hard to classify because its trial courts are largely self-supporting through the collection of revenues that go into a special fund earmarked for court operations. The state makes up the difference between revenues and budgeted expenditures.

Of the roughly $11 billion spent on state courts in 1995, local governments still provided about 50 percent. With the addition of California to the ranks of state-financed systems, the local government share is now under 50 percent. Pennsylvania is on the way to state financing, probably in a phased manner, so the state-local balances will tilt even more in favor of state financing.

The Bureau of Justice Statistics of the United States Department of Justice estimated that in 1990 the per capita expenditure on courts nationwide was $31.18.[13] This figure excludes indigent defense costs, which are included in many court budgets, and many facilities expenditures. Deviations from the national average are great. In 1990 California and New York had per capita expenditures of $48.70 and $51.82, respectively. At the opposite extreme, Arkansas had a per capita expenditure of $13.25, Mississippi $15.16, and Oklahoma $15.37. The different levels of per capita expenditure on courts are not affected to any great degree by whether the courts are funded by the state or county. There are some demographic patterns that state financing does not change.

It has been clear for a number of years that population density and urbanization are the prime factors in determining court expenditures. Those states with huge metropolitan areas and a number of other urban areas inevitably experience a level of social interaction, social disintegration, and commercial activity that drive up court workload in a geometric ratio. Moreover, personnel and other costs tend to be high in such areas. Most state court systems fall into four basic expenditure categories and should not be compared with states in other categories (Alaska and Hawaii are *sui generis*):

- states with a high level of urbanization and very large metropolitan areas (e.g., New York)
- states that are very urbanized but do not have large cities (e.g., Connecticut and New Jersey)
- states that have a more or less even mix between urban and rural areas (e.g., Illinois and Minnesota, which have one large metropolitan area in what is otherwise not a densely populated state)
- states that have relatively few urbanized areas of significant size (e.g., South Carolina, Kansas)

State financing did not insulate courts from budget problems during the recession of the early 1990s. In prior years, most state legislatures tended to defer to courts, in part because court budgets were not very large and in part because there was some recognition of the special status of courts in the governmental system. This deference decreased in the 1990s simply because of budget pressures that placed courts in competition for funds with other agencies and because court budgets had become large enough to attract serious budget

---

[13]   See Kathleen Maguire and Timothy Flanagan, eds., *Sourcebook of Criminal Justice Statistics—1990* (Washington, DC: Bureau of Justice Statistics, 1994), Table 1.5, "State and Local Justice System Per Capita Expenditures," 5.

scrutiny. At the state level, court expenditures seldom exceed 2 percent of the total state budget and are often less, but the dollar amount is often enough to awaken the interest of the legislature. In the period 1997-98, California trial courts spent close to $2 billion per annum. Connecticut, with a population 12 to 15 percent of California's, had a state judicial budget of about $225 million in the same period. The Connecticut legislature earmarks about 15 percent of the court budget for various programs it likes, a form of micromanagement that most state courts have avoided.

Even after twenty-five years of experience, any debate on state financing still produces the same hackneyed arguments pro and con. The arguments have become increasingly irrelevant, because the level of expenditures on state courts is taking local governments out of court financing. The truth is that fiscal necessity leads to state financing regardless of the advantages and disadvantages of such a step.

Proponents of state financing now rarely make extravagant predictions about the effects of state financing on caseflow or operational efficiency. The Kansas judiciary made this mistake in the 1970s and was burned in a legislative performance audit. Proponents of state financing now generally argue that it will lead to a more stable and equitable source of funding, improved allocation of resources in the system, savings of scale and other efficiencies, a more uniform system of justice, more accountability of trial courts, improved professionalism, and freedom from the compromising situations that arise when judges must handle cases involving the local entities that fund them. Opponents routinely charge that state financing will lead to undue centralization and bureaucracy, higher costs, insensitivity to local and public needs, loss of revenue for local governments, possible loss of employee jobs or diminution of benefits and status, and overdependence on one funding source.

The state-local issue usually does not involve a total transfer of financial responsibility to the state. Local officials sometimes react against the high costs of certain expenditures, such as the volatile costs of indigent defense, payment of high professional salaries to probation officers, or costs of a new court program (e.g., arbitration). If these concerns are specific, rather than general, the problems may be addressed by focusing state aid on these high-cost areas and avoiding a general shift to state financing. Even where courts are largely county funded, states have assumed some expensive trial court expenditures to grant relief to counties. Among these are probation (a court responsibility rather than an executive branch responsibility in many states), data processing, court reporting, and indigent defense. Interestingly, states have usually avoided picking up the costs of court facilities, and so many so-called state-funded systems are still dependent on local governments for the heavy expenses associated with court facilities. The truth is that every state has assumed an increased share of trial court financing. The issue, sometimes obscured by the unending debate, is how much more the state will pay, not whether the state should be involved.

Advocates of mixed state-local funding argue that it is wise to have multiple funding sources rather than to rely totally on one source, but mixed funding is so complex that it is difficult to clarify court needs for appropriating bodies and the public. In addition, mixed funding leads to a diffusion of responsibility, with the natural result that neither state nor local governments feel responsible for courts.

Underlying all these arguments is the recognition that state financing with unitary budgeting involves a major shift of power and authority to the state and the creation of an administratively cohesive (opponents might say monolithic) judicial branch. The issue is control. County commissioners do not like to raise taxes to support an organization over which they have no control or to pick up the tab for court innovations devised by the legislature. They are often willing to give up a large portion of court-collected revenues to the state to rid themselves of the trial courts. Trial court judges do not like the prospect of increasing their accountability to the state supreme court, and many would prefer to deal with county officials and be in charge of their own budget destiny. To many judges, state financing has less to do with the adequacy of financing than it does with the locus of power in a state court system.

Budgetary unification has an unwelcome corollary—pressure to produce offsetting revenues. As states have picked up a larger share of the court expenditures, they have also increased their share of court revenues and have become more concerned about the effectiveness of courts in collecting fines, fees, and costs. The amounts of money involved are huge—billions of dollars annually. Courts have been placed under pressure to raise more revenue and to impose tighter internal controls on the money passing through courts. Rarely will public discussions of state financing include references to misappropriation of court-collected revenues, but it is a serious problem, sometimes rooted in the local culture. Improved internal control of money is one of the unheralded results of state financing.

Ironically, state financing was proposed as a solution to the revenue-producing pressure counties placed on trial courts, but, in fact, state financing may only change the source of pressure from a local county commission to the far more formidable state legislature. Pressure from either level of government was deemed unacceptable in Standard 4.1 of the *Trial Court Performance Standards*: "A trial court compromises its independence . . . when it . . . serves solely as a revenue-producing arm of government."

In the state-funded Maine courts, court-collected revenues annually run between 75 percent and 80 percent of state court expenditures. During the recession of the early 1990s, an increase in revenues was the only way the Maine courts could stave off steep budget cuts. Maine has gone farther than most states in raising revenues but is hardly alone. Other state legislatures have increased fines and added a broad of array of surcharges, costs, and fees to these fines. Judges sometimes feel that their legislature sets the level of fines, fees, and costs so high that they become an alternative form of taxation, rather than a monetary sanction bearing some resemblance to the gravity of the offense charged.

Courts argue that they should not be transformed into an arm of the treasury and forced to operate like a large collection agency. As jails have filled up, financial sanctions have been used more frequently. Because it is not licit to imprison defendants for inability to pay a fine and because so many defendants claim inability to pay at once or at all, courts have somewhat reluctantly permitted deferred and installment payments of fines and instituted programs of community service in lieu of payment. Some urban traffic court judges reported that 60 percent or more of convicted defendants are going on time payments.

Even where legislators do not annually raise the level of fines, fees, and costs, they may insist that courts do a better job of collecting the revenues already prescribed by law. This is easier to do in a state-funded system. The Colorado judiciary, for example, was the first to set up a technical assistance program to help clerks and judges bring up their collection rates.

Judges recognize that the fundamental reason for enforcing monetary sanctions is that the prestige and authority of the court and the requisites of justice demand it. Nonetheless, judges continue to have philosophical and ethical concerns about whether courts should serve as revenue collectors for government treasuries. The concept of the self-supporting court has ethical implications if the court in any way uses the money it generates from judgments to pay its operational expenses. It is beyond dispute that this practice is not consistent with judicial ethics or the demands of due process. Fortunately, there are only a small number of trial courts, and one state-financed system, Oklahoma, that still use this type of financing.

On the civil side, high filing fees and costs, including the costs of a civil jury and court reporters, may deny access to justice, an issue that concerns many judges and legislators. The *Trial Court Performance Standards* deal with this in Standard 1.5, Affordable Costs of Access: "The costs of access to the trial court's proceedings and records—whether measured in terms of money, time, or the procedures that must be followed—are reasonable, fair, and affordable."

Legislators argue that there is no injustice in having defendants and court users pay a portion of the cost of court operations rather than having this spread generally among taxpayers. Legislators also observe that courts, particularly court clerks, often lobby for new fees or court costs earmarked for court purposes, so they can avoid budget constraints and have some ready money in a special fund. Courts have no great qualms over collecting money that they can keep, but express qualms over collecting money that goes into the general fund. In fact, many judges and court administrators admit that they like to have some earmarked fees that they can use more or less flexibly. Moreover, some courts have actually invoked inherent powers to keep such funds from being audited.

This "slush fund" mentality was very pronounced in locally funded courts. In Illinois, for example, the fees for marriage ceremonies performed by judges went into a special fund that could be used flexibly by judges. Court rules required that each court file an annual report on the fund, but these reports were rather casual because the amounts received in most counties were small, although large enough in some instances to fund trips by judges to educational sessions that they might not otherwise have attended. In Cook County, where the amounts in the fund were sizable, the annual report reflected more diverse use of the funds. Louisiana law permits district courts to fund their operations from a criminal fund fed by monetary sanctions imposed by the court. Such private funds invite trouble. One effect of unification is to eliminate or reduce the incidence of such private pots of money. On balance, unification has improved internal controls of court-collected funds but has certainly not freed courts from pressure to generate resources.

Budgetary unification has increased the authority of the state supreme courts by giving them monetary muscle to back up their administrative policies. It has benefited courts in the poorer parts of the state and made allocation of resources fairer. It has, overall, increased the resources available to trial courts. Most of all, it has made the creation of a third branch of government much more realistic. Courts are accountable for the state funds they receive, as they should be, but they can speak with more authority in financial matters for the whole system and not depend on a mishmash of local government budgets.

Administrative Unification

Until well into this century, there appeared to be a general consensus that state judges should be relieved of the management tasks associated with court operations so that they could concentrate on adjudication. Executive branch officials could handle financial and personnel administration, as well as facility and space needs; elected clerks could handle records management and calendaring. The underlying assumption was that judges could preserve their independence in matters of adjudication without control of the administrative aspects of court operations. As the century progressed, judges started to reject this premise and sought to protect their independence by taking administrative control of the courts.

Key to this exercise of control was judicial rulemaking authority, because it was primarily through rulemaking that supreme courts exercised administrative control over the judicial branch. In the nineteenth century, when courts were dominated by legislatures in matters of procedure and internal administration, they were not able to make much use of rulemaking power. Sometimes, legislators permitted political considerations to enter into their procedural and administrative legislation, and sometimes they imposed rigid legal constraints that inhibited effective management of court operations. But legislatures must also be credited with enacting procedural codes that were much clearer and better organized than the complex and arcane procedures found in many trial courts in the 1800s. The New York Field Code of 1848 became a prototype for legislatively enacted procedural codes.

In this century, courts have had some success in getting legislatures to recognize that there are areas where rules of court are more appropriate than legislative enactments. Courts have argued with varying degrees of success that rules of court procedure and evidence are the proper objects of procedural rulemaking. Procedural rules concern methods and stages by which a case moves from initiation to disposition and include such things as time limits for filing court papers, types of pleadings, and types of motions. Many procedural rules affect substantive matters and individual rights and have administrative and financial implications, but they are primarily designed for processing individual cases.

Courts have been less successful in obtaining legislative agreement to administrative rulemaking by courts. Administrative rules, sometimes called rules of superintendence, apply to such matters as accounting and personnel practices, recordkeeping policies, court facility standards, and case management policies. Administrative rules are the means by which high courts and judicial councils promulgate management policy for the judicial branch and are essential to a unified system.

Legislators sometimes question the right of courts to make administrative rules and may reserve the right to regulate the internal administration of the judicial branch. Legislators exercise the right to determine the venue and jurisdiction of courts, the organization of courts, the times and places of conducting court business, the number and types of judicial officers, and a variety of other matters that might be considered administrative. Most state legislatures are opposed to placing rules on a par with statutes so that a court rule could override a conflicting statute. One concern of legislators is that judges conduct their rulemaking in relative privacy, perhaps involving attorneys but rarely involving members of the general public. Many legislators take the position that if a court wants to "legislate," it must open up its processes to the public, particularly administrative rulemaking, which deals with systemic matters.

Legislators sometimes impose time standards for processing cases or place pressure on courts to be more efficient. California legislators, convinced that trial courts were not operating as well as they should, not only legislated time standards but attempted to force various efficiency measures on courts. California's trial court judges have long resisted state-level control of the judiciary and thus invited legislative intrusion into areas that should be within the judicial domain.

Administrative and procedural rules are usually developed by the same procedure and reviewed by the same committees because they affect each other. Many state courts do not draw clear distinctions between procedural and administrative rules. Sometimes, administrative rules require detailed implementation, so the supreme court uses the rules to state broad policy and administrative orders or directives to add detailed regulations. Administrative orders, like rules, may be sent out for general comment but are generally characterized by a level of administrative detail that makes it inappropriate for them to be handled through the normal rulemaking procedure.

Supreme courts have various ways of exercising their administrative authority in addition to rulemaking:

- issuance of general administrative orders or directives
- issuance of specific administrative orders to individual judges
- instructions to the state court administrator
- court decisions in cases that involve administrative issues

Quite often, a supreme court informally directs the state court administrator to perform some administrative task. Some states let the state court administrator issue directives but usually do not permit an administrator to issue a directive to a judge. The chief justice can delegate to the state court administrator the authority to transfer judges outside their courts or to recall judges to service, but these actions would normally be ratified by orders in the name of the chief justice. In states where the state court administrator is a judge, the supreme court, or even the legislature, may give the state court administrator broad authority to transfer and assign trial judges. This is the case in Connecticut.

Because the lines marking the scope of judicial rulemaking power are not clear, the relations between the judicial and legislative branches are dynamic and occasionally adversarial. In general, however, the branches usually work out an arrangement whereby the courts have rulemaking authority in procedural and administrative matters but can be, but rarely are, overridden by the legislature. Some state supreme courts have even claimed exclusive rulemaking authority under inherent powers (Arizona, Colorado, Connecticut, Idaho, Iowa, Mississippi, New Hampshire, New Mexico, Oklahoma). Two of these claims predated 1950; the rest occurred in the period 1950 to 1978, the height of the unification movement, which provided a great impetus to rulemaking.

Not surprisingly, one of the major showdowns between a legislature and a state supreme court occurred in New Jersey, when Arthur Vanderbilt was chief justice and made extensive use of administrative rules. Two problems faced by Chief Justice Vanderbilt were the intrusion of legislative politics into the courts and the relative domination of courts by attorneys. From the outset of the Vanderbilt era, the changes he instituted incurred the opposition of the bar and the legislature. Legislators were particularly incensed by his broad use of administrative rulemaking power. New Jersey law permitted the court to enact rules of practice and procedure but stated that administrative rules could be superseded by law, presumably statutes. But the court interpreted this legal provision to mean that a rule of court could only be overridden by the state constitution. This interpretation did not sit well with the legislature, but the court proceeded to use rulemaking to create positions within the judicial branch and for various detailed matters of administration; for example, the duty of municipal courts to keep books and be audited. Courts in other states also started to make extensive use of rulemaking to effect court reform, recognizing that the power of a court to manage its own operations depends heavily on the scope of its rulemaking power.

The Advent of Judicial Administration

One effect of unification, even in jurisdictions that did not fully implement it, was to highlight the increased administrative responsibility of judges. One result of the late twentieth-century reform movement was that judges started to perceive more clearly their joint and several responsibility for managing a court system that rises or falls on its ability to cope with major social and legal changes. The role of judges in the administration of the judicial branch has been termed *judicial administration*. The administrative role of a chief judge in a trial court or intermediate appellate court is important but quite different from that of a chief justice. In administrative unification, the chief justice is preeminent.

Chief justices are still grappling with how to define their administrative role in relation to the full court and professional court administrators. Given the difference between state court systems, there probably will never be a specific definition of the role of chief justice. This role has six generic components:

- goal setting and leadership
- formulation and implementation of management policy
- dealing with judges
- relationships with the bar
- relations with the other branches, noncourt agencies, and the public
- delegation and oversight of the detailed aspects of court administration

Goal Setting and Executive Leadership. A major responsibility of a chief justice is the ongoing analysis of court operations to identify needs and objectives, the institution of ameliorative programs, and the administration and funding of such programs. These activities constitute a planning process that at the state level may be performed by a judicial council chaired by the chief justice. Some states, Minnesota, for example, use a conference of chief judges to make policy recommendations for trial courts. Chief justices may assume their positions with definite goals in mind, or they may see their role as system maintenance. The goals may be improving judicial education, building new court facilities, upgrading information technology, introducing time standards for case processing or, on a more grandiose scale, reorganizing the court system. These goals may be personal to the chief and lack institutional support, or they may be incorporated into an existing court plan to which the chief is committed. The chief justice can be, and sometimes is, a change agent.

Some chiefs are by nature organizers and energizers, who can mobilize a court or court system to pursue improvement. From 1955 to 1980, a number of reformist chief justices were instrumental in leading the court reform movement, among them Chief Justice Harold Traynor in California, Chief Justice Edward Pringle in Colorado, Chief Justice Harold Fatzer in Kansas, Chief Justice William O'Neill in Ohio, Chief Justice Howell Heflin in Alabama, Chief Justice Arthur Vanderbilt in New Jersey, and Chief Justice Charles D. Breitel in New York. In 1971 alone, one-quarter of the states effected major court reforms, a testimonial to the judicial leadership in that period.

Most chief justices are not comfortable with a dynamic role. Moreover, most courts are not inclined to set goals. Nonetheless, planning is recognized as part of judicial administration, albeit a somewhat minor one. Many chief justices have, with varying degrees of enthusiasm, sponsored or cooperated with studies of the courts and commissions to explore the future of the courts. Reports and studies have often played a big role in court improvement and have been used by chief justices to foment change. At any point in time, a state supreme court may be overseeing one or more pilot programs.

Formulation and Implementation of Management Policy. Administrative rulemaking is collegial and absolutely requires the participation of all high-court justices or, in some states, a judicial council. The administrative dockets of supreme courts are a means by which a chief justice involves his colleagues in the administrative issues before the court, in particular those requiring rulemaking. The chief usually controls the administrative docket and the later implementation of administrative issues, but the involvement and education of the full court is a major responsibility. There are also, of course, informal methods of involvement that do not involve rulemaking, among them the possibility of giving some justices administrative assignments. In any event, it is difficult for a chief justice to manage without some supporting consensus among fellow judges, who are, after all, peers.

Supreme courts usually have some standing committees on rules, education, and various other matters, as well as some ad hoc committees. The chief justice may have to deal with a judicial conference or judicial council that gets involved in rulemaking or administrative issues. The chief may appoint some or all of the committees, may personally chair some committees or the judicial council, and may provide staff support to the committees or the council from the administrative office of courts. These committees play an important role in rulemaking and the proposal of policy alternatives. A chief justice involved in a major change in the court system or in court procedures can spend an inordinate amount of time dealing with reform committees.

Dealing with Judges. Chief justices and supreme courts must concern themselves with the education, behavior, and discipline of judges. Chief justices also have a particular responsibility for the morale of judges and for looking out for their compensation, retirement, and working conditions. In addition, chief justices and supreme courts deploy and assign judges. This responsibility is hard to delegate.

Chief justices have for many years had the duty of shifting judges among courts and across geographic boundaries. This can be done upon request or as a regular scheme of rotation. Routine transfers can be delegated; more-sensitive transfers may require the chief's direct involvement. The chief justice may also appoint trial and appellate judges to various committees and, if so inclined, may choose like-minded judges to extend the influence of the chief's office.

Judicial assignments of any kind cannot be made lightly. Inevitably, judges form strong opinions about what are considered unrewarding assignments and may balk at those they do not like. When judges are elected, such opposition is serious because each judge, in a sense, can argue that he is individually answerable to the voters and to no one else. This is not a very cogent argument, but chief justices cannot treat the deployment and transfer of judges, elected or appointed, as a routine personnel action.

The supreme court is ultimately responsible for judicial behavior, even though there may be a collateral right of impeachment. Every state has some body that investigates complaints about judges and may recommend disciplinary proceedings. This can take the form of a hearing before the supreme court, so the involvement of the chief justice in the administration of judicial discipline has to be limited. Nonetheless, the chief justice may be responsible for the administration of the disciplinary process and the informal methods by which disciplinary issues are resolved, such as resignation or retirement without public reprimands or sanctions. A more sensitive issue arises when a judge suffers from a disability that makes it impossible for him or her to fulfill the judicial role but may not qualify as a disability in the insurance sense of the word.

Judicial behavior encompasses much more than disciplinary matters. Often, issues of judicial demeanor in court do not reach disciplinary proportions and may be as simple as a dispute over wearing a robe. Chief Justice Howell Heflin, for example, ordered all Alabama judges to wear robes, because he felt it enhanced the dignity of the court proceedings. He encountered some opposition on populist grounds but ultimately prevailed.[14]

The education of judges is a major concern of any chief justice. Not infrequently, chief justices have to protect educational programs from cost-cutting legislators who zero in on judicial education as a "frill." In some states, chiefs have obtained funding for a judicial college that institutionalizes judicial education and develops expertise in this important area. Many states routinely appropriate money for new trial judges to attend a course at the National Judicial College in Nevada. The educational requirements for judges and the extent to which these requirements are enforced constitute a major administrative responsibility that involves policymaking by the full court and the administrative oversight of the chief. There was a time when older judges staunchly resisted such programs and had to be disciplined in some manner, but such resistance has become rare. Most judges seek educational opportunities.

Relationships with the Bar. A major responsibility of state supreme courts is supervision of the legal profession. This generally includes enactment of rules and regulations on admission to practice, attorney discipline, and continuing legal education. The implementation of administrative policies in this area normally falls upon the chief justice but is typically exercised through a staff that handles the administrative routine. Inasmuch as a state supreme court may end up hearing cases on attorney discipline, the involvement of the chief justice in this area must be limited.

There are two levels of relationships with the bar: the formal relationships, which are usually quite proper and focused on areas of common concern and agreement, and the less-public, informal relationships, where there may be deep differences of opinion between the judicial leaders of the state and some elements of the bar (the term *bar* is pretty inclusive and disguises the diverse nature of law practice and attorney concerns). Bar governance, almost by definition, will lead to some conflicts. This area of judicial administration is extremely sensitive, because no chief can afford a major split with attorneys and yet must enforce professional standards. Attorneys may pay public lip service to proposed changes, but this may conceal serious misgivings. Attorneys generally do not like to openly oppose the high court, so open communication is hard to achieve.

---

[14] The robes were paid for out of a federal grant, one of the many bizarre expenditures made under the old LEAA program.

Relations with Other Branches of Government, Court-related Agencies, and the Public. A chief justice is the official spokesperson for the judiciary in both ceremonial matters and in businesslike contacts with the various governmental bodies with which the judiciary interacts. The ceremonial role alone can demand a lot of time and is very important as a means of public education, but it is not as important as those contacts, often informal, with a governor, legislators, budget officials, and the heads of various criminal justice or public welfare agencies. The court administrative staff may carry the brunt of most external relations, but there comes a time where the top person in the branch has to take the lead. Some chief justices devote a great deal of time to nurturing relationships with those officials whose support and cooperation are important to the judiciary. Sometimes, these relationships are adversely affected by a politically unpopular supreme court decision, requiring tact on the part of the chief.

Delegation and Oversight of the Detailed Aspects of Court Administration. The above list of responsibilities is hardly exhaustive but specifies judicial administration roles that are very hard to delegate. There are numerous other administrative responsibilities that by their nature and scope must be delegated, normally to a court administrator. Letting go can be difficult for an administrative judge in an environment where judges are used to fairly authoritarian control of all facets of court operations. The opposite problem is presented by the chief who simply does not like to be dragged into administrative decision making. Striking a balance between micromanagement and aloof detachment can be hard not only for the chief justice, but for the full court.

The question of delegation becomes one of priority. Generally, the priority items are those directly affecting judges and attorneys or those of an intrinsically legal nature. Judicial involvement drops off in complex administrative and technical areas, and the degree of delegation increases commensurably. Although judges are the ultimate decision makers in matters of administration, they must of necessity rely heavily on court personnel to handle the details of personnel management, financial management, space management, and technology.

Until states started to assume the responsibility for trial court financing, state supreme courts had very minor responsibilities in budgeting, personnel management, and facilities. This changed dramatically with the advent of state financing, which required supreme court participation in personnel policies for all court employees, in budgets encompassing the whole court system, and even occasionally in trial court facility issues. This necessarily transformed the role of a chief justice into that of chief executive officer of a geographically diffuse and organizationally complex system, rather than that of titular CEO of an administratively localized system. It enlarged the court's responsibility for overseeing of the operation of the state court administrative office. State financing has been the single most important factor affecting the administrative roles of chief justices and supreme courts and the main reason why they have had to delegate so much of their management responsibility to court administrators.

It probably seemed inconceivable in 1950 that state supreme courts and chief justices would end up presiding over statewide court information systems, but this has happened in many states. Someone at the state level in the judiciary had to tie together the courts of the state in a network and to serve their informational needs, particularly the docketing and calendaring functions so crucial to case management. The areas of information technology and technology for court reporting, personal computers for judges, and electronic mail communication (very helpful for intermediate appellate judges at different locations), were among the complex matters with which justices had to deal. These functions were, of course, delegated, but the ultimate decisions on complex technology were made by chief justices and often confirmed by the full court.

Viewed in retrospect, it is amazing how much change has been effected in the authority of judges over judicial branch administration. Judges, by inclination and heritage, have not sought management roles and have often been uncomfortable in such roles, but, to their credit, they have accepted the importance of management as an aspect of judicial independence. The judiciary is still feeling its way in meeting the need for a management culture in state courts and in figuring out the judicial role in management. As tentative as this situation is, it is a far cry from the management disorder that characterized state courts only a few decades ago.

The unification movement has been crucial to the success of state courts in asserting judicial administrative independence. Without rational trial court structures, access to the state general fund, and mechanisms for administrative policymaking, state court systems would still be wallowing in chaos. By the same token, unification would count for little without improved management leadership from judges. This combination has occurred to some degree in many state court systems. The management foundations of the judicial branch are infinitely stronger than they were at midcentury.

Chapter 8
Creation of an Administrative Infrastructure: The State Component

C ourt administrators are now found at all levels of the state judicial branch. So it is hard to imagine that a short time ago there were no court administrators. The rise of this profession is one of the important, yet largely unheralded, aspects of the court reform movement of the late twentieth century.

In retrospect, professional court administration arose from a fortunate confluence of four factors: the leadership provided by bar associations, court organizations, and some visionary chief justices; the support of federal funding agencies; the general trend toward more-professional management in state and local government; and the recognition in the judiciary that courts had become complicated entities that would fall under control of the other branches unless the courts displayed some management expertise. A related but less obvious factor was that state court administration was a primary means of building a common legal culture that transcended the hundreds of highly localized cultures that shaped the American legal system. The creation of a broader legal culture was implicit in the unification movement from the outset and was a major cause for the emotional reaction against administrative unification in many states.

Origin of Court Management

By 1950, state court judges were becoming more aware of the judicial branch as an administrative entity. It was clear by then that judicial councils did not provide an adequate mechanism for court improvement and management, and so new ideas of building an administratively independent judicial branch took root. Arthur Vanderbilt's selection of Edward McConnell as New Jersey court administrator began the process of building the profession of court administration and an administrative infrastructure in state courts. Introducing court managers into the judiciary was a sharp break with tradition and an indispensable element in the drive to build a state judicial branch that was relatively independent in administrative matters.

Before 1950, the closest approximation of a state court administrator was a Connecticut court official called the executive secretary to the supreme court, a job that largely involved collecting information and producing statistical reports. By 1955, there were enough court administrators to start the National Conference of Court Administrative Officers, a professional organization open to both state court administrators and trial court administrators. In 1971 the state court administrators organized their own organization, the Conference of State Court Administrators (COSCA). By 1977, forty-six states had state court administrators, many of them possessed of significant administrative authority. By 1998, every state, the District of Columbia, Puerto Rico, and the territories were represented in COSCA.

The profession of trial court administration started establishing itself in the late 1950s. The first trial court administrator was Edward Gallas, who was appointed as administrator of the Los Angeles Superior Court in 1957. His appointment led to the creation of similar positions in other urban courts.

In 1965 trial court administrators created their own organization, the National Association of Trial Court Administrators. There was a parallel organization of elected clerks called the National Association of Court Administration. These two organizations were merged in 1985 to form the National Association for Court Management (NACM). Between 1985 and 1997, the membership of NACM increased from 980 to more than 2,300. This growth has been spectacular, considering that there were fewer than ten trial court administrators in the early 1960s.

NACM played a major role in building the profession of court administration. It provided prestige, support, education, and networking for court administrators, particularly for those who had few, if any, contacts with other court administrators. In the 1980s a frequent topic of discussion at NACM meetings was whether trial court administration was really a profession, but by 1997, the professional stature of trial court administrators was a given. Annual NACM conferences now feature major speakers, provide a wide variety of educational opportunities, and attract a wide variety of vendors to display their wares. Trial court administrators who have grown up with NACM take pride in this testimonial to the maturation of their profession.

This growth in the profession of court administration also owed a lot to various organizations that advocated the introduction of management offices into the courts. From 1913 to 1952, the American Judicature Society and the American Bar Association carried the banner of court reform, but in 1952 Arthur Vanderbilt was instrumental in founding the Institute of Judicial Administration at New York University, the first organization specifically dedicated to improving the administration of state courts.

In 1970, at the request of United States Chief Justice Warren Burger, the Institute for Court Management (ICM) was created under the leadership of Ernest Friesen, one of the early leaders in the development of court administration and former head of the United States Administrative Office of Courts. ICM started certifying and training court managers and developing the knowledge and skill base for the emerging profession. This organization, under the direction of Harvey Solomon for most of its existence, was responsible for producing many of the early court administrators and creating a network that provided some cohesiveness and mutual support within the court administration community. Denver University Law School, the University of Southern California, and American University also started programs to train court administrators. American

University was also the site of a very successful technical assistance program for courts under the direction of Joseph Trotter and Carolyn Cooper.

In 1971, again at the request of Chief Justice Warren Burger, the National Center for State Courts (NCSC) was created as a research and consulting arm of the state courts paralleling the Federal Judicial Center, which had been established in 1967. NCSC, with financial support from each state, as well as from the federal government and private contributors, provides secretariat services to various court organizations, an information service to answer inquiries on court matters, a central repository of court literature, research on various court-related issues, technical assistance and contract services to courts, and liaison with the national government on behalf of state courts. NCSC was deeply involved in improving court administration and in some of the profession's great advances, among these the development of both a national statistical database on the processing of court cases and the *Trial Court Performance Standards*.

By the 1980s, court administration at both the state and trial court level was well established and growing. State offices were concerned with administrative issues transcending particular trial courts and were not involved in the mundane affairs of trial court administration. In some sparsely settled states with few trial court administrative offices, court administration became very centralized. In some states, typically those that were urbanized and had county-funded courts, trial court administrative offices dwarfed state court administrative offices. Generally, state courts worked out a functional division between trial court administrators and state court administrators that reflected the degree of unification in the system and the demographics of the state. Most of the personnel in offices of court administration are concentrated at the trial court level, sometimes located in urban trial courts, sometimes operating at a district or regional level in rural states. Whatever the form, court administration went from being nonexistent in 1950 to having a genuine infrastructure by 1995.

Organizational support for court administration would have been much less effective if Congress had not passed the 1968 Omnibus Crime Control and Safe Streets Act to strengthen state criminal justice systems and to reduce crime. Courts were eligible for funding under this act but had to struggle to obtain these funds and objected strongly to engaging in a political wrestling match with other justice agencies to obtain block grant funds. The federal administrators assigned to the court area, notably James Swain and William Herndon, were very sensitive to court views and very supportive of the reform agenda of court leaders. Among other things, they were instrumental in providing funds to start offices of court administration, particularly at the state level. State court administration owes a lot to the Law Enforcement Assistance Administration.

State Court Administration

By midcentury, reformers and public administration scholars agreed that improved operation of the state courts required court executives entirely devoted to management. In theory, a chief justice could personally fill the executive role. In practice, this was rarely practical, because the scope of the administrative responsibilities was too large to be performed by a sitting member of the court. The profession of state court administrator developed in response to this need.

One measure of the emergence of state court administration as an important component of the judicial branch is the frequency with which state constitutions refer to the office. Twenty-one state constitutions make specific reference to an administrative director of courts, all but one within the context of appointment. Eleven of the constitutionally referenced administrators are appointed by the supreme court, six by chief justices, two by chief justices with approval of the supreme court, and one by a judicial council. The provision in Article VI of the New York Constitution is among the most comprehensive and mandatory (most constitutions use the word "may" rather than "shall" in referring to the appointive power):

> Sec. 28.a. . . . The chief judge shall, with the advice and consent of the administrative board of the courts, appoint a chief administrative officer who shall serve at his pleasure.

> Sec. 28.b.   The chief administrator, on behalf of the chief judge, shall supervise the administration and operation of the unified court system. In the exercise of such responsibility, the chief administrator of the courts shall have such powers and duties as may be delegated to him by the chief judge and such additional powers and duties as may be provided by law.

Although the term *state court administrator* is used generically to describe a person who serves the state supreme court, the chief justice, or a judicial council as the principal administrative officer of the state court system, the position has developed along different lines in each state. The range of authority, prestige, and power is great.

One factor that affects prestige is the level of compensation. Tying the salary of a state court administrator to that of the judiciary was thought to be a key element in defining the importance of the office, and in some states this link is made by law rather than by rule of thumb. In 1997 the average salary of a state court administrator was almost $91,112, roughly 87 percent of the average salary of a supreme court justice and almost the same as the average salary for a judge of a general jurisdiction court.[1] These ratios have held up for a number of years.

Who Are These Administrators? Supreme courts were slow to hire administrators from the management culture, preferring lawyers and sometimes judges as court administrators. The use of judges as administrators was heavily debated in the 1970s, but most states rejected the concept in favor of nonjudge administrators with a legal background. As time has gone on, courts have been more willing to choose lay administrators with a management or technical background.

---

[1]   Some state court administrators are, in fact, judges of the general jurisdiction trial court. This skews the comparisons a bit.

Connecticut is one of the minority of states that has judge-administrators. With one brief exception, this has also been the practice in New York. Among the states that have consistently or occasionally used judges as state court administrators are Illinois, Massachusetts, New Jersey, and Pennsylvania. The rationale for using judges is that they will be more effective than a nonjudge administrator because they understand the judicial mind, are better able to form an executive partnership with the chief, and can command more prestige and respect than an administrator who is not a judge. It has occasionally been urged that there should be both a judge-administrator and a nonjudge administrator, with the role of the former being to deal only with judges. This view reflects the deep aversion of trial judges to receiving directives from an administrator who is not a judge.

A prominent example of this preference for judges as court administrators is found in New York. In 1974 Chief Justice Charles Breitel adopted as his personal goal the improvement of court administration and appointed Judge Richard Bartlett as the first chief administrator of the New York court system. The chief justice had some major reform goals (unified budgeting, merit selection of judges,[2] and administrative unification) and felt that only a judge could command enough respect to win support for fundamental changes. His appointee, Richard Bartlett, was a highly respected judge who had served in the legislature and had been instrumental in revising the penal code and criminal procedure in New York. He had a reputation for getting things done and was quite successful within the five-year period (1974-79) that he and Chief Justice Brietel set for themselves to achieve their three major goals.

The practice in New York has been to place judges not only in the chief administrative position but also in the three principal chief deputy administrative roles. The chief deputies head the three major components of the judicial branch: the Office of Court Administration, New York City courts, and courts outside New York City. However, it has not always been necessary to be a judge at the time of appointment to one of the four top administrative positions. If the appointee is not a judge, he or she will generally be elevated to the bench in connection with appointment. Being a judge is an important part of the public persona of the chief administrative officer and the chief deputies.

Even in states that did not feel it necessary or advisable to appoint judges as state court administrators, there was a strong tendency to appoint lawyers, or someone drawn from the legal culture rather than the management culture. Ralph Kleps, the first state court administrator in California, had been an attorney experienced in dealing with the California legislature. Jim James in Kansas and Walter Kane in Rhode Island were both supreme court clerks who enjoyed the confidence of their courts and were familiar figures in their court systems. In some states, lawyer-administrators have gone from court administration to the appellate bench or trial bench.

The ideal, of course, was an administrator with some management training and also a legal background, such as Ed McConnell in New Jersey, who was a

---

[2]   He was only partially successful in achieving this goal. Trial judges are still elected on a partisan basis.

member of Arthur Vanderbilt's law firm and also had management training. Harry Lawson in Colorado was one of the first nonlawyer administrators, but he had worked for the Colorado legislature during a period of court reform and was considered to be very knowledgeable in the law and in Colorado politics by Chief Justice Pringle, who selected him.[3] Then, as now, a state court administrator had to be politically adept, able to handle interbranch relations, public relations, and the internal politics of the judiciary. The job is not technocratic, although the administrator's staff must include people who are conversant with various public administration specialties and information technology.

Each of these men displayed management ability, but they did not have a clearly defined management role and could not rely on some public administration model. These pioneers of court administration started the process of building a profession and establishing the relationships of their office to the chief, the supreme court, and the court system in general. They set the stage for the second wave of court administrators, more of whom brought a management perspective to their task.

In the early days, it was difficult for judges to define the role of a state court administrator or to determine where to find an administrator. There was no established pool of potential candidates, so courts tended to hire persons who were simply familiar figures. As the profession became more established, courts became more open to seeking state court administrators outside their small, familiar circle. The number of court administrative jobs also increased, meaning that there were more opportunities for court administrators and a more-professional recruitment process. Supreme courts looked more carefully at the pool of professional court administrators. They hired deputies from other state court administrative offices, top administrators within their own administrative office of courts, trial court administrators, and federal court administrators, but very seldom hired state court administrators from other states. Some prominent court administrators have come to their positions after holding high administrative positions in the executive branch. Another frequent supplier of state court administrators and high-ranking court managers has been the National Center for State Courts.

In 1997 seven of fifty state court administrators were women. One of the women pioneers in the profession was Betsy Belshaw, who was an assistant to Harry Lawson in Colorado and went on to be the state court administrator in Maine and Oregon. The legal system is still staunchly male in the upper-management echelons. Typically, about 10 percent of the state court administrators are women, but the increasing number of women in court executive positions in trial courts and in middle-management positions at the state level indicates that male hegemony will weaken.

---

[3]   Harry Lawson's legal acumen is such that he served for many years as a member of the faculty at the Denver University Law School, where he dealt with not only court administration but also legislation. His program supplied many court administrators and was instrumental in building the administrative infrastructure of the state courts.

What Level of Support Did They Receive? Building a relationship with the judiciary was and is no easy task. In the early days, the job of state court administrator was noted for short tenure and insecurity. Meetings of state court administrators invariably featured morbid speculation and grim humor about the turnover rate and the fate of colleagues recently dismissed or about to be dismissed. There was a realistic recognition that state court administrators could rarely obtain a similar position in another state because judges preferred to hire from within and would, in any event, be unlikely to hire an administrator who had fallen into disfavor with another supreme court.

Persons who have been interviewed for the position of state court administrator sometimes ruefully report that they scared the court by appearing as a take-charge type or as an agent of change with a number of programmatic ideas. Not infrequently, supreme courts reject renowned applicants in favor of less-threatening and more-familiar figures drawn from their own court systems. A collateral factor is the influence of the chief; sometimes, the full court will defer to the candidate favored by the chief even if the associate justices harbor some doubts about the person.

To some extent, the high turnover rate among state court administrators in the early days was a function of growing pains as judges and administrators sought to work out their relationships. But the high turnover also reflected the frequent changes in the position of chief justice and uncertainty about whether the court administrator served the full court or answered only to the chief. The weight of informed thinking was that a state court administrator should work for the court as a whole, although answering specifically to the chief justice. As a practical matter, however, few courts will overrule a chief justice who wants to fire the incumbent administrator. Thus, even those state court administrators who serve at the pleasure of the full court are peculiarly dependent on the support of the chief and particularly vulnerable every time a new chief takes office.

Not surprisingly, many court administrators tread very gingerly around their chief. There is often a note of tension and apprehension if a consultant airs controversial matters before the chief. Occasionally, the administrator wants the consultant to be the bearer of bad news, but more often, the administrator desires that nothing be said to upset the chief, lest this cause complications for the state court administrative office in general and the administrator in particular.

Although most court administrators would prefer to work with an individual administrative judge rather than a board of judges, many administrators, especially those with a highly collegial court, have to maintain communication with the full court through administrative meetings and other contacts. There are cogent reasons for having access to the full court: the court makes policy and has to be well informed; it is important for the administrator to have a sense of the dynamics of the court; the opinion of the full court about the administrator is important if he or she serves at the pleasure of the court; and, finally, the next chief may be a member of the court. An obstacle to such communication may be a chief who prefers to be the sole channel of communication with the court. Another problem is the tendency of some associate justices to go directly to the administrator on minor matters and to bypass the normal lines of authority with the chief. It is hard to set up a "send only" form of communication. Openness may invite some unwelcome intrusions. Every administrator takes a reading on how to deal with the chief and the court. This reading is not eternal; the dynamics of a court change.

The folklore in the early days was that no administrator ever got fired for proceeding too slowly or avoiding major changes. An occasional reform-minded chief might demand an activist role for the state court administrator, and there are a few instances of a chief dismissing an administrator who had been so used to keeping a low profile that becoming a leader was not feasible. In general, "slow and easy" was perceived to be the path to survival. There are some prominent examples of activist administrators trying to sell a comprehensive reform agenda to the supreme court and being dismissed for their aggressiveness. An administrator cannot get too far in front of the court and has to back off when it is clear that the court has no desire to move in a particular direction. Court consultants, who can afford to be brave, like to urge state court administrators to "lead from behind," but this can be a one-way ticket to unemployment.

Another cause of turnover was the inevitable scapegoating of state court administrators whenever administrative or judicial actions of the supreme court antagonized legislators, judges, or the general public. In Oregon, where the legislature assumed responsibility for financing the Oregon trial courts, the time allotted for transferring from local to state funding was less than a year, an almost impossible task. The goal was met by a very determined effort of the state court administrator, who became the focal point for the inevitable backlash against the rapid change and was soon forced from office.

State court administrators can be targeted by trial judges for many reasons other than state financing. A state court administrator who implements unpopular policies of the supreme court or gets heavily involved in judicial disciplinary matters can attract a great deal of opposition as a surrogate for the supreme court. One chief justice wanted to upgrade the attire of attorneys in court (the state was snowbound much of the year, leading attorneys to wear winter clothes that were somewhat informal) and told the state court administrator to issue a directive to that effect. A firestorm engulfed the hapless administrator.

In some states with a distinctly partisan process of judicial selection, a state court administrator can be dismissed for belonging to the wrong party or political faction. This is very much the case in states where the supreme court is elected on partisan lines; e.g., Alabama and Ohio. A senior NCSC consultant recalls doing a statewide study just before an Ohio election and being told not to include two major counties in the study because they were dominated by a political party hostile to the chief, for whom the state court administrator was clearly serving as a campaign advisor.

What Is Their Authority? The authority of a state court administrator depends on the perception that he or she speaks for the court in general and the chief in particular and is cloaked with the institutional prestige of the highest court and perhaps the whole judiciary. Because the power of a state court administrator is largely derivative and because judges differ in their delegation of authority, there are substantial variations in an administrator's power and prestige.

State court administrators differ in the legal basis of their authority. Some are constitutional officers, and quite a few have their functions and authority spelled out in statutes or rules. There is a difference between rules and statutes that generally spell out functions and authority and rules and statutes that impose some duty on a state court administrative office. In some states, Connecticut, for example, there are a plethora of statutory references to the state court administrator, many of them conferring relatively minor responsibilities. In Illinois, on the other hand, the supreme court took exception to the legislature naming the state court administrator in statutes. Their position was that the supreme court was in charge of the judicial branch and ought to be given the option to determine what person or agency should perform tasks assigned to the judicial branch. Thus, the court argued, statutes ought to refer only to the supreme court, not to internal components of the judiciary.

Regardless of legal references, the administrator's authority still depends heavily on the degree to which the highest court enables the administrator to execute the court's policies or to suggest policy initiatives. Key indicators of the relationship between a court and an administrator are the frequency and depth of meetings on administrative issues where the administrator is in attendance; the degree to which a court administrator sets the court's administrative agenda; the latitude of the administrator to recommend courses of action and even to disagree with the court; the degree to which the court empowers an administrator to implement the court's administrative decisions and to be a spokesperson for the court; and the ability of the administrator to run his or her office without supreme court micromanagement, particularly in personnel decisions.

The authority of the administrator ebbs and flows based on the management style of chiefs and courts. A chief or court may have a very ambitious agenda for change, which usually enhances the authority of the state court administrator, but some courts prefer a static mode, which immobilizes the state court administrator. A chief or court may become so personally involved in administrative matters that the administrator may be eclipsed; conversely, a court may become so detached from administrative matters that the administrator has a hard time catching the attention of the judges. Usually, there is some median course whereby the court signals the areas where it desires strong involvement and the areas where the chief and the state court administrator have carte blanche. These signals change, and it is up to the chief and the state court administrator to detect the changing scope of delegation.

Although the authority of state court administrators has definitely progressed beyond the mere statistical roles that characterized the profession in its early days, there are still gradations in the level of responsibility.

- A few state court administrators have a partnership role with the chief justice, have very broad executive authority over the court system as a whole with strong lines of vertical authority running down to the trial courts, are involved in programmatic initiatives for trial courts, and are generally regarded as the major court spokesperson in administrative matters. This model is restricted to unified systems and is not common even within these systems.

- Some administrators have fairly strong delegated authority in a clearly defined but somewhat limited number of functional areas, have some involvement with trial courts but not a great deal of control, and have some prestige and standing in certain areas of court administration. They do not, however, have a strong executive partnership with the chief and tend to assume a relatively low profile.

- Some administrators have a small administrative and managerial role and are concerned primarily with support to the court in legal matters transcending the adjudication of cases, in particular rulemaking, legal education, legislative drafting, superintendence of the judiciary and the bar, and litigation in which judges and courts are parties. This type of office is geared to dealing with courts through rulemaking rather than administrative involvement and is not managerially oriented.

- Some administrators have very minimal responsibilities, insignificant roles in court operations, and a few necessary administrative and legal responsibilities. This is typical of the less-unified systems, but even in these systems, activist court administrators may, largely on their own initiative, transcend the institutional limitations of their office. They move into areas where the court does not wish to be deeply involved and a statewide approach is necessary, most commonly the area of information technology.

In the early days of court administration, few state court administrators had enough longevity to acquire a personal reputation that enhanced their authority. Clearly, the strongest early model was Ed McConnell in New Jersey, who was invested with considerable authority by two chiefs possessed of strong personal executive authority. The key to his stature was his ability to make the transition from Chief Justice Vanderbilt to Chief Justice Weintraub, who was an appointee of a governor who, as a legislator, had been a strong critic of the courts and was of a different political party than Vanderbilt. Persons who expected a speedy return to the pre-Vanderbilt era were disappointed, because Chief Justice Weintraub asked Ed McConnell to remain and backed him fully; thus, by the 1960s, the authority of the state court administrative office had become institutionalized. Surviving this transition added additional stature to McConnell and made his ability to speak for the courts more difficult to challenge. Another reason for his stature was that the chief justices during his tenure remained in the background on some administrative issues, permitting him to express the mind of the court. This, of course, led to some very strong attacks upon him by persons opposed to court policy. Being the voice of the courts is not an unmixed blessing. High-profile administrators can become targets of those who are reluctant to attack the chief or the highest court. Some of these assaults can be very personal; for example, the 1996 demand of the Michigan legislature that the state court administrator resign. It can also take the form of cuts in the state court administrator's budget, as occurred in Pennsylvania during a period of particular acrimony between the legislature and the courts.

Hawaii, which is sometimes equated with New Jersey as a state with strong central authority in the chief, has at times exemplified the model where the chief's involvement is so great that it diminishes the authority of the state court administrator. In the late 1970s Chief Justice William Richardson personally directed the creation of an intermediate appellate court and did this with limited consultation with his colleagues; it was not necessary for him to delegate much authority because he was so directly involved. Alabama, in the era of Chief Justice Howell Heflin, provides another example of a chief who was so deeply engaged in programmatic reforms that his state court administrator was not perceived as a major player.

Interestingly, it is quite possible for a court administrator to acquire a strong personal position even in a court system marked by relatively collegial, frequently shifting leadership. In Alaska, Art Snowden, by dint of service from the early days of state court administration, achieved a very strong personal position in state government, providing an ongoing and familiar institutional presence for the courts. It is noteworthy that both Hawaii and Alaska started their system of court administration shortly after achieving statehood and did not have to overcome the legacy of complex localism that was common elsewhere in the United States.

Quite the reverse of the more recently admitted states are those states in the East that have judicial institutions dating back to colonial times. Delaware, for example, did not have a supreme court until 1951. Before 1951, trial court judges not involved in the decision being appealed served as appellate judges. Thus, when a supreme court was finally created, it had to defer to trial courts that dated back to the early days of Delaware by operating through an administrative board that included the chief trial court judges and the chief justice. This administrative board made policy without much reference to the state court administrator, who for years did not attend the board's meetings. In fact, the office of court administration had no defined duties until the early 1990s, when there was a definition of duties that followed the ABA Standards but did not really reflect the actual functions of the office.

Sometimes, a court administrator achieves special status stemming from perceived political influence or a reputation for political acumen. In Rhode Island, for example, the state court administrator, a former legislator, was a central figure in bringing about the resignation of a chief whose conduct had become a scandal in the late 1980s. This unique role arose from the administrator's great personal prestige in the Rhode Island system of government and politics.

There was a time when reformers in Massachusetts considered the pros and cons of having the state court administrator elected on the theory that without this type of mandate the office would have limited authority and prestige. Realistically, a state court administrator is not likely to achieve a power base independent of the court.

How Are State Court Offices Organized to Perform Their Functions? A state court administrator's authority is determined not only by delegation but by the scope of functions in his or her office. Some courts define the functional scope of their administrative office very narrowly even though they may broadly delegate authority to perform these particular functions.

Most state court administrative offices are adjacent to the supreme court in the state capital, but there are interesting exceptions to the norm. The California Supreme Court sits in San Francisco, rather than Sacramento, and the Louisiana Supreme Court in New Orleans, rather than Baton Rouge. In some states, the state administrative office is divided between two locations: Chicago and Springfield in Illinois; New York City and Albany in New York; and Philadelphia and Mechanicsburg (near Harrisburg) in Pennsylvania. The Pennsylvania court administrator sits in Philadelphia, rather than the state capital.

When state court administrative offices are split geographically, it usually leads to creation of a position of deputy state court administrator. New York, because of its size, has three deputies, two of them heading regional components of the system, but a number of state court administrative offices are too small to warrant a deputy. Some administrators, as a matter of philosophy, do not like the idea of creating an alter ego or heir apparent, feeling that it makes them expendable. Moreover, many court administrators do not like having their managers report to the deputy, feeling that it cuts them off and causes rivalries. However, a few court administrators prefer the "inside and outside" approach whereby the deputy is the manager of operations and the court administrator deals with the supreme court, intergovernmental relations, and the various court constituencies. Generally speaking, the court administrator and deputy work out a modus vivendi that permits the deputy to handle selected assignments, rather than be a barrier between the court administrator and his or her top managers. People in the courts generally sense what matters to take to the deputy, particularly where the court administrator is not easily accessible. The term deputy court administrator has no intrinsic meaning.

The internal organization and resource allocation of a state court administrative office are pretty accurate indicators of the depth and scope of the functions assigned to the office. The number of functions performed in state court administrative offices is lengthy, but they tend to fall into seven categories: external relations, superintendence and education, legal services and secretariat, administrative services, information services and report generation, trial court services, and planning, research, and miscellaneous projects. Some state court administrative offices are also involved in judicial performance evaluation, a very touchy subject that requires the protective mantle of judicial branch leaders.[4]

State court administrative offices often provide the principal liaison between the judicial branch and the legislative and executive branches of state government and generally have offices of intergovernmental relations. Where the highest state court is particularly concerned about interbranch relations, they

---

[4]   E.g., Alaska, Arizona, Colorado, Connecticut, and New Jersey.

may choose a state court administrator who has been employed by one of the other branches of state government. In addition, state court administrative offices maintain liaison with bar associations, associations of local government officials, and associations of court-related officials (elected clerks, defenders, and prosecutors).

Dealing with the media on court matters is another function of state court administrative offices. Most state court administrative offices have public information officers. Public education also falls into the realm of external relations and includes preparation of written materials explaining court organization and functions, orientation films for jurors, visits by judges and attorneys to educational institutions or civic associations, and preparation of annual reports.

State court administrative offices assist state supreme courts in overseeing judicial discipline, attorney admissions, attorney discipline, and continuing legal education for attorneys. The scope of this oversight varies by state but has the potential for a lot of tension with judges and attorneys if the highest court appears to be too stringent in disciplinary matters.

Judicial education is often a responsibility of the administrative office of courts, but some states have a separate judicial college that is largely independent. The education function can be important in maintaining good relationships with judges. A corollary of this role is training for nonjudicial personnel, which is a very major responsibility in some states.

State court administrative offices often have heavy legal responsibilities, including providing legal assistance to supreme court committees engaged in administrative and procedural rulemaking, writing summaries of opinions and legislation for judges, managing litigation involving the courts or judges (e.g., collective bargaining or personnel matters), writing advisory opinions on matters that do not involve specific cases being adjudicated in the courts, drafting legislation, and providing secretariat functions for judicial councils or conferences that recommend rules or legislation. In court systems where rulemaking has played a very large part in trial court superintendence, the legal role has been one of the major functions of the state court administrative office.

Every administrative office has some basic bread-and-butter functions common to all government agencies: budgeting, purchasing, inventory, appropriations and revenue accounting, accounts receivable, vouchers processing, personnel management, collective bargaining, and both financial and performance auditing. Internal auditing was sparked by unification, which increased supreme court responsibility for the money flow in courts and for the performance of courts generally. In state-financed systems, the number of transactions increases enormously and, thus, the size of the administrative staff increases commensurably. Some state court systems decentralize administration by delegation to trial court administrators.

State court administrative offices, in addition to the normal automation associated with office operation and management, frequently become the hub of a computerized information network for the court system or some part thereof. Such systems may include applications that support docketing and the daily functions of a trial court. The importance of information technology to courts has become so great that future state court administrators will have to have more technical skills than their predecessors. In 1998 Delaware selected as its court administrator the director of the court technology unit of the National Center for State Courts.

The administrative office of courts is expected to produce management information (e.g., time-to-disposition information) and caseload statistics. The reliability and currency of these statistics is a frequent problem, particularly where they are used to justify the assignment of judges and requests for new judges. It has been hard for court leaders to think of statistics as internal management tools that require accuracy, rather than as self-serving numbers to be waved at legislators.

Many state court administrative offices, particularly those in state-financed systems, provide a number of services to trial courts. Among these are providing technical assistance or specialized information, administering pilot projects for trial courts, administering state or federal grant programs to aid trial courts, helping trial courts obtain grants, and generally working with trial courts to institute improvement programs. Some state court administrative offices have no trial court services unit because the offices have little or no contact with trial courts.

As state court administrative offices have become more sophisticated, they have been able to provide specialized consulting in areas where trial courts lack expertise. Thus, state court administrators may have court architects to help on facility issues, caseflow management experts to help courts improve the disposition of cases, or personnel experts who can respond to queries in some of the more arcane areas of human resources management.

One service, long performed by most state court administrative offices, is the transfer and assignment of judges between courts. This function is normally fairly ministerial if the judges are rotated routinely from one court to another, as they are, for example, in the North Carolina Superior Court and the Rhode Island District Court. A similar situation exists in Illinois and New York, where trial judges outside the major metropolitan areas are regularly assigned to Cook County and New York City. In more discretionary assignments, such as a short-term infusion of judges into a backlogged court, the state court administrator may occasionally have significant power, even though a supreme court order may be required to bring about the judicial assignment.

One of the most underdeveloped aspects of court administration is planning and research. When federal grant money flowed freely to courts, many courts had planners who were largely federal grant experts able to cast court needs in the required federal planning jargon. Planning fell on hard times after the demise of the Law Enforcement Assistance Administration, but this functional area remains important and is a major differentiating factor in comparing state court administrative offices. State court administrative offices vary greatly in how much time they spend analyzing court operations and doing research. Typically, if the court has some ongoing or ad hoc group to study courts and their needs (e.g., a judicial council), the administrative office of courts assigns research and planning personnel to serve such entities. Very often, when a state legislature saddles the supreme court with administration of some discrete program that requires a court overseer or a conduit for grant funds, the planning unit, if such exists, becomes the repository for the program, because it does not fit elsewhere in the court organizational structure.

The resource allocation within a state court administrative office is the best objective indicator of the functions and priorities of the office. A quick perusal of resource allocation gives a picture of the office. Some are heavily skewed to legal services and information services; some are largely devoted to administrative services; some are heavily involved in trial court programs. Another factor in office organization is the large difference in the personnel resources within state court administrative offices. For example, New Jersey, a smaller state than Pennsylvania, has an administrative office of courts roughly four times as large as Pennsylvania's. By and large, state administrative offices of courts are not very large, most of them having less than one hundred employees and quite a few less than fifty. There are similarities but no paradigm.

What Is the Relationship of State Court Administrative Offices to Trial Courts? State court administrators are perceived by outsiders as presiding over the whole court system. In fact, they often are excluded from administering appellate courts and may, to a large extent, be excluded from trial court administration. Thus occurs the anomaly of a court administrative office with no direct involvement in the functioning of the state court system. Where this situation exists, the role of a state court administrative office encompasses only those functions extrinsic to the core functions of the courts.

Often, the attention of the state court administrator is directed toward interbranch relations, judicial education, rulemaking, legislation, and a variety of topics that transcend trial courts and have little to do with the day-to-day operations of the courts. Therefore, it not unusual for state administrative offices of courts to become remarkably detached from trial court operations. It is a truism of court administration that many employees of state court administrative offices have a very cursory knowledge of trial courts.

What ends the isolation of state court administrative offices from trial courts is the creation of a state-funded, unified court system administered at the supreme court level. Unification leads to increased use of administrative rulemaking to set policy for trial courts, unitary budgeting under the state budget process, a statewide personnel system, and, occasionally, supreme court selection of trial court presiding judges. This centralization of authority strengthens the position of state court administrators with respect to trial courts, the single biggest component of the judiciary. The size and importance of a state administrative office of courts is determined in large part by the degree to which the office is involved in trial court operations.

If the trial courts are state financed, the administrative office of courts is necessarily involved in certain aspects of trial court administration: administering the personnel system, budgeting, financial management, revenue accounting and controls, purchasing, inventory control, and, possibly, facilities. Some state-financed court systems decentralize these administrative functions in regional offices, Iowa, for example, but in general, state-financed systems require larger administrative staffs at the state level because of the increased administrative responsibilities. Budgeting alone involves the state administrative office of courts in the resource problems and operational needs of trial courts and gives the state court administrative office a strong position in relation to trial courts. It is, of course, possible for a state administrative office of courts to play an important role in trial court administration without state financing, as was the case in New Jersey before its trial court system became state financed in 1995. But as a general rule, state financing of trial courts is key to greater involvement of state court administrative offices in trial court administration.

Administrative rulemaking can, of course, take place in a system that is not unified, but the authority of the supreme court in enforcing these rules is greatly enhanced by having control of the trial court budget. The power of superintendence benefits from a financial hook. The key person in this budget process is generally the state court administrator, who will have some say in allocations and in presenting the judicial budget to state officials. This power is greater in a system where the trial court budget is centrally prepared, but it is also significant in states where the court budget is first developed at the trial court level and centrally reviewed. The state court administrative office also administers the personnel system and applies the supreme court policy. In short, once unification occurs, trial courts must look to the state court administrator for many decisions formerly made at the local level.

Some state court administrative offices are very program oriented and are, therefore, in constant contact with trial courts. The New Jersey AOC has large numbers of persons involved in implementing specific programs in trial courts and has for many years had organizational units that help trial courts with certain types of cases—specifically, criminal, civil, and family matters. Program initiatives might involve handling drug cases, centralizing preliminary hearings at one point in each county, or reducing court delay. In New Jersey and elsewhere, new pilot programs for trial courts are often initially administered by the state administrative office of courts; for example, bail programs and arbitration programs in Illinois. Where programs are funded by state or federal grants, the AOC may be the conduit for the funds and may also be responsible for overseeing the achievement of objectives that are conditions of the grant. State administrative offices of courts may oversee state reimbursement of probation officer salaries paid by counties, manage United States Department of Justice grants obtained from the state executive branch agency administering block grant programs, or be involved in the administration of the federal IV-D reimbursements for child support enforcement in trial courts (the New Jersey AOC serves as the conduit for IV-D funds).

State AOCs are also closely involved with trial courts in developing information networks. State AOCs have played an important role in developing case tracking, docketing, and related financial systems for trial courts. This undertaking does not require a high degree of administrative unification or state financing. Pennsylvania, for example, has established a statewide network for its courts of limited jurisdiction, even though these courts are locally funded. Washington, a state with a very limited degree of unification, has pioneered a statewide trial court information system.

State AOCs tend to think of their trial court outreach as a service. This is not always the perception of trial court administrators, who may regard the service as a form of control or interference. There is, therefore, a certain tension between state court administrators and trial court administrators. To some extent, this reflects the tension between trial courts and appellate courts. Trial judges often complain that they are second-guessed by appellate judges, who have limited trial experience and function in a quasi-academic environment remote from courtroom combat. Similarly, trial court administrators often regard the state court administrative office as a nuisance operation staffed by persons ignorant of the real world of trial courts. For their part, state court administrators tend to see trial court administrators as parochial, idiosyncratic, and narrowly focused on minor local concerns. These mutual criticisms are not universal and are almost institutional in nature; for the most part, they do not inhibit the generally high level of cooperation that exists between state and local offices of court administration.

A different problem is presented by major urban areas that have large offices of trial court administration in locally funded trial court systems. The trial court administrator in such a system may have more responsibility, a higher salary, and greater visibility than a state court administrator and may consider himself or herself to be more important than the state court administrator in the overall scheme of court administration. Thus, court administrators in major urban courts might consider it a step downward to become state court administrator. The state court administrator in California, one of the most highly paid state court administrators, makes less than the trial court administrator for the Los Angeles Municipal Court.

It is not unusual for a state court administrator to be effectively boxed out of any significant role in large metropolitan courts that tend to operate as independent entities. This may even apply to information systems. Some large metropolitan areas have their own computer system, which they feel to be superior to their state's system, so the state trial court network may not include some major population centers. In Maryland, some populous urban and suburban areas stayed out of the state court computer system.

Shutting out the state court administrator is normally a reflection of the power relationships between the trial court judiciary and the supreme court. Large metropolitan areas have many legislators, who will tend to side with trial judges from their district in any difference with the supreme court. There are many examples of trial court judges from urbanized areas thwarting supreme court objectives. To the extent that a state court administrator represents a threat to the autonomy of trial judges, he or she may be largely excluded from court administration in the large metropolitan areas of the state.

Trial court administrators generally answer to their chief judges and do not look to their state court administrator for directions, even though the state court administrator may take the view that he or she is the administrator-in-chief. Trial court administrators do not generally acknowledge such a relationship and tend to regard themselves as peers rather than subordinates. Even in states where the state court administrator has significant legal authority over trial court administrators (e.g., New Jersey), trial court administrators are chosen by and report to the chief judges of their courts, but may develop a somewhat schizophrenic outlook because of parallel demands made by the state court administrator. Some state court administrators feel that trial court administrators are increasingly independent of the state administrative offices of courts and perceive a trend toward localizing everything. Some state court administrators see this as a threat, but others see it as inevitable and probably beneficial.

The idea that state court administrative offices should have a dominant role stems from the historical fact that state court administration developed a little earlier than trial court administration. In some states, there was little in the way of trial court administration when the first state court administrative office was created. The major exception to this pattern occurred in states with large metropolitan courts that created trial court administrative offices before the creation of an office of state court administration. In California, for example, an office of trial court administration under Ed Gallas in the Los Angeles Superior Court predated the appointment of Ralph Kleps as the first state court administrator. Ed Gallas recalls that Ralph Kleps offered some suggestions on court operations in Los Angeles County and was told to mind his own business. Historically, this may the first test of power between a state court administrator and a trial court administrator.

More common than the California situation was the absolute dearth of a trial court administrative structure. In the less-populated, nonurban states, many functions were centralized in the state administrative office of the courts when state financing occurred because there were no administrative offices at the trial court level or, at best, an administrative office in one or two relatively urban counties. In the western plains area, trial court administration arrived late and in some states was instituted in a only a few urban areas; Nebraska, for example. Thus, it occurred that many administrative functions that might normally be performed at the local level were carried out at the state level. Centralization occurred less by design than by sheer necessity. The modern tendency is to delegate back to the local level when trial court administrative offices are created.

State court administrators and trial court administrators are still working out their relationship, but the incredible thing is that they even exist. As recently as 1960, few people would have envisioned the existence of a large and dynamic administrative network in courts, but court administration is here to stay. No contemporary supreme court would dream of not having a state court administrator, because state court administration has become an integral part of the judicial branch and a principal means to advance the administrative independence of the judiciary.

Chapter 9
Creation of an Administrative Infrastructure: The Trial Court Component

Trial court administration was slow to catch on but is now as firmly entrenched as state court administration and much more pervasive in its effects. What happens at the state level is important, but the ultimate test of court administration is the ability of trial courts to function justly, effectively, and efficiently.

Organizational Form of Trial Court Administration

The central figure in trial court administration is the judge charged with administrative responsibility for court operations. In a small court, each judge may be an independent administrative entity, but usually one judge is designated as the chief judge. This judge may be assisted by a trial court administrator if the size of the court warrants it. Aside from these generalities, there are few universal statements to make about the organization of trial court administration, because it reflects the variety of organizational forms within state and local government in the United States.

The most obvious variable is court size. Much of the United States is still served by judges in rural circuits encompassing several counties. Normally, judge-caseload ratios in rural areas are below the average for the state, so problems of delay and backlog may not be very pressing. The modern trend is to have at least three or four judges in even the smallest circuits so that there is some internal backup in the event of recusal, vacations, or illness. One of the circuit judges may serve as chief by election of fellow judges, rotation, seniority, or supreme court appointment, but the level of required administration may not be high, so the chief may carry a full load and not have a trial court administrator. In rural circuits where there is little opportunity for specialization, each judge handles a full range of cases. In this environment, the chief judge is not some remote authority figure but the first among equals. Individual judges have a high degree of administrative autonomy.

At the other end of the spectrum are huge metropolitan courts with hundreds of judges laboring in relative anonymity on specialized calendars and shifting at intervals from one subject matter division to another. There are a number of large urban and suburban courts with twenty-five to one hundred judges that share some of the characteristics of the very large metropolitan courts:

- management by a hierarchy of administrative judges under a chief judge, who is a full-time administrator somewhat removed from day-to-day court operations

- a number of subject matter areas or geographical units, each with its own administrative cadre

- a large trial court administrative office headed by a trial court administrator with significant authority and a public presence that dwarfs that of most judges

- a highly impersonal, noncollegial atmosphere

In between the rural and urban extremes are a variety of different administrative configurations. As courts grow in number of judges, there is a point when relatively low-key, collegial management gives way to a more bureaucratized system. It is not clear at what point this occurs, but signs of centralization invariably appear when a court reaches fifteen to twenty judges. Some would argue that this phenomenon occurs when a court has ten or more judges. In any event, one of the most difficult transitions in court administration is that from a collegial court to a court with much more concentrated management authority. The argument can be made that courts ought never to group judges in units above ten in number and that maximum accountability and productivity occur when there is a team ethos rather than an impersonal collective administration. It is in theory possible for a large, multijudge court to create a team environment and to organize support personnel around teams of judges, but this rarely happens.

Many courts do not have a trial court administrator or, for that matter, a chief judge. There are whole states, Arkansas and Mississippi, for example, where there is no tradition of presiding judges, much less trial court administrators. By comparison, some states place every state trial court in an administrative infrastructure (for example, Connecticut, Iowa, Maine, New Jersey, New York, and Pennsylvania). Thus, a trial court infrastructure built around one or more judges supported by a trial court administrative office is not a universal structural condition. Even existing infrastructures may have little in common, other than the basic functions common to any government entity, such as budgeting, personnel, and automation. In seeking information and ideas, chief judges and administrators seek contact with trial courts of similar size and structure, recognizing that there is no generic form of trial court administration.

Trial court administrative structure is also shaped by court organizational structure and jurisdiction. Organizationally unified trial court systems have characteristics not found in less-unified court systems. The major distinction between an organizationally unified system and a highly fragmented system is that the latter will either lack chief judges and trial court administrators or, more commonly, will have a patchwork system of trial court administration that exists in a few places and follows no particular pattern.

In states with very fragmented court organization (e.g., Georgia and Tennessee), you do not find a coherent statewide system of trial court administration. By contrast, a one-tier statewide trial court system lends itself to a compact and fairly uniform system of trial court administration, such as that in Iowa and Minnesota. A state with a one-tier court system does not always develop, however, a full-blown system of court administration. Illinois has a one-tier trial court system and a chief judge, but offices of court administration range from huge in Cook County to practically nonexistent in some downstate areas.

In two-tier trial courts, the chief judge of the higher court and his administrator can serve both court levels, but very often the lower-tier court has its own chief and, perhaps, its own administrator. Before adoption of a constitutional amendment permitting unification of superior and municipal courts in California, there were often a number of court administrative offices in the same county, one office for the superior court and a separate office for each municipal court.[1] The patent inefficiency of this practice caused the California legislature to enact legislation to facilitate the merger of administrative offices. Responding to this legislation, courts in some counties created a single office of court administration. This practice has become the norm in California because the great majority of courts have used the constitutional authority to unify.

Sooner or later, most states with a two-tier system consider adopting a form of vertical administration to reduce costs of administration and to coordinate the functions of both tiers of court. Maine adopted a vertical form of regional court administration to replace the use of administrators at each level. The state is divided into regions with a single administrator for all trial courts in each region.

There are states where the trial court administrator is in charge of a statewide tier of the trial court. This is true in Massachusetts, where both the superior court and the district court have a chief judge and administrator for the whole state, as well as some local administrators. The District Court of Maryland also has a chief judge and administrator exercising statewide authority over all district court locations. The statewide administrator is technically a trial court administrator but is in some ways like a state court administrator.

There are a variety of special jurisdiction courts, typically juvenile or family courts that have their own chief judge and administrator, but the most frequent form of special jurisdiction court is the ordinance court, typically a municipal court. Court reformers have grappled with the place of municipal courts in the unified system and never really solved the puzzle of how they fit into the scheme of trial court administration. States with unified court systems have treated municipal courts in a variety of ways: leaving them outside (e.g., Colorado and Kansas), having ordinance cases heard by state trial courts with the fines being remitted to the municipality (e.g., Illinois), or letting municipal courts choose between their own courts or state courts (e.g., Alabama).

The term *municipal court* is very confusing. In New Jersey, a municipal court handles ordinance violations and has a major role in handling criminal cases arising under state law. In Ohio and California, municipal courts serve as limited jurisdiction courts to handle civil and criminal matters arising under state law, as well as ordinance violations. However, a pure ordinance court does not get involved

---

[1]   California municipal courts handle state cases and constitute the limited jurisdiction tier of the state court system.

in procedural complexities and is essentially a traffic court. Municipal courts in cities like Phoenix, Seattle, and Houston are among the biggest courts in their states and have large offices of court administration. Municipal court administration is almost a separate profession.

Chief Judges

Trial court administration is directed by administrative judges bearing various titles, such as administrative judge, chief judge, or presiding judge. In any large court, the chief judge is assisted by a cadre of administrative judges, each in charge of a component of the court. In virtually every large trial court and in many smaller trial courts, a trial court administrator works with the chief judge. Commonly, there are other managers exercising responsibilities for various components of the court, such as the probation office or clerk's office. The trial court administrator may or may not have an overseer role with respect to these court managers, but, in any event, the chief judge-court administrator tandem is in most courts the heart of the trial court administrative system.

Chief judges often have the responsibility for assigning judges to some geographic or subject matter component of the court. This task is rarely pro forma and involves some difficult decisions about individual judges. The chief may have to take into account the skills, experience, and speed of judges to make the best use of their service. The recall of senior judges, the use of parajudicial officers, and choice of divisional administrative judges also are sensitive matters that may have to be handled by chief judges. The choices made in these various assignments have a great deal to do with the operational success of the court.

Although chief judges of trial courts are usually not involved in the formalities of judicial discipline, they may, in the interest of the court and public, have to intervene informally when a judge's health, work ethic, or behavior is causing a problem. The chief judge may decide, for example, to have other judges temporarily or partially assume the duties of a judge who cannot fulfill the role. One argument in favor of a master calendar is that a court can compensate for judges who cannot do the job but are not really disciplinary problems in the more extreme sense of the word. A court protects its own to preserve the image of the judiciary, if this can be done without sacrificing the effectiveness and efficiency of the court. Some trial courts have gone to great lengths to cover for an alcoholic judge. An occasional malady of trial judges is the condition of being "trial shy." Some judges simply reach the point where they cannot make themselves preside over a trial, because of the tension, the second-guessing, and the fear of failure and criticism. Dealing with such issues is an aspect of administration that may involve the privacy and rights of a judge, retirement issues (always a primary concern), and fairness to parties affected by the actions of a judge who may be having troubles.

Chief judges do not have direct control over admission, discipline, and continuing education for the bar, but are very much involved with attorneys in disciplinary matters. Trial courts are often a source of complaints about attorneys. Chief judges often become involved when judges impose sanctions on attorneys for failure to comply with rules or contumacious conduct. The chief judge is, in a sense, the ultimate protector of the court's dignity and authority in the face of challenging behavior.

Chief trial court judges usually have an important administrative role in personnel, budgeting, and facilities regardless of who funds their courts. Their personnel role is diminished somewhat in a state-funded system inasmuch as they have little to do with presenting the budget or forming personnel policy. They have the responsibility of complying with the budgetary guidelines and personnel policies emanating from the supreme court (or judicial council in some states). Nevertheless, budgeting and personnel management involves chief judges of trial courts at a level of detail not possible or desirable at the state level.

In dealing with other agencies of government, the chief judges' local role is very similar to that of the chief justice at the state level, but chief trial judges are more intensely involved with the everyday aspects of court administration. Some chief judges prefer a fairly detached role, but many feel it very important to be deeply involved in the community and are highly accessible to persons outside the judicial branch. Relations with local government officials and court-related agencies are crucial to court operations and necessarily involve the chief judge. Occasionally, a chief judge may find that relations with local appropriating bodies have deteriorated to the point where it is necessary to mandate appropriations for the court and to become involved in the strategy of litigation. Inherent powers conflicts are an unwelcome corollary of the chief judge's responsibility to see that the court has adequate resources.

A principal responsibility of an administrative judge is caseflow management. Because caseflow management is integral to adjudication, it requires substantial judicial leadership at all levels, even though there must be a support apparatus directed by an administrator acting under delegated responsibility from the court. The literature supports the idea that a crucial factor in successful caseflow management, perhaps the single most important factor, is the forceful leadership of a chief judge. Many chief judges evaluate themselves by the success of their courts in disposing of the matters placed before them.

Generally, the chief judge of a trial court is seen as an august figure. Persons external to the court and court employees may perceive him or her as powerful. This, of course, may be true where the traditions of the court support the idea of a strong chief, where the legal definition of the chief's authority is clear and broad, and where the political ethos of the community enhances authority of the chief.[2] Where the selection of the chief is by the supreme court or another appointing authority outside the court, the chief judge is much freer to pursue management objectives without establishing a total consensus and thus enjoys enhanced authority.[3] Sometimes, the supreme court or the chief justice will elevate a relatively junior judge to the position of chief judge, an event unlikely to occur if the

---

[2]   The political aspects can be very important in courts where the chief judge is seen as dispenser of court positions and judicial assignments to the politically faithful.

[3]   Presiding judges are chosen by the supreme court in Vermont and Kansas; by the chief justice in Maine, South Dakota, and Oregon; by the chief justice with supreme court approval in Iowa; by

court itself is making the choice. In such situations, senior judges may be a bit resentful, feeling that they have been slighted and that the new chief judge is primarily answerable to external power centers. It should be added that chief judges selected by an external appointing authority do not receive carte blanche to run roughshod over the other members of their courts and do not usually assume a management style markedly different from chief judges chosen by their peers. Deference to fellow judges is particularly prudent in courts where all the judges are elected, and even the most junior judge can rightfully assert that he or she answers to the people directly and is an independent force.

The perception of power is often misleading. The chief judge may not have the authority attributed to him or her and may be a figurehead held on a tight leash by fellow judges. There may be factions or an established hierarchy of senior judges who exercise the real power in the court. Some courts are divided along political lines, even to the point where different parts of the court system are under control of different political parties. Some chief judges have a very narrow role, restricted to such matters as judicial assignments and calendar control. Chief judges have to make some delicate decisions on judicial assignments and must have an idea of the abilities and work habits of their peers. There are painful times when a chief judge must confront the poor demeanor, disabilities, or poor work habits of judges. This obligation is harder in a highly collegial court than it is in a more impersonal court. Many chief judges spend much of their time placating fellow judges and are reluctant to take any step that might produce some opposition.

In some courts, there is a regional chief judge and administrative judges at the county level, the role of the former being largely concerned with supra-county matters, such as transfers of judges and court reporters between counties, while the county administrative judge deals with the full court. The regional administrative judge is one step removed from day-to-day operations and may be no more than a figurehead.

Where a chief speaks out on a controversial issue, there is no guarantee of support from fellow judges. Where a chief judge gets too far in front of the court or does not reflect the court's views, the power of the chief may evaporate, because it is built largely on voluntary compliance. Often, an heir apparent is waiting in the wings, the next judge up on the rotation or selection process. People who have had the opportunity to attend en banc administrative meetings of trial courts can quickly pick up the power relationships and are sometimes surprised to see a chief judge overridden or shunted to one side. The public deference paid to a chief judge by peers does not always extend to private meetings.

Trial Court Administrators

The roles, pay levels, and skills of trial court administrators are so varied that it is sometimes hard to think of them as members of the same profession. The

the chief administrative officer in Connecticut (the state court administrator is a judge); and by the governor in Delaware and Rhode Island. It is no coincidence that these are all state-funded trial court systems.

salaries for court managers range from $30,000 per annum to well over $100,000 in some metropolitan courts. Court executives in large California counties have bigger salaries than the judges they serve. Salary variation is only to be expected because the level of management expertise required in a large court is far beyond the modest requirements of a very small court. The former is truly a chief executive officer. There are probably three different professional levels among trial court administrators: administrative assistants, middle-management types, and executives. Because of these gradations, there is no guaranteed upward mobility in the profession, because distinctly different skills are required at each level.

Court consultants are disappointed that so few trial court administrators achieve high stature in the eyes of judges, but this situation is not altogether surprising. At one time, judges used to appoint their secretaries as trial court administrators. It has taken years for the profession to gain status. This transition has been speeded by the certification and education of trial court administrators through the Institute for Court Management and professional associations, such as the National Association for Court Management. Despite the common certification process, the profession now contains a very diverse group of administrators.

There is a category of trial court administrators that might be called the "intruders." These are the court administrators who have very marginal roles carved out of local turf over the resistance of elected clerks and local government officials and with limited support from judges. These trial court administrators may be professionally competent but lack a clear mandate and are always operating in the cracks of the system or in new areas that no one else has claimed. These administrators have marginal positions and are politically vulnerable unless they have strong ties to the chief judge. Very often these ties do not exist.

There is a growing category of trial court administrators who could be termed the "technicians." With court technology becoming increasingly complex, some courts are seeking trial court administrators with technical expertise as their primary qualification. These individuals may not have many management responsibilities, which allows them to concentrate on their area of expertise. Judges generally recognize that they are not competent to manage technology and technological development and are more likely to delegate in this area than they are in areas where they feel more comfortable; caseflow management, for example.

There is a category of trial court administrator that might be termed "high-level administrative assistants" with some largely routine responsibilities in personnel administration, purchasing, space problems, and budgeting, but a very small role in caseflow management or court programs and a low-profile role in interbranch relations. This situation is subject to change. It is not unusual for a trial court administrator to move in and out of caseflow management based upon the desire of each new chief judge to handle this function personally or to share authority. The reverse may be true. Before state financing of trial courts, trial court administrators in New Jersey were largely concerned with case management issues and various court programs. After state financing, they had to allocate much more of their time to budgeting and personnel matters.

Some trial court administrators qualify as the "strong manager" type. By definition, this person has a broad and clear definition of authority from the chief judge and the trial court and is invested with the power to execute court policy in administrative matters, to handle a large part of interbranch relations and public relations, and to play an important role in caseflow management and various court improvement programs. This role entails at least a limited partnership with the chief judge so that the position of trial court administrator is elevated above the level of administrative assistant. This role can only exist in a court where the trial court structure is administratively coherent and the trial court administrator is truly the chief administrative officer for the whole court.

Court managers known as "entrepreneurs" are not wedded to traditional bureaucratic methods and are more inclined to "wheel and deal" and to think of faster and cheaper ways to accomplish objectives. These individuals are invaluable in times of limited resources because they can find odd pots of money and free services, form budget coalitions, and drive hard bargains. Judges, conscious of the dignity of the court, are not generally enthusiastic about entrepreneurs who place a premium on innovative and adventurous management. This feeling derives in part from the perceived unseemliness of such a style and, perhaps, from reluctance to let court managers do what it might seem inappropriate for a judge to do.

Finally, there is the "fixture," the type of administrator whose longevity gives him or her a special security and respect. Trial court administration has only been around a short time, so few persons fit this category. In a court where the chief judge position shifts frequently, an experienced trial court administrator who has survived several chief judges can become the rock of stability and the resident institutional memory. This longevity increases the stature of the trial court administrator, making it increasingly difficult for an incoming chief to dismiss the administrator, minimize the position, or convince the full court that the administrator must go, because no can imagine the court without the incumbent administrator.

Judge and Administrator Relationships in the Performance of Administrative Functions

The manner in which a particular court handles its administrative responsibilities is determined by how many duties the chief judge delegates to the administrator. Some judges totally immerse themselves in details and eclipse their administrators, and others delegate some functions. Others go so far as to form an executive partnership, but this is rare. A trial court reaches its administrative apogee when the judge and the administrator constitute a team and the court, rather than an executive branch agency or an elected local official, has control of functions that are central to court administration.

Most administrative functions can be delegated to an administrator, the exception being the decisions and pronouncements that directly affect judges. These must be done in the name of the chief judge and include calendar assignments, determination of vacation schedules and backup procedures, judicial discipline, room and parking space assignments, and any other matters where it would be awkward and inappropriate for a trial court administrator to be involved.

The chief judge handles liaison with his peers in administrative matters, so trial court administrators may have limited contact with the full court even if they are selected by and serve at the pleasure of the full court. In large courts, administrators may deal with committees of judges or administrative judges for divisions of the court, but in general, they rely on the chief judge as an intermediary. Both the chief judge and trial court administrator have to retain the goodwill and support of trial judges and fulfill the judges' administrative expectations. Sometimes, disagreements between the chief judge and his or her colleagues can lead to dismissal of the trial court administrator, who is offered as a sacrifice.

The first trial court administrators were delegated very few responsibilities and had to fight their way into the system over the objection of judges. One senior trial court administrator recalled that when he was hired, the judges of his court would not dream of inviting him to their en banc meetings on administrative matters. He kept after the chief judge and was finally permitted to come and make a report, for which he was given ten minutes. One day, the judges asked him to stay on longer, because they were going to discuss the issues he raised. After awhile, the judges got used to him and thought he was helpful, so they decided that he should attend their administrative meetings. One judge thought this was outrageous and said he would not attend a meeting with the administrator present, but he had no backers. The trial court administrator then became a regular at the meetings. It took years to achieve this status by which time the administrator had been around longer than most of the judges and provided, among other things, the institutional memory.

Because the scope of trial court administration and the degree of delegation vary, administrative functions have to be viewed almost one by one. A key function is budget preparation, which is normally delegated to an administrator, who may in turn delegate to a budget officer.

Many people assume that a trial court is a coherent administrative entity that submits a single budget prepared by the trial court administrator under the direction of the chief judge and the court. This may be true in a few places, particularly if the trial courts are financed from the state general fund and permitted to develop a budget. Quite often, however, clerks, probation offices, and various other court-related agencies have separate budgets, so the chief judge may do no more than forward all the separate budgets for the trial court system.[4] Sometimes, the court-related agencies directly submit their budgets to the appropriating body. Complicating the picture is that court budgets may be submitted to the state for some items of expenditures and to the county for others.

Sometimes, a chief judge and trial court administrator will prepare a budget restricted to the direct expenses of judges and the expenses of the court administrative office. Historically, this occurred because trial court administrators had no established place in the overall court structure and carved out very small roles for

---

[4]   The most common example of budgetary independence is the budget of an elected clerk. In Virginia, the clerk is not only independent but actually budgets for the court. The power of Virginia clerks has clearly inhibited the development of trial court administration throughout the whole state.

themselves. Under state financing, trial court administrators normally become state employees and end up with the responsibility for preparing a court budget request to the state on behalf of all the state-financed functions of the trial courts.

An indicator of the relationship between the chief judge and the adminis-trator is budget presentation. The chief judge may make a ceremonial appear-ance and turn over the presentation to the administrator, turn over all budget mat-ters to the administrator, make the presentation but refer questions to the admin-istrator or court budget officer, or simply do it all. Appropriating bodies expect a symbolic judicial appearance but generally prefer dealing with court managers, who are more conversant with procedures and details and less likely to be impe-rious. Moreover, court managers have probably been in communication with the other branches before the presentation, which is often a public confirmation of arrangements made in advance.

Normally, trial court administrators and judges are united on asserting the position of the judiciary in budgetary matters, but there are instances when trial court administrators have resigned rather than pursue a confrontational course. This typically arises when a trial court administrator has established close work-ing relationships with officials in the other branches and is overridden by a new chief judge who feels the court should be more aggressive in dealing with appro-priating bodies.

Probably, the most precarious role of an administrator is serving the needs of individual judges. These needs may concern personal computers, furniture, books, maintenance problems in their offices or courtrooms, personnel problems, problems with court-related agencies, scheduling problems, or security prob-lems. Some of the requests from judges are bizarre; for example, an urgent request from a judge to find out if he was covered by workers compensation for the collapse of his seat in court. Judges may also depend on the administrative office and the chief judge to oversee and provide staff support for judicial educa-tion, judicial conferences, and meetings of administrative committees of judges. The list is infinite.

Some chief judges and administrators feel these requests from judges to be a nuisance, particularly if these requests involve some petty problem, but more commonly, they are very careful to respond to judges' requests, however minor, and give them high priority. Even though the ultimate test of credibility for the chief judge and administrator is the budget and the resources made available to judges, budgetary successes may not atone for consistent neglect of day-to-day judicial concerns, particularly parking.

It has always been a standing joke in the court community that more trial court administrators lose their jobs over the assignment of judicial parking spaces than for any other reason. This is not just a legend. Anyone familiar with courts has seen examples of the parking priority. Once in a downstate Illinois court, a frantic public address announcement called for the owner of a particular vehicle to report to the sheriff immediately. Deputies roamed the halls quizzing every-body on their knowledge of the car until the owner was apprehended, marched off surrounded by deputies, taken to his car, issued a summons, and then ordered in disgrace from the parking lot. The misdeed—parking in a judge's space. At a national conference of court administrators, a training video focused on the handling of parking spaces for judges and ended with the judge (played by a prominent trial court administrator) firing the hapless administrator.

A more recent priority is the physical security of judges, a task that often falls to law enforcement officials but generally involves trial court administrators, as well. Rural courts throughout the United States, once thought to be beyond the violence zone, now feature security checkpoints. Prisoner security is a concern in courthouse construction and is closely related to the security of judges. Many judges have tales of security lapses. A trial judge in Providence, Rhode Island, told the tale of a prisoner escape from court, even though the court was awash in sheriff's deputies and police officers. A defendant who was a police informer and addict suddenly realized that the police were no longer protecting him and fled in desperation rather than go to certain destruction in the local correctional facility. He was apprehended a long distance from the court after having outrun a posse of overweight deputies, who were not very zealous in pursuit. The judge remarked that she had noticed one deputy moving out of her sight to the right as the defendant started his flight to the left.

Chief judges often rely on the trial court administrator to be a troubleshooter, because trial courts can be dynamic and a bit wild. A courthouse in the full throes of a busy court day can be a scene of frenetic activity and hourly emergencies. These problems are often referred to the chief judge or trial court administrator. A major breakdown in court operations or case scheduling can be embarrassing and frustrating, so each day presents a new administrative challenge to keep things moving along without major fiascoes.

Some days the emergency events can seem incessant—missing court reporters, inadequate number of jurors, missing files, breakdowns in sound systems, or leaks in the roof. Other days are calm, but deceptively so. Trial court administration, at least that part of it concerned with day-to-day operations, is rarely without unexpected challenges. However, trial court administrators in a number of courts have very little to do with day-to-day court operations and deal mainly with the routine and impersonal aspects of public administration. In such courts, problems are referred to chief judges, clerks, or other high-ranking court officials. The solution of these emergency problems is very important to trial judges, but handling the diverse problems of a trial court is an art, not a science.

Many trial court administrators concern themselves with bread-and-butter functions common to most administrative offices of government: budgeting, personnel management, financial management, purchasing, contracting, inventory, facility and space management, and management of the office of trial court administration itself. Some trial court administrative offices have large staffs devoted to financial and personnel administration, but many still do not. Traditionally, courts relied on executive branch agencies to perform many of these administrative functions, particularly in locally financed court systems. Elected clerks still often control revenue collection and cash accounting.

The relationship between trial court administrators and elected clerks is one of the sensitive issues of trial court administration that cannot be treated in textbooks. Clerks are often unfairly characterized as unprofessional politicos in contrast to more highly trained trial court administrators, but many clerks are very capable and have the experience, legal knowledge, and "street smarts" to run a good office.[5] Under the unification, more clerks have become appointed civil service employees and, thus, more likely to come under the supervision of trial court administrators, but the great majority of clerks are still relatively autonomous constitutional officers. They may overshadow a trial court administrator who has a limited role, or they may be very cooperative. The clerk-administrator relationship remains one of the unresolved administrative issues and leads to occasional rifts, particularly in matters of personnel and data processing.

Personnel issues have a great potential for creating a rift between trial court administrators and judges. There are touchy situations where a trial court administrator is in the position of trying to restrain judicial personnel decisions that may not accord with current personnel laws, collective bargaining agreements, and prevailing personnel policy.[6] Judges, long used to special prerogatives in choosing and terminating employees in close contact with them, have not always adapted well to modern personnel practices. For example, supreme court justices temporarily in charge of the Philadelphia trial courts under a supreme court order discharged a number of older employees without reference to prevailing federal law on discrimination, resulting in a number of lawsuits. Many trial court administrators report heated discussions with judges over the applicability of Fair Labor Standards and other labor laws to court employees.

Human resources management has become very complex because of many federal and state regulations. The Civil Rights Act of 1964 and many subsequent laws and regulations on discrimination have been followed by the Americans with Disabilities Act and the Occupational Safety and Health Standards Act. Laws against harassment in the workplace have created a whole new aspect of human resources administration. The list is lengthy, almost beyond the ability of a generalist administrator to master, requiring them to locate personnel gurus. They also have to educate judges.

In the highly politicized trial courts, a number of personnel issues arise that may place the administrator in the position of making personnel moves that suit local political objectives but are legally and ethically indefensible. The most common problem is the hiring of unqualified persons because they are referred by political leaders or are related to a judge. A personnel study in the Philadelphia Court of Common Pleas revealed that many personal employees of judges were compensated well beyond the standard for the particular job and that there were some other significant aberrations in pay scales. Judicial leaders permitted the court employees to vote on whether they wanted to accept the study; to no one's surprise, they rejected it.

---

[5]   Connecticut has traditionally required that its top tier of clerks be attorneys. The clerks in Connecticut are appointed, which makes this requirement possible.

[6]   In unionized court systems, the trial court administrator often becomes the chief management negotiator, because it is inappropriate for judges to serve as advocates of the management cause and judges of labor disputes.

In one southern court, where nepotism is a time-honored practice, a municipal court judge hired his brother as a reporter and hired a second reporter who could actually perform the function. This is obviously inappropriate but beyond the power of a trial court administrator to rectify. Actually, trial court administrators are often products of the local political culture and lively defenders of the prevailing ethos.

In the Civil District Court of Orleans Parish, Louisiana, the trial court administrator was dismissed for going to law enforcement authorities to report a dummy employee who was receiving checks and that court employees were being "loaned" to a state senator. In the same court, there were defalcations from a garnishment fund in the clerk's office. The trial court administrator consulted the chief judge before reporting the problems, but the full court voted to discipline the administrator by dismissal. The administrator subsequently sued those judges on the court who voted for his dismissal. The case was settled out of court without resolving the underlying issues, but this incident provides a somewhat flagrant example of what can happen when a trial court administrator has to challenge his or her court on an issue of legality in matters of financial and personnel management. What makes such confrontations unique is the inequality of the combatants, a court employee versus the judiciary.

There is an ongoing need for liaison with other branches of government, the media, the bar, court-related agencies, and the public. This may include legal confrontations on inherent powers issues and litigation management, which, if it occurs, can occupy a great deal of the time of a chief judge and court administrators, to say nothing of the strain on interbranch relations. Some courts have ongoing battles with appropriating bodies and executive branch officials, so administrators in such courts find that participation in this struggle is a major part of their role. The Essex County (New Jersey) Superior Court, in the days of county financing, always seemed to have one or more suits going against the county. A major function of the trial court administrator was managing litigation.

Any court engages in external relations to some degree, but some courts minimize external contact by assuming an aloof, somewhat defensive posture, whereas other courts have very active outreach programs. Trial court administrators usually reflect the attitude of the court. In the introverted courts, the chief judge tends to be a remote authority figure who asserts judicial independence forcefully rather than subtly and relies upon one-way communication rather than dialogue. The trial court administrator in such courts is inhibited from building close working relationships with noncourt agencies and officials and becomes the agent of the chief judge in fighting the outside world.

In an extroverted court trial court, the chief judge and designated judges spend a great deal of time working with citizen groups, government officials outside the judicial branch, and the heads of the various court-related agencies—bar associations, law enforcement agencies, health and welfare agencies, child protective agencies, prosecutor offices, public defender offices, probation offices, and the offices of elected clerks and sheriffs. Great effort is put into making the public aware of courts and making sure that members of the public are treated with respect and dignity. The trial court administrator in such courts is generally not a well-known public figure but is active in communicating with the staff and with the heads of various government agencies. The trial court administrator is recognized in the government and criminal justice community as a spokesperson for the courts.

Balancing the mundane and ad hoc aspects of court administration is the need to seek long-term improvement through identification of needs and implementation of programs to meet these needs; i.e., the planning process. The issuance of the *Trial Court Performance Standards* in 1994 provided a valuable frame of reference for determining needed areas of planning for improvement, but most trial courts do not engage in planning. The rare court that has a planning process is characterized by pilot programs testing some innovation or improvement. Such miscellaneous programs often end up under the aegis of a trial court administrator, because they do not fit neatly into the existing organizational and budgetary structure. These programs may include bail agencies, special treatment for domestic violence, alternative dispute resolution, court interpretation, assistance to pro se litigants, and a variety of other programs that are essential to the continuing improvement and modernization of trial courts.

Trial courts are swamped with paper and information and constitute a natural constituency for computerization. Trial courts were somewhat slow in climbing on the technology bandwagon but eventually grasped the importance of technology to judicial independence, court management, interagency relationships, and efficiency. Caseflow management, with its sophisticated information needs, was a major catalyst in sparking computerization in the courts.

In the early days of computer development, when centralized mainframe systems were in vogue, most courts depended on the executive branch of local government to supply whatever computer services trial courts required. Often, court applications did not command much priority, so courts increasingly sought to develop dedicated systems under court control. The rise of personal computers and more decentralized systems facilitated this move toward independence in computer use and development. Quite commonly now, courts have computer systems under control of the judicial branch. Sometimes, the system is a statewide judicial branch information system that serves trial courts through the state administrative office of courts. Sometimes, the system is a local system under control of the trial court judiciary. Almost inevitably this function is assigned to the trial court administrator.

Efficiency was another concern driving computerization and other forms of technology development. Use of sound recording and computer-aided transcription in lieu of traditional court reporting was controversial, sometimes pitting court administrators against court reporters and those judges who were very comfortable with the stenographic method. Courts were placed under pressure by appropriating bodies to deal with their labor-intensive systems and to modernize, further heightening the demand for technological advancement. Technological expertise is of such prime importance to courts that it is increasingly viewed as a major component of trial court administration and a necessity in building management credibility with the other branches.

Caseflow Management:
The Quintessential Trial Court Administrative Function

Two aspects of trial court administration are unique: jury management and caseflow management. The mutual interest of judges and trial court administrators in these two areas provided a basis for joint efforts to improve the courts and to win confidence for the embryonic profession of court administration. Because jury management was often under the control of a clerk or jury commission, trial court administrators used caseflow management as the main vehicle for establishing the profession. Caseflow management concerns the scheduling of cases, the deployment of judicial resources, and the development and implementation of procedures for processing cases through a court until the point of disposition.

Caseflow management appeared as a major aspect of trial court and appellate court administration in the late 1970s, when court literature identified court delay as the key issue of trial court administration and created a broad interest in procedures for the expeditious disposition of cases.[7] The term *caseflow management* apparently originated in a study of the District of Columbia courts about a decade earlier. Maureen Solomon, a member of the study team and a leader in developing caseflow management, attributes the idea of strong judicial control over case scheduling to Ed Gallas, the first trial court administrator.

The very nature of caseflow management brought judges and court administrators into close working relationships in adjudication of cases, the central mission of any court system. This development led to new job classifications related to case management; great advances in information systems for docketing, case differentiation and scheduling; better use of judicial time; and a variety of changes in the rules of criminal and civil procedure. Caseflow management made the concept of an executive partnership between the chief judge and court administrator a more likely possibility and enhanced the prestige of trial court administration.

Analysis of court delay revealed many causes—haphazard scheduling, lenient continuance policies, lack of judicial accountability for case disposition, inadequate information on case status and time to disposition, and a variety of other causative factors. Transcending all these factors was a more fundamental cause—courts lacked control over their own process of case adjudication. Lawyers very often controlled the civil and domestic relations calendars; prosecutors controlled criminal calendars; elected clerks, elected sheriffs, probation offices, and law enforcement agencies affected case processing in many ways that

---

[7] Concern with delay and the necessity for court management started appearing regularly in the literature from about 1978 onward. Some of the initial works were Thomas Church et al., *Justice Delayed: The Pace of Litigation in Urban Trial Courts* (Williamsburg, VA: National Center for State Courts, 1978); Ernest C. Friesen, Maurice Geiger, Joseph Jordan, and Alfred Sulmonetti, "Justice in Felony Courts: A Prescription to Control Delay," 2 (1979) *Whittier Law Review* 7; Larry Sipes et al., *Managing to Reduce Delay* (Williamsburg, VA: National Center for State Courts, 1980). About ten years later the developments in caseflow management were described in Barry Mahoney et al., *Changing Times in Trial Courts* (Williamsburg, VA: National Center for State Courts, 1988).

were not subject, at least directly, to court control. To a large extent, caseflow management was a euphemism for assertion of judicial control over the process of dispute resolution. In the lexicon of the court administration scholars, courts had to change the "legal culture."

The elements of successful programs to overcome court delay and change legal cultures have been publicized.[8] Judges and court administrators have been sensitized to the lexicon and procedures of caseflow management in education sessions, by articles and books, and by actual experience in addressing the problems of court delay. The various aspects of caseflow management include time standards, early screening and disposition of cases, innovative calendaring techniques, alternative dispute resolution, supportive technology to track cases and develop management information, systems analysis to identify bottlenecks, procedural changes, enforcement of deadlines and stringent standards for continuances, forceful judicial leadership, ongoing communication with the various agencies and the bar, case differentiation, discovery controls, pretrial conferences, and a variety of other means of obtaining some control over the movement of cases through the courts. Underlying many of the changes introduced through caseflow management is the concept that courts have an obligation to parties that transcends the prerogatives of lawyers. Lawyers, though usually publicly supportive of caseflow management, often harbor deep reservations about its implicit challenge to bar control.

One means of establishing court control and court accountability to the public was the use of time standards. The American Bar Association has produced time standards for trial and appellate courts that were widely referenced but coexisted with various speedy trial laws and local standards. There are obvious constitutional reasons for speedy trial laws, but they pertain only to criminal cases, do not deal with the time between procedural events leading to disposition, and are not infrequently waived by defendants. Moreover, some exceed the national time standards set for criminal cases. Time standards provide a better management tool for moving cases and impose more discipline on courts, attorneys, and court-related agencies. Even though delay prevention is certainly not the only criterion of a good court system or a guarantor of substantive justice, it is measurable and reasonably visible to appropriating bodies and the general public. Caseflow management is built around time standards and is thus very crucial to the way courts are perceived and the way they are treated by the other branches. A court that cannot move cases is a court that lacks management credibility and is prone to interference from outside the judiciary.

One of the big contributions of caseflow management has been a more sophisticated differentiation among cases to identify various times tracks and levels of complexity. The traditional categories of cases—civil, small claims, traffic,

---

[8]   Very early in the development of caseflow management, the researchers identified key principles of successful delay reduction programs: individual responsibility, early court intervention, continuous judicial control, trial date certainty, and information to support case management. See Maureen Solomon and Barry Mahoney, *Toward Excellence in Caseflow Management* (Williamsburg, VA: National Center for State Courts, 1991).

misdemeanor, felony, juvenile, domestic relations, and probate—were too broad for caseflow management purposes. Criminal cases had to be sorted out according to more-detailed factors, among them: seriousness of the charges; likelihood of a plea based upon the defendant's history and the nature of the charges; possibility of diversion; case complexity in terms of parties, issues, and witnesses; drug involvement and search-and-seizure problems; and the jail status of the defendant. The main purpose was to identify likely pleas and to dispose of such cases quickly. Civil and family cases were divided along various tracks, some of them emergency situations (temporary restraining orders, protective orders); but most of them were divided along lines of complexity, amounts in issue, discovery needs, and required time to disposition. The effect of this analysis was almost immediately to encourage alternative dispute resolution for categories of cases that probably did not require the attention of a judge or even an attorney and that could be resolved quickly, cheaply, and fairly by some parajudicial official. For the cases in the other tracks, rules of procedure could be tailored to the needs of the particular category, and judicial manpower could be allocated more efficiently.

The many agencies that interacted with the trial courts were also affected by the emergence of caseflow management. Caseflow management lent great impetus to interagency-coordinating groups and placed judges in the position of coordinator-in-chief rather than the despot ruling by judicial fiat. The coordinating role required a lot of negotiation and consensus building, so judges emerged as the heads of a diverse system of support groups and agencies. In the criminal area, the relationships were pretty well-established, because judges were used to working with a loose coalition of prosecutors, defenders, law enforcement agencies, probation agencies, detention officials, bail agencies, jailers, and diversion programs. Coordination in the family area was more difficult because agencies dealing with health, shelter, social welfare, and child services approached their tasks with a very different view than judges. This led to some serious problems when the needs of children, as perceived by the social agencies, collided with the due process view of the court.

Judicial independence, which could have easily taken the form of a relatively aloof position in regard to court-related agencies, gave way to a more complex coordinative process in which caseflow management forced judges to take a more active role in solving problems. This was a realistic acceptance of the fact that many causes of court delay are beyond the power of a judge; for example, the volume of police activity, prosecutor-screening devices, the availability of drug-testing facilities, and efficient service of process by a sheriff. Even choices of attorney can cause problems over which courts have limited control. In New Jersey, for example, backlogs have resulted because the one or two companies that dominate medical malpractice insurance use only one or two attorneys.

The real problem in caseflow is a built-in inertia that must be continuously challenged, which is one reason why a strong chief judge is the most important element in a court delay program. It is unrealistic, however, to think that strong pressure can be continuously applied. Typically, courts have spates of activity when they move cases with unprecedented speed and then a period when the pace becomes more relaxed.

Most judges like to see the court functioning efficiently and effectively and support methods to improve caseflow, but there is a price to be paid—more pressure on judges. Caseflow management literature tends to come down on the side of individual judge calendars, which fix responsibility for case disposition by each judge and provide a basis for comparison of output among judges. Sometimes, these comparisons are quite unfair because the mix of cases assigned is rarely even in terms of the amount of time required to dispose of individual cases. Moreover, it may be difficult to shift cases quickly or to back up a judge when every judge is running an individual calendar. Many courts, particularly large courts, favor a master calendar or some mix of an individual judge and master calendar. The master calendar permits a chief judge or divisional administrative judge more latitude in assigning cases and making the best use of available judges. The truth is that some judges work much faster than others or are more adept at settling cases. Some judges may be inexperienced or prone to error, defects that can be ameliorated by an administrative judge in control of a master calendar system. Given these situations, it is not unusual or surprising that some tensions arise between administrative judges and trial judges. The more productive judges may feel that they are carrying too much of the workload. Some judges may feel that they are not being given their share of interesting judicial assignments or are being placed in a position where their "numbers" will look bad and cause a negative public reaction. Some judges may not like the idea of being a cog in a case-processing system and fail to cooperate with the administrative judge. Case management means more pressure on judges as well as attorneys.

Caseflow management has encouraged more innovative use of staff and more use of teams. Support of case management requires a lot of ingenuity, knowledge of the court and court procedures, knowledge of how litigating attorneys work, knowledge of individual attorneys and their styles (some are chronic settlers or procrastinators), analytical and statistical ability, and a thorough grasp of information technology and the intricacies of case tracking. Operating the system requires an ability to track individual cases and a level of technical sophistication that was not present in most courts even a decade ago.

New job classifications have emerged to reflect this phenomenon, the major ones being case manager and case coordinator, positions that are part of the chief judge's office, rather than that of a clerk of court. It is not uncommon in large courts to have a case coordinator in each major division and an overall case manager with a staff. The coordinators support a divisional administrative judge but are part of the larger support team that supports the chief judge. Many cases will never reach a judge and must be tracked to conclusion. Those cases that are dismissed, diverted, referred to an alternative form of dispute resolution, or settled with little or no court involvement constitute the bulk of the caseload. The judge handles those matters that bubble up to the top and absolutely require the action of a judge. The judge is not a solo act and requires a strong support team. Old practices die hard, but the technological revolution is changing the nature of court staffs and the relationship between judges and staff in the disposition of cases.

The team concept is evolving and can apply even in a master calendar situation where the teams are organized around case type rather than a judge.

The details of court administration are less important than the significance of its existence. There is now a well-established court administrative system at the state level and trial court level. The expansion at the trial court level has been nothing less than phenomenal, giving the judiciary a management infrastructure unknown and largely unanticipated at midcentury. Chief judges and trial court administrators have been the shock troops in the creation of a real judicial branch.

PART IV

The New Reform Phase

Chapter 10

The Old and New Agendas

The reform agenda of the twentieth century was conservative, firmly rooted in the legal-judicial culture, and very introverted. It stressed judicial independence as a defense against external domination. As essential as this phase of reform was, it was not an end it itself. It laid the basis for more serious reforms that could only be effected by a mature, self-confident judiciary. Such changes are starting to occur.

Even the modest twentieth-century reforms caused controversy. In retrospect, it is amazing that so much heat has been generated by a reform as mundane as unification. People rail against unification as if it were some anti-Jeffersonian conspiracy designed to crush out any trace of local autonomy and initiative, or they simply say that it hasn't worked. Proponents tend to equate it with good government and enlightenment, the type of thing that any progressive, decent person would embrace. It does not have to work, because it is intrinsically good. The critics are enjoying a resurgence, because unification, like any reform movement that has been around awhile, generates a countervailing force. The truth is that unification has never been as pernicious or as beneficial as the combatants would have us believe and has been applied quite pragmatically. The essential point is that unification has occurred on a large scale and probably had to occur to introduce some coherence into state court systems. It is a truism that you have to centralize in order to decentralize rationally. Whether unification is an imperfect instrument is not terribly important. It is an important historical reality.

Another reality is that unification was not a populist concept arising from the grass roots. It originated in the upper reaches of the legal profession and the judiciary with theoretical contributions from legal thinkers. Although court reformers received some voter support in instituting unification, the public has never warmed to unification as an ideal. The possible reasons for this relative indifference are that the public simply does not appreciate what the courts have accomplished or, more likely, that the reforms were largely in-house, structural adjustments that did not really affect the treatment of citizens by the courts or alter negative public perceptions of courts and lawyers.

A third reality is that the court reform movement reached its apogee almost simultaneously with a powerful public backlash against the whole legal system. There is a great irony in the parallel development of a vigorous court reform movement and a mounting public aversion to the legal culture shaping the court reform movement, but it is not surprising. The court reform movement and unification, as beneficial as they were in many regards, were introverted and reinforced the view that the judicial branch was a beleaguered fortress, defending its independence against various outside forces. Consequently, reformers only belatedly started to deal with the emerging social and technological trends that called for a more user-oriented, outward-looking judiciary.

Public dissatisfaction with courts and the legal system is so high that in 1998 every major court organization and the ABA made building public trust and confidence a priority issue. But the issue did not arise out of the blue. The first survey of public opinion about courts took place in 1978 and reported that the general public and community leaders were dissatisfied with the performance of courts and ranked courts lower than many other major American institutions.[1] Only 23 percent of the national sample of members of the public reported being extremely or very confident in their state and local courts.

The situation has not improved. Survey after survey reconfirms the negative public perception of the 1978 survey.

> A series of recent surveys at the state level report continuing problems. Only between 22 and 48 percent of the public has high confidence in the judicial system or thinks the judicial system is doing an excellent or good job. Several common themes that contribute to low levels of public trust emerged from the state surveys, including perceptions of case processing delay and backlog, racial and ethnic bias, income bias, and poor customer service.[2]

The public opinion surveys are pretty consistent in what they report about citizen concerns. These concerns are not restricted to issues of timeliness, fairness, courtesy, and lack of protection for society. The public is concerned about the integrity of the judicial process itself—its lack of accountability, poor methods of judicial selection and discipline, political intrusion, and the ability of attorneys to manipulate the court system. The public is also concerned about the barriers that decrease public access to courts and the justice system.

A number of citizen complaints focus on the need to be served and to be treated with respect.

- There is a perceived need for judges to be more involved with the people they serve and in problem solving, even if this means ending the near monopoly of lawyers on the time and attention of judges and changing the nature of the judicial role.

[1]   Yankelovich, Skelly and White, Inc., *The Public Image of Courts: Highlights of a National Survey of the General Public, Judges, Lawyers and Community Leaders* (Williamsburg, VA: National Center for State Courts, 1978).

[2]   David Rottman, Hillery S. Efkeman, and Pamela Casey, A *Guide to Court and Community Collaboration* (Williamsburg, VA: National Center for State Courts, 1998), 5.

- There is a perceived need for courts to reach out to the community and to involve citizens to a larger extent in the operations of the courts.

- Courts are being asked to be more innovative and flexible in handling cases in areas of high public concern, or that require specialized treatment and expertise.

- There is a demand for greater access to court information and for increased information sharing and networking.

- There is powerful push to make courts more performance oriented and more responsive to user needs.

- Courts are being asked to end their relative isolation and to form partnerships in the public and private sector.

Perhaps more threatening is public skepticism about the legal system itself. What judges and lawyers take for granted may seem absurd and unworkable to the average citizen. There is mounting evidence that the whole adversarial system is losing credibility, because it serves neither truth nor justice well and seems to favor the affluent and influential.

Judges and lawyers tend to attribute negative public views of the legal system to ignorance and to call for more intensive public education. The assumption is that if the public really understood the process, they would change their views. There is, of course, the possibility that the public perception is correct and that judges and lawyers should change their views. Although this possibility is conceded, the idea of systemic change almost always plays second fiddle to such programs as improving court-media relations, forming speaker bureaus to talk the public into submission, and instituting improved curricula in schools. These programs have some merit but, to some extent, miss the point. Citizen complaints stress the need for courts to end their absorption in the self-contained legal world, to play a more active and service-oriented role in the outside world, and to reexamine the whole adversarial system.

These complaints are being heard and are drawing courts out of a defensive shell. Until recently, the court reform movement concentrated on eliminating the organizational and administrative weaknesses of courts and on improving the behavior, training, and qualifications of judges. It is increasingly clear that the court community senses a change in the objectives of court reform and is laying the groundwork for different types of change. There is a natural progression from administrative improvements to more fundamental changes in the legal system. The specifics remain to be decided, but at least four general areas of change stand out:

- further modifying the adversarial system of justice
- adapting the role of judges to the expanded social responsibilities of courts
- creating the open and service-oriented court

- dealing with the specialized user needs and federally imposed specialization

Judicial leaders are defining a new vision of court reform. In the 1990s the Conference of Chief Justices addressed bias in courts, lack of professionalism among lawyers, and waning public confidence in courts. These are not issues of court reorganization and administration. They go respectively to the fairness of the judicial system, relationships between courts and lawyers, and the relationship of courts to the citizens. These issues symbolize the nature of the reform agenda that is now starting to address such fundamental matters as the integrity of the justice system, the integrity of the legal profession, and the role of judges in stemming the social pathologies of our era. The new reform era will profoundly affect the way courts deal with the outside world, particularly court relations with the community, court users, noncourt agencies, and the private sector. It will also alter the way state courts organize and proffer their services.

Courts, in their deliberate way, are redefining their objectives and taking on tougher problems. Fortunately, the state judiciary is now in a better position to address its fundamental problems than it was fifty years ago. The state judicial branch of government everywhere is more cohesive, professional, and self-confident. Moreover, state court systems have spawned a variety of professional organizations that are assuming more responsibility for systemic improvement. Foremost among these is the Conference of Chief Justices. There was a time when state judiciaries had little communication with and support from one another. Now, judicial leaders meet regularly, communicate even more regularly, and constitute a force for reform. It would be unrealistic to state that CCJ has been a powerful force for reform, but the potential is there. Chiefs look at what other chiefs are doing and are much more susceptible to external example and exhortation. The same could be said of organizations of court administrators. There is a support network for change that did not exist a few decades ago.

The new reform agenda has not been clearly articulated, but it exists in inchoate form and is already being partially implemented. The earlier reform agenda is by no means completed; each year, there are new attempts to increase state financing or to achieve a higher state of organizational or administrative unification. New and old reforms will run parallel to one another and occasionally conflict.

The new reform agenda will be less mechanistic and more diverse and challenging than the old agenda. If it is to be implemented, it will require judges to take on issues with which they may be a bit uncomfortable. Symbolic of the controversial issues confronting the state judiciary is the unhealthy condition of the legal profession. Leaders of the bench and bar are concerned but find this issue hard to deal with.

There are some lessons to be learned from the medical profession, which has been thrown into turmoil by failure to respond to public concerns about the trends in medical practice. The medical profession has literally imploded. Implosion occurs when a profession becomes so egocentric and so impervious to the needs of those it is supposedly helping that it collapses under the weight of its myopic avarice and invites external control. This is occurring in the medical profession because doctors, at some point, decided that a medical degree entitled them to a prodigious income and lost their ethical compass. A popular revolt ensued, and doctors are being herded into managed health care plans where they are salaried employees. People sought alternatives to expensive medical services by turning to acupuncture, chiropractors, and homeopathic and herbal treatments. One aspect of the revolt was the rise of the medical malpractice industry, which thrives on the increasing impersonalism of medical practice and the public perception that doctors do not care very much about their patients. Even medical schools decided that admission should be based on factors other than high grades in science, such as interest in actually helping someone. Doctors attempted to use the noble professional concept of the doctor-patient relationship to stave off external control but fell victim to the public skepticism that they had so abundantly fueled. The irony of this conflict between the medical profession and the American public is that American doctors have never been more skilled and better prepared. Technocracy does not substitute for the human dimension.

Hospitals, rough medical equivalents of courthouses, have turned into bureaucratic, money-driven organizations that have become indifferent to patients, who are a captive audience with few alternatives. Doctors receive some attention because of their stature, but patients have to fight for it. Patients seek information and participation but encounter the stone wall of the staff and the professional esoterica of the doctors. People exit from hospitals with very much the same attitude as persons who have gone through the adversarial process in court—"Never again!" If buildings can have souls, it is certain that hospitals and courthouses are among those buildings that lack them.

The revolt against the medical profession is being duplicated to some extent in the legal profession. Tort reform is only the opening salvo in a popular uprising against a profession that is overpopulated, arrogant about its prerogatives, too often shoddy and unethical, and frequently driven by monetary fantasies. The personal injury bar overreached itself so far in medical malpractice that it caused a counterrevolution. The public figured out that they were going to end up paying for the big awards through higher medical and insurance costs and that doctors were being forced into practicing expensive defensive medicine at the expense of their patients.

Lawyers have started suing one another for professional malpractice or routinely seeking new trials for criminal defendants on the grounds of inadequate representation. Defense lawyers in criminal cases are so routinely accused of incompetence upon appeal or postconviction review that they paper their files with protective material and file every motion in the book. They are every bit as cautious as doctors practicing defensive medicine are.

Another indication of decline in the legal culture is the rise in incivility among attorneys and in their relationships with courts and court users. This has prompted some courts to adopt standards for civility, which are basically pleas to be courteous. The D.C Bar *Voluntary Standards for Civility in Professional Conduct* apply to judges and include a large section on discovery, which is often the occasion for incivility. General Principle I of these rules captures their spirit.

1.   In carrying out our professional responsibilities, we will treat all participants in the legal process, including counsel and their staff, parties, witnesses, judges, and court personnel in a civil, professional, and courteous manner,
at all times and in all communications, whether oral or written. We will refrain
from acting upon or manifesting racial, gender, or other bias or prejudice
toward any participant in the legal process. We will treat all participants in
the legal process with respect.

It seems bizarre the court would have to issue specific standards for treating people with respect, but this is what the legal profession has come to. This
situation is not simply a matter of a coarsening of manners but a blow at the Rule
of Law that remains heavily dependent on the civility of attorneys and judges. In
commenting on the effect of the D. C. standards, Judge Noel Kramer of the D.C.
Superior Court observed:

> Based on my recent experience, I would say that the voluntary standards have
> not yet uniformly permeated the consciousness of the lawyers practicing in
> the District of Columbia. . . . One can't help but wonder if the lack of enthusi-
> asm for the practice of law found among large segments of the bar doesn't
> stem from this atmosphere of incivility.[3]

Lawyers, like doctors, trot out honored concepts to defend what they are
doing and how they are doing it. A standard defense of shoddy ethics and incivility is that vigorous advocacy is incompatible with standards that restrict a
lawyer's ability to advance the cause of a client. The lawyer-client relationship is
used to fend off assistance from judges or court personnel to clients who are
being poorly served by their attorneys. Due process is employed to justify spu-
rious suits, which, even if successful, would enrich lawyers at the expense of practically everybody else. The O. J. Simpson case, for all its excesses and aberrations, has become a symbol of a profession run amok and a justice system where
money talks and witnesses say whatever they think will help their side. Even
worse, the case is a symbol of a judicial profession that is a passive observer of
the adversarial process in its worst manifestations. Meanwhile, on the fringes of
the profession, thousands of attorneys scrap for survival under the not-too-vigi-
lant eye of the state judiciary. The medical profession has started the process of
limiting the number of doctors. Will the legal profession be far behind?

The public formed a very clear and negative perception of the medical profession but found their views ignored for a long time. The public perception of the
legal profession is every bit as unflattering. Enlightened bar leaders are quite
aware of these perceptions and have, to their credit, called upon their fellow attorneys to heed the warning signs. W. Seaborn Jones, 1998 president-elect of the
Association of State Bar Presidents and a prestigious Georgia attorney active in bar
reform programs for years, aptly summed up the state of the legal profession:

[3]   "Lawyers Roundtable: Civility in the legal Profession," 13:1 (1998) *The Washington Lawyer*, 35.

Too many of us striving for the private practice, big bucks from the legitimate legal work that needs to be done but is not out there in sufficient quantity to feed all of us who want to do it.

Too many of us are willing to take on worthless/less than legitimate legal business because there isn't enough good stuff to go around.

Too many of us for whom the practice of law is purely a business and not a profession, giving rise to the perception that many of us put our own interests before our clients.

Too few of us willing to do the low paying pro bono work that needs to be done.

Too few of us who are willing to take on matters for the middle class at rates which the middle class can afford.

Too much strain on lawyers to find enough work to do and then do it, often without adequate supervision.

Too many beginning lawyers practicing without any supervision and a decline in the quality of supervision received by beginning lawyers employed by experienced lawyers.

Too many of us who are willing to do whatever the client dictates for fear of losing that client.

Too much temptation to take on any type of legal work we can get, whether or not we are competent to do it.

An increasing amount of dishonest and unethical conduct brought on by all of the above.

A lax, slow-to-action, self-administered disciplinary system.

Too much unfortunate "We Will Get It All For You" advertising.

Too many bad lawyers on television and elsewhere which lead beginning lawyers to believe that a confrontational approach serves their clients best.

A decline in civility and professionalism among experienced lawyers who should know better.

Too much competition from non-legal entities (banks, insurance companies, "do-it-yourself" services), and more to come with improving computer technology.

Too little interest, time and energy being spent on analyzing our problems and correcting them.

Too much self-denial, retrenchment and reluctance to change the system in order to correct the problems which have developed.

Expect these problems to worsen, not improve, unless bar leaders who appreciate the seriousness of the situation undertake meaningful reforms.[4]

Seaborn Jones stresses the need for a mentoring system, because he has clearly defined the problems of the legal profession as cultural. Ethics courses in law school and CLE courses, as essential as they are, do not change a culture, but senior attorneys can and should pass on the traditions of the legal profession. This, ultimately, is how a culture is nurtured and sustained.

A big difference between the legal profession and the medical profession is that the former includes judges. Judges regulate the profession but are part of it. Judges have to be detached from lawyers but are dependent upon them. Judges are not, however, just a group of lawyers who have donned robes but honored members of the profession who have a special status that enables them to provide leadership if they choose to do so. They can play a major role in uplifting the profession, or they can watch it decline while they privately decry what they publicly ignore. Tinkering with the rules of ethics or requiring more courses in how to be ethical does not suffice. The problem goes deeper.

Judges in the late twentieth century showed leadership in building a stronger state judiciary. This was the easy part, because it did not mark a sharp break with legal tradition. Reforms were justified by such principles as separation of powers, judicial independence, and inherent powers, all of which emphasize the defense of judicial prerogatives. Unfortunately, concepts that were aimed at preserving the right of judges to adjudicate without coercion have been used to reinforce an essentially introverted, exclusionary culture. Lawyers, who operate under the protective mantle of the judiciary, are the principal beneficiaries of this insular culture.

It is obvious that the relationship of judges to lawyers is being tested. The institutional culture of the judiciary is fixated on the transcendental importance of attorneys, but lawyers, as important as they are to the functioning of the courts, are only one group of court users and a partially endangered species. Judges have obligations to the public and litigating parties that transcend professional bonding. It may be an exaggeration to say that judges have to choose between the people and the legal profession, but this is not far from the truth. Judges truthfully and almost invariably comment that most lawyers conduct themselves professionally, but the percentage of shoddy practitioners appears to be increasing. At first, this change was reflected in the off-the-record comments of many judges, but judges are now going public.

---

[4]   Extract from a letter of August 20, 1997, used with permission of writer.

At their 1996 annual meeting, the Conference of Chief Justices adopted a resolution expressing concern over the level of professionalism among attorneys. This resolution called for a study of lawyer conduct on a state-by-state basis and the development of a plan to help the judiciary to effectively deal with lawyer conduct and professionalism.[5] The plan is very broad in its scope, involving law schools, bar associations, appellate courts, and the role of individual judges. It addresses education, discipline, lawyer regulation and admission to practice, behavior in court, interstate cooperation, and public outreach. The plan shows that the upper judiciary recognizes that judges will have to either exercise stronger leadership to make the legal profession more accountable to clients and to judges or run the risk that legislatures will attempt to regulate the legal profession as they have the medical profession.

In the final analysis, the battle for the integrity of the legal profession will be won at the trial court level. Supreme courts may point the way, but trial court judges deal with the everyday reality of professional decadence and incompetence. The fortitude, dedication, and example of trial court judges will have a lot to do with the outcome of the battle to upgrade the legal profession, but they will need help from bar leaders.

Judges can view the problems of the legal profession more objectively than those of their own profession, even though the problems of the judiciary have been set forth in numerous studies and reports. The judiciary suffers from a lack of institutional humility. This is the single greatest obstacle to the achievement of the new agenda, because if you do not see yourself as you are, you stagnate.

Judges have great authority and, due to the tradition of judicial independence, more latitude in their actions than other public officials. They receive, quite properly, a lot of deference from those persons working for them and from people appearing before them. The high perch on the bench, the robe, and the various other accoutrements of position invest judges with prestige. It is fitting that they should have a special dignity as the dispensers of justice, but this can be a heady experience that clouds reality.

Judges quickly become isolated from social interactions and constraints that curb undue hubris in other professionals. They lack reality checks, except in the narrow and restricted world of appellate justice, and tend to kill messengers with bad tidings. If judicial independence means freedom from listening to anyone other than another judge, the price is too high. It is quite possible to have strength and dignity on the bench and still be open to legitimate criticism and fresh, even disturbing ideas. Many judges are quite open, but as an institution, the state judiciary is much too self-absorbed.

Organization theorists like to distinguish the self-correcting, self-aware organization[6] from the more traditional hierarchical authoritarian model. The judicial branch, directed by an authoritarian hierarchy and driven by rules, clear-

---

[5]   A *National Action Plan on Lawyer Conduct and Professionalism*, which was jointly published by the American Bar Association and the National Center for State Courts in 1999.

[6]   Called by some a "learning organization." See Peter M. Senge, *The Fifth Discipline: The Art and Practice of the Learning Organization* (New York: Currency Doubleday, 1990), 5.

ly falls in the latter category. In operational practice, this organizational form does not necessarily lead to strong centralized management at the state level or within a specific trial court. There is an underlying "do your own thing" philosophy rooted in the state judiciary, so the judicial branch has the defects of an authoritarian organization without the benefits of decisiveness and order, the worst of both worlds.

Like leaders of many organizations, judges have an unstated concept or model of how the judiciary should operate. They may not articulate it or even be consciously aware of it, but they instinctively adapt to it. A major element of self-awareness is recognizing an inchoate concept and starting to question assumptions. This is particularly crucial in courts and legal systems where mythology has great influence and the nonessential becomes frozen in perpetuity.

Courts are not exemplars of self-awareness and self-evaluation. Thus, when the *Trial Court Performance Standards* came out in 1994, the twenty-two standards and their sixty-eight related performance measures were hailed as the harbinger of a new era. For the first time, courts had some common criteria of performance that could be adapted to different court environments. The purpose of the national standards was to change the management culture of the courts by building self-awareness and ongoing self-assessment into court management.

Despite the overwhelmingly favorable reaction to the standards in the court community, they have not gained acceptance in actual practice. Few, if any, general jurisdiction trial courts have embraced the standards as an integral part of their management system. This is due in part to the highly structured, somewhat cumbersome packaging of the standards, but it also reflects the reluctance of courts to look closely at their performance, particularly in the core function of adjudication.

The standards and their supporting measurements were developed primarily for general jurisdiction courts with the idea that they would also have some applicability to limited jurisdiction courts. Ironically, the fullest implementation of the standards in the United States has occurred in a limited jurisdiction court, the Los Angeles Municipal Court. This is no ordinary municipal court. It is the largest court of its kind in the United States with about ninety judges and a budget in excess of $100,000,000 annually. It has a larger budget than some state court systems.

The Los Angeles Municipal Court took about five months to start the measurement of the standards and eighteen months to ascertain which of the sixty-eight measures were applicable. Some were not adopted because they did not pertain to a municipal court or were too cumbersome or not as good as measures that the court already had in place. By doing this total assessment, the court was able to decide the efficacy of the measures and make a preliminary assessment of court operations. Some interesting aspects of this process are noted below:

- The assessment included a technique that permitted Touch-Tone™ phone users to provide their perceptions of the court in response to a questionnaire. Various user surveys indicated dissatisfaction with the hours of the court and the methods of setting cases on the calendar—complaints that the judges took seriously.

- To measure the equality and fairness of the court's decisions and actions, attorneys were surveyed and samples of sentences and bail decisions were reviewed. An interesting result was that there was no evidence of discrimination by race, ethnicity, gender, or age.

- A survey of criminal cases revealed that only 60 percent of the defendants had paid the money ordered, leading to follow-up steps to improve this performance.[7]

- Surveys of appellate decisions in traffic cases were conducted to ascertain the reasons for reversal of decisions on traffic infractions.

- As a result of the data on security measures, almost immediate changes were effected in court security practices for weapons screening and access to internal hallways.

Based on experience gained in measurement, the court made a commitment to continue the self-assessment practice on a more selective basis, applying some measures on an ongoing basis and others periodically. The effort to deal with all the standards at once proved exhausting, but the standards have survived in a more feasible form and are being incorporated into the management of the court. This would not be considered a major management innovation outside the courts, but it stands out in the judicial world where self-evaluation is not part of the management ethos and is rarely practiced on a regular basis. But it is exactly this type of self-awareness and openness that is necessary to the success of the new reform agenda.

The great unknown for court leaders is the ultimate effect of telecommunications and computer technology on courts. So far, courts have used technology to automate certain functions but have not dealt with the fact that information is more than the contents of documents. The tasks and processes that make up the system are also a form of information. As information systems integrate all types of information and the court starts to become a self-aware, self-correcting system, there will be fundamental changes in time-honored court practices. Technology has proven a great force for cultural change and has transformed whole industries; banking, for example. Courts will be no exception, but no one clearly per-

---

[7]   A high percentage of convicted defendants in United States courts pay fines on an installment basis or a deferred lump-sum basis. Most courts do not have an automated accounts receivable system, forcing them to rely on surveys to judge their effectiveness in collection. Performance measurement identifies such gaps in the information system.

ceives exactly what form this cultural change will take. Technology will be a major, but somewhat unfathomable factor in the new reform agenda.

Fortunately, the court reform movement of the twentieth century brought the courts much closer to a modern management model. What might have seemed utopian in 1950 is a real possibility now. There are signs of fundamental change in the offing and greater judicial receptivity to public opinion. In short, the time is right for some risk taking based upon frank self-assessment. This does not portend spectacular and dramatic changes, because the judiciary approaches reform like a stately ocean liner altering its course. The course change of the liner does not attract much notice at first, but at some point everyone realizes that the direction and destination have changed. Courts are starting to move in the direction of the new agenda and are preparing to realize the bright promise of the earlier reform agenda.

Chapter 11

A New Look at the Adversarial Process

In *High Noon*, Gary Cooper is preparing to meet a group of desperadoes in a gunfight. Grace Kelly tries to dissuade him by pointing out that he has no one to help him, is outnumbered, is up against some of the best gunslingers in the West, and is endangering their life together. Gary observes that there are certain things a man just has to do. He then goes out to blow away the bad guys in what has to be the ultimate form of dispute resolution. The problem, as Grace pointed out, was that the whole thing made no sense. She articulated the human dimension of the adversarial system.

The Aversarial Process: The Human Dimension

Any dispute involves tension and strain for all concerned, but the formal adversarial process seems to exact a particularly heavy toll, one that appears to many laypersons as out of proportion to the social and individual benefits it yields. Even trial judges often suffer from stress. In high-profile trials, judges are concerned about making reversible errors and about keeping control over the court, particularly if attorney behavior is provocative. Judges are constantly second-guessed by appellate courts, the media, and the bar. Some accept this as an occupational hazard; others find it hard to live with. Many judges hate hearing marriage dissolution proceedings because of the almost violent emotional irrationality that erupts. Judges suffer from emotional exhaustion more than most persons realize.

Trial lawyers also emerge from big trials emotionally, physically, and mentally exhausted. They, perhaps, pay a bigger price than anyone else, because their professional reputation and sometimes their compensation depend on the outcome of the trial. They do, however, have one advantage over lay participants in the adversarial process. They know what to expect.

Witnesses, jurors, and the parties to the case are less able than lawyers to cope with the tribulations and idiosyncrasies of the adversarial process. Many are irritated or frustrated by their experience, and some come away with negative attitudes about the system. A common refrain is, "There has to be a better way!" This reaction generally stems from the way they were treated, but it sometimes stems from a conclusion that the justice system is defective.

The average trial is not very exciting or emotionally stressful for jurors. The jurors start out apprehensive and proceed to boredom and irritation with the endless legal bickering and disconnected, seemingly irrelevant flow of evidence. Some trials are exciting and some very excruciating. In trials involving gruesome or morally offensive subject matter or the death penalty, jurors often become upset. It is also very upsetting to be on a hung jury, particularly if some jurors are taking a position that is clearly at odds with the instructions and the facts. However, the real problem for most jurors is the sense of being herded about and having no control over anything. You become Juror #7 and sink into the maw of a system, which seems mindless, inefficient, arcane, defiantly impersonal, and unconcerned about anyone other than judges and lawyers. Jurors can see the late start of court, the long lunch hour, and the total disregard for anyone's time except that of the judge, the attorneys, and an occasional big-shot witness.

Witnesses are often shaken by their experience. They may have to rearrange their schedule two or more times because of continuances. Once the court day arrives, they often are asked to sit alone in a witness room where they have time to wonder what is going to happen to them in court. By the time they are called, they are nervous. Some witnesses are terrified over retaliation from a vengeful spouse, neighbor, or, perhaps, criminal defendant. When they enter the court, particularly an imposing high-ceilinged court, they usually feel great trepidation. The opening questions, even if known in advance, seem a little bit different than expected. Objections interrupt the flow of testimony and make everything less coherent. The judge issues a warning about the phrasing of a response. What is worse, a witness may have to recount some traumatic or embarrassing experience in a public setting and suffer shame. By the time the cross-examination comes, the witness is not at all sure that the direct testimony amounted to anything and is totally confused by the evidentiary rulings that seemed designed to wreck any continuity and clarity. The opposing counsel may seem threatening, deceptively smooth and friendly, or just plain obnoxious. It is clear that the purpose of the cross-examination is to prove that the witness is untrustworthy, unobservant, and prejudiced, if not a downright liar. Being a witness in a formal court proceeding can be very intimidating.

This is not to say that the discomfiture and fear of some witnesses offers a rationale for ending trial by combat, only that the unwillingness of witnesses to talk freely in open court is a problem that must be dealt with. Many witnesses would prefer to give their testimony on video in an office so that they do not have to appear in court at all. Although this may not be feasible, the legal system cannot expect witnesses to tolerate the way they are treated. A subpoena is no substitute for a reexamination of current procedures.

It is noteworthy that ten states will admit indirect testimony of children in evidence. Some states allow children to testify on videotape or through closed-circuit television, while other states will admit hearsay evidence concerning a child's statements about abuse, and still others will allow previous testimony by the child to be admitted. These departures from the normal rules of confrontation cannot be totally transported into the adult realm but are indicative of how gruesome the trial process can be for those forced to go through it.

There are, of course, professional witnesses—police officers and various expert witnesses. Their problem is not fear but getting someone to believe what they say. The skepticism about police testimony is reaching crisis proportions in some courts. One urban jury panel laughed uproariously when asked in voir dire if any of them would trust the testimony of a police officer more than that of a civilian. Contempt for expert witnesses is also high, but lawyers love them because the use of experts permits lawyers to transcend actual empirical evidence of cause and effect and to rely on opinion evidence that makes up in credentials what it lacks in integrity. It is a mystery to laypersons why their opinion is considered worthless when the purchased testimony of experts is valued. There is mounting pressure on judges to exclude "junk science" from getting to juries or to call their own experts. This is another example of how the public expects judges to stand for the integrity of the adversarial process, rather than to accede to attorney game plans.

Probably the most frustrating aspect of the adversarial process is the plight of a person or corporation sued vindictively or without valid cause. A person or corporation in this situation may decide either to buy off the attacker, rather than suffer the tribulations of litigation and the attorney costs, or to dig in and fight for vindication. If the defendant is victorious, the high attorney fees for defense may transform the triumph into a sad occasion. The idea that the loser should pay for attorney fees is anathema to the American trial bar, so the adversarial system provides an open field for the unscrupulous plaintiff. Without such constraints, there no incentive for defense counsel to shorten the proceedings and limited risk for the unscrupulous plaintiff.

The experience of a party to litigation can be traumatic and frustrating. You have to talk through an intermediary, who charges you for translating your thoughts into legally acceptable form and who seems to have no incentive to speed things up or render them less complex. Your star witnesses cannot talk directly but only through the artificial device of attorney questions. Truth and clarity seem to be incidental to the process, if not directly hostile to it, and you seethe in frustration as facts get twisted or omitted. The judge seems to be above it all and occasionally intervenes to enforce the rules of combat, which make no sense to you but apparently make sense to the attorneys. The jury looks confused, and you wonder what they are thinking and if they are as confused as you are. At one point, the other lawyer elicits an answer unfit for the ears of a layperson, and the judge tells the jury to blot it out. You cannot blot it out and wonder if they can. Everything seems to drag on, and no one seems to care. The lawyers talk to the jury, and you wonder if either lawyer really understands the case. You are apprehensive, but your lawyer is hopeful because several jurors nodded when he made a point, and he does not think they like the other lawyer. The jury comes back with a verdict in your favor, and your lawyer is jubilant. He should be; he came out well. You got much less than you expected and wasted twenty-four frustrating months waiting for this moment.

The above experience is obviously not universal, but it is common. Although many parties may have unrealistic expectations, disappointment with the adversarial system is very understandable. People want to be heard in their own way without being badgered by attorneys or placed in an intimidating environment. In a variety of not-too-subtle ways the laity is informing the legal profession that the current process is dehumanizing.

The formal adversarial process is costly and traumatic to all involved. Anyone who experiences the full gamut of the litigation process comes away scarred. Trials occur in very few cases, but trial lurks as the horrible fate that will await people who do not plead guilty or settle their civil disputes. The laity may love trials on TV, but they sure hate them in person.

Alternatives to the Formal Adversarial System

Alternative dispute resolution (ADR) offers one way to avoid the more abrasive aspects of the adversarial process. This alone is enough to recommend ADR to many people. ADR also offers a solution to the daunting cost and complexity of the legal system. For many people, access to justice is not a practical reality.

Although Utah has effected a number of changes to enhance access to justice and has been among the more progressive states in this area, a study revealed that there were still serious obstacles to access. Referring to this study in a December 2, 1997, speech before the Utah Bar Foundation, Chief Justice Michael D. Zimmerman stated:

> That study has made it abundantly clear that there is no way that those who need those services can pay for them in the current market and in the current lawyer-based legal processes. For much of the public, what the law is means little, because they have no realistic access to the law's machinery. And they do not see lawyers as very concerned about the problem.

> To the extent that we resist changes that increase access because increased access by those without full legal representation is disruptive of our existing way of doing business, I think we are in danger of finding ourselves in the same situation as doctors before the managed health care revolution. Professionally myopic, unduly wedded to old models that work for the insiders, but not for the public, and quite proud of the quality product our expensive machinery can produce, without paying much attention to the fact that most people cannot afford it.

After speaking of expansion of ADR, more use of paralegals, use of clerks in a paralegal capacity, and support for pro se litigants, he observed that these cheap alternatives serve an important purpose: "While it may provide what some see as less than perfect justice to the parties in that context, we have to recognize that it is better than unobtainable perfect justice."

The relatively inflexible and formal nature of the adversarial system does not suit most disputes. Many disputes do not require that the judge play a direct adjudicative role. The traditional model with the judge as the major actor is giving way to a different model in which the primary role of judges is to ensure that disputes are fairly resolved, but not necessarily to preside over all cases themselves. In the newer model, judges are at the peak of a network of diverse alternative dispute resolution mechanisms characterized by speed and informality and by a relatively high degree of pro se representation, as is now common in family courts. The role of the judiciary is to oversee this diversified process, handling only those cases that require error correction or that by their nature require the direct exercise of judicial responsibility. This model has been used in juvenile courts for a number of years.

The idea of judges as the pinnacle of a flexible and relatively informal dispute resolution process is a new paradigm that is unfamiliar to many appropriating bodies. Moreover, it sometimes conflicts with a populist view that all persons deserve consideration of their case by a judge, rather than being diverted to some "bargain basement" forum labeled as an alternative to formal adjudication. It is sometimes argued that "second-tier justice" is basically a denial of access to justice. There is, however, a strong counterargument that alternative dispute resolution is the best means of tailoring justice to the nature of each case to provide more timely and less costly decisions.

The diversified dispute resolution model, sometimes called the multidoor court, suggests an alternative to the addition of judges as caseloads rise or change in composition. No longer are caseload figures translated into a certain number of new judgeships. The old weighted caseload methods have limited application in a multidoor court using a mixture of parajudicial officers, counselors, neighborhood conciliators, and attorney-arbitrators. Moreover, legislatures may be loath to create new judgeships, leaving courts little choice but to experiment with less-costly, more-flexible models of dispute resolution. However, ADR has not been fully accepted and remains on extended probation in many jurisdictions due to a populist belief that every citizen is entitled to a judge, concern over the caliber and training of quasi-judicial officials, concern that reliance on such officials will undercut requests for new judges, and the belief that mediators, conciliators, and arbitrators complicate the adjudication process without really resolving anything.

ADR is not always as cheap or speedy as it is supposed to be but seems to appeal to court users more than the formal process. It is a less formidable forum and appears to be more solution oriented than the court-centered process. Many judges look down on ADR and would consider it demeaning to preside over such an informal process, although judges sometimes preside over settlement conferences. A settlement conference is basically designed to muscle the parties into "splitting the difference," but is less an exercise in dispute resolution than it is the application of judicial pressure to settle.

ADR, whatever its defects, comes closer to what the average person requires for dispute resolution and offers an escape from high attorney fees. The cost of legal services is one of the main reasons ADR exists. Many parties to litigation are dissatisfied with the legal fees, particularly if the person paying the fee has been unsuccessful in the case. In contingent fee cases, the law firm may actually pay a lot of the costs and collect them later on if the suit is successful. This should be appreciated by the client but is often a bone of contention when the combined legal fee and up-front costs equal or exceed the recovery by the plaintiff. It is a rare plaintiff that can pay for the hourly rate of a trial lawyer and the costs of litigation, meaning that lawyers have largely priced themselves out the market, except in cases that are so strong that the risk factors in a contingency arrangement are minimal. On the other side, insurance companies and corporations complain that defense lawyers run the meter. Neither the civil plaintiff bar nor the civil defense bar is well loved.

The formal adversarial system has alienated enough people to create large demand for alternatives. There are very few, if any, court systems that have not offered some form of ADR. The uses of ADR are legion and still being explored, but certain types of court-annexed civil arbitration and mediation are pretty well established: the use of arbitrators and mediators in civil damage suits, the use of divorce commissioners in uncontested divorces, and the use of quasi-judicial officials to handle traffic, small-claims, and other routine high-volume cases. At some point, court-annexed ADR has to be accepted as integral to court operations or rejected as not worth the effort. If courts keep ADR in limbo or even reject it, courts run the risk of having various forms of ADR grow up outside the court, because ADR does serve an important public purpose.

ADR was spawned in the earlier era of reform. Its integration into the legal culture is an issue for the new reform agenda.

The Adversarial Process: The Mythology

Laypersons are starting to question some of the cherished practices of judges and lawyers and to point out the mythological nature of the formal adversarial process. It seems odd to many people that the legal system and legal procedures are organized around the trial when, in fact, only a minuscule percentage of cases ever reach the trial stage. Initial filings and charges establish the issues, discovery occurs, evidence is marshaled, depositions are taken, various discovery and dispositive motions are made, issues are honed for trial, certain facts are stipulated, and witnesses are lined up. The decks are cleared for the final dramatic event, the trial. The irony in all this is that the whole legal system is set up to prevent trials.

The whole thrust of caseflow management is to minimize the number of trials and to devise ways to force cases to exit the system quickly by settlement, entry of a plea, or some other disposition. In fact, the system would founder if there were too many trials, because the courts simply cannot accommodate the event around which everything is organized. The courts have to ration the trials and must, for constitutional reasons, favor criminal trials. Trials have become a luxury, yet trial courts cannot bring themselves to limit the time of litigating parties the way that appellate courts do. The right to trial by jury drives the whole system but maintains its legal force simply because the system has figured out a way to keep the right from being exercised, even to the extent of making parties pay the jury costs in civil cases.

One of the myths in civil litigation is the role of the discovery process. Theoretically, discovery and pretrial activities sharpen issues, eliminate surprises, and reduce the case to a few factual issues to be decided at trial. In actuality, the discovery system has been undercut by lack of professional respect among attorneys and failure to respond fully, if at all, to interrogatories and motions to produce. The San Francisco Superior Court has two commissioners who do nothing but handle discovery disputes, which often arise out of pure incivility. The Arizona courts have replaced their old discovery rules with a form of disclosure that increases pressure on parties to be forthcoming with requested information. Discovery is a long, tortuous process that is a primary cause of trial court delay and a major irritant to parties in litigation and to judges.[1] Litigators who want to win at all costs are not playing by the rules.

Another myth is the idea that justice will be served by having two skilled advocates present different facts or draw different inferences from the same facts. The problem is that the advocates are rarely equal and that facts are often obscured and occasionally distorted. Justice may occasionally be served by this process, but this is more of a fortuitous occurrence than a logical result. The "crap shoot" atmosphere in the trial process is one of the major deterrents to litigation and is sometimes hailed as a means of curbing litigious behavior. This whimsicality may, however, only motivate people to seek different forums.

The criminal courts provide a great example of the conflict of myth and reality. Judges handle some trials and pretrial proceedings that are genuinely adversarial, but these cases constitute a small percentage of the judicial caseload. Mainly, a judge ensures the legality of an assembly line that depends on the cooperation of defendants in conceding their guilt. Judges spend a considerable amount of time taking guilty pleas and sentencing defendants. It is common knowledge that any criminal defendant who has the temerity to ask for a trial and loses can forget about probation, because the system cannot tolerate resistance to the assembly line. Defense attorneys do a little bargaining on behalf of their clients but are indispensable in keeping the assembly line moving. We cannot afford an adversarial system, so we settle for the myth.

Protecting the Integrity of the Adversarial Process

The most cogent voices for reform of the adversarial system are judges who must preside over this process and have the best seat in town to observe its operation. In the mid-1990s two experienced trial judges, Harold J. Rothwax of New York City and Burton S. Katz of Los Angeles, wrote very strong critiques of the criminal justice system.[2] Judge Rothwax had served as a defense attorney for the Legal Aid Society, and Judge Katz had served as both a prosecutor and a private

---

[1]   Some judges get involved in discovery issues in chambers and take actions that are not on the record or reviewable. This is another gray area but perhaps necessary to establish some control over a case.

[2]   Harold J. Rothwax, *Guilty: The Collapse of Criminal Justice* (New York: Random House, 1996), and Burton S. Katz, *Justice Overruled: Unmasking the Criminal Justice System* (New York: Warner Books, 1997).

criminal defense attorney. Their books did not raise novel issues but had great impact, because the authors spoke with authority and knowledge and were able to document their views with concrete examples drawn from their own experience. The most striking feature of the two books was the insistence of the authors that the criminal justice system had lost its integrity and public respect by treating truth as irrelevant and assigning it a low value.

If the two judge-authors were not so well versed in the actual workings of the criminal justice system, it might be easy to dismiss their lofty view about truth as academic or unduly moralistic. After all, only prosecutors are assigned the role of seeking the truth, and they may not be very enthusiastic about revealing exculpatory evidence or insisting on police honesty in describing how evidence was collected. Criminal procedure gives the defendant wide latitude to suppress the truth and play the odds. Defense strategies tend to change as the prosecutor's case is revealed through pretrial discovery. "I am innocent" becomes "I did it in self-defense" and finally "I was mentally deranged." Very seldom are defendants well served by the truth, except in Perry Mason books.

Juries are supposed to seek the truth and often do, but some jurors may lie in voir dire to get on a jury so that they can "send a message." Even a truth-seeking jury discovers that the rules of evidence ensure that they do not receive the full truth—God forbid! The whole jury trial system is rife with absurdities that defy common sense and defeat the pursuit of truth. Judges routinely instruct jurors to draw no inference from the fact that the defendant exercises the constitutional right not to testify, but any normal juror will infer that the defendant is afraid of the truth.

Judge Rothwax, who became increasingly frustrated by these absurdities, observed that the rules of criminal procedure should be directed toward the pursuit of truth, not its suppression:

> Let us remember that legal procedure is a means, not an end. Therefore, the purpose of the procedure should be to enhance the law, not to delay or defeat the law's intention. I believe it stands to reason that a primary objective of procedural rules should be to facilitate the discovery of truth.[3]

Judge Katz, who became something of a media celebrity after leaving the bench, had the experience of hearing the views of a wide range of citizens who called in to ask him questions. He drew an interesting conclusion from these calls:

> What unites most of my callers, regardless of their viewpoint, is a deep sense of unease. They sense that something has gone wrong. Worse, some things may never have been right. They feel lied to, cheated. American justice has been sold to us as a bright beacon of truth and justice, the greatest system in the world. But it does not look that great on TV. Has Uncle Sam played a cruel joke on us? Who gets justice? Who doesn't? And why? Is truth always irrele-

---

[3]   Rothwax, *Guilty*, 31-32.

vant? Are defense attorneys, judges, police, and prosecutors interested in anything besides winning?

Public perceptions about justice are important. Even if inaccurate, they become self-fulfilling. My callers perceive that lawyers, judges and the police care little about the truth. Procedures, rules, technicalities, strategies, clever practices, yes. Justice and truth, no. My callers are right.

Judge Katz cited five reasons for agreeing with his callers and writing a book. All of his reasons involved the disrespect for truth that is corroding the system of justice.

- The struggle between the police and the appellate courts in applying formulaic standards on search and seizure has kept truth from jurors and led to farcical police accounts of how they gather evidence.

- The adversarial system is encouraging adherence to arcane rules and procedures, sanctifying form over substance, and rewarding trickery and technique at the expense of truth.

- Jurors are succumbing to public pressures, yielding to their biases, and engaging in "payback" verdicts.

- The public and legislatures are seeking easy and cheap ways to look tough on crime and settling for appearances rather than a really effective system.

- The "abuse excuse" and other diminished-capacity defenses encourage the misuse of expert witnesses, the inflammation of passions, and misinformation. He terms this "psychiatric fraud far adrift from the calm waters of truth."[4]

The large metropolitan courts where Judge Rothwax and Judge Katz served are not average American courts, but their frustration is hardly unique among trial judges. Their views on reforming the system are a bit different in detail, but their descriptions of the adversarial process in criminal cases are eerily similar. At no time, however, do they suggest that the adversarial process be scrapped. They do not, on the other hand, think that the existing problems are susceptible to a quick fix or minor reforms. They call for fundamental changes in the criminal justice system, especially the rules of criminal procedure.

This view is not confined to judges. Ed McConnell, the original court administrator, and the president of the National Center for State Courts for many years, observed in a 1996 interview that the next wave of reform would address the procedures governing civil and criminal cases. He linked this to the history of the National Center for State Courts, which during his tenure was instrumental in the major administrative and organizational reforms of the 1970s and 1980s but by

---

[4]   Katz, *Justice Overruled*, 3-4.

the 1990s was seeking to redefine its relationship to court improvement. He predicted that the courts would start looking at procedural fundamentals and that the National Center for State Courts would have an important role in this process.

The Adversarial Process: Jury Reform as a Microcosm of the New Agenda

The state judiciary is well aware of the weaknesses in the adversarial system, but very often cannot directly address them because the solution lies in legislation, changes in the rules of procedure and evidence, and changes in the case law of the state. There have nonetheless been some significant changes. Nowhere is this more evident than in the area of jury reform.

No area of court operation is more integral to the American legal system than the use of juries to decide facts and, in a few states, even to decide the sentence. No area of court operation involves citizens so closely in the legal process and brings them into closer contact with legal culture. No area of court operations, except perhaps caseflow management, is closer to the concerns of judges. Unfortunately, no other area of the legal system is so shrouded in myth.

According to myth, jurors are blank slates on which attorneys write conflicting hieroglyphics. Information is filtered to the jury though an archaic legal mesh that is supposed to screen out evidence that laypersons cannot handle. In theory, insurance coverage and attorney fees should not be factor during jury deliberations, but jurors routinely figure the net recovery of a plaintiff after subtracting the contingency fee. They may take into account that a defendant is probably uninsured, as, for example, in an intentional tort case. When determinate sentencing became a fad in legislatures, there was fear that jurors might balk at conviction in some cases if they knew the severity of the fixed sentence, so they had to be shielded form this terrible truth. However, streetwise or well-informed jurors are not ignorant of legislative actions and do discuss the nature of the sentence if they think the defendant is one of the marginal loser types who so often get nailed to the wall in narcotics cases. The idea of entrusting the jurors with the truth simply runs head-on into the legal myth that they are putty to be shaped by trial lawyers and judges.

Another myth is the ability of attorneys to detect possible bias in prospective jurors and that peremptory challenges to remove such likely enemies is a good way to obtain a fair and impartial jury. The vehicle for fairness is the voir dire process, a preliminary examination to determine the fitness of prospective jurors to serve and sometimes a vehicle for not-too-subtle indoctrination by attorneys. Whether attorneys or judges interrogate prospective jurors, voir dire results in the removal of some jurors for cause and others because they have been peremptorily challenged. The latter challenges are limited in number by the rules and based on the sixth sense that Juror #12 is unsympathetic or on some dubious consultant strategy for screening out unfriendly jurors. A juror dismissed due to a peremptory challenge may greet this occurrence with joyful relief, but some jurors are offended by rejection and feel demeaned. Finally, both sides run out of challenges and settle for a jury that may be even worse for them than the one that was originally seated. The use of peremptory challenges is anachronistic because the federal courts have created restrictions on the use of such challenges to exclude persons on the basis of race[5] or gender.[6] If "peremptory" means what the dictionary says it means, the courts are in the process of abolishing it. The whole system would improve if peremptory challenges were officially abolished and jurors were dismissed only for cause. Jury panels would be reduced in size, and jurors would not have to be put through a demeaning experience. The ultimate protection of the parties is random jury selection, not the instincts of the attorneys about individual jurors. The myth, however, dominates.

Another classic example of the legal mind in action is provided by jury instructions. The theory is that the jury weighs the facts and makes a decision based on the legal instructions provided by the judge. The instructions are supposed to initiate the laypersons into the mysteries of the law so they can make an informed decision. Instructions are usually a case of too much, too late. Jurors have often made up their minds before the instructions and sometimes cannot understand them after they have been rendered. Instructions tend to be boilerplate formulas guaranteed to withstand appeal and are written in legalese. The idea that jury instructions ought to be written in English is just catching on.

If ever an institution seemed impervious to change, it was the jury system. Yet, modern jury management became the first area of concentration for many courts and the primary example of social science research challenging legal mythology. The recent history of jury reform captures the ethos of the early court reform movement and the nature of the second-wave reform movement that is germinating. It symbolizes the achievements of twentieth-century court reform and signals the type of achievements that are to come.

From a sociological and political perspective, the jury system has gone through enormous changes in a little more than three decades. In 1960 juries were much less representative and far more homogeneous than they now are. In some states, women were not involuntarily called to jury service, and members of minority groups were excluded. Legislatures granted numerous exemptions from jury service under pressure from particular groups, to the point where jury service was less a public duty than an imposition on the small body of remaining eligible citizens. Compounding the problem was inadequate source data to draw jury lists so that some elements of the population were never included. Moreover, the process of choosing citizens for jury service was not random in many areas. Friends of county officials and persons looking for extra income might be favored. The system was neither democratic nor truly representative of the population.

This faulty system was challenged and dramatically changed. The civil rights movement and automation played a big role in the changes, but hardly explain the depth of the phenomenon. The jury system has been largely democratized. This carries with it the possibility of a wider range of views and values

---

[5]   *Batson v. Kentucky*, 476 U.S. 79 (1986).

[6]   *J.E.B. v. Alabama*, 114 S. Ct. 1419 (1994)

on a jury and more opportunities for sharp divisions and inability to achieve una-nimity. As the jury system has become more cross-representational, it has come under increasing fire as an institution. Jury deadlocks are thought to have increased; juries are deemed incapable of handling the testimony in complex cases; and juries are accused of nullifying the law by simply ignoring their instruc-tions on the law. Jurors, for their part, voice criticisms of the closed, legalistic nature of the adversarial system and call for a more active juror role at trial.

To gain insight into the closed world of the law, it is helpful to track the his-tory of jury innovations over the last decade or two, starting with William Pabst, an engineer whose experience as a juror in the 1960s led him to champion improved jury management. An early pioneer in quality control, he quickly per-ceived the inefficiencies of the jury system and the extravagant waste of public funds. Perhaps more significantly, he was distressed by the waste of citizens' time and the lack of concern for jurors. The inefficiency of the system was a ter-rible imposition by the legal culture on the citizens. He conveyed his ideas to Judge Oliver Gasch of the District Court for the District of Columbia, who became a supporter.

With a small grant from the Law Enforcement Assistance Administration (LEAA) Pabst did a preliminary jury study and concluded that $300,000 per year could be saved in the District of Columbia by good jury management, and the scientific study of juries commenced.[7] A principal collaborator of Pabst was G. Thomas Munsterman, a fellow engineer, who is currently acknowledged as the top expert on juries. In 1974, under another LEAA grant, Pabst and Munsterman produced A *Guide to Juror Usage* and in 1975 A *Guide to Jury System Management*, which focused on efficient use of jurors in large courts with juror pools.[8] The authors enunciated seven rules of jury use, which are still largely intact. More significantly, the application of an engineering approach to court management raised a series of questions that simply did not get asked in a legal environment where the convenience of judges and lawyers transcended concerns for citizens. Two questions were posed: "How many people do you really need to pull in for jury service? Is there any need for them to be here every day?" As simple as these questions were, they had not been asked. The engineers quickly provid-ed quantitative and empirical means to determine how many persons had to be called and gave courts quantitative benchmarks to evaluate their success in jury management. This methodology, simple by engineering standards, was a novel-ty in courts and saved many citizen hours and tax dollars.

Pabst and Munsterman founded the Center for Jury Studies in 1978 and broadened the scope of their jury work. Tom Munsterman was a pioneer in the

---

[7]   Pabst was not alone. There were some parallel studies and projects by the Institute for Judicial Administration, by Westinghouse with the help of Maureen Solomon, by the American Bar Association in 1970, and by the Cleveland Court Management Project under Fran Bremson. What distinguished the work of Pabst and his colleagues was a very vigorous quantitative methodology brought over from industrial engineering.

[8]   In 1972 the Federal Judicial Center came out with some jury guidelines, which were more in the nature of discrete suggestions than a systematic scheme.

struggle for the one-day/one-trial system that effectively eliminated the burdensome practice of calling citizens to juror service for long periods. About 40 percent of the United States population now live in jurisdictions where this innovation applies, a remarkable achievement in the cautious legal world.[9] Tom Munsterman was instrumental in using automation to merge various lists, such as voter rolls, tax rolls, and motor vehicle lists, into a comprehensive juror list, thus assisting in the process of jury democratization. Through publications and newsletters, jury management became a special topic and a recognized area of court management. In the early 1980s the Center for Jury Studies started to provide technical assistance and became a regularly funded, recognized repository for information on juries. In 1982 its scope and stature were enhanced by incorporation into the National Center for State Courts, then emerging as a major force in court reform. In less than a decade, jury management had won national acceptance.

In 1983 the National Center for State Courts published a set of standards for juries, which marked a shift from the quantitative emphasis of early jury studies that focused on efficiency and techniques. The concern was shifting to qualitative matters, which included the treatment of jurors, their accommodations, their orientation, their convenience, their role in the trial, and their general ease in a strange and sometimes intimidating environment. From this point onward, studies tended to focus on the future of the jury system and the role of jurors; for example, the NCSC publication *Jury Trial Innovations*, among other issues, dealt with the problem of juror stress, a topic that did not rank high on the conversational list in the lawyers' lounge.[10] The clear trend was to more deeply examine the place of laypersons in the adversarial process and to raise some serious questions about the underlying assumptions of the legal culture.

Jury reform had moved into a more controversial area. Empirical data clashed with the legal myth that jurors were passive, intellectually limited observers. In fact, the legal model of the ideal juror is almost totally the opposite of what empirical studies tell us about jurors, as pointed out by Judge B. Michael Dann of the Superior Court for Maricopa County (Arizona):

> Despite overwhelming evidence from social science research and accepted truths about the educational process, the legal establishment remains largely resistant to proposals that would modify the present trial model to allow for more juror participation in general and improved communications with jurors in particular. Indeed, there are even reported instances of courts moving in directions contraindicated by the empirical data.[11]

---

[9]   The first use of this innovation, which predated the Munsterman initiative, occurred in Houston under the aegis of Judge James Stovall, an early advocate of trial court administration. Texas law prohibited more than one voir dire for a juror, which made it senseless to hold a juror on service. This was the origin of the reform.

[10]   This 1997 collection of thought-provoking articles was edited by G. Thomas Munsterman, Paula Hannaford, and G. Marc Whitehead.

[11]   B. Michael Dann, "'Learning Lessons' and 'Speaking Rights': Creating Educated and Democratic Juries," 68 (1993) *Indiana Law Journal*, 1236.

Judge Dann contrasted the elements of the legal myth with the elements of an empirically based model he labels the "Behavioral-Educational Model." The latter model is based on the premise that jurors want to be active participants and are educable.[12]

Legal Model	Behavioral-Educational Model
1. Passive—acted upon	1. Active—takes responsibility for one's part in the learning
2. Merely observes	2. Actively participates
3. Empty vessel to be filled	3. Possesses existing frames of reference
4. Object of one-way, linear communication	4. Participant in interactive process
5. Complete and accurate recorder of information	5. Selective and otherwise imperfect recall of evidence
6. Suspends judgment until end of case regarding: a. evaluation of evidence b. decision on the issues	6. Actively processes information as received: a. evaluates, classifies, etc., evidence b. frequently makes decisions prior to deliberations
7. Does not give feedback until verdict	7. Continuous feedback during trial and deliberations
8. Because of "recall readiness," substantive jury instructions are best given at end of case	8. "Cognitive filters" used during trial; instructions should also come at beginning of trial
9. Takes into account all evidence	9. Selects evidence that best fits frame of reference or tentative verdict choice; forgets some, confused by others
10. Well-served by adversarial system	10. Frustrated and confused by adversary system, which interferes with learning
11. Effective representative of community; role enhances participative democracy	11. Loss of sense of power and control; reduced satisfaction; importance of jury denigrated

Current jury reform proposals tend toward the behavioral-educational model as outlined by Judge Dann. The reforms that have been adopted in Arizona and other states are noted below.[13]

---

[12] Ibid., 1246-47.

[13] For a description of Arizona's jury reforms, see Janessa E. Shtabsky, "Comment—A More Active Jury: Has Arizona Set the Standard for Reform with Its New Jury Rules?" 28 (1996) *Arizona State Law Journal* 1009-33.

- The judge gives legal instructions and explains the nature of the case at the beginning of the trial, or perhaps the legal instructions are given just before the closing arguments so that the jurors can measure the summations against the legal criteria.

- Interim summations are given by counsel so that jurors are not lost in a sea of discrete facts and confused.

- Jurors can pose written questions through the judge and seek interim clarifications.

- Legal instructions are written in understandable English and related to the case. The judge can offer additional verbal explanations if asked, even after deliberations have started.

- Written copies of instructions go into the jury deliberation room along with notebooks containing documentary evidence.

- Jurors can take notes and bring them into deliberation room.

- Additional argument by counsel is permitted if jury becomes deadlocked on specific points.

- Jurors can discuss the case with fellow jurors as the case progresses.

- Law should permit less-than-unanimous verdicts if constitutionally permissible.

These proposed changes are bound together by the concept that a trial is a quest for truth and that truth is sometimes ill-served by the adversarial process as it now exists. Judges and lawyers are uneasy when jurors get involved and sense, probably correctly, that this modest lay intrusion is the first step in a more serious challenge to the adversarial system. The people want "in." This popular desire for inclusion, respect, and the right to challenge or circumvent the legal culture is understandable and was probably inevitable. It is not confined to juries but extends to all areas of court operation.

The jury reforms have mirrored the broader trends in courts. The first step is recognition that the system is defective. This is followed by introspection and analysis and then some changes in the way the system is managed and organized. That's the easiest part because it does not impinge on the legal culture. When jury reforms were centered on better jury lists, nice jury lounges, more courtesy toward jurors, and video orientations, there was limited resistance. These reforms have been very positive. In general, jurors think more highly of the legal system after they have served than before. Jurors are a major client of the courts and have been better accommodated in recent years than they were at midcentury.

When jury reform turned to reducing or eliminating peremptory challenges to restore some integrity to the jury process, the response in legal circles was not enthusiastic. When the proposed reforms threatened to give jurors a bigger role in the adversarial process, the legal culture assumed a defensive posture. This type of reform, which is starting to occur on a limited scale, is illustrative of the new reform agenda.

A more radical change in presenting evidence to jurors is the video trial. The effect of video records of court proceedings and the use of video depositions will affect appeals, the rules of evidence, the role of witnesses, and perhaps the whole question-and-answer method of eliciting testimony. Courts could tell parties to reduce their case to a five-hour video expurgated in advance, with some jury instructions at the beginning and some at the end. Video testimony at trial could be arranged in logical order and would be free of interruptions and the usual courtroom jousting, thus reducing the showman role of lawyers and focusing the jurors on the facts. One ironic result of the video trial would be to perpetuate the passive role of the juror. The video trial may or may not be feasible economically or legally, but it is symbolic of the challenges confronting the adversarial system.

The new reform agenda will require willingness on the part of judges and lawyers to reexamine the underlying premises of the legal system, which runs the risk of becoming an anachronistic insider game. The rules of evidence and procedure are part of the problem, although more of an effect than a cause. The underlying precepts of the rules of civil procedure are no longer valid, because notice pleading assumes discovery, and discovery assumes a higher level of professional ethics than is being exhibited in some parts of the United States. The same might be said for the limited discovery of the criminal process, where the "win at any cost" philosophy is more entrenched. Many judges will say "discovery still works," but this view is not shared by many experienced court observers who have been analyzing caseflow management data over the years. The discovery problem is the major flaw in the system.

The adversarial process symbolizes the best and the worst in the legal system. It is possible to modify its negative elements without destroying the institution, but there are still members of the legal profession who fear even modest change—fear that it will open up a deluge of unwelcome reforms. Indeed, that is a risk but one that has to be taken if the integrity of the adversarial system is to be protected. The truth is that the process is already being changed in a number of small ways that will have a cumulative effect, but, at some point, judges, legal scholars, and bar leaders will have to promote more fundamental changes. This may be the single most difficult task on the new reform agenda.

Chapter 12

Broadening the Role of Judges and the Concept of Justice

itizen expectations about the powers of a judge to help them may be unrealistic, but they are rooted in idealism. Citizens expect fairness, but they also want judges to appreciate their plights and to protect them. They do not need touchy-feely jurists, but they do want judges who are attuned to the people coming to court and involved in problem solution. In fact, judges have been responding by assuming a variety of responsibilities that go beyond the confines of the traditional adjudicative role. This very fundamental change is occurring without much fanfare but is one of the most important aspects of the new reform agenda.

The changing role of judges reflects a changing view about the meaning and scope of justice. *Doing justice* is not a self-explanatory term. Its meaning may have to be inferred from the way a system of justice conducts itself. It is apparent from observation that the meaning of justice is being expanded.

The Role of Judges

The changing role of judges in most noticeable in the exercise of juvenile and family court responsibilities where judges, as a matter of law, have a continuing obligation to oversee the execution of their orders and engage in executive rather than judicial functions. This postadjudication role may be more important and time-consuming than adjudication and may occasionally go beyond mere oversight to mandating provision of services by executive branch agencies or administering social service and detention programs that are under court aegis.

These administrative, protective, and rehabilitative roles go beyond the family area. They encompass court oversight of guardians and protection of persons who are being committed or have been committed for reasons of mental disability or incompetence, and they extend into the criminal area, particularly in diversion programs and in sentencing. Legislators prefer a robotic, nondiscretionary form of sentencing, but judges fight to retain sentencing discretion, because they have to balance the common good against the fate of an individual. Although very few criminal defendants go to trial, judges sentence everyone convicted of a crime, so sentencing is arguably the most important judicial function. Sentencing is a very personal proceeding, which judges sometimes agonize over and often involves use of rehabilitation programs, community-based corrections, and a variety of alternatives designed to break a pattern of recidivism or substance abuse.

The legal culture has traditionally perceived the judge as a dispassionate arbiter, but many people appearing before a judge are seeking a protector, healer, or advocate, not a detached referee. This socially involved role takes the courts into many areas that were once considered executive turf and often requires judges to assume responsibility for seeing that mandated services to families are provided. The new role places judges at the pinnacle of a network that includes many noncourt agencies and makes the judge a coordinator and facilitator more than an adjudicator.

Juvenile and family courts are points of entry for individuals needing social services. Judges in such courts engage in therapeutic jurisprudence and are not just detached arbiters of legal disputes. Courts do not necessarily want to run social programs but have a public responsibility to ensure that judicial orders are enforced or that governments actually provide the services mandated by statute. This involves courts in the social service delivery system.

The point-of-entry phenomenon also applies to pro se litigation, mental health, and domestic violence. Courts simply cannot avoid being involved in the care and treatment of those persons who have a legitimate right to invoke the authority of the courts. Courts and other agencies are often addressing the same aspects of social pathology in an individual or a family but are not in communication with one another. Some of these persons are "revolvers," mentally ill persons who constantly reappear before the court. There is a growing movement toward involuntary outpatient commitment aimed at intervention at an early stage.

Court involvement can simply consist of referrals to a service provider, but courts have sometimes teamed up with service providers or provided entirely court-based services through, for example, a nonprofit affiliate of the court. Courts must find out what services are available from social agencies and institutions, what services are needed, who pays for the services, and whether the provided services comply with court orders. Ultimately, courts end up monitoring the services they order.

Courts have to address access to legal assistance in an array of cases stemming from family issues. This encompasses the appointment of lawyers in child neglect and abuse cases where various members of the family require attorneys, representation of indigents in paternity suits or child support enforcement proceedings, and representation of juveniles charged with delinquency. These legal costs can be quite staggering, because some of these proceedings may require multiple hearings over a long period. Sometimes, these legal fees would not be paid by government officials but for the intervention of a judge.

One important aspect of the family issue is domestic violence. Some idea of the dimensions of the problem is provided by the domestic violence program of Dade County, Florida, which from the outset had the primary goal of preventing fatalities. In 1995 the county court had four judges assigned to domestic violence cases and several other judges in branch courts. The domestic violence court is open to issue restraining orders twenty-four hours a day, seven days a week. There is a special intake office for domestic violence cases, and there are coordinators who are attorneys and assist both petitioners and respondents, as well as the court. The coordinators make referrals to appropriate social agencies. The prosecutor and defender offices also have separate domestic violence divisions. This constitutes a problem for the public defender because of the possible conflict situation if criminal charges are filed.

Domestic violence is not just an urban problem. Judges in rural areas are wrestling with the need to set up domestic violence programs in sparsely settled multicounty areas. Placing quasi-judicial officials in each county is a possible solution (shades of the much-maligned justice-of-the-peace system). The very nature of these programs makes the judge an advocate and protector and creates a very different judicial environment. The key issues are common to just about any jurisdiction:

- necessity for consistency of judges so that conflicting orders are not made
- emotional burnout of judges if they specialize in family cases
- inadequate case histories of violence
- necessity of judicial involvement in building domestic violence programs
- need to train judges and court personnel on how to handle domestic violence cases, particularly at times of high danger and risk where quick response may be crucial
- need of special intake programs in high-volume areas
- monitoring the linkage between dissolution suits and domestic violence suits so that there can be no abuse of the domestic violence program to gain tactical advantage in a divorce suit
- necessity of cooperation between the judicial and executive branch agencies and an end to turf wars, because domestic violence programs demand a high level of interbranch cooperation

The issues in the family area are clearly not traditional issues of case adjudication. Judges may even attempt to control executive agencies, to order expenditures, or to supplant these agencies by placing programs directly under court administration. Some judges feel that courts, because of their duty and authority to determine the services and treatment to be provided, are compelled to fill the void caused by lack of executive branch response or by inefficiencies and lack of coordination. This shocks judicial purists and raises some fundamental questions.

- Should judges confine themselves to a strict adjudication role in family and juvenile cases?
- Should courts be involved in providing social services, or should they be strictly confined to referral?

- Do courts have the responsibility and authority to fill gaps in the social service delivery system by setting up their own programs and bypassing executive branch agencies?
- If courts perform executive functions, should they be evaluated at budget time by the criteria applicable to executive branch social service and treatment agencies?
- What control should courts exercise over the other branches that are providing social services according to a court order? Can a court mandate that a state or local government provide a particular service?

Regardless of how one answers these questions, the genie is out of the bottle and is not going back in. Judges have been thrust into a different role, one with which many are unhappy. A court administrator observed that the judges of his general jurisdiction court tended to view judges of the nearby family court as social workers in black robes. He was, therefore, surprised to see a judge of his court conducting an awards ceremony in his courtroom. A number of defendants in drug cases had successfully completed a rehabilitation program under the terms of their sentence and were being individually congratulated by the judge, who came down from the bench to express his personal pleasure in their progress. Therapeutic justice is not limited to family courts.

One of the most cogent summations of this change in the judiciary was presented by Chief Justice Michael D. Zimmerman of Utah in a speech to the Utah Bar Foundation. Commenting on a pending proposal for a family court, he stated:

> At root, this challenge is a demand that judges and courts assume a stronger administrative, protective, or rehabilitative role toward those appearing before them, that they become more involved in what some have termed "therapeutic jurisprudence." This is in contrast to the more traditional "dispassionate magistrate" model of judge that most of us are used to. Those arguing for more involved judiciaries note that when certain types of matters come into court, the court becomes the entry point into the governmental system of individuals needing social services. The demand is that judges and the judicial system become more expert in these problems and active in seeing that those services are provided, rather than simply dealing with only those manifestations of their problem that fit within our traditional civil or criminal law tasks. This may involve simple coordination with social service agencies, or it may involve ongoing supervision of the provision of those services.
>
> It is the demand for just such deeper involvement by judges that underlies much of the push for a family court. Specifically, the family court proposal is grounded upon the claim that the present system divides jurisdiction over family problems along lines that make sense to lawyers, judges and the law, but not to the family unit. The argument is that a family court, augmented by broader social services, would do a better job of dealing with the many manifestations of a dysfunctional family. It is not enough for the courts to treat the symptoms individually, be they divorce, child custody disputes, incidents of

child abuse and neglect, or of juvenile crime. Rather, the family itself should be the focus of attention. The motto of the family court proposal is "one family, one judge." And the judge in this motto will almost certainly function as a supervisor and monitor of social services to the family.

The family court proposal has implicit within it this demand for more involved judging, but that same underlying demand is becoming evident in other areas. The drug court model that has gained much recent attention is also premised on such therapeutic judging. The judge coordinates and cooperates with various agencies in helping addicts beat their habit. This is done by supervising the defendant's progress through repeated visits to court, with the judge alternatively encouraging those who are toeing the mark, and threatening those that do not with jail. The program seems to work, and I am certain we will see strong pressure for it to expand. But be honest—the demand for such involved judging has large cultural implications for the judiciary.

For many years, those across the country occupying positions analogous to our district and appellate judgeships and constituting the vast majority of judges, have largely organized their judiciaries around their vision of the world. These judges have tended to see the "dispassionate disinterested magistrate" model of judge that they learned about in law school, the one who sits passively while lawyers present their two contending visions of reality, as the preferred model. Those judges have tended to look down on those involved in person-centered judging, such as juvenile or family court judges.

But as the public and legislatures, not to mention the federal government, increasingly demand more participation and coordination by the judiciary in the addressing of social problems that evidence themselves in courts, the judiciary is going to have to face a new cultural reality. The detached magistrate model of their law school days will increasingly not be the preferred model in the trial courts. More trial judges are going to have to become more adept at entering into the management of people's problems, and the coordination of social services to address those problems. And more of the resources of the judiciary are going to be committed to supervising and providing such services, a fact which has large implications for our ability to handle our more traditional work in the old, relaxed manner.

Many of you may say that the judiciary can and should resist these demands because they fundamentally change the nature of the court system and its adversarial premises, and will require shifting funds from our traditional core functions to newer, less central activities. I suppose that these pressures can be resisted for a while, but I think that resistance is futile, and probably unwise.[1]

---

[1]   Extract from a speech by Chief Justice Michael Zimmerman to the Utah Bar Foundation on December 2, 1997.

Sitting in judgment is still the key function of a judge, but it no longer defines the role of a judge. A number of judges would prefer a more varied and challenging role and would like responsibilities that permit them to have a positive effect on the system and on the lives of the people coming before them. They would like trial courts to be a great source of ideas and creative leadership. Unfortunately, the judicial culture does not foster creativity or reward the mover and shaker. Judges with strong leadership potential are often those who will never be chosen by their peers as chief judge. In states where the chief judges are appointed by the chief justice or the supreme court, leadership skills can be rewarded, but all too often these potential leaders never get to be chief judge or are frustrated by their peers when they do.

It is interesting to see which judges end up in specialty courts. They may be low in the pecking order, but, on the other hand, they may simply be judges who want to be more involved in solving problems. Because unification tended to homogenize trial judges in the name of efficiency, separatist impulses were not encouraged. The push for specialization is not just a demand of special-interest groups but an outlet for those judges who prefer a less traditional role. The term *open court* usually refers to public access and participation, but it can apply equally to opening the judiciary to different career paths.

The Nature of Justice in the Modern Era

The expanding role of judges reflects a broadening of the concept of justice. In the legal world, the word *justice* is frequently bandied about, but no ever defines it. According to Black's Law Dictionary (revised fourth edition), justice is a virtue, "the constant and perpetual disposition to render [every person his or her] due." However, this generic definition leaves much to be desired. Rendering others their due takes many forms.

In criminal cases, this virtue generally takes the form of distributive justice, which assigns to each person the proper criminal sanction under the law. In civil cases, this virtue often amounts to enforcing commutative justice, which is the justice owed by one person to another, as in honoring a contract or observing due care in actions. The strict, mechanical justice favored by some legislators is a caricature of justice; real justice must ultimately deal with the application of law to a specific situation and to specific organizations or individuals. Judges have to consider the dignity and worth of an individual in a way that is not possible in the legislative process.

When judges speak of justice, they tend, quite naturally, to focus on the core role of the judiciary. They are usually referring to their application of the law to arrive at a substantively correct and fair decision or to their role in ensuring procedural fairness and protection of rights at all stages of a proceeding. Not often stated, but implicit, is the judiciary's long-standing role in adjudicating internal partnership and corporate disputes and rights in property. This role is a very important element of justice, which is sometimes taken almost for granted in court administration literature. The types of property matters are numerous, among them condemnation, eminent domain, inheritance, rights in personal and real property, conservation of property of disabled or incompetent persons, receivership of property on behalf of creditors, and landlord-tenant matters.[2]

The traditional judicial roles in litigation and property matters do not sum up the meaning of justice in the contemporary court scene. Courts, for example, have always had a protective role, but in recent years this role has increased greatly in importance, sometimes eclipsing more traditional roles. Protective justice takes the form of placing vulnerable persons, among them the mentally incompetent, the aged, the neglected child, or the abused wife, under the protection of the court. A temporary restraining order, a protective order, or an interim support order all have the quality of a quick intervention to prevent harm or suffering when the moving party, or his or her representative, has a right to invoke the aid of the court. Judges supervise a staff that may be dealing with guardians, intake processes for abused wives or scared children, and heart-wrenching instances of mental breakdown. If the judge's attitude is unsympathetic and bureaucratic, the staff will reflect this. The persons who are seeking help are largely helpless and vulnerable to degrading treatment.

The conflict between foster care and adoption advocates places courts in the middle of a major dispute that is rocking the social welfare world. Courts can easily end up supervising a plethora of foster homes through their staffs or other agencies. The children placed in those homes are, or should be, under court supervision but are, unfortunately, left pretty much on their own or continually shunted from one home to another. This is a denial of protective justice.

Ameliorative justice takes the form of repair. Some court action is an attempt to return a person to a prior healthier position; for example, compensatory damages fixed by a jury or by a judge in a bench trial. Some courts have a mediation and counseling program for marital dissolution cases or programs for counseling families that are being torn apart by dissension. This type of help reflects a social policy in favor of preserving marriages and families and sometimes encounters opposition from the divorce bar, which has no incentive to see families heal. Courts can also promote healing by using their authority to compel treatment for substance abuse as an alternative to more-punitive sanctions. This is not just an act of mercy but a relatively pragmatic decision that benefits society by ending a cycle of addiction that leads to criminal recidivism.

Enforcement justice is simply using court orders and judgments to protect the integrity and credibility of court authority and, in some cases, to ensure that the beneficiaries of these orders or judgments receive their due. One of the weakest aspects of the American justice system is lack of follow-through. What purpose does it serve to render a fair decision and then fail to enforce it? Enforcement jus-

---

[2]   Landlord-tenant cases are usually relegated to a court of limited jurisdiction, a housing court, or some quasi-judicial official because the cases are numerous, do not involve large amounts of money, and are considered legally simple. Even though these cases often involve eviction and the fundamental need of shelter, they are minor matters by the logic of court administration.

tice is most obvious in the supervision of child support, the payment of restitution, or the enforcement of money damage judgments in civil cases. It also extends into the realm of fine and fee collection, where courts have been rather lax to the detriment of their own credibility.

Conditional release on bail or probation is tied to avoidance or performance of certain acts, some of them rehabilitative in nature. Quite often, the supervising agency is part of the judicial branch and subject to direct administrative control of the judiciary. Sometimes, courts contract for misdemeanor probation.[3] In the desire to relieve prison overcrowding, supervisory agencies have been swamped with the inevitable result that conditions of release are not strictly enforced. The public is not well served by lax supervision, nor is a probationer well served if a rehabilitative condition of probation is ignored. Some courts give probation violations very low priority.

Corrective justice is the due of any litigant who relies upon an appellate system to correct errors that occur in the trial. Some parties simply cannot afford the time and money to make an appeal or even to fight an appeal in a case that they have won. In the latter situation, they may settle for something less than they are due to avoid appeal. Interestingly, indigent criminal defendants may be in a better position to obtain appellate justice than those who are paying for the appeal themselves. California, for example, has a large system of appellate defenders working through nonprofit corporations that are publicly funded. In states where appeal takes the form of a trial *de novo* in a higher trial court, the process is redundant, wasteful, and ineffective. In any event, trials *de novo* are all too often a denial of corrective justice.

A greatly neglected aspect of justice is the just administration of courts and cases. In a sense, caseflow management is a manifestation of administrative justice, so judges who make ad hoc, arbitrary administrative decisions about case processing are guilty of administrative injustice. Administrative justice is also due to a person who makes inquiries of the court, seeks to file papers, or relies upon the court to keep records correctly. Court users are entitled to justice in these particulars and to courteous treatment. Some courts bring to memory the early days of restaurant desegregation in the South when proprietors had to permit access to formerly excluded persons but were surly to those who exercised their right to be treated justly.

Equity, viewed in a nontechnical sense, represents the highest and purest form of justice and is an integral part of the American legal system. It provides equal protection of the law but recognizes that justice must be occasionally tempered by the distinctive nature of the parties and situation. Equity has always represented the triumph of justice over technicalities and, in fact, originated as an intervention to compensate for the rigidities of the common-law writs. In criminal law, the legislature looks at a social problem, but the judge looks at an

---

[3]   Florida has used this method quite frequently. In Pinellas County, misdemeanor probation has been provided by the Salvation Army.

individual. The day that this distinction is blurred will be the end of judicial justice. There are interstices, ambiguities, and gross inequities that may find their way into positive law. A judge does not have to "make law" to moderate or prevent that which is unconscionable. People still look to the courts as the ultimate guardian of justice.

The difference in the future is that judges and courts will be asked to provide justice on a broader plane. The progress made in the late twentieth century has laid the groundwork for a more inclusive definition of the judicial role and the meaning of justice. This raises fear of judicial tyranny and intrusive activism, but judges are not seeking a new role. It is being thrust upon them by the social exigencies of contemporary American society. All too often, courts become the place where the "buck stops."

The broader dimensions of justice have implications for caseflow management, probably the premier court administration reform of the late twentieth century. Caseflow management was an attempt to change the management culture of courts and to encourage strong judicial leadership under the banner "justice delayed is justice denied." Yet, curiously, this important innovation reflected some of the narrowness of the twentieth-century reform agenda. It was and is still focused on dispositions and getting cases out of the system without undue delay. A disposition is recorded when the case is resolved by settlement, plea, dismissal, or trial verdict. At this point, the court has done its job. The case is no longer pending or part of the backlog. Unfortunately, this management philosophy has limited application to large areas of court activity where the court has an ongoing role, as, for example, in foster care, mental commitments, and guardianships. Family and juvenile cases do not lend themselves to crisp dispositions and tend to remain in the system with many modifications of judgments and frequent hearings. Even where an order is entered, the court may be involved in postdisposition enforcement proceedings. Child support enforcement is by definition a postadjudication activity and yet may occupy many court employees and require frequent court appearances by delinquent payers. Even the important sentencing role of a judge is beyond the scope of caseflow management. The main limitation of caseflow management is that it is case oriented, not person oriented.

Some court administrators moan that their courts have been transformed into enforcement courts, meaning simply that the enforcement of court orders and judgments is becoming as important as entering an order or judgment. Small-claims courts may rapidly process cases to conclusion but remain lax in enforcing the judgments that could be easily obtained. Courts may fail to enforce judgments against criminal defendants paying fines and fees on an installment basis. A court that does not enforce its judgments is not much of a court, no matter what its record is in speeding cases to disposition. This court administrators' complaint makes sense only if the sole role of a judge is to move cases to disposition. This, however, is not true. The measurement of trial court performance must be multidimensional, because justice is multidimensional.

The problem of the new reform agenda is not defining or championing a new role for judges or a broader concept of justice. These are upon us. The issue is adapting to this reality. This entails moving from the mind-set that governed the old agenda to the philosophy that is already shaping the new reform agenda. As Chief justice Zimmerman observed, adherence to outmoded paradigms of the judicial role is probably "unwise."

Chapter 13

The Open Service-oriented Court

O One way to look at a court is to regard it as a castle of justice surrounded by moats. You can enter with difficulty, do what you have been summoned to do by the lords, and leave without upsetting them. On the other hand, the court can be open to discussions with the citizens of the outside world, be ready to accept their good ideas, and even to go out to find their needs and to serve them in their own vicinity. The latter court is interested in citizens; the feudal court tolerates them. The ideal is to eliminate the feudal court and replace it with the open service-oriented court.

Open Proceedings

The very first standard in the *Trial Court Performance Standards* (1.1) states: "The court conducts its proceedings and other public business openly." This standard requires openness to be the norm and suggests that denial of public access be in accord with the law and reasonable public expectations. This standard also specifies that proceedings be accessible and audible. This standard encompasses "physical access" and requires accommodation of the physically handicapped not only as parties and witnesses but as jurors. This is a much broader concept of openness than has existed in the past.

Open court proceedings for adults have long been considered a constitutional right, an important check on the abuse of power. Openness can also benefit the judiciary because the court's actions are seen by the public and, thus, the court is less likely to be engulfed in rumors and innuendo. Yet, some of what happens in courts is not open, usually because it happens in chambers or in a private colloquy at the bench during a trial. There are also some categories of cases that have traditionally been closed to public view, notably juvenile proceedings.

The privacy of juvenile proceedings is based on the perceived best interest of children and has long been a required feature of both delinquency and abuse/neglect proceedings. Juvenile courts are supposed to have a less intimidating environment and to cushion juveniles against the harshness of the adult system. Their problems are shielded from public view, as is their identity. This privacy also applies to files because these may contain sensitive materials about internal family occurrences and revealing psychological profiles. This privacy places a special burden on judges to avoid being arbitrary as there is less scrutiny of their actions by the public.

Unfortunately, privacy exposes courts to uniformed criticism for what is supposedly happening behind closed doors or, conversely, shields them from warranted criticism. Juvenile advocates are starting to question whether privacy is in the best interest of children and the juvenile justice system. Judges are starting to express similar views, because it is hard for them to counter unjust criticism. Although judges are not enthusiastic about public monitoring of their courts, particularly by lobbyists for some cause, seasoned observers can sometimes serve as a buffer against unfounded criticism of the judiciary and be an ally in effecting needed changes. On the other hand, public ignorance about the juvenile justice system can translate into either lack of political and financial support for the system or bizarre legislation. Furthermore, failure to share information undermines the ability of agencies to provide effective services to children and their families. The persons most adversely affected by this situation are children.

The trend to openness, even in juvenile matters, is demonstrated by experiments with open hearings in some of the most sensitive matters. In 1998 the Minnesota Supreme Court authorized each judicial district to conduct a three-year pilot project on open hearings for child protection, permanent placement, termination of parental rights, and subsequent state ward reviews. This is one of many steps being taken by states to open up the juvenile process.

Collaboration with Citizens

The desire for openness does not stop with court proceedings. There are numerous civic groups and court-monitoring groups that seek to open up the administrative processes of the courts, asking the not unreasonable question, "Why is the administrative decision-making process of the courts private inasmuch as these decisions do not involve adjudication?" Courts appear to be public entities run in privacy. Judges are reluctant to use citizen advisory groups, to appoint nonlawyers to court committees, and to obtain citizen input in court administrative matters that affect the general public, as, for example, in the administrative rulemaking process.

Some senior court administrators place a lot of emphasis on citizen involvement on court committees, seeing it as a way to make the legal culture more responsive to court users and the community. Some judges are very receptive to this, but this type of citizen involvement bothers many judges who are convinced that only lawyers can really understand the needs of a court. Judges do appoint prominent citizens to court reform committees, but the idea of ongoing association with lay persons in matters pertaining to the management of a specific court is not generally palatable.

Volunteers are the best link between the court and the community and are extensively used in some courts, even for supervision of probationers. In 1995 there were some 6,000 volunteers in the New Jersey courts alone. Many courts have since hired volunteer coordinators. Some courts actively recruit volunteers through community colleges, senior citizens groups, and churches.

Volunteers can become effective advocates for courts with the community, but they can also be very clear sighted critics of the courts. They are sometimes treated as flunkies, as do-gooders, or as a means of keeping down personnel costs. They are not always recognized as the valuable resource they are in opening up communication between the court and the community. They cannot be expected to lead cheers for the court if they are not treated properly or heeded when they make suggestions for improvement. Courts are, therefore, starting to include more volunteers on court committees, because they are demonstrably interested citizens with some knowledge of the problems faced by courts.

Inviting the citizens into the court is only one aspect of court-community relations. Courts have to make some outreach into the community. In October 1995 over 1,000 court and community leaders across the country participated in the first National Town Hall Meeting convened under the auspices of the National Center for State Courts and the American Judicature Society to explore ways courts and communities can collaborate to improve the public's trust and confidence in the justice system. The event was symbolic of citizens' desires to work more closely with courts and concentrated on programmatic and attitudinal innovations. The collaboration of the community and the courts on the systemic level was aptly described by Chief Justice Shirley Abrahamson of Wisconsin:

> Court and community collaboration is a sustained, two-way commitment to ensuring that the justice system is open and effective for all. It is not a one-shot event aimed at solving one isolated problem or satisfying one special interest group.[1]

Court-community collaboration, like many "innovative ideas" in courts, is not new. There have been a number of "grassroots" efforts, many of them originating in a community that perceived some means of improving the justice system. Chief Justice Shirley Abrahamson described the phenomenon as follows:

> Throughout the country, courts are coming together with the communities to improve how courts respond to the needs and interests of the public. Volunteer service programs, court advisory councils, and public opinion surveys are but a few examples of the diverse approaches being used to connect courts more effectively to the communities they serve. We call these efforts "court and community collaboration" because they stem from and require public involvement in decision making about how the courts should function.[2]

---

[1]   Rottman, Efkeman, and Casey, *Court and Community Collaboration*, 2.

[2]   Ibid., note 1.

Typical of these collaborative efforts are:[3]

Navajo Nation Peacemaker Court	The cultural traditions of the Navajo nation did not lend themselves to dispute resolution through an adversarial process, giving birth to a system of peacemakers, who are individuals respected for their wisdom and ability to resolve problems through discussion. The people choose the peacemakers who operate under the aegis of the regular court system in settling disputes.
Franklin County (Massachusetts) Futures Lab Project	This eminently "grassroots" project was an offshoot of the work of a futures commission that produced a report recommending various improvements in the delivery of justice in Massachusetts. The purpose of the "lab" was to establish a mechanism for obtaining community feedback about court problems and possible enhancements. The centerpiece was a task force that involved all elements of the community and sought to involve persons perceived as pessimistic about the process. The project has led to proposals for pilot reform projects by reaching out through town meetings and conferences and using working groups to make reform ideas concrete.
Oakland County (Michigan) Youth Assistance Program	This is a long-standing program to keep juveniles out of the justice system and to strengthen families by use of youth assistance offices throughout the county to operate local programs and counseling services. The offices make extensive use of volunteers, but the court assigns professional caseworkers to coordinate volunteers and community-organizing activities.
Juvenile Conference Committees (New Jersey)	This long-standing program features Juvenile Conference Committees composed of citizen-volunteers appointed by the presiding judge of the family division. There may be ten or more committees in a county, each serving some local community. The committee makes recommendations on cases involving first-time juvenile offenders with minor offenses and monitors compliance.
Juvenile Justice Councils (Florida)	Like so many contemporary changes in courts, court-community collaboration draws much inspiration from juvenile and family concerns. The Florida legislature has authorized county juvenile justice councils, which are

---

[3] Ibid., Appendix A, "Site Reports."

vehicles for collaboration and structured to ensure broad community participation. The focus is on juvenile delinquency, where it has been amply demonstrated that it takes a comprehensive community effort to redirect the behavior of the large percentage of juvenile offenders who are not hard-core miscreants.

Court visionaries see a time when courts will be neighborhood based for many purposes and even located in public-housing projects. A forerunner of this may be the experimental Midtown Community Court in New York City. This court collaborates with the community to address quality-of-life offenses like prostitution, disorderly conduct, shoplifting, minor drug possession, and property defacement. The court includes a community advisory board and provides a good illustration of effective information sharing among courts and court-related agencies. The appeal of this type of court is that it focuses on offenses that may go unchecked or unnoticed in a high-volume criminal court but can destroy a neighborhood. Another interesting feature of the Midtown Community Court Project is that it attracted funding from the Fund of the City of New York, a private nonprofit organization. This type of court requires above-average resources and poses the same problem raised by any innovation in court structure that carves up court resources into little chunks.

Public Service Considerations

As the Midtown Community Court illustrates, an important aspect of openness is court location. This is also an aspect of public service because inconvenient location and inconvenient hours are inconsistent with the goal of public service. One innovation that resonates with the public is reducing the need for persons to come to a central courthouse for just about any service; for example, filing court papers. In geographically large and well-populated counties, such as the urban and metropolitan counties of California and Florida, court facilities have frequently been decentralized.[4] The problem is determining what functions must be centralized and what functions can be provided by an outreach facility. The need to have holding facilities for prisoners and jury courtrooms requires that some types of proceedings be centralized. This same rationale applies to highly resource-dependent functions that require a concentration of services at one point. There is, however, no need for every court facility to be a full-service location. The more routine and voluminous matters lend themselves to treatment in outlying facilities that are simple in structure and convenient for the public. It may well be that outlying court locations will be located in public buildings, such as regional libraries. Maryland has encouraged limited jurisdic-

---

[4]   There may be an opposite trend in sparsely settled states where the number of court facilities is excessive in relation to population.

tion courts to house themselves in state buildings with agencies that have a lot of in-person contact with the public.

Having court sessions on Saturday or in the evening can be a great boon to citizens who find it necessary to leave work to accommodate the regular court hours. As obvious as this is, many courts find it difficult to overcome opposition from judges, court employees, and unions. These off-hour sessions could be held in outlying locations for the many less-serious matters that constitute the principal volume of most courts, but even this raises many objections. Some legislatures have concerned themselves with this issue of service, so it is not unlikely that recalcitrant courts may find themselves facing a statutory mandate.

Convenience does not guarantee courtesy and respect. A senior court administrator recounted the experience of his state in introducing Total Quality Management to court personnel. A consultant was enlisted to explain the concept to a group of court employees and started talking about a customer orientation. Before he progressed very far in his presentation, he became aware of snickers and barely suppressed laughter. Finally, he paused and asked his audience what was so funny. One senior clerk said the talk seemed unreal because the people they had to deal with were mostly "slobs and jerks." So much for customer orientation.

A number of court administrators report that they have received similar reactions from judges when court users were described as customers. Part of the problem is that the term *customer* suggests the world of commerce and retail sales. The term *client* does not work because it has such an explicit legal connotation. *User* seems to be a more acceptable term. The problems of terminology probably reflect the confusion within the courts about exactly who they are serving.

Sometimes, court reformers speak of serving the public, but exactly who composes the public? The "general public" consists of the great majority of citizens who only have occasional contacts with a court. There is a "public" composed of opinion leaders, such as members of the media, citizen observer groups, business organizations, labor leaders, leading officials in government agencies, and legislators. There is a third constituency composed of persons who have experiences with the courts and its procedures, such as jurors, witnesses, and trial attorneys. Finally, there is an "inside group," judicial officers, persons employed by the court, and the organized bar. Courts have to be more specific about what "public" they are trying to serve.

The term *customer* is unpopular among some court people, but the term includes anyone who receives or uses what a governmental entity provides or produces or whose success or satisfaction depends on an action of a governmental entity. Courts have a broad array of customers, among them criminal defendants. Persons accused of crime depend heavily on court to the dispense justice fairly and are, in that sense, customers.[5]

---

[5]   It should be noted that court customers may be sharply divided on how the court should act. Criminal defendants may not favor speedy case processing, whereas other customers, such as prosecutors, may favor speedy disposition because that is how they achieve "success or satisfaction."

Customers may be internal or external. Some court agencies exist primarily to serve components of the court, rather than the public. The beneficiaries of these services are considered internal customers (e.g., a judge receiving computer support from the court's computer division). The majority of court customers are individuals or organizations outside the court, among them attorneys, law enforcement officers, and litigants. There is a widespread public perception that judges see attorneys as their only customers.

Very often, a governmental body has both internal and external customers. A clerk may provide services to both judges and attorneys. It is not unusual for two government units to be both providers of services and customers to one another. Probation agencies, for example, provide presentence reports to judges, but judges handle probation violation hearings instituted by probation agencies.

The definition of *customer* is ultimately less important than attitudes. Judges and court employees have a hard time with customer service for a variety of reasons. Many people come to court under some form of compulsion and do not want to be there. It is very hard to see prisoners exiting from a sheriff's van for their day in court and think of them as customers. Moreover, the nature of the judicial process is such that there are losers in many proceedings, hardly satisfied patrons. There is also a complacency based on having a perceived monopoly on the services being provided. "Where else can they go? We control the whole process."

There is a necessary linkage between customer orientation and quality. Courts must be willing to change their way of doing business to meet the needs of the persons they serve. Judges and court employees need some help and guidance in reordering their thinking, because they may not have developed a public service orientation. If they feel they have a monopoly that makes them impervious to public criticism, they must learn that the existence of a monopoly creates a particular social responsibility to be attentive to the needs of persons coming to court.[6] Excellence in performance is a necessary corollary of a changed disposition toward public service.

Working with dedication, courtesy, and concern is what eventually separates the service-oriented court from the court that is going through the motions sluggishly. Unfortunately, many courts are still in the latter category, largely because they function as bureaucracies where employees are treated with the same low respect that they in turn show to the public. The inherent problem is the idea that there is an aristocracy composed of judges served by a group of underlings who live to make judges happy. Fortunately, this is changing. The demands of technology, the complexity of court management, and the plethora of social programs under court aegis have introduced many more-educated, highly trained employees into the courts and narrowed the lord-serf gap. Judges themselves are perceiving that they can be more effective if surrounded by a highly trained team to

---

[6]   The monopoly on adjudication is not total by any means. There are many alternative dispute resolution methods that are not court annexed. To some extent, this phenomenon has been driven by dissatisfaction with the service provided by courts.

which they can delegate many important functions. The stage is set for an era in which court employees will be able to take more initiative and reach outward to court users, to the community, and to noncourt agencies.

People who come to court are very often scared, confused, or over-whelmed, so many courts are trying to look at their operations from a citizen's perspective. Those courts that adapt this perspective treat people better, often starting with those persons who have special needs (for example, the elderly, who will become increasingly important recipients of court services). It is only in recent years that some courts have gotten serious about language difficulties and set up interpreter programs and bilingual service centers. (The development of standards governing selection and performance of interpreters is just under way with the formation of a consortium of interested states, but interpretation in courts is still quite whimsical.) Despite the passage of the Americans with Disabilities Act, most courts are simply not equipped to deal with the needs of persons with physical disabilities, although many new courthouse designs are reflecting more consideration of these needs.

Nowhere has the indifference and coldness of courts been more evident than in the treatment of women who have been victims of violence or harass-ment. Humiliating interrogations of women by quasi-judicial officials and court employees have frequently revealed a callous disregard for women com-plainants. Women emerge even more dehumanized than when they entered. Unfortunately, this is not an aberration caused by a few cranky employees. It is symbolic of the fortress court, where the peasants stand outside and beg for jus-tice and feel grateful if they are noticed.

Courts are changing and starting to do a better job of addressing the needs of court users. Among these promising initiatives are specially trained intake teams for victims of domestic violence, location of publicly funded legal offices and court clerical staff in large mental health institutions, and aggressive outreach and training programs to upgrade the availability and skills of court interpreters. Each of these needs may be viewed as discrete, but from a management perspective they are tied together by the need of the court to be aware of user concerns.

The number of pro se litigants has increased to the point where courts are introducing programs to help them. A good example is the Self-Service Center of the Maricopa County (Arizona) Superior Court, which provides information, instruc-tions, and simplified forms for use in divorce, paternity, child support, guardian-ships, and conservatorships (probate will be added later). The forms are subject to tight quality control and are designed to minimize legal jargon. Because of the large Spanish-speaking population, the program is bilingual. The center is helpful to pro se litigants and to anyone who has to deal with the court system.

The assistance to litigants in Maricopa Family Court is interdisciplinary and is based on partnerships with other county agencies to keep costs down. The family court provides linkages to many social service providers, inasmuch as many people who are experiencing domestic difficulties have problems in other areas of their lives. Self-represented litigants are also linked to attorneys for legal advice and limited service on a reasonable-fee basis, because many liti-gants want some advice from attorneys but not necessarily full-scale representation. Litigants are also linked with mediators. Any fee arrangements with attorneys or mediators do not involve the court. A major positive feature of the program has been the assistance provided by the Arizona Bar Association.

Maricopa County has demonstrated that self-represented litigants can, with the help of a good program, negotiate the system fairly well and that the court owes them this opportunity, but no more. They have to put in a significant effort of their own to supplement the aid received from the court, so there is no incentive to pursue frivolous litigation. Moreover, a line has been drawn between procedural advice and substantive advice. The court tries to confine its aid to procedural matters, but the distinction between these areas is not always clear. This self-help approach produces cost savings for the court by reducing the amount of time spent by court personnel on personally doing everything for litigants. It is hoped that the program will reduce the amount of extra time judges spend in "churning" cases that have been sidetracked or delayed by procedural errors made by self-represented litigants. It is also possible that the program will be extended into landlord-tenant matters, probate, mental health, and civil suits generally.

Information Sharing

The ability of court users to obtain access to court information or to provide information to courts without going to the courthouse is improving, but a long way from ideal. Giving court users the ability to communicate from afar or bringing court services to court users is very embryonic, because the positive attitude that must accompany information sharing may not be present. The more progressive court systems have used technology to serve public information needs by providing access through personal computers, by information kiosks at strategic locations, and by twenty-four-hour telephone service with a variety of recorded information, such as juror call-in systems and calendar information. It is still difficult to overcome the idea that people come to the court, not the court to the people.

Even this tradition would be marginally acceptable if the information were readily available from a clerk. Even assuming a high level of clerical cooperation, the requestors find that asking clerks for information is inconvenient, slow, and sometimes unsuccessful. The misfiling of a record or its removal to the office of a judge, prosecutor, or attorney kills access. Normally, litigants make inquiries, but there are many other possible inquirers—businesses affected by a case, researchers, journalists, credit companies, and many other potential users. Information is guarded and doled out. Sometimes, court information is viewed as a commodity to be sold. The Maricopa County (Phoenix) Superior Court is providing free Internet access to its large court database docket. Anyone with Internet access can use the database. Yet courts often charge for electronic access.

Even though electronic filing of court papers has been discussed for years, only a few courts have attempted it. One major obstacle is the lack of technological capability among lawyers not associated with a large firm, a condition that will change rapidly as the legal system moves toward electronic case citations and broader networking among attorneys. There is also a lack of standards to govern information interchange. Control of information is important to many people, making them leery of easy access to or improper use of their information. Verification of information received from others is also a legitimate, if somewhat exaggerated, concern. Court control over filings and clerical empires are threatened. Moreover, there are often a plethora of anachronistic statutes and rules that reflect the practices of an earlier era. Some of these legal provisions even make it impossible to accept fax pleadings.

A classic illustration of court attitudes toward open access to information is provided by the controversy over universal electronic citations that would place court opinions in the public domain almost as soon as they were issued. The American Bar Association took a lead role in devising a proposed universal citation protocol that would be common to all courts and built around a sequential case-numbering system by year and by court and use of paragraph numbers to identify sections of a court opinion. This anticipated the transition from the volume and page citations of the print medium to an electronically based legal research system.

Many appellate courts already make their slip opinions available on the Internet or on bulletin boards. A few states already use parallel electronic and print citations, and the West Publishing Group incorporates these electronic citations into its printed volumes. Nonetheless, many state and federal judges expressed great reservations about the ABA proposal. The United States Judicial Conference, reflecting the expressed view of a great majority of federal judges, refused to endorse the ABA proposal and saw it as vaguely threatening. The Conference of Chief Justices expressed reservations about the proposal and was privately hurt that the views of the conference had not been solicited. Some state supreme courts flatly rejected the ABA proposal and took the position that it reflected an attack on the time-honored print medium. The objections raised about the ABA proposal were rather weak, but more surprising was the indifference of some high courts to the many users of court information lined up in favor of what is an almost inevitable change.

The only one on the side of the judges is West Publishing Group, which is fighting a losing battle to maintain its monopoly over court information that should, by any standard, be in the public domain. The whole footnote system and the West additions to the court opinions it publishes and sometimes edits (West is the official reporter for many state appellate courts) are being rendered obsolete by full-text search capability. Lined up in favor of the ABA proposal are independent publishers, law schools, law librarians, and many bar associations. The appeal of electronic citations to small law firms and individual practitioners is cheap and easy access to the full range of legal materials without buying costly printed volumes. Some bar associations have filed petitions urging their state's highest court to adopt electronic citations, but the appeal of electronic citations goes beyond the legal world. Researchers and businesses of all kinds have an interest in court information. In the face of all this, the judges have been a little slow to react.

Courts have problems in sharing information not only with the public but also with the agencies with which they interact. This is not necessarily the fault of courts, as other government entities are often possessive of their own information. This has been a problem in the criminal justice area for years. When the Law Enforcement Assistance Administration focused attention on crime and criminal justice agencies in the early 1970s, analysts soon announced the then novel concept of a criminal justice system that included the courts and various justice agencies. Courts were at first reluctant to accept their inclusion in the system but have, over the years, been increasingly drawn into sharing information with criminal justice agencies and a variety of other agencies; for example, motor vehicles departments.

Information technology is forcing courts and noncourt agencies into information networks, but this does not come easily in a bureaucratic environment. For years, the development of integrated criminal justice information systems languished because of parochial attitudes and exaggerated fears of security breaches, mostly emanating from the law enforcement component of the system. This insular mentality frustrated the ability of the criminal justice system to pass along identifying information on an individual. Instead, each component of the system protected its own database and separately entered the same information about a defendant. For many years, eliminating repetitive data entry was the unfulfilled aspiration of persons engaged in criminal justice information systems. Fortunately, this cultural primitivism seems to be changing. Consultants long frustrated by the intransigence of criminal justice agencies are reporting breakthroughs in cooperation and openness among criminal justice agencies and some promise of adapting the criminal justice culture to current technological possibilities.

Information technology is forcing more cooperation among the agencies involved in helping troubled families, because crucial information is in the possession of other agencies. Some courts, such as domestic violence courts, must have quick and easy on-line access to information files in various locations. Family courts are starting to assign all matters related to one family to an individual judge to prevent contradictory orders, to better constrain violent family members, and to provide a focal point for all information on a particular family. Moreover, court information is crucial to many other agencies, especially welfare and health agencies. Courts often find social agencies irritatingly bureaucratic and can react to this frustration by staying out of an information network where the court is a key component but not the principal beneficiary. Even at the cost of losing federal funding, some courts have been reluctant to tie themselves to welfare agencies in such matters as child support enforcement and foster care. Generally, however, courts are accepting the need to be part of a larger system transcending the judicial branch.

The electronic interchange of information is necessary to realize the full value of computerization. Although most courts are using computerized case management systems to speed and improve their work, the cost of paper handling and conversion of paper-based information to an electronic format is eating up most of the productivity gains that computer systems provide. The National Center for State Courts has designed JEDDI (Judicial Electronic Data and Document Interchange) to facilitate the electronic interchange of information, including transmission of images and documents, between courts and the governmental agencies with which the courts interact. There is even a civil JEDDI project to link up courts with credit agencies. As in most court-related projects on information sharing, cultural barriers are the main impediment to implementation.

Collaboration with Noncourt Agencies

Courts need to cooperate with other agencies in many areas other than information sharing; budgetary matters, for example. Common sense suggests that courts should approach appropriating bodies in conjunction with other governmental bodies engaged in addressing a common problem and perhaps even take the lead. Domestic violence, for example, cuts across many agency lines, involving prosecutors, defenders, and a variety of social agencies. However, the traditional court approach is to address the budget need as a workload problem for the courts: "The number of domestic violence cases has gone up 10 percent. Give us more money." Legislative bodies, both state and local, are fed up with the "go it alone," input-centered budget approach of courts. A budgetary alliance based on problem solution is far more persuasive.

The most comfortable partnerships are those with bar associations and legal aid groups because they are within the fraternity, but there are many others forms of joint action: state-local partnerships; city-county partnerships, public-private partnerships, and creative use of nonprofit affiliates. These forms of cooperation would have shocked judges at midcentury but are now occurring with enough frequency to indicate that the judiciary is more receptive to joining with others to meet public needs. Below are a few examples of this emerging trend.

- Courts and social service agencies are putting employees at the same locations so that members of the public can receive a full range of information and services without having to go to multiple locations.

- Courts are establishing 501(c)(3) affiliates to obtain supplemental program funding in areas where public funding is unlikely and even to operate social programs that are not being provided by government agencies, or, at least, not being provided very well.

- Courts using personnel from other governmental agencies in regional facilities to provide mini-outreach centers for the courts, one example being the librarians in regional libraries.

- Courts have formed partnerships with community colleges to provide education programs that traffic violators can attend as an alternative to harsher sentences.

- Courts have used 501(c)(3) corporations for privatized design-build-finance court construction projects.

- Courts have made themselves the site of software development and teamed with software companies in developing, testing, and marketing court products.

- Courts have teamed with nonprofit affiliates of private corporations to combine private grants and public funding in the construction of court facilities.

- Courts have worked with urban redevelopment corporations in the renovating decaying areas by locating court facilities in target areas in return for private aid in funding construction.

- Courts have located traffic and small-claims facilities in or near high-volume mall areas to serve people where they congregate and to obtain cheap rentals from a developer or mall operator anxious to increase the flow of potential customers.

- Cities and counties are forming partnerships to fund court facilities and programs.

- Some courts have actually formed condominiums with private entities when occupying space in private buildings.

There are legitimate objections to some of the above arrangements, the most common being conflict of interest. The salient point, however, is the willingness of courts to come out of sanctuary and seek allies in the cause of court improvement. This can take the form of involvement in a criminal justice information system, networking with treatment providers, or budgetary alliances. Social involvement means more than "therapeutic jurisprudence."

There is not a single issue of openness and access that is not being addressed by some state court. Moreover, there is a general awareness of the importance of this particular issue. The movement is in the right direction but its pace is slow, because the culture of the state courts has not been shaped by concepts of openness, access, and public service. Changing this "closed court" culture is a major aspect of the new reform agenda.

Chapter 14

The Assault on Unification: Specialty Courts and Special Interest Groups

For several decades state courts have struggled mightily to bring order out of chaos. They now find themselves struggling against powerful interest groups dedicated to subdividing the trial court system into specialized courts or, if necessary, to avoiding the state courts entirely. What makes this movement toward specialization so potent is that it is supported and sometimes led by federal agencies and by state executive branch officials aligned with these federal agencies. The court community sees its control of its own house eroding under this challenge. One of the prime casualties will be the concept that trial courts should be unified and that trial judges constitute a pool to be deployed in whatever part of the court they are needed.

Advocates of specialty courts base their position on the necessity to focus resources on a specific problem and to obtain judges who have the expertise and desire to handle that problem. The underlying assumption of the specialty court advocates is that the unified courts will give low priority to their agenda. They prefer to carve out a court segment dedicated to their concerns or, failing this, to bypass the state courts entirely. Opponents assert that fragmentation into specialty courts defeats rational allocation of resources and is an overly rigid means of dealing with problems. They feel that flexible shifting of resources and creation of specialty divisions by rule of court can meet specialized needs. They point out that the trendy problem of today may not be the problem of tomorrow and that you cannot create rigid structures to deal with transitory social phenomena. The pro-unification forces are losing, in part because the state courts have not been very responsive to specialized needs, in part because the pro-specialization forces are so varied and strong.

Juvenile and Family Court Initiatives

There has been a strong lobby for separate juvenile and family courts for many years. The movement has had a second wind, fueled by a variety of federal programs and a surge of support in many state legislatures. In the flurry of contemporary activity, it is easy to forget that the movement for separate juvenile courts started well before the twentieth-century unification movement. Chicago had a juvenile court as early as 1893.

Because juvenile courts were already institutionalized in many places, they were largely exempted from organizational unification and, in effect, grandfathered into the unified court systems. When, for example, the Connecticut courts were unified in the late 1970s, juvenile courts remained in separate buildings, with their own staffs, and even their own venue districts. Juvenile courts judges became superior court judges, so juvenile courts were technically part of the one-tier trial court system. In practice, they maintained a separate identity because this was demanded by the juvenile court movement.

Most states, unlike Connecticut, located juvenile courts only in urban areas with sufficient population to warrant a full panoply of support services. These courts were not affected by unification. Interestingly, these courts often had juvenile probation officers paid by the local government, whereas some state executive branch agency provided juvenile probation services elsewhere in the state. In general, juvenile courts had a far different staffing pattern than adult courts. Because so many juvenile matters were settled informally without judges, juvenile courts had a number of professionals, such as probation officers and caseworkers. Therefore, the salaries and the ratio of staff to judges were higher than those of adult courts. It was simply easier to leave these courts separate. The historical pattern has been reinforced by federal funding programs in the Department of Justice that reinforce the isolation of these courts. One counterforce has been the "get tough with juveniles" slant of recent state and federal legislation. This has made juvenile delinquency proceedings more like adult proceedings and encouraged more transfers of juvenile cases to adult court.

Some states combine domestic relations and juvenile court functions, which they consider fundamentally linked, into family courts. Small states like Delaware and Rhode Island have created structurally separate statewide family courts. The modern tendency is to add child support enforcement, adoption, and foster care to the family court mix and to see the various personal problems of a troubled family as interrelated. This favors the family court over the traditional juvenile court. However, both approaches now have substantial federal funding support. Much of this funding takes the form of a percentage reimbursement of state and local expenditures. The IV-B, IV-D, and IV-E programs of the Social Security Administration are focused on family components of courts and are reimbursement programs.

It is no secret that most judges do not like family and juvenile cases. This has fueled the demand for separate juvenile or family courts staffed by judges who want to be there and who share the ideology that shapes such courts. Legislatures are still often pressured by interest groups to create special jurisdiction courts, usually family courts. In the mid-1990s, family advocacy groups in Michigan obtained legislation requiring a family division in every circuit court. This legislation transferred many family-type issues from probate courts to circuit courts without transferring any support staff and created divisions in a number of circuit courts that did not have sufficient volume to warrant a specialized division. Court officials and family advocates have since ironed out some of the their differences, but the legislation created organizational structures that made no sense from an administrative viewpoint. Courts in areas with a large volume of family cases could create divisions on their own by rule, but the statute imposed a single solution for a problem that had to be dealt with flexibly. This is the classic dilemma posed by the creation of courts to serve specialized needs.

The Boutique Courts

The danger of fragmentation is exacerbated by the "federalization" of many issues traditionally handled by states. The federal government, never particularly sensitive to the role and prerogatives of state courts, has been a force in the creation of specialty courts. Federal officials have used their grant money to encourage states to set up special courts according to federal specifications and to keep them separate from the court system. These special-purpose courts have been dubbed "boutique courts." Although the term may include specialty courts that are not federally funded, it has a definite federal connotation.

The Department of Health and Human Services and the state courts have continually struggled over the so-called IV-D Program and child support enforcement. Some states now have child support enforcement magistrates who are parajudicial officials of the state judicial branch but are federally funded to carry out federal program objectives.[1] Some states carry out their child support enforcement programs with absolutely minimal state court involvement, frequently by choice of state judicial leaders. The HHS ideal is for state courts to be their agents in executing federal policy and to keep all child support enforcement activities separate. HHS frankly prefers administrative courts but testily tolerates state court "intrusion" into their program.

Federal grant programs in the Department of Justice, notably the drug court and victim assistance programs, are slightly more sensitive to state court prerogatives, but not much more. Fortunately, a few DOJ officials have a state court background and have raised their lonely voices to suggest that state courts should, in fact, be respected and involved, rather than excluded. Unfortunately, state court systems can be their own worst enemy, choosing indifference and opposition when their only real alternative is to get in front of the mob and lead it to some sensible goal.

Because state judges have been uncomfortable in the treatment coordinator roles being thrust upon them, the federal government has emerged as a major advocate for programs demanding better coordination between courts and social services. Nowhere is this more apparent than in the rise of drug courts. These courts, for the most part, divert nonviolent addicts to treatment without formal adjudication and try to break the cycle of substance abuse that makes repeaters of so many drug users. The key to drug courts is a close working relationship between treatment providers and judges.

---

[1]   The salary of a state court judge cannot be reimbursed under the IV-D Program, but this is largely a matter of nomenclature. The salary and office expenses of some limited jurisdiction state judges are being reimbursed because they have assumed a title that meets the requirements of federal law.

Since the inception of the Miami drug court in 1989, the number of drug courts has increased at an accelerating pace. As of June 1, 1998, there were 430 drug courts in various stages of development, including adult drug courts, family and juvenile drug courts (a newer phenomenon), tribal drug courts, and rural drug courts. Only 124 of these drug courts were more than two years old on this date, testifying to the quick expansion that is occurring. These courts have grown up outside the mainstream court community, which has been slow to see the significance of the movement.

Federal authorities recognized this remarkable growth, which now encompasses forty-eight states, the District of Columbia, Puerto Rico, and Guam, and placed federal support behind the state and local efforts. Title V of the Violent Crime Control and Law Enforcement Act of 1994 authorized federal grants for drug courts and led to the creation of the Drug Court Program Office (DCPO) within the Office of Justice Programs of the United States Department of Justice. Unlike some federal programs, the drug court program has sought to prevent the creation of structurally separate drug courts and to build cooperation between drug courts and the state court systems. There are, however, those in the drug court community who would like to keep drug courts quite separate from the mainstream court community, although drug courts have much in common with juvenile and family courts in the administration of therapeutic justice.

Experiments to meet urgent problems attract the attention of federal funding agencies, which provide resources unavailable at the state and local level. Federal involvement, however benign in intention, usually ends up as the tail wagging the dog as resources are poured into some relatively small area of court activity that becomes disproportionately large and difficult to mesh with other court activities. State court judges are justly concerned about the federalization of their court systems, because it is a real threat to the structural coherence of state courts and to judicial independence. Chief Justice Michael Zimmerman of Utah captured this concern:

> The price of appearing to resist such initiatives from the federal government can be large. An instructive example not well known is the recently established program to strengthen child support collection nationwide. One element of this program is to require that states determine paternity in simplified administrative proceedings. The federal government is intent on taking these determinations out of courts and away from juries, which they see as slow and unduly cumbersome ways of determining such questions. To this end, the federal legislation requires that if a state has a statute or constitutional provision that precludes these determinations from being shifted to administrative agencies and out of courts, such as a mandate that a jury trial be available, the state has three years to repeal such provision or face a draconian cut in funding for the child support program. It seems unlikely that any state will long resist such pressure.
>
> On a national level, state court leaders think that we are on the verge of a virtual avalanche of legislation, essentially federalizing aspects of the state

courts by mandating how we do business in specific areas. I think our only hope is that we get out in front of the parade if we are to have chance of gaining credibility with the public and the other branches of government and getting them to help us in gaining control over how these new programs run and how they are integrated with our more traditional way of doing business. We should be part of the solution, not part of the problem.[2]

Rather than appealing to principles of federalism that have little impact on Congress or the national executive branch, state courts find themselves seeking to influence the ways federal initiatives are applied at the state level. In fairness, some of the federal programs, despite their bureaucratic idiosyncrasies, are addressing problems that state court leaders have ignored.

Special Demands of Business Groups

There is a struggle under way to control the decisions of state court judges on issues that affect business. On one side are ranged the trial lawyers, labor unions, and Democratic interest groups. The pro-business side is composed of corporations, small businesses, manufacturers, hospitals, insurance companies, and various trade associations. Because medical malpractice has been linked with "tort reform" in business cases, doctors are often part of the business coalition. The contending forces have locked horns in judicial elections, and they have battled in nearly every state legislature. Business forces have had considerable success in legislatures but have seen state appellate judges override their legislative victories. The special demands of business groups must be considered against this backdrop.

Many years ago, businesses started avoiding state courts in corporate contract disputes. They often included arbitration clauses in contracts so they could exercise some control over the selection of arbitrators and assure themselves that the arbitrators understood the business issues of their particular industry. They could not, however, avoid the state courts entirely and frequently complained that the courts were so absorbed in family and criminal cases that they neglected civil dockets. In states with a big corporate presence, courts were asked to devote more time to business cases.

Some states attempt to meet this need with a separate court, such as the Delaware Chancery Court. So many corporations are chartered in Delaware that the court system has always been very responsive to the requests of business groups for service. New York allocates some judges and courtrooms exclusively for business cases. Some court observers view small-claims courts and landlord-tenant courts as "business courts" despite the populist origins of these courts. Many jurisdictions use these courts as vehicles to help landlords or lenders. This

---

[2] Extract from a speech by Chief Justice Michael Zimmerman to the Utah Bar Foundation on December 2, 1997.

is not necessarily a bad use of these courts, but it is not considered politic to refer to these courts as business oriented. The problem is that it is hard to determine exactly what a "business case" is. It appears to be whatever the commercial litigating bar says it is, making it difficult for courts to be responsive.

Not openly stated, but clearly part of the business agenda, is the desire to control the caliber of judges hearing business cases. There is great skepticism in the commercial litigating bar about the ability of many state court judges to handle complicated issues. Although the lawyer-generalist is becoming rarer because the complexity of law has forced a high degree of specialization, the judiciary clings to the idea that any judge is capable of dealing with complex legal, technological, and scientific issues. In bench trials, a great deal of time is spent educating the judge, sometimes to no avail.

There is increasing doubt about the logistical ability of state courts to handle complex mass torts at either the trial or the appellate level. In fact, mass torts place great strains on state trial courts, which, after all, are high-volume courts with limited resources. Such cases, with their records of daunting size, can overwhelm state appellate courts. Some state courts are assessing expenses against the parties in such cases rather than having the public treasury bear the full brunt.

The issue that has roiled the state courts and led to widespread criticism of the judiciary is product liability litigation. The opposing sides have fought for control of the highest state appellate courts and have manipulated the electoral process. The "tort reform" groups have invoked federal help in their crusade to limit the liability of manufacturers and their distributors, not to mention their insurers.

The perception among many corporate attorneys that state courts are not an appropriate forum for complex corporate litigation arises in large part because of the way state courts have handled product liability. In the landmark case of *Henningsen v. Bloomfield Motors, Inc.*, 161 A. 2d 69 (N.J. 1960), the New Jersey Supreme Court held that a relationship of privity was not necessary to bring a product liability suit against a manufacturer or dealer. In 1962 California adopted the standard of strict product liability (*Greenman v. Yuba Power Prods., Inc.*, 377 P. 2d 897 (Cal. 1962)). Encouraged by the *Restatement (Second) of Torts* § 402A (1965), many other states adopted strict product liability as a legal standard.

Product liability law remained in a state of flux in the 1970s but tended generally to favor plaintiffs and to lead to higher damage awards. Liability insurance rates increased, resulting in attempts to curb the effects of strict product liability.[3] A major shift in legal thinking and responsibility was going on as courts and legislatures attempted to balance protection of users against the social need to encourage the manufacture and sale of useful products. A number of societal goals were involved, but not usually in a clear or consistent way. Among these

---

[3]   The term *strict liability* is unduly frightening. Basically, strict liability shifts the focus of proof from the due care taken in the production process to the nature of the product itself. It did not leave product sellers defenseless.

were providing an incentive for product safety, compensating those who sustain loss or injury from unsafe products, allocating loss or risk fairly, and ensuring accountability in mass marketing.[4] In many instances, government regulatory agencies intervened to achieve one or more of these objectives. Parties frequently protected themselves with contractual provisions. In addition, courts had to face the complexity of the market and distribution chain. Inevitably, there was concern among product sellers and insurers about the slowness and vagaries of the common-law process. This was exacerbated by decisions that appeared to be unduly creative in discerning new rights. Business groups called for certainty.

During the Carter administration, the Department of Commerce became concerned about complaints from businessmen and insurers over the adverse effect of product liability litigation on international competitiveness, new product development, and the economic well-being of American producers. Many of the business complaints focused on high insurance rates, which, for purposes of product liability, are figured on a national level. This concern among product sellers sparked a series of studies and proposals resulting in the Model Uniform Product Liability Act (UPLA).

The introduction to the UPLA provides an interesting insight into the thinking of its framers on the role of state courts:

> The current system of having individual state courts develop product liability law on a case-by-case basis is not consistent with commercial necessity. Product sellers and insurers need uniformity in product liability law so they will know the rules by which they are to be judged. At the same time, product users are entitled to the assurance that their rights will be protected and will not be restricted by "reform" legislation formulated in a crisis atmosphere. Thus, the Model Law meets the needs of product users, sellers, and insurers.

The above paragraph is a strong criticism of the condition of product liability law in state courts, with some implied pressure to adopt the model law or be superseded in the name of "commercial necessity." The model act attempted to legislate certainty.

On balance, the UPLA provided a fairly evenhanded attempt to encourage a common statutory approach to product liability cases, but it failed to attract support. It did, however, lend some momentum to the forces mobilizing against strict product liability. In the 1980s this counterforce was successful in swinging the legal pendulum toward the defense side with a series of laws that were grouped under the heading of "tort reform." These laws were hotly opposed by the personal injury bar and actually became an issue in the 1992 presidential campaign. These reform laws have some points of similarity but are largely responsive to local concerns. In general, they reflect attempts to modify what

---

4   One of the difficult balancing acts in product liability law is the interplay between the UCC and product liability statutes. The presence of contract law and warranties in product liability suits makes it hard to draw clear lines.

appeared to be an exceedingly pro-plaintiff orientation in the early development of strict product liability.

The most common issues addressed by state laws are statutes of limitations; statutes of repose; definitions of defects; restrictions on admissibility of evidence; compliance with government standards defense; duty to warn; alteration, modification, or misuse defense; contributory negligence;[5] retail vendor's defense; notice requirements; limitation of damages; change of collateral source rule; ceilings on awards; separate trials on liability and damages; and sanctions for frivolous suits. Most legislation has been designed to protect defendants, particularly nonmanufacturer defendants in the chain of distribution. Case law, to the extent that it can be summarized on a national level, has also moderated various aspects of strict liability. During the 1980s, the pro-plaintiff tilt of the previous decade was slowed down and in some instances reversed, but the corporate bar remained suspicious of common-law state judges and the capacity of state judges to handle complex issues with great economic consequences.

The issue of "junk science" captures some of the concerns emanating from the business community. The silicon breast implant cases led to bankruptcy for the huge corporation that was held liable for damages to women who used the product. Informed scientific opinion eventually coalesced around the proposition that the methodology used by experts for the plaintiffs had no scientific validity. By then, the corporate defendant was financially destroyed.

The United States Supreme Court weighed in with its opinion in *Daubert v. Merrell Dow Pharmaceuticals*.[6] This case set forth in dicta a standard of reliability for the admissibility of scientific evidence, in effect making federal trial judges the gatekeepers to exclude scientific evidence not based on a valid scientific methodology. In observing that the many *amicus* briefs in the case concerned scientific method and matters far afield from the expertise of judges, Chief Justice Rehnquist expressed concern over making trial judges into amateur scientists to determine what evidence should go to a jury. Many attorneys feel the same way, and not just those on the plaintiff side. If there are doubts about federal judges, there are at least as many doubts about state judges. Can the fate of an industry rest on such a frail reed?

One solution is to federalize all issues affecting national corporations and to take state courts out of the picture. As the common law is overridden by federal and state statutes and regulations, the common-law state judges are diminished in importance, as is the personal injury bar in the state courts. The concepts of pain and suffering and punitive damages are being curtailed to keep down insurance rates and the costs of goods and services. The civil jurisdiction of the state courts is eroding, in part because of economic issues beyond their control, in part because they may, in fact, be unequal to the complexities of a modern industrial system.

---

[5] Strict liability in torts normally carries a standard of comparative responsibility. States that do not recognize comparative damages have had to deal with this issue.

[6] 509 U.S. 579 (1993).

Underlying the malaise about the role of state courts is that they are being forced to regulate business practices through the jury system. Harassment and discrimination suits filed against an HMO under a patient bill of rights are typical of the cases that involve mini-regulation of business practices. Juries replace government administrative agencies, a frightening specter in some regards because jurors have very little knowledge of the impact of their decisions and no responsibility for what they have done. It appears that politicians who want to change or control some part of the economy resort to a bill of rights that opens up the economy to the high-stakes gambling casino that is our litigation system. Judges often are blamed for strange trial results over which they have no control.

The state courts are receiving pressures from many directions and a lot of criticism, some of it unfair. Some of the special interest groups leading the assault are not admirable in their objectives or methods and simply want to twist the courts into a mold that suits their purposes. The critics, whatever their agenda, have one thing in common: a belief that state courts are unresponsive to user needs and incapable of addressing the social, scientific, and economic needs of a modern society. State courts are trying to be responsive, to the extent that it is proper to do so, but are contending with a number of restless constituencies.

State chief justices are painfully aware of the impact of special interest groups on the courts and the common law. They are even more concerned about the aggressive expansion of federal law into areas long considered to be within the state domain and increasing federal encroachment upon the administrative authority of the judicial branch and the state legal system. The Conference of Chief Justices has, for about ten years, spoken out frequently on these issues but without great expectation that their conference resolutions can slow down the federal juggernaut. Nonetheless, specialty courts and the federal role in shaping state legal systems will be major items on the new reform agenda, requiring a far different type of leadership than that exercised to effectuate the old agenda.

Chapter 15
Leadership Challenges

J udges from foreign countries often visit the National Center for State Courts to learn about state court systems. Interestingly, the models they look for are administrative, not adjudicative. Many come from countries with civil-law systems and do not draw many analogies between their role and that of American judges, who operate in the common-law tradition with a jury system. They can, however, appreciate court administration. This interest was so pronounced that the National Center for State Courts developed a monograph for foreign judges that explains court administration in the United States.[1]

Court administration in the United States is a new phenomenon and most certainly a work in progress. Its imperfections seem quite glaring and its needs endless, but foreign visitors see it for what it is, a marvelous step forward for courts. We need this perspective, because Americans get so absorbed in the pursuit of "progress" that they forget where they started and how far they have come. By any standard, state courts have come a long way in managing the judicial branch. The legal myth of separation of powers has been given substance by the creation of organizational forms and administrative infrastructures that enable courts to direct their own operations. This truly great advance does not always get due recognition. Without this fundamental change, many other important advances in courts would not have occurred.

The reform movement of the late twentieth century affected states differently, but few were untouched by it in some way. The movement will be remembered for a number of beneficial changes in state courts:

- making progress in merit selection of judges and modifying the political aspects of this process
- bringing courts of limited jurisdiction into the state judiciary and introducing a higher degree of professionalism in these courts
- making great progress in judicial education and substantial progress in judicial discipline
- introducing professional management into the courts

---

[1]   Robert W. Tobin, *An Overview of Court Administration in the United States* (Williamsburg, VA: National Center for State Courts, 1997).

- heightening awareness of case delay and introducing caseflow management
- introducing jury management
- involving state government in the financing of trial courts
- introducing organizational coherence into state court systems
- building administrative systems with professional credibility
- promoting more active judicial leadership and increasing judicial awareness of responsibility for the performance of the court system

This is an impressive list even though it does not capture all the advances made in state courts. These beneficial changes are, however, only a start in the right direction. The reform agenda of the last half-century is unfinished. Politics still plays too large a role in the judiciary; there are still many eccentric local aberrations that reflect poorly on the courts; some states still have chaotic organizational structures; judges have much to do in superintending the legal profession and their own profession; and many judges are still uncomfortable with administrative and executive responsibilities.

Looking back on the great judges in the Arthur Vanderbilt tradition, one perceives that these men were skillful political figures who had the courage and vision to create something out of almost nothing. Because the traditions and institutions of the judicial branch were not conducive to strong leadership from a chief, these early leaders were, to a large extent, on their own. In retrospect, their successes were quite phenomenal. Their achievements included major court reorganizations, shifts of trial court funding responsibility to the states, and major increases in the authority of supreme courts over the court system and judges. One could argue that these leaders were the beneficiaries of a general trend to state government reform after World War II. But the judicial branch was by far the weakest of the three branches and inherently less able to reform itself. Early judicial leaders needed a personal political style to compensate for lack of power. Fortunately, they institutionalized some of their achievements by constitutional or other legal changes. Otherwise, their legacy would have faded when they left office. Their great contribution was leaving a strengthened branch so that their successors could exercise leadership with less political struggle.

The early leaders sometimes encountered resistance from state and local officials who were unused to an assertive judiciary, but these leaders had the advantage of dealing with issues within their sphere—court structure, court administration, rulemaking, court financing, and the selection, education, and discipline of judges. It was hard for officials in the other branches to deny that judicial leaders had valid interests in these matters. The voters could also perceive the legitimate interest of the chief justice in these issues and sometimes indicated their approval or disapproval of the chief's position by their vote in a constitutional referendum.

Early judicial leaders also had definite reform goals. Their agenda was clear—unifying courts and upgrading the judiciary. Many judicial leaders shared this vision, so the reform movement was not a series of isolated events. Judges throughout the nation were urging each other on and forming support groups. The triumphs in one state invigorated the leaders in other states. Even though the reform agenda played out differently in each state, judicial leaders gained strength in pursuing a shared vision. Even some states where judicial leadership was not strong partially achieved the reform agenda.

The great judicial leaders had the ability to state a vision in simple and compelling terms. Their greatness did not lie in dreaming up visions, but in their ability to apprehend and mobilize support for ideas whose time had come. The great judicial leaders of the late twentieth century made the judicial branch a coherent reality. They also lent their prestige to upgrading the state judiciary by improving the selection, discipline, and education of judges. These reforms were not just discrete items on a list of good things to do but a means of ensuring the integrity of the system. When Arthur Vanderbilt brought about the administrative unification of the New Jersey courts, he did not view unification as an end in itself. He was trying to insulate the New Jersey judiciary from the political ethos of the state and to protect the court system from corruption. Yet, to this day many persons comment on the New Jersey reforms as centralization run wild and miss the point that Vanderbilt and his heirs did a pretty good job of ensuring the integrity of the system.

All court reform revolves round two perennial questions: Does our justice system have integrity? Do we show respect and concern for the people who rely upon the courts for justice? One reason the formal adversarial system is under fire is that it is perceived as lacking both integrity and respect for persons. The system stands accused of producing a shoddy form of justice that is divorced from the truth, that demeans those who participate, and that denies access to many who might invoke the aid of the system. Even though twentieth-century court leaders made major steps in establishing the system's integrity, they did not usher in a perfect system. Moreover, they put much less emphasis on treatment of the public than they did on reforming the system itself. Improving court organization and administration and upgrading the judiciary are fundamental to serious reform but constitute only a beginning. Much remains for the judicial leaders of the next millennium.

It must also be remembered that most chiefs in the late twentieth century did not attempt to emulate Vanderbilt's reformist zeal and assumed a low profile. It is not realistic, even now, to expect that most chiefs will be dynamic leaders, but it is realistic to expect that they will feel responsible for the performance and integrity of the court system. They need not be crusaders, but they can take leadership steps commensurate with their personal political skills and the culture of their system. Chief justices are now more amenable to leadership than they were a few decades ago. This is a silent tribute to those chiefs who blazed the trail.

There are some lessons to be learned from the past. One is that the nature of judicial leadership varies by type of issue. In matters of interbranch relations, only the chief justice can speak with ultimate authority for the judicial branch, because the chief justice personifies the branch and has to be its political champion. The chief justice is also the natural leader in any struggle to protect the integrity of the court process and the judiciary when problems transcend the local level. Some chiefs are politically astute, an attribute that is sometimes scorned but probably indispensable to effective leadership. The chief justice has to build support within the supreme court and elsewhere in the branch and negotiate the political system within the bounds of the ethical codes that bind a judge.

The issues raised by the twentieth-century reforms were primarily those where the chief justice had to be out front. The issue of system integrity remains crucial but is starting to share the stage with the other great fundamental premise of court reform, respect for the persons who come in contact with or rely upon courts. Because the new reform agenda is more person oriented, the role of the chief justice will probably be reduced and somewhat less political and confrontational.

Contemporary judicial leaders have some positive leadership legacies from the early reform era. Most are now officially the chief executive officers of their court systems. Methods of selecting chiefs have been slowly changing toward longer terms and away from automatic rotation. Supreme courts are more accustomed to administrative rulemaking. The authority of chief justices and supreme courts has been increased by unification, particularly budgetary unification. A number of states have made skillful use of futures commissions, trial judges, and judicial councils as part of their leadership schemes and have stimulated a flow of ideas to ensure the vitality of the system. Some big battles have already been fought and won. Finally, there is a court administrative support system that is both a source of ideas and leadership.

The interstate and intrastate networks of judges and court employees that have grown up since midcentury are other legacies of the reform movement. The Conference of Chief Justices constitutes a particularly valuable leadership resource if the organization's potential can be realized, particularly on issues of federalism. The chiefs have made some progress in winning independence from the other branches of state government but are losing the battle to prevent federalization of the state court system. The federal presence is growing rapidly with no end in sight. There is a crucial need for state chief justices to show national leadership. This will necessarily involve the Conference of Chief Justices and, on federal imposition of unfunded administrative responsibilities, the Conference of State Court Administrators. These organizations are not really constituted for active leadership on behalf of state courts and have been slowly moving toward active engagement with federal authorities. Individual chiefs have started to work more with elected federal officials in their own states, but this still occurs infrequently. This inertia has to end, because the integrity of state courts depends on the ability of state judicial leaders to right the imbalance in judicial federalism.

State court administrators play important subsidiary leadership roles and may occasionally be the prime movers in an important change. Some state court administrators have been successful in conceptualizing reform ideas and obtaining supreme court support. This is sometimes called "leading from behind," but the term does not capture the importance of ideas in bringing about change. Ideas can come from many sources, among them judicial councils, citizen groups, legislators, and planning bodies. But a state court administrator who is gifted at conceiving and articulating ideas is a particularly potent leadership force because of close ongoing contact with judicial policymakers.

Some state court administrators have the personality and political skills to lead reform efforts. Sometimes, a prescient or relatively inactive high court may entrust a state court administrator with leadership on key issues where the court and the chief decline the honor or feel that the particular skills of the administrator make him or her the natural leader. There is no inherent reason why a state court administrator cannot be a strong leader if he or she has the support of the chief and the court, particularly of the former. This makes the state court administrator a target, but this is the price for stepping out front.

Because the early reform issues centered on unifying and upgrading the trial court judiciary, the forces of reform came from the central level of the judicial branch. Many trial judges were opposed to these reforms, so trial judges were not a not a likely source of leadership. Moreover, the issues transcended any one court and required state-level action. Here and there trial judges assumed leadership in these reforms, but the main reform impetus came from the top appellate court or some other state-level entity. Some of the legitimacy and acceptance of the twentieth-century reforms were lost because there was not enough leadership emanating from the trial courts.

As the nature of court reform becomes more "grassroots," the leadership role of trial judges becomes very important. Appellate judges do not deal with the public or, for that matter, with most of the bar. They can advocate changes in the way trial courts do business, perhaps even mandate some actions, but the real leadership will have to come from trial courts. Typically, chief trial judges take the lead, but occasionally a trial judge simply takes up some cause and becomes the acknowledged leader. It is argued that unification stifled trial court leadership, and there is some truth in this. Chief trial judges and trial court administrators in a unified system may become mechanisms for implementing state policies and may not be innovative or reformist in their orientations. Many of the interesting trial court innovations have occurred in states where trial courts have broad management.latitude.

There is no necessary connection between unification and passivity at the trial court level. Great latitude can be given to trial court leaders within a unified system. This is not just an option but a real necessity in the second wave of reform. Moreover, the courts that are free to experiment will attract the best trial court administrators, and there are some capable members of this profession who can bring ideas, vigor, and management ability to their courts in the same way that a state court administrator can at the state level. There have been great chief judge-administrator teams at the trial court level, as there have been at the state court level. A form of unification that inhibits this type of trial court creativity and leadership is a caricature of reform. Intelligent decentralization is the hallmark of a unified system that is responsive to the public and uses local leadership capabilities. The truth is that trial judges understand many problems much better than appellate judges and will not only bear the primary burden of implementing many reforms but may be the original moving force behind the reforms.

It is not unusual for ideas that originate in trial courts to suffer from parochialism and tunnel vision, just as it not uncommon for ideas conceived at the state level to be impractical and trendy. Any successful court system will figure out some way to take advantage of state and local strengths. Responsible leadership requires a process for generating ideas, translating them into realistic form, and focusing energy on the most important ideas for change. Unfortunately, this process can at times become mechanistic and quite divorced from the fundamentals of the system. Nothing is more frustrating than to see a court caught up in all types of trendy court improvement projects while the core of the system decays and the public is ignored. The danger of all reform agendas is that they can become self-justifying and lose touch with reality.

Although it can be truly said that a new reform agenda is emerging, it does not represent a spectacular break with the past. It is more a change of emphasis from institutional matters to relations with the public and the community. How leaders in the court deal with this change will vary greatly, but the real leadership challenge is not championing whatever passes for current reformist wisdom, but constantly going back to basics. Sometimes, a reform agenda can become a distraction from reality. ADR can become a gimmick for avoiding changes in the basic litigation system; improved caseflow management can become divorced from the fundamentals of justice; and providing Internet access to court records can become a public relations coup. In the end, every court leader is forced to consider the fundamental integrity of the justice system and to respect people and their needs—that is to say truth, justice, and human dignity. State courts have tried with some success to provide a system with integrity, but with much less success to provide a system governed by respect for human dignity. The battle for integrity continues. The battle to create a person-oriented court is under way. Courts require a human dimension that has been sadly lacking.

Index

A

Abrahamson, Shirley, 235
Accountability, in investigations of judicial misbehavior, 126–127
    judicial independence and, 15–16
Act of Settlement (1701), 6
Adams, John, 12
Administrative Office of the United States Courts, 121
Administrative orders, 147
Administrative rulemaking, role of chief justice in, 150
Admiralty courts, in colonies, 8
Adoption, in family courts, 248
    protective justice and, 229
Adversarial system, alternatives to, 210–212
    criticism of, x–xi, 213–215, 259
    human dimension of, 207–210
    jury reform and, 216–222
    mythology of, 212–213
    public opinion of, 94, 197
    role of truth in, 214–215
Age Discrimination in Employment Act (1967), 20
Agencies, noncourt, court cooperation with, 244–245
Alabama, court reform in, attitude of blacks toward, 64
      chief justice participation in, 48. See also *Heflin, Howell.*
    elected clerks in, 71, 72
    federal block grant funds and, 49
    judicial elections in, 30
      tort reform and, 40
    justices of the peace in, 64
    role of local judges in, 58–59
    special courts in, 52
    state court administrator in, 165
Alaska, state court administrator in, 165
Alternative dispute resolution, 210–212
    in caseflow management, 189
    role of trial court administrator in, 186
    status of, 211
    uses of, 212

American Academy of Judicial Education, 130
American Bar Association, 14
 court reform and, 140, 156
 early support of merit selection of judges by, 123
 ethical aspects of judicial political activity defined by, 31–32
 Model Rules of Professional Conduct, 82
 racism in, 89
 section on judicial administration in, 121
 Standards of Judicial Administration, 17, 133, 140
 Standards Relating to Court Organization, 134
 universal electronic citations proposal of, 242
American Judicature Society, court reform and, 156
 creation and contributions of, 119
American Law Institute, common law and, 87
American University, 156, 157
Americans with Disabilities Act, 184, 240
Anglo-Saxon legal system, 5
Appeals, from limited jurisdiction trial courts, trials *de novo* and, 52
Appellate courts. See also *Supreme courts, state.*
 collegial tradition in, 105–107
 corrective justice and, 230
 intermediate, before 1950, 21–22
 jurisdiction and powers of, in early republic, 9
 mass tort cases in, 252
 restricted access to reports of cases in, 86
 state financial responsibility for, 139
 vs. trial courts, 171, 172
Appellate judges, career paths of, 46
 common law and, 87
 corruption among, 128, 129
 issue-specific pressures on, 40–41
 selection of, 30, 124
  in New York, 34–35
Appellate Judges Seminar, 129
Arizona, court user orientation in, 240–241
 judicial selection in, 30
 nonlawyer real estate transactions in, 86
Arkansas, judicial election in, 30
 law and equity courts in, 55
Arraignment, disorder during, 62
Arrest warrants, issued by justices of the peace, 56
Articles of Confederation, prolegislative slant in, 8–10
Attorney general, state, as career path for judges in appellate courts, 46
Attorney-client relationships, court regulations of, 97
 judicial bypass of, 93–94
Attorneys. See *Lawyers.*
Audits, of trial courts, 69–70
 by elected clerks, 73

B

Baar, Carl, 4
Bail, conditional release on, 230
Bail agencies, trial court administrator and, 186
Bail bondsmen, 75, 76
Bail hearing, in District of Columbia Court of General Sessions, 101
Bailiffs, 69, 77
Banks, local trial court arrangements with, 69
Bar. See *Lawyers*.
Bar association(s), governing of, role of chief justices in, 151
    of City of New York, 121
    local, challenges to incumbent judges by, 36–37
    role in merit selection of judges, 123
    state, 95–96
        conflicts of with judiciary, 96–97
        integration of, 95–96
        regulation of, 95–97
    state court administrator liaison with, 167
    vs. groups challenging legal turf, 97
Bar examinations, local control of, 95–96
Bartlett, Richard, 159
Belshaw, Betsy, 160
Bench warrants, 76, 77
Bench-bar conflicts, 96–97
Bias, in justice-of-the-peace system, 64
    in legal profession, 89–90
    in potential jurors, 74, 216
Bilingual service centers, for court users, 240
Bills of attainder, 9
Bills of pain and penalty, 9
Bird, Rose, rejection of in retention election, 29
Blackstone, 6, 7
Bond, forfeiture of, 76
Boutique courts, 249–251
Boyle, John, 107
Breitel, Charles D., 35, 149, 159
Brown, Edmund "Jerry," 31
Buchanan, President James, in *Dred Scott* case, 14
Budgeting, by elected clerks, 71, 181n.
    court cooperation with other agencies in, 244
    disputes over, 66
        inherent powers suits and, 17–18, 66–67
        legislative revenge for political decisions and, 13, 36, 38, 45
    inequities in, in locally funded trial courts, 67–69
    judicial independence and, 3, 4, 15
    relationships between prosecutors and courts in, 79
    role of chief judge in, 177
    role of trial court administrator in, 170, 181–182
    for sheriff's deputies, 75, 75n.

unification of, ix, 18, 133, 139–146. See also *State financing*.

unitary, under state financing, 67

Burger, Warren, 156, 157

Business groups, state court decisions and, 251–255

C

Calendar function, attorney control over, 97–98

    caseflow management and, 190

    of elected clerks, 71

    police control over, 78–79

California, administrative offices in, 172, 175

    appellate defenders in nonprofit corporations in, 230

    attitude of judges in higher courts to those in lower courts, 137, 137n.

    commission to investigate complaints of judicial misbehavior in, 126

    judicial selection in, 31

    municipal courts in, 175

    retention election in, 29

    state court lobbying in, 49

    state financing in, trial court inequities and, 67

California Trial Court Budgeting Commission, 113–114

Canons of Judicial Ethics, American Bar Association, 31–32

Capiases, 76

Cardozo, Albert, 123

Cardozo, Benjamin, 122–123

Caseflow, through courts, police department role in, 77–79

Case manager or coordinator, caseflow management and, 190

Caseflow management, administrative justice and, 230

    attorney-judge relationships and, 97–100

    categorization of cases in, 188–189

    chief judge's role in, 177

    components of, 188

    definition of, 187

    limitations of in broader concept of justice, 231

    in Ohio, 110

    trial court administrator's role in, 179, 187–191

Caseload, allocation of, in Kentucky, 136

        in two-tier court system, 136–137

    statistics on, state court administrative office and, 168

Cases at law, vs. cases at equity, 54–55

Catholic associations, judicial profession and, 89

Center for Jury Studies, 218–219

Chancellor, governor as, 6

    role of in early English courts, 5–6

Chancery (equity) courts, 6, 55

Chase, Samuel, impeachment of, 12, 13

Checks and balances, separation of powers and, 10–14

Chief court administrator, in Connecticut, 105

Chief judge(s), authority of, 107, 177–178

    relationships of, with trial court administrator, 180–187

    relationships of, with other judges, 178, 180–181

responsibilities of, 176–177
 roles of, administrative, in budgeting, 181n., 181–182
  in caseflow management, 189
  in trial court administration, 176–178
  leadership, 261
  symbolic, 104
 in trial court structure, 173
Chief justice(s), administrative role of, dealing with judges in, 150–151
  delegation of details of administration by, 152–153
  goal setting and executive leadership in, 149
  implementation of management policy in, 150
  models of, 105, 106
  relationship with bar in, 151
  relationship with court-related agencies in, 152
  relationship with public in, 152
  state financing and, 152
 as change agent, 149
 leadership role of, 12, 259–260
 legislative influence of, 48
 relationship of with state court administrator, 161–162
Child neglect and abuse, legal access and, 224
Child support enforcement, caseflow management and, 231
 in family courts, 248
 federal support for, 249
  conflicts with state courts over, 249
 legal access and, 224
Children, as witnesses, 208
 in foster homes, 229
 privacy of juvenile court proceedings and, 233–234
Circuit courts, 52, 54
 in colonies, 8
Citizen groups, relationships with, trial court administrator and, 185
 unification movement and, 133, 135
Civil cases, categorization of, in caseflow management, 189
Civil Rights Act, 184
Clerks, elected, administrative services provided by, viii, 71, 72, 181n.
 factors favoring independence from judicial control, 71–73
 fees of, 71–72
 functions of, 70
 jury system and, 73–74
 opposition of to state unification, 70–72
 political power of, 72
 relationships of, with trial court administrators, 183–184
  with trial court judges, 70–73
Client trust funds, court regulations of, 97
Clinton, William, 84
Codes, vs. common law, 87–88
Colonies, administration of by king and Privy Council, 7
 court system in, 6, 8
 local law in, 8

Colorado, inherent powers suits in, 18
    water courts in, 54
Common law, development of, 6
    resentment of, 87–88
    vs. codes or statutes, 87–88
Common-law courts, 5
Computer-aided transcription, role of trial court administrator in, 186
Computerization, electronic sharing of information and, 243–244
    for compilation of juror lists, 219
    in courts, effects of, 205–206
    role of trial court administrator in, 186
Conference of Chief Justices, judicial federalism and, 19–21
    legal specialization and, 88
    legislation on product liability and, 88
    new court reform agenda and, 198, 260
    regulation of legal profession and, 95, 203
    universal electronic citations and, 242
Conference of Senior Circuit Judges, 120
Conference of State Court Administrators, 156, 260
Congress, judicial review of by Supreme Court, in early republic, 11–12
Connecticut, executive system of court management in, 105, 155
    legislative interference in court system by, 9, 45
    local bar examinations in, 96
    localism in, 63
    one-tier court system in, 138
    selection of judges in, 125
    state court consolidation in, 52–53
    statutory references to state court administrator in, 163
Conservatorships, standards for, federalization of law on, 21
Constable, in jury selection for justice-of-the-peace juries, 65
Constitutional Convention, interbranch relationships in, 9
    judicial review issue in, 10–11
Constitutions, state, judicial branch status and, 3
    state supreme court judicial review function and, 12–13
Contempt power, of judges, 13
Conti, Samuel, 113
Controversial issues, in election of judges, 40–41
Cook County, Illinois, 69
    Chief Judge John Boyle of, 107
    courts of, DePaul University Law School graduates in, 46
        localism in, 61
    marriage ceremony fees in, 145
Cooper, Carolyn, 157
Corporate legal offices, in-house, conflicts of with organized bar, 97
County courts, 52
    functions of, 56–57
    of Massachusetts Bay Colony, 7, 7n.
County funding, of local trial courts, inequity of, 67–69
Court administration, achievements of, 257–258

as career, origins of, 155–157
    state court component of, 157–172. See also *State court administrator.*
    trial court component of, 173–176. See also *Trial court administrator.*
collaboration with citizens and, 234–237
detail and background information in, 108
judicial administration in, 148–153
    role of chief justice in, 149–153
judicial independence and, 15, 21–23
in trial courts, early 20th century, viii–ix
    increased expenses for in 1970s, 141
    localism and, 57–58
unification of, creation of infrastructure in, ix–x, 155–172
    goals of, 133
    importance of, ix–x
    inherent powers suits and, 18
Court committees, public participation on, 234–235
Court days, for police officers, 77
Court delay, caseflow management and, 187n., 187–189
    causes of, 187
    discovery process and, 213
    reduction of, 188, 188n.
Court employees, attitudes of toward public service, 238, 239, 240
    chief judge and, 177
    command structure for, 111–112
    in locally funded trial courts, inequities in, 69
    misuse and theft of court funds by, 69–70
    state court administrators and, 170
    trial court administrators and, 184–185
    unification movement and, 133
Court facilities, chief judge and, 177
    legislative interference in court system concerning, 45
    local financing of, 143
Court information. See also *Information.*
    electronic filing of, 241–242
    sharing of, 241–244
    systems of. See also *Information networks.*
        role of chief justices in, 152–153
Court interpretation, programs for, 240
    role of trial court administrator in, 186
Court management. See also *Court administration.*
    judicial independence and, 4
    Trial Court Performance Standards and, 204
Court of Assistants, of Massachusetts Bay Colony, 7
Court reform. See also *Unification.*
    agendas in, changes in, 195–206
        in first stage, 195–196
        in new stage, 197–198, 222
    caseflow management in, 98. See also *Caseflow management.*
    elite bar and, 100–101

leadership in, achievements and advantages of, 258–259
    for new agenda, 260
    role of Conference of Chief Justices, 198
    support systems for, 140, 149, 198, 260
  milestones in, 257–258
  need for change in legal profession and, 198–202
  origins of, 119–121
  state bar associations and, 95
Court reporters and reporting, focused state financing of, 143
  trial court administrators and, 186
Court sessions, off-hour, 238
Court users, confusion about, 238–239
  with special needs, 240
  terminology used for, 238
Court venue, 54
Courtesy, in court employees, 238
Courthouse. See also *Court facilities*.
  role of in community, 58, 59
Court-related agencies, court collaboration with, xi
    with elected clerks, 70–73
    with police departments, 77–78
    political control of jury system and, 73–74
    with prosecutors and public defenders, 79–80
    with sheriffs, 74–77
  in caseflow management, 189
  information sharing with, 243
  management limits and, 111–112
  relations with, with chief judge, 177
    with chief justice, 152
    with local trial court, 70–80
    with state court administrator, 167
    with trial court administrator, 185
Courts. See also *State courts*; *Trial courts*.
  boutique, 249–251
  expenses of, factors influencing, 142
    per capita, 142
  general jurisdiction. See *Trial courts, general jurisdiction*.
  history of, vii–viii, 5–8
  jurisdiction of, congressional control of, 27
  justice-of-the-peace, 55–56
  limited jurisdiction. See *Trial courts, limited jurisdiction*.
  local patronage system and, 45
  multidoor, 211
  municipal. See *Municipal courts*.
  off-hour sessions of, 238
  open, changing role of judges and, 228
    collaboration of with citizens, x, xi, 234–237
    collaboration of with noncourt agencies, 244–245
    information sharing and, 241–244
    proceedings in, 233–234

public service considerations in, 237–241
 reform movement and, xi
operations of, costs of, responsibility for, 145
organization of, after unification, 134–139
 early 20th century, vii–viii, 52–58, 115, 135
political influence on, inappropriate, 33–46. See also *Political process.*
public access to, 196
public service considerations in, collaboration with citizens and, 234–237
 cooperation with noncourt agencies and, 244–245
 information sharing in, 241–244
 location and, 237–238
 off-hour sessions and, 238
 treatment of users with special needs and, 240
revenues from, misappropriation of, 144
 state financing and, 144–145
rural. See *Rural courts.*
specialty, 54
 arguments for and against, 247
 boutique courts and, 249–251
 family and juvenile courts and, 247–249
 judges in, 228
 product liability law and, 251–255
 reform movement and, xi–xii
structure of, in 1950, 135
urban, 171, 173, 174. See also *Municipal courts.*
vs. appellate courts, 171, 172
Courts of last resort, before 1950, 21–22
 leadership categories in, 105–107
 number of members on, 106n.
Criminal cases, categorization of, in caseflow management, 189
Criminal courts, adversarial system and, 213
 changing roles of, xi
Criminal defense attorneys, in Rhode Island legislature, judicial selection by, 38
Criminal justice information systems, 79
Cy-pres relief, legislative jurisdiction over, in early republic, 9

D

Dacey, Norman, *How to Avoid Probate,* 86
Dade County, Florida, domestic violence program in, 224–225
Dann, B. Michael, 219–220
Data processing, focused state financing of, 143
Daubert v. Merrell Dow Pharmaceuticals, 254
D.C. *Bar Voluntary Standards for Civility in Professional Conduct,* 199–200
De Tocqueville, Alexis, on public role of lawyers, 85
Debt collection agencies, conflicts of with organized bar, 97
Declaration of Independence, 7, 8
Defendants, sued vindictively or without valid cause, 209
Delaware, bipartisan judiciary in, 43
 state court administrator in, 165
Delaware Chancery Court, 102, 251

Democratic party, in Pennsylvania Supreme Court, 43
    in Philadelphia judgeships, 44
    in South, in partisan judicial elections, 39–40
Denver University Law School, 156
DePaul University Law School graduates, in Chicago courts, 46
Deputy state court administrators, 166
    in New York, 159
Detroit, fiscal crisis in 1970s, state financing and, 141
    Recorders Court in, appellate court control of, 61
Dewey, Thomas E., 129
Differentiated case management, in New Jersey, 99
Discovery, attorney attitudes toward, 99
    problems with, 199, 212–213, 222
Disorderly conduct, 237
District courts, 52, 54
    in Texas, 57
District of Columbia, Court of General Sessions in, 101
Diversity issues, judicial elections and, 41n., 41–43
Diversity-of-citizenship cases, jurisdiction of, 10, 19
Divorce, legislative, in early republic, 9
Domestic relations law, federalization of, 21
Domestic violence cases, changing role of judges in, 224–225
    court cooperation with other agencies in, 243–244
    court intake teams for victims of, 240
    role of trial court administrator in, 186
    special courts for, 54
Douglas, Stephen, 82
Dred Scott case, 12, 14
Drug cases, caseflow through courts and, 78
Drug Court Program Office, 250
Drug courts, 54
    changing role of judges and, 227
    federal programs for, conflicts with state courts over, 249–250
Drunken driving charges, pressure on judges from, 37
Duekmejian, Governor, 31

E

Education, judicial. See *Judges, education of.*
Elderly, protective justice and, 229
Election districts, diversity issues and, 42
Electronic information systems, 243–244. See also *Information; Information networks.*
    controversy over universal electronic citations and, 242
    filing of court papers and, 241–242
Emergencies, trial court administrators and, 183
Environmental courts, 54
Equity, as form of justice, 230–231
    in early republic, 9
Equity courts, 6, 8
Erickstad, Ralph, 32
Ervin, Sam, 46

Ethics, judicial, 35, 127
    of self-supporting court, 145
Ethnic associations, judicial profession and, 89
Executive branch, assumption of judicial functions by, 9–10
    disputes with judiciary over budget matters, 16
    organization and development of, 4
    reform of, 121
    relationships with other branches of government, 3–5. See also *Interbranch relationships.*
    trend toward specialty courts and, 247
Expert witnesses, 209

F

Family courts, 54
    additions to, 248
    assistance to litigants in, 240–241
    changing roles of, xi
    separate, 248
Family issues, agencies dealing with, 189
    attorney compensation in, 92
    caseflow management and, 189, 231
    categorization of, in caseflow management, 189
    changing role of judges in, 223–228
    information sharing with court-related agencies and, 243
    in lower-tier courts, 136
    protective justice and, 229
Fatzer, Harold, 149
Featherbedding, 69
Federal Circuit Court of Appeals, 129
Federal courts, early changes in, 120–121
    Federalist influence on, 10–12
    relations with state courts, 18–21, 249–251, 254–255, 260
        habeas corpus review of state court convictions and, 20
        state court jurisdiction and, 19
Federal grants, court planning process and, 110–111
    state court administrative office and, 170
    for family and juvenile courts, 247–249
    for judicial education programs, 130
    for special courts, and fragmentation in state courts, 247, 249–251
    for state courts, 48–49
Federal Judicial Center, 157
Federal judiciary, elite bar and, 100–101
    nonrepresentative ideology of, 42
Federal law, judicial interpretation of, 11
Federal question jurisdiction, state court jurisdiction and, 19
Federal Trade Commission, regulation of legal profession by, state court resistance to, 95
Federal treaties, judicial interpretation of, 11
Federalist, The, 3
Federalists, federal court system and, 10–11

judicial review by Supreme Court and, 11–12
Federalization. See also *Federal grants*.
    Conference of Chief Justices and, 19–21
    main issues in, 19
    of state court system, 18–21, 249–251, 254–255, 260
Fees and fines, attorney, 92, 93
      court regulation of, 97
      public perception of, 86
    court-collected, misuse and theft of by court employees, 69–70
      state financing and, 144–145
    earmarked for court operations, 145
    of elected clerks, 71–73, 73n.
    filing, access to justice and, 145
    inability to pay, community service and, 144–145
    installment payment of, 205n., 231
    legal, 211–212
    for marriage ceremonies, 145
    nonpayment of, sheriff functions and, 77
    retained by justices of the peace, 64
    retained by municipal court judges, 65
Field, Stanley, 35
Fifth Street Bar, 101
Financial aspects, of localism, 66–70. See also *Budgeting; State financing.*
    inequitable county funding of trial courts and, 67–69
    inherent powers suits and, 17–18, 66–67
    shift toward state financing and, 66
    slush fund mentality in, 145
    transition to state financing in, 69
Florida, Dade County, domestic violence program in, 224–225
    elected clerks in, 73, 73n., 74
    juvenile justice councils in, 236–237
    local bar examinations in, 96
Ford, Gerald, 84
Fortas, Abe, nonjudicial functions performed by, 14
Foster care, caseflow management limitations and, 231
    in family courts, 248
    protective justice and, 229
Franklin County (Massachussetts) Futures Lab Project, 236
Friesen, Ernest, 156
Fuchberg, Jacob D., 35
Fund of the City of New York, 237
Futures commissions, 111

G

Gallas, Edward, 156, 172, 187
Gallup poll, of public perception of lawyers, 83, 83t
Gasch, Oliver, 218
Georgia, election of judges in, 28, 30
Government legal service, judicial career paths and, 46
Government relations offices, in judicial branch, 48

in National Center for State Courts, 48
Governors, judicial appointment by, 29, 31
in California, 31
judicial branch and budget and, 3
Greenman v. Yuba Power Prods., Inc, 252
Guardianship cases, caseflow management limitations and, 231
court oversight of, changing role of judges in, 223
federalization of law on, 21
fees for, 92
Guide to Juror Usage, A, 218
Guide to Jury System Management, A, 218
Gulley, Roy, as state court administrator, 113

H

Habeas corpus, federal, review of state court convictions and, 20
Hamilton, Alexander, 11
Harris poll, on public opinion of lawyers, 82
Harvard Law School, common law and, 87
Hawaii, executive system of court management in, 105
relationship of state court administrator and chief justice in, 165
Health care legislation, federalization of law on, 21
Heflin, Howell, 32, 48, 58, 107, 149, 151
court reform and, 64
state court administrator and, 165
Henningsen v. Bloomfield Motors, Inc., 252
Henry II, King, 5
Herndon, William, 157
Hoffman, Julius, 89
Holdings, in common law, 87
How to Avoid Probate (Norman Dacey), 86

I

Idaho, judicial elections in, 30
Illinois. See also Cook County, Illinois.
geographic balance in supreme court in, 43
inherent powers suits in, 18
judicial election in, 30
marriage ceremony fees in, 145
one-tier court system in, 138
status of elected clerks in vs. judges, 73, 73n.
Illinois Supreme Court, state court administrator and, 112–113
Impeachment, of judges, 13, 126
of Samuel Chase, 12, 13
Indiana, election of judges in, 28
Indigent defense, courts and, 79–80, 80n.
focused state financing of, 143
increased expenses for in 1970s, 141
in paternity suits, legal access and, 224
Information, open access to, court attitudes toward, 241–244
Information networks, criminal justice, 243

electronic, 243–244
    role of chief justices in, 153
    state court administrative office and, 167–168, 170–171
Inherent powers, rulemaking authority and, 148
Inherent powers suits, administrative and budgetary unification and, 18
    interbranch relationships and 16–18, 148
    limitations on, 18
    in local trial courts, 66–67
    vs. judicial review, 16
Inns of Court, 90
Insolvency, legislative jurisdiction over, in early republic, 9
Institute for Court Management, founding and role of, 156
    judicial education and, 130
    trial court administrators and, 179
Institute of Judicial Administration, 129
    founding of, 156
Institutional trust departments, conflicts of with organized bar, 97
Insurance companies, conflicts of with organized bar, 97
Interbranch relationships, vii
    in delivery of social services, 226
    historical development of, 8–9, 22
    judicial independence and accountability and, 16
    role of chief judge in, 177
    role of chief justice in, 259
Interest groups, challenges posed by, 37, 247
Internet, access to court database docket in Maricopa County (Arizona), 241
    legal citations on, 242
Iowa, one-tier court system in, 138
    state financing in, status of elected clerks in, 72

J

Jacksonians, attitude of toward judiciary, 13–14, 28
James, Jim, 159
Jay, John, treaty negotiated by, 6, 14
Jefferson, Thomas, 84, 90
    attitude of toward judiciary, 12, 13, 28
    objection to power of federal court system, 10–11
Jeffersonians, impeachment of Samuel Chase by, 13
Johnson, Albert W., 129n.
Johnson, Lyndon, 14
Joint Committee for the Effective Administration of Justice, 129–130
Jones, W. Seaborn, state of legal profession summed up by, 200–202
Judges, accountability of, public demand for, 13–16, 27
    administrative vs. trial, 190
    allocation of, 44, 62–63, 136
    appointment of, 30, 31, 38
        by governor, 28
        by legislature, 28–30, 38
    assignments of, role of chief judge in, 176
        role of chief justices in, 150

role of state court administrators in, 168

attitudes of, to adversarial system, 94, 197, 213–216
    to alternative dispute resolution, 211
    to court-collected revenues, 145
    to management, 103–105
    to pro se litigants, 97
    to public service, 83–85, 239
    to state financing, 66, 68, 144

behavior and discipline of, ix, 126–129
    reform of, 126–127
    role of chief justices in, 150–151
    role of state court administrator in, 167

buried bench warrants and, 76

in business cases, skepticism of corporate bar about, 252, 254–255

checks on, in various states, 13

collegial tradition among, 105–107

in colonies, 8

compensation of, 65, 92, 125–126

conflicts of interest in, 69

demeanor of, 151

education of, ix
    funding for, 130, 151
    reform of, 129–130
    role of chief justices in, 151
    role of state court administrator in, 167
    specialized, 91

and elected clerks, relationships of, 70–73

election of, viii
    campaigns for, 33–36
    controversial issues in, 37, 40–41
    diversity issues in, 41n., 41–43
    drunken driving platforms and, 37
    early history of, 28
    for supreme courts, 30
    for trial courts, 30
    ideological posturing in, 36
    methods of, 30
    nonpartisan and partisan, 28–29, 39, 123
    nuisance candidates in, 34n.
    political influence on, 43–44, 128
    public demand for, 13, 85
    reform of, 28–30
    vs. appointed, 31

evaluation of, by attorneys, 92–93, 252, 254–255
    reform of, 131–132

in family and juvenile courts, 248

federal, 42
    vs. state, relationships between, 18–21

in general jurisdiction courts, condescending attitude of to judges in lower court,
    136–137

impeachment of, 13, 126
incompetent, community acceptance of, 60
language of, in municipal courts, 65
and lawyers, 81–102, 202–203
    common orientation of, 83–85, 239
        in financial relationships, 92
        in maleness and ethnicity, 89–90
        in mutual evaluations, 92–93
        in shared professional rites, 85–88
        in training and development, viii, 90–91
    public perception of, 81–83, 197
    tension with, 93–102
        in caseflow management, 97–100
        in elite bar, 102, 252, 254–255
        in modifying adversarial system, 94
        in need to protect client from attorney, 93–94
        in superintending legal profession, 94–97
lay, 56–57, 122
legislative removal of, 13
management perspective in, 103–116
    attitudes toward, 103–105
    avoidance of risk in, 110–111
    broad view needed for, 108–109
    collegial tradition in, 105–107
    command structure in, 111–112
    insistence on privacy in, 114–115
    methods of based on legal models, 107–108
    reluctance to delegate in, 112–114
    use of rules and directives in, 109–110
minor, need for, 138–139
and myth of solo generalist, 88–89
nonjudicial functions assumed by, 14
parking spaces for, 182–183
participation of in legislative process, 47–50
personal employees of, compensation of, 184
political involvement of, 44–45, 50, 122, 124
    career advancement and, 32, 46, 124
    fear of reprisal at polls or at reappointment and, 36–40
    in lobbying in different states, 49–50
    in local patronage system, 44–45
    use of agents for, 48
problem behavior and discipline of, intervention of chief judge in, 176
professionalism of, viii–ix
    reform and upgrading of, need for, 121–132, 203–204
public involvement with, need for, 196–197
relationships of, with chief justices, 150–151
    with state court administrators, 112–114
    with trial court administrator and chief judge, 180–183
retention elections for, 29, 30, 37–38, 72

role of, changes in, 223–228, 261
    in alternative dispute resolution, 210–211
    in caseflow management, 189
    in local communities, 58–60
    political and communal, 85
    symbolic, 59
roles of, reform movement and, xi
in rural areas, 62–63, 135–136
security of, 183
selection of, by merit, ix, 119, 122–125
    diversity issues and, 42
    in early republic, 27–28
    ethical aspects of, 31–32
    hybrid systems of, 30
    methods of besides election, 30. 122–125
    political process and, viii, 31–32
        origin and development of, 27–32
        original insulation of from popular control, 27–28
        reformist position toward, 27
        state court administrator turnover and, 162
    in specific states, 30–31
as state court administrators, 112–113, 159
stress of trials on, 176, 207
transfers of, 150, 168
"trial shy," 176
types of, in single-tier court states, 138, 139
visiting, in local areas, 60–61
Judicial administration, 148–153. See also *Court administration.*
Judicial branch, administrative weaknesses of, 4, 20, 22
    historical development of, 3–23
    interbranch relationships of. See also *Interbranch relationships.*
        government relations offices for, 48
        inherent powers and, 16–18
        state court administrators and, 166–167
    legal concepts underlying, 5
        checks and balances, 10–14
        differentiation of functions and, 7–10
        inherent powers, 16–18. See also *Inherent powers.*
        judicial federalism, 18–21
        judicial independence, 14–16. See also *Judicial independence.*
        separation of powers, 5–7. See also *Separation of powers.*
    organization and upgrading of, after 1950, 23, 121–132
    political activism of, 46–50. See also *Political process.*
    structure of, unification of, 134–139
Judicial Conference of New York, 120
Judicial Conference of the United States, 120
Judicial councils, 119, 120, 155
Judicial Councils of the Circuits, 121
Judicial Electronic Data and Document Interchange, 244

Judicial ethics, 35, 127, 145
Judicial federalism, 18–21. See also *Federal grants; Federalization.*
    Conference of Chief Justices and, 19–21
    main issues in, 19
Judicial independence. See also *Separation of powers.*
    "accountability" of judicial branch and, 15–16
    administrative requirements of, 1–23
    and budgeting, 3, 4, 15
    definitions of, 14–15
    as excuse for management failure, 116
    factors contributing to, 15
    legal concepts of, vii, 3–5, 14–16
    and privacy in administrative policymaking, 114–115
    separation of powers and, 4, 14–15
Judicial review, development of, separation of powers and, 10–14
    in early republic, 11
    in state supreme courts, 12–13
    vs. inherent powers, 16
Judiciary, early leaders in, achievements and advantages of, 258–259
Judiciary Subcommittee on Separation of Powers, 46
"Junk science," 254
Jurors, ideal, 219–220
    in current adversarial system, myths about, 216
    participation of in trials, 220–221
    peremptory challenges of, 216–217, 221
    selection of, racial problems in, 74
    stress of trials on, 208, 219
Jury commissions, 73
Jury instructions, development of, 14
    myths about, 217
Jury management, 219
Jury system, and truth, 214
    in business cases, 255
    changes in since 1960, 217–219
    criticism of, 218–219
    elected clerks and, 73–74
    qualitative judgments on, 219
    reforms of, x, 216–222
        current suggestions for, 221–222
Jury Trial Innovations, 219
Jury trials, in justice-of-the-peace courts, 64–65
    public demand for, 13–14
Justice, access to, 210, 224
    administrative, 230
    in adversarial system, 213
    ameliorative, 229
    broadening concept of, 228–232
    commutative, 228
    corrective, 230

definition of, 228
disrespect for truth and, 214–215
distributive, 228
enforcement, 229–230
in litigation and property matters, 228–229
protective, 229
supervisory, 230
therapeutic, 224, 226, 250
Justices of the peace, authority of, 56
complaints about, 63–65
currying police favor by, 64
education and, 64
jury trial with, 64–65
retention of fees by, 64
traffic fines and, 64
courts of, 52, 55–56
Juvenile cases, caseflow management limitations and, 231
increased costs of in 1970s, 141
legal access and, 224
in lower-tier courts, 136
Juvenile Conference Committees, 236
Juvenile courts, 54
changing role of judges in, xi, 211, 223–228
privacy in, 233–234
separate, 247–249
historical roots of, 248
Juvenile Justice Councils, 236–237

K

Kane, Walter, 159
Kansas, status of elected clerks in, 72
Katz, Burton S., 213–215
Kefauver, Estes, 129n.
Keith, Sandy, 32
Kennedy, John F., 14
Kentucky, court structure in, before and after unification, 135–136
judicial elections in, 30
state judicial review in, 13
Kentucky District Court, formation of, 136
King, as chancellor, 5–6
judicial control by in colonies, 8
role in English legal system, 5–6
King, John, 32
King, Martin Luther, assassination of, 101
King in Council, 5, 7
King's Bench, 5
Kleps, Ralph, 159, 172
Kramer, Noel, 200

L

Landlord-tenant cases, 229n.
Language, of judges in municipal courts, 65
Larsen, Rolf, 126
Law cases, vs. equity cases, 54–55
Law enforcement agencies, courts and, 77–79
    relations with judges, 37
    relations with justices of the peace, 64
Law Enforcement Assistance Administration, 110–111, 157
    court reform supported by, 140
    funding for judicial educational programs through, 130
    jury research studies and, 218
    planning function and, 168–169
Law firms, specialized, 88
Law schools, judicial selection from, in local courts, 46
    University-based, rise of, 91
Lawson, Harry, 112, 160
Lawyers, admissions to bar, role of state court administrator in, 167
    appointed, indigent defense and, 79–80
    caseflow management and, 98–100
    in colonies, 8
    compensation of, in family cases, 92
        judicial approval of, 92
    court attire of, 162
    discipline of, by judges, 96–97
        intervention of chief judge in, 176–177
        state court administrator's role in, 162, 167
    diversity-of-citizenship jurisdiction and, 19
    elite, role in state courts, 100–102
    honesty and ethical standards of, public perception of, 82, 83, 83t, 196
    incivility among, 199–200, 213
        judicial rules for, 110
    incompetent, judicial protection of client from, 93–94
    in local bar, challenges to incumbent judges by, 36–37
    and judges, 81–102
        common orientation of, 83–85
            in financial relationships, 92
            in maleness and ethnicity, 89–90
            in mutual evaluations, 92–93, 99
            in shared professional rites, 85–88
            in training and development, 90–91
        public perception of, 81–83, 83t, 196
        tensions between, 93–102
            in caseflow management, 97–100
            client protection from attorney and, 93–94
            in elite bar, 100–102
            judicial superintendence of legal profession and, 94–97
            modification of adversarial system and, 94
    judicial campaign contributions by, 31, 128

and myth of solo generalist, 88–89
profession of. See *Legal profession*.
public opinion of, 81–83, 83t, 196
relations with elected clerks, 71
specialization among, 88–89, 100–102
as state court administrators, 159
in state courts, viii, 21
    vs. elite bar, 100–101
in state legislatures, 85
stress of trials on, 207
visiting, in local areas, 61
Leadership, judicial, in court reform movement, 134, 257–262
    in upgrading legal profession, x, 151, 202
Legal assistance, access to, 210, 224
Legal culture, creation of, state court administration and, 155
    public dissatisfaction with, x, 195–197
Legal education, apprenticeship model of, 90–91
    continuing, state court administrator and, 167
Legal profession. See also *Lawyers*.
    indications of decline in, 199–200
    judicial regulation of, 94–97, 151
    socioeconomic cleavage in, 100–102
    state bar associations and, 95–96
    status of, 199–202
    upgrading of, 91, 102
        leadership of judges in, x, 202
        need for, 198–202
Legal research, by judges, 91
Legal source materials, restricted access to, 86
Legalese, 87
Legislation, federal, preempting state law, state-federal tension over, 20–21
    on product liability, 20–21
Legislative process, judicial participation in, 47
Legislative reapportionment, 36
Legislature(s), administrative rulemaking by courts and, 147–148
    appointment and reappointment of judges by, 38
    control of court budget by, 3, 16
        patronage system and, 44–45
    function of, in early republic, 9
    judicial activism and, 47, 49–50
    organization and development of, 4
    pressure for court-collected revenues in, 144–145
    protection of court budget from interference by, 45
    reform movement of, 121
    relationships with other government branches, 3–5. See also *Interbranch relationships*.
    revenge on judiciary for unpopular decisions, 13, 36, 38
Licht, Frank, 32
Lincoln, Abraham, 82
Litigation, role of trial court administrator in, 185

governments, administrative services provided by, viii
   relationships with, role of chief judge in, 177
      role of chief justices in, 152
      role of state court administrator in, 167
      role of trial court administrator in, 185
   shared state-local funding of courts and, 143–144
Local patronage system, 44–45
Localism, community acceptance of, 60
   fiefdoms in, 61
   financial aspects of, 66–70
      increased costs of trial courts and, 66, 140–141, 144
      inequitable nature of county funding and, 67–68
      inherent powers suits and, 66–67
      insulation and involvement in local politics and, 68–69
   general and limited jurisdiction courts in, 62–63
   idiosyncrasies in, 59–60
   influence of on court organizational structure, 52–58
   judicial, 51–52
      flaws of, 51–52, 70
      purposes of, 51
   justices of the peace and, 55–56, 63–65
   municipal courts in, 65
   nostalgic aspects of, 58
   relations with court-related agencies in, political control of jury system and, 73–74
      with elected clerks, 70–73
      with police departments, 77–78
      with prosecutors and public defenders, 79–80
      with sheriffs, 74–77
   rules of procedure in, 62
   treatment of visiting judges and attorneys in, 60–61
   urban and rural court styles in, 61–62
   variations in standards, procedures, and professionalism in, 58–65
Los Angeles, court of, financing of, 67
      localism in, 61
Los Angeles Municipal Court, performance standards in, assessment of, 204–205
      implementation of, 131
   trial court administrator in, 171
Los Angeles Superior Court, 172
   trial court administrator of, 156
Louisiana, judicial elections in, 30, 31
   local bar examinations in, 96
   political enmity between prosecutors and judges in, 37
   slush funds in, 145

M

MADD (Mothers Against Drunk Driving), challenges to incumbent judges by, 37
Madison, James, 12
Magistrates, in single-tier court systems, 138

Maine, court revenues in, 144
    trial court administration organization in, 175
Management methods, of judges, avoidance of risk and, 110–111
        based on legal models, 107–108
        collegial tradition and, 105–107
        command structure and, 111–112
        insistence on privacy and, 114–115
        judges' attitudes toward, 103–105
        reluctance to delegate and, 112–114
        systemic approach to vs. detail approach, 108–109
        tendency to use rules and directives in, 109–110
Manorial courts, of Maryland, 8n.
Manton, Martin T., 129
Marbury, William, 12
Marbury v. Madison, 6, 12
Maricopa County (Arizona), help for pro se and family court litigants in, 240–241
    Internet access to court database docket in, 241
Marshall, John, 6, 11–13
Maryland, legislative assumption of judicial functions in, 9
    manorial courts of, 8n.
    political influence on judicial elections in, 44
    status of elected clerks and, 72
    trial court administration organization in, 175
Masonic lodges, judicial profession and, 89
Mass torts, state courts and, 252
Massachusetts, attitude of judges in higher courts to those in lower courts, 136–137, 137n.
    early colonial court system in, 6, 7, 7n.
    Franklin County Futures Lab Project in, 236
    legislative control of court budget in, 45
    trial court administration organization in, 175
    undifferentiated government authority in, 7n., 7–8
Mayors' courts, 56
McClellan, John, 46
McConnell, Edward, 112
    management method of, 107–108
    need for changes in justice system and, 215–216
    as state court administrator, 155, 159–160, 164
Media, lawyers' use of, public opinion of, 82
Medical profession, similarities of with legal profession, 198–199
Mental disability or illness, commitment for, caseflow management limitations and, 231
        changing role of judges in, 223–224
    increased expenses for, 141
    protective justice and, 229
Mental health institutions, publicly funded legal offices in, 240
Merit selection, of judges, ix, 119, 122–125
Michigan, confusion in family and circuit courts in, 248–249
    judicial election in, 30, 31
    Oakland County Youth Assistance Program in, 236
    Supreme Court of, inherent powers suits in, 18

Minnesota, judicial elections in, 30
    one-tier court system in, 138
    pilot programs in open hearings in juvenile matters, 234
Minorities. See also *Racial divisions.*
    in state court judgeships, 41
Mississippi, judicial elections in, 30
    justices of the peace in, 64
    law and equity courts in, 55
Missouri, inherent powers suits in, 18
Missouri Compromise, 12
Missouri Plan, 119
    arguments for and against, 29–30
    judicial selection under, 29
    for merit selection of judges, 123–124
Model Code of Judicial Conduct, 131
Model Rules of Professional Conduct (American Bar Association), 82
Model Uniform Product Liability Act, 253
Montana, judicial elections in, 30
Montesquieu, 7
More, Thomas, 6
Mothers Against Drunk Driving, challenges to incumbent judges by, 37
Municipal courts, 52
    administrative organization of, 175–176
    court unification and, 56
    functions of, 56
    localism in, 65
    in one-tier court states, 137
Munsterman, G. Thomas, jury research by, 218–219

N

National Association for Court Management (NACM), role in profession of court adminis-
    tration, 156, 179
National Association of Court Administration, 156
National Association of Trial Court Administrators, 156
National Center for State Courts, 32
    creation and role of, 157
    electronic interchange of information and, 244
    government relations offices in, 48
    role of in new reform agenda, 215–216
    standards for juries and, 219
    support for court reform by, 140
    in urban court budget dispute, 68
National College of Trial Judges, 129
National Commission on Criminal Justice Standards and Goals, 130
National Conference of Court Administrative Officers, 155–156
National Judicial College, 91, 129–130, 151
National Town Hall Meeting, court-community relations and, 235
Navaho Nation Peacemaker court, 236
Nebraska, retention election in, 37–38

Nepotism, 185
  in local trial courts, 69
Nevada, judicial election in, 30
New Jersey, administrative office of courts in, 170
       appointment and reappointment of judges in, 38–39
       bipartisan judiciary in, 43
       court budget in, insulation of from legislative control, 45
       differentiated case management in, 99
       executive system of court management in, 105
       inherent powers suits in, 18
       Juvenile Conference Committees in, 236
       legislative assumption of appellate function in, 9
       legislative opposition to administrative rulemaking in, 148
       municipal courts in, 175
       state court lobbying in, 49
       state financing in, status of elected clerks and, 72
       trial court judges in, 68
New Jersey Judicial Council, 121
New Mexico, judicial selection in, 30
       state court lobbying in, 49
New Orleans, separate courts for civil and criminal cases in, 54
New York, business cases in, 251
       court of appeals in, judicial selection for, 34–35
       election of judges in, 28, 34–35, 44
              political influence on, 35, 44
       inherent powers budget dispute in, 17, 17n.
       judges as state court administrators in, 159
       legislative assumption of appellate function in, 9
New York City, court structure in 1950, 135
       financial condition of, court reform and, 133–134, 141
       Midtown Community Court in, 237
       separate courts for civil and criminal cases in, 54
New York Court of Appeals, 123
New York Supreme Court, 17, 17n., 122, 123
New York University Institute of Judicial Administration, 156
New York University School of Law, 129
Nixon, Richard, 84
North, Oliver, 31
North Carolina, judicial elections in, 30, 39–40
       judicial rotation in, 63
       state financing in, status of elected clerks and, 72
       state funding of courts and prosecution in, 79
North Carolina Republican Party v. Hunt, 39
North Dakota, judicial elections in, 30
       localism in, 63
       public hearings on vacant judgeships in, 115
       Rule on Rules in, 115
       state court lobbying in, 49–50

O

Oakland County (Michigan) Youth Assistance Program, 236
Occupational Safety and Health Standards Act, 184
Ohio, judicial elections in, 30
        need for fund raising in, 33–34
        school funding and, 40–41
    municipal courts in, 175
    political influences on unification of court system in, 34
    supreme court in, geographic and political balance and, 43
Ohio Supreme Court, 110
O.J. Simpson case, 200
Oklahoma Supreme Court, judicial misbehavior in, 128
Omnibus Crime Control and Safe Streets Act (1968), 157
O'Neill, William, 32, 110, 149
Open court. See Courts, open.
Orders, as court management tool, 109–110
Oregon, judicial elections in, 30
    scapegoating of state court administrator in, 162
    Supreme Court in, judicial campaign for, 35–36

P

Pabst, William, jury research by, 218–219
Parajudicial officials, 99
Parental Kidnapping Prevention Act, cause of action under, federalization of law on, 21
Parker, John J., 14, 121
Parliament, and king, court system under, 6
Parties to litigation, stress of trials on, 209
Patronage, local, courts and, 44–45
Pennsylvania, administrative model in, 106–107
    early colonial court system in, 6, 9
    inherent powers suits in, 17, 17n., 18
    judicial elections in, 30
    supreme court of, impeachment of judges in, 13, 126
        inherent powers budget dispute in, 17, 17n.
        one-party domination of, 43
"People's" courts, in colonies, 8
Philadelphia, courts in, dispute over state financing in, 68–69
        localism in, 44, 61
        supreme court takeover of, 68, 68n.
Philadelphia Court of Common Pleas, 68
Physical disabilities, court accommodation of, 240
Pilot programs, in open hearings in juvenile matters, 234
    role of state court administrative office in, 170
    role of trial court administrator in, 186
Pittsburgh, trial court system of, 61
Plaintiffs, unscrupulous, 209
Planning and policymaking, by courts, 110–111
    role of chief justice in, 148
    role of state court administrator in, 168, 170

role of trial court administrator in, 186
unification movement and, 133
Plea bargaining, 93
Police officials, relations with judges, 37
relations with justices of the peace, 64
as witnesses, 77, 209
Police prosecutors, in New England, 78–79
Political parties, bipartisan balance of, 43, 44
judges' responsibilities toward, 45
representation issues and, 43
role in judicial elections, 39, 43–46
in New York, 34–35
in Oregon, 35–36
Political process, in court decisions, public perceptions of, 33
in court systems, viii, 21
diversity issues and, 41–43
fear of reprisals and, 36–40
inappropriate intrusions of, 33–46
integration of judiciary with prevailing political milieu and, 43–46
in political campaigns, 33–36
political quid pro quo and, 40–41
in judicial selection, ambivalence toward, 27
origin and nature of, 27–32
reformist position toward, 27
judicial independence and, 15
judicial involvement in, 46–50. See also *Judges, political involvement of*
local. See also *Localism.*
geographic jurisdiction of trial courts and, 54
municipal courts and, 65
personnel issues involving, 184
resistance of Supreme Court to, 12
state court administrator turnover and, 162
unification movement and, 133
Politicians, lawyers as, 84
Pound, Roscoe, 119
Presidents, lawyers as, 84
Pringle, Edward, 112, 149, 160
Prisoners, security of, 183
Privacy, in administrative process of courts, 234
in juvenile court proceedings, 233–234
in management and administrative policymaking, 114–115
in rulemaking, 147
Privy Council, colonial administration and, 7
Pro se litigants, 210, 211
assistance to, role of trial court administrator in, 186
changing role of judges and, 224
conflicts of with organized bar, 97
court programs for, 240–241
Probate, fees for, 86, 92
legislative jurisdiction over, in early republic, 9

Probate courts, 54
Probation, focused state financing of, 143
        increased expenses for in 1970s, 141
        supervisory justice and, 230
Product liability law, 252–255
        adverse effects of, 253
        issues of state law addressed in, 254
        societal goals in, 252–253
        state-federal tension over, 20–21, 102, 254–255
        vs. case law, 88
Property defacement, 237
Property tax, 41
Prosecutors, and trial courts, 79
        political challenges to incumbent judges by, 37
        role in bond forfeiture, 76
        role of in early 20th-century courts, viii
        and truth, 214
Prostitution, 237
Providence, Rhode Island, arraignment court in, 62
        Bench-bar conflicts in, 96
        police department of, scheduling of criminal cases by, 78–79
Public access, to courts and justice system, x, xi, 196–197, 234–241
            collaboration with citizens groups and, 234–237
            collaboration with noncourt agencies and, 244–245
            information sharing and, 241–244
            location of facilities and, 237–238
            off-hour sessions and, 238
            treatment of users with special needs and, 240
Public defenders, 79–80
Public education, state court administrator and, 167
Public opinion, of adversarial system, 94, 197
        of courts and legal culture, 81–83, 86–87, 195–197
Public relations, role of chief justices in, 152
        role of trial court administrator in, 185–186
Publicity, lawyers' use of, public opinion of, 82

R

Racial divisions, in jury selection, 74, 217
        in justice-of-the-peace system, 64
        in legal profession, 89–90
Real estate transactions, fees for, 86
Recall, of judges, 126
Reform agenda, changes in, 195–206
        early, vii,ix-x
Religion, colonial court system and, 8
Report of the Commission on the Future of the California Courts, diversity issues in, 41
Republican party, in south, in partisan judicial elections, 39–40
Retention elections, elected clerks' political power and, 72
        in California, 29, 29n.
        in Missouri, 123

opposition in, 37–38
    for rejection of judges, 29, 29n., 30
Retirement, mandatory, 127
Rhode Island, change in method of selection of judges in, 38
    legislative assumption of judicial functions in, 9
    political diversity in court system in, 43
    Providence, arraignment court in, 62
        bench-bar conflicts in, 96
        police scheduling of criminal cases in, 78–79
    state court administrator in, 165
Rhodes, Jim, 30
Richardson, William, 165
RICO, civil jurisdiction under, federalization of law on, 21
Rockefeller, Nelson, 135
Rosenman, Samuel I., 122
Rothwax, Harold J., 213–215
Royal courts, origin and development of, 5
Rule of Law, 6
Rulemaking power, administrative, 146–148
      judicial vs. legislative control and, 147–148
      role of chief justice in, 150
      trial court budget and, 170
    interbranch relationships and, 16–17
    and responsibilities of state court administrators, 164
    unification movement and, 133
    use of, 119, 120
    U.S. Supreme Court authority for, 120
Rules, as court management tool, 109–110
    for acrimony between attorneys, 110
    local, variations in, 62
    procedural, 146, 147
    regulatory, common law and, 87–88
    superintendence, 147
    vs. statutes, 147
Rules of criminal procedure, need for changes in, 215
Rules of evidence, and legal monopoly, 87
    development of, 14
Rural areas, domestic violence in, 225
Rural courts, allocation of judges in after unification, 135–136
    limited jurisdiction vs. general jurisdiction, 63
    localism in, 61–63
    number of judges available for, 62–63
    organization of, 173
    rules of procedure in, 62

S

San Diego, court financing in, 67
Scheduling (calendaring), attorney control over, 97–98
    caseflow management and, 190
    by elected clerks, 71
    by police in Providence, Rhode Island, 78–79

School choice, judicial elections concerning, 40
School funding, judicial election concerning, 40–41
Scientific evidence, standard of reliability for, 254
Security, in courts, 75
    of judges, trial court administrators and, 183
Sedgwick County District Court, 103
Sentencing, caseflow management and, 231
    changing role of judges in, 223
    criminal, jury involvement in, 13
Separate But Subservient, 4
Separation of powers. See also *Judicial independence.*
    administrative management and judicial independence and, 4, 21–23
    at Constitutional Convention, 9
    checks and balances and, 10–14
    differentiation of functions and, 7–10
    as general concept, vii, 5–7
    history of, 3–5
    interbranch relationships and, 6, 10
Seriatim opinions, 12
Settlement conference, 211
Sheriffs, 74–77
    bail bondsmen and, 75–76
    deputies of, 75, 75n.
    functions of, 74, 76–77
    professionalism of, 74
    role in segregation and desegregation of public facilities, 74
Shestack, Jerome J., 82
Shoplifting, 237
Silicon breast implant cases, 254
Sirica, John, 94
Smith, Al, 123
Snowden, Art, 165
Social problems, court reform agenda and, x, xi
Social science research, in jury system changes, 217-221
Social service agencies, in caseflow management, 189
    court cooperation with, 141, 244, 249
        changing role of judges in, 224–228
Solomon, Harvey, 156
Solomon, Maureen, 187
Sourcebook of Criminal Justice Statistics, 83
South Carolina, judicial selection in, 30, 125
South Dakota, state financing in, elected clerks and, 72
Special interest groups, challenges posed by, 37, 247
Specialty courts, arguments pro and con, 247
    boutique courts and, 249–251
    family and juvenile courts and, 247–249
    judges in, 228
    product liability law and, 251–255
    in reform movement, xi–xii

Standards of Judicial Administration (American Bar Association), 17, 133, 140
Standards Relating to Court Organization (American Bar Association), 134
State attorney general, as career path for judges in appellate courts, 46
State court administrators, authority of, 147–148, 162–165
    compensation of, 158
    constitutional appointment of, 158
    deputy court administrators and, 166
    functions of, 166–169
    geographic location of office of, 166
    intervention of in inherent powers suits, 18
    judges or lawyers as, 112–113, 158–159
    leadership role of, 260–261
    management methods of, 106–108
    in New York, 159
    origins of profession of, 155–157
    personal characteristics of, 158, 161–162
    professional organization of, 166–169
    qualifications and background of, 158–160
    in reform movement, ix–x
    relationships of, with chief justice, 161–162
        with judges, 112–114
        with supreme court, 161–163
        with trial court administrators, 157, 171–172
        with trial courts, 169–172
    responsibilities of, 163–164
    support for, 161–162
    turnover rate among, 161–162
    women as, 160
State courts. See also *Courts; Trial courts.*
    bias in, 41
    business cases in, 251–255
    civil jurisdiction of, erosion of, 254–255
    elite bar in, 102
    exclusive control of legal profession in, 94–95
    federal grant programs for, 48–49
    federalization of, 18–21, 250–251, 254–255, 260
    geographic balance in, 43
    local governmental political influence on, 43, 50, 52–58. See also *Localism.*
    political influence of, 49–50
    political intrusion into, 50. See also *Political process.*
    public confidence in, 83, 84t
State financing. See also *Budgeting.*
    administrative role of chief justices in, 152–153
    arguments pro and con, 143–144
    implementation of in specific states, 141–142
    of trial courts, 139–146
        arguments pro and con, 143–144
        in court reform movement, 140
        fiscal relief for local governments and, 140–141

opposition of elected clerks to, 71–72
partial, 143–144
pressure to raise court revenues and, 144–145
shift of power with, 144
statistics on, 142
structural or administrative unification and, 140, 169–170
State Justice Institute, 48
Statutes, common law and, 87–88
vs. rules, 147
Stevens, Harold A., 35
Story, Joseph, 91
Stovall, James, 35
Street crimes, federalization of law on, 21
Stress, of trials, 207
on judges, 176, 207
on jurors, 208, 219
on lawyers, 207
on witnesses, 208
Superior courts, 52
in colonies, 8
Supreme courts, state, administrative authority of, 20, 146–147
changes after 1950, 22
and federal habeas corpus review, 20
inherent powers disputes involving, 17–18
judicial review function and, 12–13
management models in, 105–107
in reform movement, ix
relationships with federal courts, 19–21
Surveys, in passing unification, 135
Swain, James, 157

T

Taft, William Howard, 84–85
federal court changes and, 120
Team support, in caseflow management, 190, 191
Technology, caseflow management and, 190
court lag in implementation of, 110–111
in compilation of juror lists, 219
decreased reliance of judges on attorneys and, 91
effects of in courts, 205–206
increased expenses for, 141
in information sharing, 241–244. See also *Information networks*.
role of trial court administrator in, 179, 186
Telecommunications, in courts, 205–206
Telemarketing fraud, prevention of, federalization of law on, 21
Tennessee, geographic balance in supreme court in, 43
law and equity courts in, 55
retention election in, 38

Term limits, 36
Texas, county court system in, 57
    general jurisdiction courts in, 57
    judicial elections in, 30, 31, 40
Time standards, in caseflow management, 188
Title companies, conflicts of with organized bar, 97
Torbert, Bo, 32
Tort reform, 199, 251
    judicial election concerning, 40
    and product liability litigation, 252–255
Total Quality Management, 238
Town and village courts, 52
Traffic courts, local politics and, 65
Traffic fines, justice-of-the-peace compensation and, 64
Traynor, Harold, 149
Trial commissioners, in Kentucky, 136
Trial court administration, origins of profession of, 156
Trial court administrators, 178–180
    administrative role of, caseflow management and, 187–191
        in budgeting, 181n., 181–182
        elected clerks and, 183–184
        liaison with public and governmental agencies, 185–186
        mundane functions of, 183
        personnel matters and, 184–185
        in serving needs of individual judges, 182–183
    compensation of, 178–179
    functional division with state court administrative office, 157
    management styles of, 179–180
    organization of court structure and, 173–176
    relationship of with chief judge, 176, 180–186
    status of, 179, 261
    vs. state court administrators, 171–172
        in major urban courts, 171–172
Trial Court Performance Standards, 131, 186
    developed by National Center for State Courts, 157
    implementation of, 204–205
    judicial independence and accountability and, 15–16
    open court proceedings in, 233
    purpose of, 204
Trial courts. See also *Courts; State courts.*
    administration of, judicial independence and, 21–23
        management styles in, 107
        organization of, 173–176
        role of chief judges in, 176–178
        weakness of prior to 1950, 22
    audits of, 69–70
    changes in, after 1950, 23
    divisions in, and weakening of political message, 49–50

expenses of, 141–142
general jurisdiction, 52, 54
    merit selection of judges in, 124–125
    relation to lower courts, 136
    small pool of judges in, 62–63
inherent powers suits in, 17, 18, 66–67
jurisdictional rigidity and looseness in, 52–54
leadership role of, 261
limited jurisdiction, appeals from, 52
    condescending attitude toward, 136–137
    criticism of, 55–56
    in Kentucky, 135–136
    judges available for, 63
    lack of professionalism in, 55
    in New York City after unification, 135
    unification movement and, 133
localism of. See *Localism*.
mass tort cases in, 252
municipal. See *Municipal courts*.
ordinance, administration of, 175
organization of, size and, 173–174
    variations in, 174–175
prosecutors and, 79
public confidence in, 83, 84t
rural. See *Rural courts*.
services to, by state court administrative office, 168–172
sheriffs and, 77
single-tier, 134–135, 137, 138
special jurisdiction, administration of, 175. See also *Specialty courts*.
state financing of, reasons for, 66–70. See also *State financing, of trial courts*.
Two-tier, 134–135
    administrative organization of, 175
    allocation of caseload in, 136–137
    in Kentucky, 135–136
upgrading of, ix, 203
urban, 173–174. See also *Urban courts*.
Trials, rationing of, 212
Trials *de novo*, 52, 230
Tribunals, administrative, 9–10
    in royal courts, 5
Trotter, Joseph, 157
Truman, Harry, as county judge, 7n.
Trusts, legislative jurisdiction over, in early republic, 9
Truth, current jury reforms and, 221
    in justice system, 214–215
Turnage, Jean A., 32

U

Unification. See also *Court reform*.
    administrative, ix, 146–148
    budgetary, ix, 139–146
    controversy over, 195
    elected clerks opposition to, 70–71
    public indifference to, x, 195
    state court administration and, 155
        involvement with trial courts, 169–170
    structural, ix, 134–139
    threats to from specialty courts and special interest groups, 247–255
Uniform state laws, common law and, 87
United States Administrative Office of Courts, 156
United States Constitution, 9
    judicial interpretation of, 11–12
    separation of powers and, 10–11, 27
United States Department of Justice, Civil Rights Division of, 74
    Office of Justice programs of, 250
    state court regulation of legal profession and, 95
United States Judicial Conference, 46
    universal electronic citations and, 242
United States Supreme Court, building of, 120
    judicial review function of, 11
    rulemaking power of, 120
University of Southern California, 156
Urban courts. See also *Municipal courts*.
    disorder in, 62
    large, vs. supreme court and state court administrative office, 171–172
    localism in, 61
    organization of, 173–174
    protection of from rural legislators, 45
Utah, judicial selection in, 30

V

Vanderbilt, Arthur, 112, 121, 133, 149, 155, 156, 164
    achievements of, 259
    administrative rulemaking authority of, opposition to, 148
Venue, in general jurisdiction trial courts, 54
Vermont, election of judges in, 28
    localism in, 63
Victim assistance programs, federal, conflicts with state courts over, 249
Video arraignments, sheriffs' role in, 74
Video trials, 222
Violent Crime Control and Law Enforcement Act (1994), 250
Virginia, early colonial court system in, 6
    elected clerks in, 73, 181n.
    judicial selection in, 30, 31, 38, 125
    state court influence in, 49

Voir dire, 216
Volunteers, as link between court and community, 234–236
Voter education, unification movement and, 133, 135
Vouchers, for school choice, judicial election concerning, 40

W

Wallace, George, 32, 58
Wallace, Jack, 58–59
Warren, Earl, 14
Washington, inherent powers suits in, 18
    judicial election in, 30, 39
Water courts, of Colorado, 54
Webster, Daniel, 82
Weintraub, Chief Justice, 164
West Publishing Group, universal electronic citations and, 242
West Virginia, budget dispute in, 3
    elected clerks in, 72
    judicial elections in, 30
    justices of the peace in, 64–65
Wilentz, Chief Justice, 38–39
Williams, G. Mennen (Soapy), 32
Wills, probate of, fees for, 86
Wisconsin, judicial elections in, 30, 40
    one-tier court system in, 137–138
Witnesses, stress of trials on, 208
Women, harassed or abused, court treatment of, 240
    in legal profession, 89
    prevention of gender-based crimes of violence against, federalization of law on, 21
    in state court judgeships, 41
Wythe, George, 90

Z

Zimmerman, Michael D., 210, 226–227, 250–251

About the Author

Robert W. Tobin is a senior staff associate with the National Center for State Courts (NCSC), where he has specialized for many years in court finance. He has conducted major statewide studies of court finance in Alabama, Arkansas, Illinois, Louisiana, Ohio, and other states. He has also conducted finance studies at the county level, most recently in Orleans Parish, Louisiana, and Pinellas County, Florida. He has written numerous articles, monographs, and reports on court administration and court finance, among them: *Planning in State Courts: Trends and Developments, 1976-78* (1978); *The Administrative Role of Chief Justices and Supreme Courts* (1979); *The Transition to State Financing of Courts* (1981); *Status of State Court Financing 1989* (1989); *NACM Trial Court Financial Management Guide* (1993); *Managing Budget Cutbacks* (1994); and *Internal Control of Court-collected Funds* (1995). He has also conducted many projects in general areas of court administration, such as caseflow and calendaring analysis. Before his service with NCSC, he was a professor of government at the University of Miami, a trial lawyer with the Department of Justice, and a management consultant. He holds B.S.S. and LL.B. degrees from Georgetown University, LL.M. and J.S.D. degrees from Columbia University, and an M.A. from the University of Miami.

About the National Center for State Courts

The nation's state chief justices founded the National Center for State Courts (NCSC) in 1971 with the support of Chief Justice of the United States Warren E. Burger. NCSC is a non-profit organization dedicated to improving the administration of justice by providing both leadership and service to the state courts through direct technical assistance and consulting, research and technology, information and education, government relations and association management, and international exchange and cooperation.

For More Information, Contact:

The National Center for State Courts
www.ncsconline.org

WILLIAMSBURG, VA
300 Newport Avenue
Williamsburg, VA 23185-4147
DENVER, CO
1331 Seventeenth Street, Suite 402
Denver, CO 80202-1554
ARLINGTON, VA
2425 Wilson Boulevard, Suite 350
Arlington, VA 22201

> Association Services (800) 616-6165
> Consulting (800) 466-3063
> Court Information (800) 616-6164
> Education-ICM (800) 616-6160
> Government Relations (800) 532-0204
> International Programs (800) 797-2545
> Publications (888) 228-6272
> Research (800) 616-6109
> Technology (888) 846-6746

0-595-32277-8

Printed in the United States
206150BV00001B/97-1023/A